RESURRECTION REALISM

Resurrection Realism

Ratzinger the Augustinian

Patrick J. Fletcher

CASCADE *Books* • Eugene, Oregon

RESURRECTION REALISM
Ratzinger the Augustinian

Copyright © 2014 Patrick J. Fletcher. All rights reserved. Except for brief quotations in critical publications or reviews, no part of this book may be reproduced in any manner without prior written permission from the publisher. Write: Permissions, Wipf and Stock Publishers, 199 W. 8th Ave., Suite 3, Eugene, OR 97401.

Cascade Books
An Imprint of Wipf and Stock Publishers
199 W. 8th Ave., Suite 3
Eugene, OR 97401

www.wipfandstock.com

ISBN 13: 978-1-62564-021-5

Cataloguing-in-Publication data:

Fletcher, Patrick J.

Resurrection realism : Ratzinger the Augustinian / Patrick J. Fletcher.

viii + 270 pp. ; 23 cm. Includes bibliographical references.

isbn 13: 978-1-62564-021-5

1. Benedict XVI, Pope, 1927–. 2. Catholic Church—Doctrines. 3. Augustine, Saint, Bishop of Hippo—Contributions in theology. 4. Resurrection. 5. Catholic Church—Doctrines—History—20th century. I. Title.

BX1378.6 .F56 2014

Manufactured in the U.S.A.

The Catholic Edition of the Revised Standard Version of the Bible, copyright © 1965, 1966 by the Division of Christian Education of the National Council of the Churches of Christ in the United States of America. Used by permission. All rights reserved.

To my wife, Corinne,
whose tireless devotion to our family
made all this research possible.

Contents

Introduction   1

Part One—Ratzinger the Augustinian

1. Augustine on Resurrection: Characteristics of an Augustinian Theology   13
2. Apologetics and Proclamation in Ratzinger's Theology of Resurrection   72

Part Two—Crucial Distinctions in Ratzinger's Theology of Resurrection

3. The Body-Soul Distinction   103
4. The Distinction between Death and Resurrection: The Intermediate State   134
5. The Body and the Flesh? The *Leib-Körper* Distinction   159

Part Three—Ratzinger the Realist

6. Matter in Ratzinger's Theology of Resurrection   181
7. Conclusion   247

   Bibliography   259

Introduction

F or if the dead are not raised, then Christ has not been raised. If Christ has not been raised, your faith is futile and you are still in your sins.

—1 Corinthians 15:16–17

The Resurrection of the Body: Contested throughout History

The doctrine of the resurrection of the dead—also called the resurrection of the body and the resurrection of the flesh—has always been, and remains, central to Christian faith. In the Apostles' Creed, Christians profess their belief in the *carnis resurrectionem*,[1] and in the Nicene Creed they assert their expectation of the *anāstasin nekrōn*.[2] Tertullian (160–220) declared that "the resurrection of the dead is the confidence of Christians; by it we are believers."[3] But this belief has been a source of controversy from the earliest days of the Church, being debated and defended by generations of theologians throughout history.

Irenaeus (d. 202), for example, avowed that the denial of the resurrection is at the root of every heresy: "For whatsoever all the heretics may have advanced with the utmost solemnity, they come to this at last, that they blaspheme the Creator, and disallow the salvation of God's workmanship,

---

1. *Enchiridion Symbolorum* par. 1. Hereafter cited as *Denzinger*, along with the corresponding paragraph number.

2. *Denzinger* 86.

3. Tertullian, *De Resurrectione Carnis* 1. My translation. Latin text from *Tertullian's Treatise on the Resurrection*, 4. "Fiducia Christianorum resurrectio mortuorum: illam credentes hoc sumus."

which the flesh truly is."[4] By the time of Augustine (354–430), the most serious opponents of the resurrection were those who followed the philosophy of Plato. Augustine notes the philosophical climate of his day:

> Yet on no other point is the Christian faith contradicted so passionately, so persistently, so strenuously and obstinately, as on the resurrection of the flesh. Many philosophers, even among the pagans, have argued at length about the immortality of the soul, and in their numerous and various books have left it on record that the human soul is indeed immortal. But when it comes to the resurrection of the flesh they never falter, but openly and plainly deny it. So flatly do they contradict us on this that they declare it impossible for earthly flesh to ascend to heaven.[5]

The Challenge of Platonic Dualism

The pagan philosopher Plato (428–348 BC) continued to exert an extraordinary influence in Augustine's time through those philosophers who followed and expounded his philosophy. Many of Plato's statements on beatitude, however, suggest that what is required is the soul's liberation from the body rather than that body's resurrection. In the *Phaedo*, Plato suggests that "if we are ever to have pure knowledge, we must escape from the body and observe matters in themselves with the soul by itself."[6] In Plato's anthropology, the separation of soul from body occurs at death,[7] so that "those who have purified themselves sufficiently by philosophy live in the future altogether without a body; they make their way to even more beautiful dwelling places."[8]

This Platonic dualism, or tendency to view soul and body as two disparate entities (one of which is ultimately non-essential to human nature), presents a strong challenge to Christian faith in the resurrection of the body. Centuries after Plato, the Platonic philosopher Plotinus (205–270

---

4. Irenaeus, *Adversus Haereses* IV, preface, 4. English text from vol. 1 of *The Ante-Nicene Fathers*.

5. Augustine, *en. Ps.* 88(2).5. English text from *Expositions of the Psalms 73–98*. Unless otherwise noted, I will use the abbreviations for Augustine's works found in Fitzgerald and Cavadini, *Augustine Through the Ages*, xxxv–xlii.

6. Plato, *Phaedo* 66d.

7. Ibid., 64c.

8. Ibid., 114c.

AD) further developed Plato's thought. Within his system (later dubbed "Neoplatonic")[9] the goal of the soul is ecstatic union with the One, which requires the abandonment of the body and materiality.[10] Plotinus' combative disciple, Porphyry (234–305 AD), carried this idea further, stating that true beatitude requires that *"corpus esse omne fugiendum"* (every kind of body is to be shunned).[11] Such a view clearly contradicts Christian faith in the resurrection of the *body*.

Augustine is important in the resurrection debate because he learned and accepted the Platonism of Plotinus and Porphyry, yet when he became a Christian he eventually rejected those beliefs of the "Platonists" which he considered to be incompatible with Christian faith in the resurrection. In other words, the Platonic "dualism" which saw the body as a lower-order reality to be left behind was not unconsciously assumed by Augustine, but rather explicitly considered and rejected. In this respect, Augustine's theology of resurrection is highly significant in the development of Christian doctrine, for it was developed in conscious opposition to this Platonic dualism.

Ratzinger, Augustine, and the Modern Situation

In the nineteenth and twentieth centuries, some theologians suggested that Platonic dualism had infiltrated Christian thought to the point that biblical faith in bodily resurrection had essentially been replaced by the Platonic idea of the immortality of the soul. Notably, Oscar Cullmann (1902–99), a Lutheran exegete, claimed that "1 Corinthians 15 has been

9. Although contemporary usage refers to Plotinus and his successors as "Neoplatonists," I will in general follow the usage of Augustine himself and simply use the term "Platonists." Although it is true that Plotinus and Porphyry made innovations on Plato's thought (Augustine himself is aware of this, e.g., *civ. Dei* 20.30), they were considered by themselves and by Augustine as disciples of Plato, and therefore Platonists.

10. For an introduction to Plotinus' doctrine of emanation and beatitude, see Bowery, "Plotinus, *The Enneads*" and Copleston, *History of Philosophy*, 1:464–72.

11. Cited by Augustine in *civ. Dei* 22.26 and elsewhere. It is not certain from which of Porphyry's works this passage derives since many are no longer extant. A similar idea is expressed in Porphyry's *Sententiae ad Intellegibilia Ducentes* 7, which states that the achievement of *apatheia* (impassibility) results in freeing the soul from the body. See Porphyry, *Sentences*, 796. It is most likely, however, that the passage is from the no longer extant *De regressu animae*. In *civ. Dei* 10.29, Augustine states that "Porphyry, in those very books upon which I have drawn so freely, and in which he wrote of the soul's return [*De regressu animae*], so frequently teaches that the soul must leave behind all union with a body [*omne corpus esse fugiendum*] in order that the soul may dwell in blessedness with God." When citing *De Civitate Dei* I will follow Dyson's translation.

sacrificed for the *Phaedo*."[12] This accusation naturally raises questions about theological anthropology and the compatibility of the body-soul schema with Christian thought. The chief problem is whether the notion of a postmortem soul, separated from its body while it awaits the resurrection, is compatible with the Christian view of the human being, which sees both body and soul as essential to human nature.

Joseph Ratzinger (b. 1927), who became Pope Benedict XVI in 2005 until his resignation from the papacy in 2013,[13] has written extensively on the topic of resurrection, most notably in his 1977 book *Eschatologie*[14] in which he defended the concept of the soul and argued that the Catholic Church's view of death and resurrection is not in fact dualistic. Ratzinger's theology of resurrection is important not only because of its significant contribution to the current debate, but also because of the prominence of the person whose theology it is. It is therefore notable that until now, his eschatology has received relatively scant attention.[15]

Ratzinger's Augustinian Influence

Ratzinger has repeatedly claimed to be influenced by the thought of Augustine. His doctoral dissertation, *Volk und Haus Gottes in Augustins Lehre*

---

12. Cullmann, *Immortality of the Soul*.

13. I will use the name Joseph Ratzinger to identify the author of his privately published works (those works published before his election to the papacy, his Jesus of Nazareth series, etc.). I will use Benedict XVI to indicate the author of his works penned as Pontiff (encyclicals, homilies, etc.).

14. The current edition is Joseph Ratzinger, *Eschatologie—Tod und Ewiges Leben*, 6th ed. (Regensburg: Friedrich Pustet, 2007). Hereafter cited as *Eschatologie*. Although this is still considered the 6th edition, the addition of a new 2006 foreword by Benedict XVI means that the pagination is no longer identical with the original 6th edition from 1990. Published in English as *Eschatology: Death and Eternal Life*, 2nd ed., trans. Michael Waldstein; translation edited by Aidan Nichols (Washington, DC: CUA Press, 2007). Hereafter cited as *Eschatology*.

15. Only one major study has been dedicated to Ratzinger's eschatology: Nachtwei, *Dialogische Unsterblichkeit*. Ratzinger's theology of resurrection is dealt with as a minor theme in Sonnemans, *Seele*, and in Wohlmuth, *Mysterium der Verwandlung*. A recent book chapter dealing directly yet rather unsystematically with Ratzinger's eschatology is Marschler, "Perspektiven," 161–91. Astoundingly, there has been no treatment of Ratzinger's eschatology in English. Aidan Nichols' chapter on Ratzinger's eschatology in his *Theology of Joseph Ratzinger*, 155–87, is simply a synopsis (without discussion) of one work (*Eschatologie*). This chapter is unaltered in the new edition of the work, *The Thought of Pope Benedict XVI*, 2nd ed., 110–33.

von der Kirche,[16] dealt with Augustine's ecclesiology. As early as 1969, he stated that "I have developed my theology in a dialogue with Augustine, though naturally I have tried to conduct this dialogue as a man of today."[17] More recently, Benedict XVI has declared that "when I read St. Augustine's writings I do not get the impression that he is a man who died more or less sixteen hundred years ago; I feel he is like a man of today: a friend, a contemporary who speaks to me, who speaks to us with his fresh and timely faith."[18]

If, then, Joseph Ratzinger was so deeply influenced by the thought of Augustine, then an important question arises: is Ratzinger's theology of resurrection "Augustinian"? Although Ratzinger has indicated that he was impacted by the personalism of Augustine's *Confessions*,[19] there are few other indications of where any Augustinian influence might lie. In 2009, Joseph Lam Quy expressed wonder that the theme of Augustine's influence on Ratzinger's thought had hitherto been dealt with only marginally.[20] Indeed, references to the "Augustinian" character of Ratzinger's theology are common, but textual support for these references is not.

What Is "Augustinianism"?

When it is claimed that Ratzinger is Augustinian, what is often meant is that his ecclesiology or his anthropology is marked by a pessimism toward human nature and an emphasis on the need for grace. In other words, Ratzinger's "Augustinianism" is often seen only with respect to Augustine's

16. Ratzinger, *Volk und Haus Gottes*. This is also published as vol. 7 of *Münchener Theologische Studien*.

17. Ratzinger, "Glaube, Geschichte und Philosophie," 543. The English translation is from Nichols, *Theology of Joseph Ratzinger*, 27.

18. Benedict XVI, General Audience, January 16, 2008, par. 7. Also, compare Ratzinger's comments in a television interview with the station Bayern-Alpha on September 4, 1998: "Meine große persönliche Begegnung war aber Augustinus, der für mich gar kein Mensch der Vergangenheit ist, sondern sein Leben liegt so gegenwärtig vor uns und er spricht so unmittelbar, daß ich ihn als einen Zeitgenossen, ja als einen Weggenossen meines eigenen Lebens empfinde" ("Joseph Ratzinger im Gespräch mit Martin Lohmann," 8).

19. Ratzinger, *Milestones*, 4. "[The] encounter with personalism was for me a spiritual experience that left an essential mark, especially since I spontaneously associated such personalism with the thought of St. Augustine, who in his *Confessions* had struck me with the power of all his human passion and depth."

20. Quy, *Theologische Verwandtschaft*, 12. He notes that in studies of Ratzinger's thought, Augustine has hitherto been dealt with only under the general theme of patristic influence.

anti-Pelagian writings. This position is evident in books by James Corkery, Thomas Rausch, and Giancarlo Zizola.[21] Such a characterization, however, has been called into question by Tracey Rowland, who has suggested that "contrary to many hastily prepared editorials at the time of his election to the papacy, Ratzinger's Augustinian dispositions should not be construed as having anything to do with wanting the Church to retreat from the world, or wanting her scholars to close down conversations with the rest of non-Catholic humanity. Unfortunately, in popular parlance the adjective 'Augustinian' has often been tarred with a Calvinist brush."[22] Rowland suggests that Ratzinger's Augustinianism is found chiefly in his epistemology, his emphasis on the relationship between truth and love, and his interest in beauty.[23] And although Rowland's work laudably attempts to come to a greater understanding of Ratzinger's "Augustinian preferences,"[24] this is unfortunately done without any textual references to Augustine.

The situation mentioned above sums up well the current state of scholarship on Ratzinger's relationship to Augustine, which is in general full of assertions but lacking in evidence. This is particularly true on the issue of the resurrection of the body. Even in Quy's book (which is dedicated to the Augustinian nature of Ratzinger's theology), there is no treatment of Ratzinger's theology of resurrection at all.[25] This situation is highly unfor-

21. Corkery, *Joseph Ratzinger's Theological Ideas*. Corkery states that in Ratzinger's theology, "Augustinian footprints are highly discernible: a preferring of the humility of faith over the pride of philosophy; a defence of the 'city of God' against the powers of the 'earthly city'; and a recognition of the duality that lies deep within human beings who, even when desiring the good, cannot embrace it" (25). He goes on to suggest that, from reading Augustine, "Ratzinger has been aware of how much humanity depends on the grace of God and how much human nature, as manifested in its concrete historical incarnations, is in discontinuity with it" (25–26). In a section titled "An Augustinian Pessimism," Rausch (*Pope Benedict XVI*, 47–52) argues that an acceptance of Augustine's notion of original sin leads Ratzinger to be suspicious of the human intellect, to emphasize grace over nature, and to reject Rahner's supernatural existential. Also, Duquesne and Zizola, *Benôit XVI ou le Mystère Ratzinger*, 165. Here, Zizola identifies Ratzinger's Augustinianism only with respect to ecclesiology. In this regard, he states that Ratzinger follows Augustine in seeing the Church as a mystery (rather than simply an institution), but expresses a strong break with the values of the world and a pessimism about man's future, believing that the Church is engaged in a struggle that will endure until the end of time.

22. Rowland, *Ratzinger's Faith*, 9.

23. Ibid.

24. Ibid., 149. Here, Rowland states that "at a time when everyone is saying that the key to Ratzinger is to understand his Augustinian preferences, some effort has been made in this book to explain in greater detail what this means."

25. Part III of Quy's book is on eschatology, yet the issue of resurrection and the twentieth-century debate over the soul is avoided entirely.

tunate, given both the importance of Augustine in the development of the Christian theology of resurrection and the significance of the purportedly Augustinian Ratzinger in the modern debate.

If Ratzinger's "Augustinianism" is to be properly evaluated in a specific area of his theology (in this case, on the resurrection), this cannot be done on the basis of bald assertions regarding how pessimistic or optimistic he is; it must be based on the comparison of texts and ideas. One cannot extract highly generalized themes from Augustine's thought (e.g., the emphasis on interiority, or a supposed stress on grace over nature) and attempt to use them as universal standards to determine whether a modern theologian is "Augustinian" in a specific area. This is because such general themes are not necessarily important to Augustine himself in his writings in those areas. As an example, it may be true that there is a certain "pessimistic" character to many of Augustine's writings on original sin but this does not mean that "pessimism" is therefore a universal characteristic of his theology as a whole. In other words, a proper evaluation of what is "Augustinian" should respect the integrity and diversity of Augustine's thought, allowing him to speak for himself in each particular area of his theology. If one wants to see what an "Augustinian" theology of resurrection looks like, one need not look far: Augustine himself provided one. This is the only legitimate way to test whether Ratzinger's theology of resurrection can legitimately and meaningfully be described as "Augustinian."

Method and Aim of This Book

I will therefore attempt to answer the question about the Augustinian nature of Ratzinger's theology of the resurrection of the body by first considering Augustine's theology of resurrection in its own right, noting its key characteristics. This will then allow a concrete evaluation of Ratzinger's theology of resurrection from an Augustinian standpoint. In this way, it will be determined not only whether Ratzinger's theology has captured a certain element of the Augustinian spirit, but how his actual assertions relate to what Augustine thought and taught about the resurrection.

Until now, the only study of Ratzinger's eschatology that has attempted to examine his theological development over time was Nachtwei's work, which was completed twenty-five years ago. The question is thus also open as to whether Ratzinger's position vis-à-vis Augustine is static or has changed over time. And if it has changed, has it been in a direction toward, or away from, Augustine's thought? Some Ratzinger scholarship asserts a certain retreat toward more conservative ideas after the year 1968. If this is the case, might this be reflected in his theology of resurrection?

The aim of this book is twofold: to examine Ratzinger's theology of the resurrection of the body from an Augustinian standpoint, determining how and to what extent Ratzinger's theology is in continuity with Augustine's, and to consider Ratzinger's contribution to the twentieth-century resurrection debate.

General Outline

Examining Augustine's Theology of Resurrection

In chapter 1, we will identify and consider four important characteristics of Augustine's theology of the resurrection of the body. First, we will note how Augustine's theology is marked by attention to the importance of apologetics and the proclamation of the Gospel. Second, we will observe the importance of anthropological duality in Augustine's theology of resurrection. This duality encompasses the distinctions (1) between body and soul, (2) between death and resurrection, and (3) between the physical body and corruptibility. The third Augustinian characteristic is the strong emphasis placed on matter in the resurrection, while our fourth and final characteristic of Augustine's theology of resurrection is the importance of beauty.

Ratzinger's Theology of Resurrection in Light of Augustine's

Having determined our four Augustinian characteristics, we will proceed to consider Ratzinger's theology in light of them. In chapter 2 we will consider Ratzinger's apologetic approach to the resurrection. We will see that he (unlike Augustine) began his eschatology in conscious opposition to Platonism and only gradually came to accept the value of certain elements of Platonic anthropology. It will also be demonstrated that his estimation of the value of what might be called the modern worldview has depreciated over time. The result is that Ratzinger, for whom the proclamation of the good news has always been important, has moved from a position that gave the modern scientific worldview an important role in theology, to a more critical view of the natural sciences and of their influence on modern thought. This chapter will show that the more mature view of Ratzinger's corresponds with Augustine's, which sought in Platonism confirmation of the resurrection but did not define the resurrection on the basis of Platonic presuppositions.

In chapters 3, 4, and 5, we will examine Ratzinger's theology from the point of view of the anthropological duality characteristic of Augustine's theology of resurrection. Although Ratzinger was at first suspicious of the body-soul schema, which he considered to be a Greek concept incompatible with Biblical thought, he came to see it as essential to the content of Christian faith. Further, Ratzinger's more recent works argue for an intermediate state in which the soul awaits the resurrection. In order to describe this waiting period, Ratzinger utilizes the concept of *memoria*-time developed by Augustine in Book XI of the *Confessions*. This aspect of Ratzinger's anthropology is therefore strongly Augustinian. Chapter 5 will conclude by showing that in his earlier theology, Ratzinger utilized a distinction deriving from German phenomenology that allows one to differentiate between a body as a center of experience and a body as a physical entity. It will be demonstrated that this distinction, similar to one made by Augustine in his early works between body and flesh, was later abandoned by Ratzinger due to its connection to the theology of "resurrection in death" against which Ratzinger has argued with such vigour.

Finally, in chapter 6, we will consider the question of the materiality of the resurrection in Ratzinger's theology. We will see that Ratzinger has moved from an eschatology (partly influenced by Teilhard de Chardin and Karl Rahner) that tended to see eschatological fulfillment as a process, toward a more realist and even "physicalist" view of the resurrection in which the matter of this world is transformed and elevated into a new mode of existence. This newer view of Ratzinger's stresses the connection between resurrection and the corpse, and emphasizes God's ability to intervene in the biological world. Ratzinger's more recent theology thus corresponds more closely to Augustine's mature work (as found in, e.g., *De Civitate Dei* XXII) in that both tended toward a greater "physicalism" in their understanding of the resurrection.

We will also see that the fourth Augustinian characteristic (beauty), which Rowland has rightly recognized as important to certain areas of Ratzinger's thought, is not clearly apparent in Ratzinger's theology of resurrection. This is partly because Ratzinger's eschatological works exhibit a strong reservation toward imagery. I will suggest that Augustinian images of resurrected life would enhance Ratzinger's theology, providing it with greater inspirational potential.

Towards an Augustinian Realism

As a sort of conclusion, I will attempt a very limited "synthesis" of some key ideas from Augustine and Ratzinger, in order to point toward an answer to some of the important questions concerning the risen body. My intention here is to articulate a way of thinking about the resurrection that retains the deep insights of Augustine, yet incorporates some of the newer intuitions of Ratzinger. In this way, this section could be considered as a concrete verification of Ratzinger's Augustinianism, inasmuch as it is an essay at testing his theology against the standard he has so often set for himself, the standard of Augustine's own theology, which he finds so relevant even today.[26]

---

26. Benedict XVI, General Audience, January 16, 2008, par. 7. "In St. Augustine who talks to us, talks to me in his writings, we see the everlasting timeliness of his faith; of the faith that comes from Christ, the Eternal Incarnate Word, Son of God and Son of Man. And we can see that this faith is not of the past although it was preached yesterday; it is still timely today, for Christ is truly yesterday, today, and for ever."

Part One

Ratzinger the Augustinian

1

Augustine on Resurrection

Characteristics of an Augustinian Theology

First Augustinian Characteristic

Apologetics and Proclamation

Augustine the Platonist Christian

One of the reasons for Augustine's importance in the development of Christian thought is his deliberate engagement with Platonism. Like many other church fathers—the Cappadocians, for example—Augustine struggled to express his Christian faith using the philosophical tools available to him from the Platonic philosophy that he had learned. Augustine, however, did not do this without careful deliberation. He did not take Platonism for granted, and thought deeply and repeatedly about the compatibility of the thought of Plato and his intellectual descendants with the Christian faith he had received from the Church. In other words, Augustine was not simply a church father for whom Platonism was as natural and unconscious as the air he breathed. Partly because his initial embrace of Platonism was a conscious choice made in adulthood, and partly because of his own inquisitive personality, Augustine did not take for granted the compatibility of the two systems: Platonism and its intellectual progeny on the one hand, and the Church's tradition on the other.

This is not to say, however, that Augustine's understanding of the relationship between Platonism and Christianity did not undergo development. In fact, his thought progressed throughout his life in what might be described as a sort of purification whereby those elements of Platonism that he eventually found to be incoherent and in conflict with the truths of his faith were gradually expunged. One example of this was his evaluation of matter and the body. Although some have argued that Augustine remained a sort of crypto-Platonist throughout his life,[1] it appears clear to me (and to a great many other scholars) that Augustine's conversion to Christianity was a genuine one.[2] Rather than describing Augustine's Platonism in terms of "syncretism" or "influence," James McEvoy has identified the situation as one of "discernment" whereby Augustine adopted those Platonic doctrines that were in accord with his faith and rejected those that were not.[3]

From a stylistic standpoint, it is also apparent where Augustine's loyalty belongs. Lance Richey has pointed out that the rather free interpretations Augustine often gives to passages from Plato and other philosophers reveal his lack of deference to them.[4] Augustine shows far greater reverence for Scripture than for the writings of any philosopher.

Kerygmatic Apologetics

It is universally accepted, even by his detractors, that Augustine was a stunning rhetorician. He had a remarkable ability to shred his opponents' arguments to tatters and was a master of the *reductio ad absurdum*. It is

---

1. For example, Alfaric, *L'évolution intellectuelle*, 379. "c'est au Neoplatonisme qu'il s'est converti plûtot qu'à l'Evangile."

2. Consider, for example, Gilson, *Being and Some Philosophers*, 31. "What makes the greatness of St. Augustine in the history of Christian philosophy is that, deeply imbued with Neoplatonism as he was, yet he never made the mistake of devaluating being, not even in order to extol the One. There is a great deal of Neoplatonism in Augustine, but there is a point, and it is a decisive one, at which he parts company with Plotinus: there is nothing above God in the Christian world of Augustine, and, since God is being, there is nothing above being."

3. McEvoy, "Neoplatonism and Christianity."

4. Richey, "Porphyry, Reincarnation and Resurrection," 136.

also true that the Platonists—particularly Porphyry—were the target of many of Augustine's rhetorical salvos. Yet Augustine's approach to Platonism is not one of constant controversialist bombardment. In fact, much of his writing praises the Platonists for their ingenuity and for the truths they have discovered. But Augustine is not content with congratulations, however deserved they may be; his overarching plan is to show how the truths of Platonism are fulfilled by the revelation that comes in Christ and the Church.

If the atmosphere in the Roman Empire at the turn of the fifth century was comprehensively molded by Platonism and its "metaphysical disqualification of the body and of everything in us which, because of the body, was dependent on crude matter,"[5] then it is not surprising that an intellectual like Augustine would seek to proclaim the Gospel in a way that would affirm—as much as possible—the truths already embraced by the culture at large.

In this case, Augustine's kerygmatic *apologia* has a dual thrust: it is directed both to the Christians living in a very Platonic world and to the Platonists themselves. This is a point of decisive importance: for Augustine, Platonism does not represent a philosophy to be shunned but rather a group of people to be saved. This is fundamental to his attitude toward Platonism. Augustine would have encountered Platonists on the streets and in the marketplace. Some were his acquaintances.[6] Augustine's apologetic approach to Platonism is thus not one of outright rejection but rather selective affirmation.

Of all the philosophies, Augustine believed that Platonism came closest to the truths in Christianity.[7] The "Platonic philosophers, whose name is derived from that of their teacher, Plato," confess a God "Who is above all that belongs to the nature of the soul . . . Who made not only the visible world . . . but also every soul whatever."[8] Augustine goes on to remark

---

5. Marrou, *Resurrection*, 9.

6. Marius Victorinus, for example.

7. Augustine, *civ. Dei* 8.5. "No one has come closer to us than the Platonists." When citing Augustine, I will normally provide an accepted English translation. When I consider a consultation of the Latin text to be helpful in elucidating Augustine's meaning, however, I will provide it as well.

8. Ibid., 8.1. Also, *civ. Dei* 8.5 where Augustine expresses his desire that the two forms of pagan theology (the mythical, pertaining to myths about the gods, and the civil, pertaining to temple rituals) would give way "to the philosophy of the Platonists, who have said that the true God is the author of all things, the illuminator of truth, and the giver of happiness."

that many Christians are amazed to discover that Plato's understanding of God was so consistent with the truth of Christianity.[9] Yet in spite of these important truths, the Platonists lack the goal of all philosophy: Christ the incarnate God.[10]

One of the most influential of the Platonist philosophers was Porphyry, a disciple of Plotinus. Yet while Augustine can praise him for his brilliance and discovery of truth, in the end he laments that Porphyry did not discover what he was really seeking: "If only you had known Him [Christ]; if only you had entrusted yourself to Him for healing, rather than to your own virtue which, being human, is fragile and infirm, or to most pernicious curiousity."[11] This concern for the man himself is characteristic of Augustine's approach to Platonism as a whole. There is admiration for the brilliance of the system, and sorrow that it cannot follow its own truths to their ultimate end. Augustine does not simply want to refute Porphyry; he wants to evangelize him.

Fundamental to this approach is the presupposition that Platonism and Christianity are not fundamentally opposed, although they may be in conflict on particular points. This view is not universally shared by modern theologians, however, as the modern de-Hellenizing movement gives evidence. When Platonism and Christianity are seen as fundamentally opposed, most theologians prefer to reject Platonism. For Augustine, however, Platonism was a lighthouse of truth on a raging sea of competing philosophies and mythologies which might for a time prevent shipwreck, yet was ultimately found to be only a reflection of the true Light, whose fulfillment and correction it required.

Augustine's Rhetorical Strategy

The Structure of *De Civitate Dei*

Because Augustine's thought with respect to Platonism developed throughout his life, we will focus our attention on his mature works, particularly *De Civitate Dei Contra Paganos* (*The City of God Against the Pagans*, written between 412–26). This work, as its name suggests, is a sort of *apologia*

---

9. Ibid., 8.11.
10. See Augustine, *civ. Dei* 9.15.
11. Ibid., 10.28.

Augustine on Resurrection

against the entire pagan world. And since much of that world was shaped by Platonism, Augustine deals with it in considerable detail. The overall structure of *De Civitate Dei* can be used as a frame within which to set Augustine's rhetorical relationship to Platonism.

Augustine himself describes the organization of the twenty-two-book work as consisting of five parts:

> Let the first contain the first five books, in which I write against those who claim that the worship of the gods—or, as I should rather say, of evil spirits—leads to happiness in this life. Let the second volume contain the next five books, written against those who think that such deities are to be worshipped by rites and sacrifices in order to secure happiness in the world to come. Let the three following volumes contain four books each: I have arranged this part of the work in such a way that four books describe the origin of that City, four its progress—or, rather, its development—and the final four the ends which await it.[12]

Much of the first part of the work (Books I–V) rebuts the pagan accusation that the recent sack of Rome was punishment for Rome's apostasy from the worship of the gods when it became Christian. The third and fourth parts deal largely with questions about creation, and salvation history as recorded in the Old Testament. Of particular interest to us are the second part (Books VI–X), where Augustine considers what could effectively be called pagan soteriology and eschatology, and the fifth and final part, where he considers the last things (judgment, hell, heaven).

Looking at the structure as a whole, we glimpse Augustine's rhetorical plan. First, pagan philosophy and mythology are shown to be impotent as regards both earthly (part 1) and heavenly (part 2) happiness. This is true as regards heavenly happiness because even though Platonic philosophy correctly identifies God as the ultimate *telos* of the human being, no pagan sacrifices or rituals are capable of providing adequate mediation between the human and the divine. Augustine praises the Platonists for their discovery of truth by means of philosophy, yet chastizes Platonists like Porphyry for being inconsistent by their approval of superstitions like the practice of theurgy, whereby rites were performed to obtain favors from gods or other celestial beings.

---

12. This is an excerpt from a letter the full Latin text of which is found in Lambot, "Lettre inédite de S. Augustin." The English translation is from Dyson's introduction to his edition of *City of God*, xiii.

For Augustine, the only real solution to the dilemma of mediation is the incarnation of the Son of God, which the Platonists cannot accept because of their rejection of the flesh. Augustine outlines the Christian doctrine of creation (part 3) and God's action in that creation through his revelation to Israel, which culminates in the incarnation (part 4). Finally, having explained *how* we are saved, Augustine describes *what* salvation is (part 5). It is here that Augustine responds to the objections of Porphyry on the bodily nature of beatitude, appealing to the natural world and the shared heritage of human reason.

On the question of the resurrection, we will see that Augustine's rhetorical strategy (in *De Civitate Dei*) consists in (*a*) defusing objections to resurrection in principle, (*b*) affirming and accepting certain truths held dear by the Platonists, (*c*) pointing out the inadequacy of the Platonic system as it stood and its need for Christian fulfillment, and (*d*) demonstrating that the resurrection of the body is supported by insights from Plato and other Platonist philosophers. We will now examine each of these points in detail.

The Credibility of the Resurrection: Miracles and the Natural World

Augustine employs various arguments for the credibility of the resurrection which are not explicitly directed against Platonic philosophy but which seek to prove its reasonability by appealing to the natural world and to the power of God, something even the Platonists did not deny. These arguments answer the rational objections raised by opponents, thereby opening the way to other, positive arguments *for* the resurrection.

Miracles

One of the supposed attractions of theurgy was the possibility of obtaining miracles. Although the worldview of the time was not completely mythologized, there is no question that Platonists, as well as regular Roman citizens, accepted the idea of frequent miraculous interventions by divine beings. In *De Civitate Dei* 22.8, Augustine provides an immense catalogue of miracles that he has either witnessed or knows of personally. The list is staggeringly long, comprising more than thirty-eight hundred words in the Latin text. Augustine begins by stating that the point of miracles is to testify to "that one grand and saving miracle of Christ's ascension into heaven in the flesh in which he rose."[13] Since Augustine's purpose is to use his catalogue of miracles as evidence for the resurrection of the body, it is telling that virtually all of the miracles listed are bodily healings. They point not only to the possibility of miraculous events, but point more specifically to God's power to heal and transform the body.

The Natural World

In response to those who find miracles simply unbelievable, Augustine counters with examples from the natural world which, considered objectively, are just as wonderful as miraculous healings and even the resurrection of the body. For Augustine, the created world is "beyond doubt a miracle greater and more excellent than all the wonders with which it is filled."[14] The fact that anything exists at all is more wonderful than any events that might occur within that created world. And although it may be difficult to imagine that a body completely decomposed in the tomb could ever rise again, we ought to "consider equally the hidden and daily miracles of nature."[15]

Augustine's point is that the difference between the natural and the miraculous is sometimes only one of perception. In *De Trinitate* Book III, he declares that we call something a miracle if it is sufficiently out of the ordinary or unexpected, while if miraculous things happen over and over again, we call them natural.[16] In *De Civitate Dei*, he provides examples of various natural phenomena which at first glance appear utterly amazing, yet after continued experience seem merely natural. Such examples

13. Augustine, *civ. Dei* 22.8.

14. Ibid., 21.7.

15. Augustine, *s.* 362A.2. My translation, from the end of this longer passage: "Hoc autem solum solet quasi movere homines, quomodo resurgant consumpta corpora quae propterea sepeliuntur, quia offendunt oculos cum (con)sumuntur; quia cara nobis erant cum animabus quas habebant, recedentibus autem inde animabus iacent ea quae diligebamus et nolumus ante conspectum illa corrumpi, propterea sepelimus. Cum ergo dicitur quod sint resurrectura, intendis, cor humanum, quid nunc fiat, et non credis quod futurum est? Nam si perpendas et recte iudices, parum consideras secreta et cotidiana naturae miracula . . ." The text of this newly discovered sermon is taken from Schiller, Weber, and Weidmann, "Sechs neue Augustinuspredigten." Consider also *s.* 242A.2 where Augustine states that the resurrection is "rehearsed over and over again by daily evidences. Nature cries it aloud."

16. Augustine, *Trin.* 3.11. For an English translation, see vol. 5 of The Works of Saint Augustine. Unless otherwise noted, all English citations of *De Trinitate* are from this edition.

include the properties of lye, magnets, charcoal, and diamonds.[17] From his detailed descriptions of these substances—Augustine is particularly impressed by a friend's story about tricks one can play with magnets[18]—one glimpses Augustine's fascination with the natural world, or with what we would today call "science."

Resurrection and Birth

Of all these everyday, "natural" occurrences, Augustine considers the creation of new human beings to be the most worthy of awe. The problem, from an epistemological point of view, is that we deem the birth of new human beings to be unremarkable. Yet in fact this event ought to fill us with more wonder than the resurrection of bodies: "At least in the tomb you can see cinders, you can see bones; in your mother's womb there was nothing. You can see this, at least the cinders are there, at least the bones are there. As for you, before you existed, there were neither cinders nor bones; and yet you were made, when you didn't exist at all."[19] Augustine's point is simple: "He, therefore, who can create what was not, can He not restore that which already existed?"[20] This birth-resurrection analogy is used by Augustine—it seems to this author—more than any other argument in defense of the resurrection's credibility.[21] Interestingly, however, it is almost only used in his sermons, and is not mentioned in *De Civitate Dei* or the *Enchiridion*. While the argument certainly would be easy for the uneducated to understand (which would explain its use in his sermons), it is not clear why Augustine would be hesitant to use it in controversies with the Platonists. Perhaps he eventually discarded the argument, which would explain its absence from later works like *De Civitate Dei* and the *Enchiridion*. On the other hand, since for the Platonists the process of conception and birth was less of a wonder and more of a curse (involving imprisonment in a body), it is possible that Augustine elected to avoid this analogy when disputing with them.

17. Augustine, *civ. Dei* 21.4-6.

18. Ibid., 21.4.

19. Augustine, *s.* 127.15. English translation from vol. III/4 of The Works of Saint Augustine.

20. Augustine, *s.* 361.12.12. English translation from Augustine, "Sermons 361 and 362" (trans. John A Mourant). Unless otherwise noted, all citations from *Sermons* 361 and 362 are taken from this edition.

21. Examples of this argument include, but are probably not limited to, *s.* 127.15; *s.* 242.1; *s.* 242A.2; *s.* 264.6; *s.* 316.12.12; *s.* 362A.2; *Trin.* 3.11.

The Power of God

Another argument that Augustine often invokes when he anticipates strong objections to the resurrection is God's power, which even the pagans accept.[22] Although this is not itself a positive argument for resurrection, it is designed to eliminate the objection that the resurrection is impossible. In this way, it clears the way for his other arguments. The Platonists acknowledged an all-powerful God. Augustine thus reminds them that "God is certainly called 'Almighty' precisely because He is able to do whatever He wills."[23] Later in the same work, he maintains that for those who doubt the resurrection of the body, God's omnipotence alone is enough argument.[24]

Augustine is using the Platonists' acceptance of an all-powerful deity to unhinge their objections to resurrection in principle. If there truly exists an omnipotent God (as the Platonists admit), then events like resurrection cannot be dismissed out of hand. Augustine wants to utilize belief in the God of the philosophers as a first step toward faith in the Christian God of the resurrection.

The Truth of Platonism

Although *De Civitate Dei* is in many ways an attack on pagan philosophy, it is not a rejection of the whole of it.[25] Augustine recognized that the Platonists had, by their own methods, discovered profound truths. The greatest of these concerned the *telos* or goal of human existence. Augustine notes that while all the other philosophers have attempted to locate the ultimate human good in the mind, or body, or both of these, the Platonists recognize that the one true Good of human beings is found not in man but God.[26] "This, therefore, is the reason why we prefer the Platonists to all others: because, while other philosphers have exhausted their ingenuity

---

22. See, for example, *s.* 240.2; *s.* 242.7; *s.* 362.15.18; *civ. Dei* 21.7; 22.25.

23. Augustine, *civ. Dei* 21.7.

24. Ibid., 22.25.

25. Ibid., 8.1. "For I have not undertaken this work in order to refute the vain opinions of all the philosophers, but only those whose opinions have to do with theology (which Greek word we understand to signify reason or discourse concerning divinity); and not, indeed, all of those."

26. Ibid., 8.8. "The Platonists say that a man is happy not in the enjoyment of the body or in the enjoyment of the mind, but in the enjoyment of God . . . as the eye enjoys light."

and zeal in seeking the causes of things and the right way to learn and to live, these, by knowing God, have discovered where to find the cause by which the universe was established, and the light by which truth is to be perceived, and the fount at which we may drink of happiness."[27]

The Value of Porphyry

While Augustine esteemed the Platonists in general for seeing God as the human goal, he particularly approved of certain aspects of Porphyry's philosophy. Although there is ongoing debate as to whether Plotinus or Porphyry ought to be considered the greater influence on the thought of Augustine,[28] this particular squabble is ultimately irrelevant for us since Porphyry is unquestionably more important in the discussion of human beatitude. Porphyry was a philosopher of towering importance in Augustine's time,[29] yet probably due to his anti-Christian polemic, none of his writings survive intact today. Nonetheless, fragments remain in citations from Augustine and other writers.

Augustine shows particular admiration for how close Porphyry came to Christian doctrine. He notes approvingly that, for Porphyry, beatitude is not simply union with a transcendent One, but a "return to the Father."[30] Augustine later cites Porphyry's explanation of how God effects moral transformation in human lives: "For God indeed, who is the Father of all, has no need of anything; but it is good for us to adore Him by means of justice, chastity, and the other virtues, and to make our whole life a prayer to Him by imitating Him and seeking to know Him. For seeking to know Him purges us, while imitation of Him deifies us by causing our disposition to resemble His."[31]

---

27. Ibid., 8.10. Augustine also notes that Plato said that happiness only comes from virtue (cf. *Gorgias* 470D), and that since God is the highest good, the philosopher will only be happy when he enjoys God (*civ. Dei* 8.8).

28. For an introduction to this debate, see Richey, "Porphyry, Reincarnation and Resurrection," 129–30.

29. Evangeliou, "Porphyry's Criticism of Christianity," 52. "Porphyry was the recognized defender of Hellenic polytheism and a formidable foe of Christianity." Evangeliou's position, however, is that Augustine and the Church helped forge a false alliance between the contradictory philosophies of Christianity and Hellenism.

30. Augustine, *civ. Dei* 10.30. "He [Porphyry] says also that God put the soul into the world so that, having come to understand the evil nature of material things, it might return to the Father."

31. Ibid., 19.23. Augustine adds that "Porphyry certainly spoke well proclaiming God the Father and in telling of the conduct by which He is to be worshiped; and the

Further, Augustine lauds Porphyry for his awareness that there are two *principia* by which we are cleansed: God the Father, and God the Son (who is the intellect or Mind of the Father).[32] Augustine later points out that Porphyry also posits a third entity between the Father and his Intellect or Mind, and calls these three gods. Porphyry, then, does "to some extent see as it were a kind of shadowy image of what we should strive towards."[33]

Augustine also credits Porphyry with holding an elementary doctrine of grace. "You [Porphyry] confess that there is such a thing as grace, however; for you say that it has been granted only to a few to reach God by the power of their intelligence.... Beyond doubt, then, you acknowledge the grace of God, not the sufficiency of man."[34]

It would seem that Augustine even made use of an element of Porphyrian anthropology in his understanding of beatitude. Several scholars have remarked on Augustine's concept of the soul's post-death "spiritual vision" in Book XII of *De Genesi ad Litteram* and its dependence on Porphyry's notion of the spiritual soul.[35] Although Augustine does not attribute this concept to Porphyry, Gerard Watson suggests that there was a good reason for this: given Porphyry's bad reputation in Christian circles (he had written a work called *Against the Christians*), Augustine feared that any argument based on an insight of Porphyry's would be rejected out of hand because of its provenance.[36] Whether this is true or not, it is clear that in Augustine's view, Porphyry was a Platonist worth borrowing from.

Although John O'Meara's thesis—that the whole of *De Civitate Dei* is essentially a response to Porphyry[37]—may go too far, we can at least

---

prophetic books of the Hebrews are full of such precepts, whereby the life of holy men is enjoined upon us or praised." It is uncertain which work of Porphyry's Augustine is citing.

32. Ibid., 10.23.

33. Ibid., 10.29.

34. Ibid.

35. These include Watson, "St. Augustine, the Platonists and the Resurrection Body"; Finan, "Modes of Vision in St. Augustine"; O'Donoghue, "The Awakening of the Dead"; O'Meara, "Parting from Porphyry"; Te Selle, "Porphyry and Augustine." Te Selle (144) notes that Augustine would have found this concept in Porphyry's *De regressu animae* (*On the Return of the Soul*).

36. Watson, "St. Augustine, the Platonists and the Resurrection Body," 231.

37. O'Meara, *Charter of Christendom*, 75. "The chief negative target of [*The City of God*] is the work or works [of Porphyry] which I shall refer to as the *Philosophy from Oracles*. It is as an answer to the *Philosophy from Oracles* that the *City of God* in the context of its own times can best be understood."

agree with Richey when he concludes that "it is clear that Augustine read Porphyry closely and intentionally dealt with and accepted parts of his theory of the soul's destiny."[38]

The Problem of Mediation

While the Platonists had achieved the feat of discovering a single, transcendent God who is the source of all things, some of them displayed what Augustine saw as a glaring inconsistency in their approval of theurgic rites. For the Platonists, however, such practices could be seen as necessary based on the hierarchy of being which they professed, in which the spiritual was placed above the material, with various intermediate beings filling in the space between man and God.[39] Porphyry's vision of ultimate beatitude was union with "the Father,"[40] but achieving this union was not a simple task. Eugene Te Selle explains the Porphyrian necessity of mediation: "If the human soul is alienated from God, he cannot be accurately known or eagerly sought without the mediation of finite symbols, events, or persons which cross the chasm and meet the soul in its actual situation."[41]

In *De Civitate Dei*, Augustine explains that for the Platonists there are essentially three kinds of souls.[42] They are, in descending order of perfection: gods, demons, and men. Interestingly, all three have bodies. The bodies of the gods are made of ether,[43] while the bodies of demons are similar to the gods and far superior to ours.[44] What is important, however, is that the demons were considered to have "an eternal body, like the gods,

---

38. Richey, "Porphyry, Reincarnation and Resurrection," 137.

39. See, for example, O'Meara, "Parting from Porphyry," 360.

40. For example, Augustine, *civ. Dei* 10.30. "Porphyry . . . said that the purified soul returns to the Father, that it may never again be held fast in the defiling contagion of evil."

41. Te Selle, "Porphyry and Augustine," 125. Te Selle suggests that Augustine may have borrowed his concept of mediation from Porphyry. If this were the case, it would be another example of Augustine making use of Platonic concepts to proclaim the Gospel.

42. Augustine, *civ. Dei* 8.14.

43. Ibid., 8.21.

44. Ibid., 8.15. It is certain that the bodies of the demons are superior to ours. It is unclear to me, however, whether their bodies were considered to be ethereal, like the gods, or in some intermediate form between flesh and ether. In any case, Augustine's argument is unchanged.

but a flawed soul, like that of men."[45] In this way, demons were seen as being capable of mediating between humanity and the gods, since they shared something in common with each.

Books VIII, IX, and X of *De Civitate Dei* are largely an assault on the notion that union with God (or the gods) can be brought about by the mediation of demons. Augustine is especially critical of Porphyry, who held that a philosopher had no need of theurgy since he could ascend to God by the *intellectual* soul, yet nonetheless recommended theurgy to the common people lacking intellectual ability, since theurgy purifies the *spiritual* soul.[46]

Augustine's response to the claims of Platonists like Porphyry regarding theurgy is relatively simple. While it is possible that demons could be mediators since they share with us a fallen soul, and with the gods an eternal body, they can only be mediators of misery.[47] They are entirely unworthy of our worship since in them, the most important part (the soul, which rules the body) is just as corrupt as our own.[48] The demons share our misery, yet are incapable of freeing themselves from it—even by death, since they cannot die.[49]

If, then, we are to have a mediator, it would need to be someone who could share—at least temporarily—in our misery in this life, and who would simultaneously be God.[50] The only mediator capable of bestowing true happiness, of course, is Jesus Christ, the God who became man. We need no other mediators "because a God Who is blessed and bliss-bestowing has become a sharer in our humanity, and so has furnished us with all that we need to share in His divinity."[51]

Augustine, then, essentially flattens out the Platonic system of mediation: the supreme God bypasses all the intermediaries and unites himself directly with the lowest level in the Platonic chain of being. This means

---

45. Ibid., 9.9. While imperfect, not all demons were considered evil. Augustine notes that the Platonists believed in the existence of "good demons or . . . angels" (*civ. Dei* 10.1).

46. Ibid., 10.9.

47. Ibid., 9.15.

48. Ibid., 9.9.

49. In *civ. Dei* 9.10, Augustine cites Plotinus as saying that God was merciful in giving men mortal bodies since doing so provides them a means of escaping these miserable bodies. The demons, however, have no such possibility.

50. Ibid., 9.15.

51. Ibid.

that superhuman beings—angels and demons—need not be worshiped since our salvation has been arranged directly by God himself. It also implies a complete reevaluation of matter, since God has become flesh: "For there are two wholesome lessons of no small importance which His incarnation reveals to us at the present time: that true divinity cannot be contaminated by flesh; and that demons are not to be thought better than ourselves because they do not have flesh."[52]

Although Porphyry had posited different forms of purification for the different parts of the soul (one for the intellectual soul and one for the spiritual), Augustine proclaims that our Savior has taken on the *whole* of human nature.[53] Christ's mediation is thus the universal means of the soul's deliverance that Porphyry had sought, but been unable to find.[54]

Why, then, did Porphyry—who lived during the period of the Church—not accept Christ as the Mediator? Augustine, defending Porphyry, suggests that perhaps the Church had not grown large enough at that time to convince him that it was more than a passing sect.[55] He finds Porphyry guilty of a certain intellectual dishonesty, suggesting in numerous places that the theurgic rites which he adopted from "Chaldean masters" (and *not*, Augustine emphasizes, from Plato) were considered by Porphyry himself to be of rather dubious value, yet were recommended by him to reward his Chaldean teachers.[56]

Ultimately, however, Augustine attributes Porphyry's rejection of Christ to pride.[57] Unable to accept that the supreme God could take on something as lowly as flesh, Porphyry dismissed the possibility of an incarnation. It was this same dismissal of flesh and bodies which led Porphyry to attack the other Christian doctrine of the body: the *resurrectio carnis*.

---

52. Ibid., 9.17.

53. Ibid., 10.32. "This way cleanses the whole man, and prepares each of the parts of which a mortal man is made for immortality. We need not seek one purification for the part which Porphyry calls intellectual, and another for the part he calls spiritual, and another for the body itself; for our most true and mighty Purifier and Saviour took upon Himself the whole of human nature."

54. Ibid., 10.32.

55. Ibid.

56. Ibid., 10.11; 10.28.

57. Ibid., 10.24. Also, *civ. Dei* 10.29. "It is, presumably, a matter of shame for learned men to leave the school of Plato and become disciples of the Christ Who by His Spirit taught a fisherman to think, and to say: in the beginning was the Word, and the Word was with God, and the Word was God."

Given Augustine's respect for Porphyry, it is interesting to note that in responding to him, Augustine never suggests any intellectual flaws in his opponent. He attributes Porphyry's errors to the influence of friends, and to pride (a moral failing). Augustine would rather impugn Porphyry's morals than the excellence of his intellect.

Porphyry's Objections to the Resurrection

Porphyry was the only well-known Platonist to have disputed with Christians over the resurrection of the body. As a Platonist, he was bound to reject both the incarnation and the resurrection, since matter and flesh were seen as antagonistic to perfection and divinity. Yet according to Augustine, the Platonists wanted to reject matter not because it was ontologically evil but because it was morally problematic: "The Platonists are not, indeed, so foolish as the Manichaeans; for they do not detest earthly bodies as the natural substance of evil [*mali naturam*],"[58] but they hold that every element was made by God, the Creator. "Nonetheless, they hold that souls are so influenced by earthly limbs and dying members that they derive from them their unwholesome desires and fears and joys and sorrows."[59]

For the Platonists, then, the material world was not created by an evil being (as in some Gnostic mythology) but by God the Creator. It was thus not evil in itself, but only with respect to its ability to weigh down the soul and distract it from its divine vocation. Yet this was still reason enough to shun the body. Much of Augustine's writing on the resurrection is a response to Porphyry's famous dictum *ut beata sit anima, corpus esse omne fugiendum.*[60]

Corpus esse omne fugiendum

Augustine's chief bulwark against this attack is, of course, the incarnation. Yet for those for whom this was not a sufficient defense, Augustine provides further reasons based on the teachings of the Platonists themselves. We find this response in Books X and XXII of *De Civitate Dei*, as well as in *Sermons* 241 and 242.

---

58. Ibid., 14.5.

59. Ibid.

60. Ibid., 10.29; 22.26. The passage likely derives from Porphyry's no longer extant work *De regressu animae* (*On the Return of the Soul*).

Part One: Ratzinger the Augustinian

His main tack is essentially to place the opinions of Plato and Porphyry in opposition to each other. He does this by first noting that not even the writings of the great Plato are sacrosanct: "If it is thought improper to change anything which Plato taught, why did Porphyry himself make so many changes, and these of no small significance?"[61] Most significant of these is the belief, held by both Plato and Plotinus, in perpetual reincarnation. According to this idea, the blessed souls of the human dead would eventually experience a period of forgetfulness and would then long to return to a body. They would then return and animate the bodies of other humans, or even animals.[62] Porphyry, however, rejected this idea of cyclical, eternal reincarnation, holding that the soul—once purified—would enter beatitude with "the Father" and never again suffer the pain of this world.[63]

Augustine illustrates the absurdity of a supposed beatitude which is always followed by more misery. If these souls know they are going to again be miserable, they cannot be happy, and if they do not know, then they are ignorant. But can true beatitude consist in ignorance? This leads to the question of why anyone would teach such a doctrine in the first place. As Augustine sarcastically intones in *Sermon* 241, "Tell me, please, even if all this rubbish were true, wouldn't it be better not to know it?"[64]

Porphyry, however, receives glowing praise for parting ways with Plato on this issue: "Here is a Platonist dissenting from Plato and taking a better view; here is one who saw what Plato did not see, and who, even though he came after so great and so distinguished a master, did not hesitate to correct him; for he preferred truth to Plato."[65] Having shown the

---

61. Ibid., 10.30.

62. Ibid. For Plato's opinion that the souls of the dead may return to the bodies of animals, see *Phaedo* 81E; *Phaedrus* 249B; *Republic* 10.619D; *Timaeus* 42C. For the same view in Plotinus, see Stobaeus, *Eclogae Physicae* I.52.

63. Augustine, *civ. Dei* 10.30. "He [Porphyry] says also that God put the soul into the world so that, having come to understand the evil nature of material things, it might return to the Father, and never again be defiled by contact with them.... [H]e acknowledges that the soul, once cleansed of all evil and established in the Father's presence, will never again suffer the ills of this world." This does not mean, however, that Porphyry rejected all reincarnation; he simply rejected (1) eternal, cyclical reincarnation, and (2) the possibility of being reincarnated in the body of an animal. One of his reasons for rejecting the latter was the absurdity of a mother being reincarnated as an ass, and having her own son ride on top of her.

64. Augustine, *s.* 241.5. English translation from vol. III/7 of The Works of Saint Augustine. Augustine makes the same point in *civ. Dei* 10.30.

65. Augustine, *civ. Dei* 10.30.

Platonists that it is reasonable to reject cyclical reincarnation, Augustine now moves to demolish the Porphyrian objection that every kind of body is to be shunned. He does this by pointing out that when the Platonists condemn bodies, they do not really mean bodies as such, but the corruptible bodies possessed by fallen human beings. He indicates that Plato himself held that the stars are ensouled bodies, and are gods.[66] He alludes to *Timaeus* 41 A-B, where the gods are given immortal bodies.[67] And he reminds Porphyry of his own belief that there is a soul of the universe, thus making the universe one great body which, as Augustine points out, Porphyry does not advocate shunning.[68]

Augustine's strategy, then, is to prove to the Platonists that their philosophy is not as anti-corporeal as they might at first think. By making the careful distinction between corruptible and incorruptible bodies, he shows the Platonists that their beliefs are not incompatible with a bodily resurrection, or even an incarnation. "What is required to ensure the soul's blessedness, then, is not an escape from any kind of body whatsoever but the acquisition of an incorruptible body. And what incorruptible body could be better adapted to the joy of those who rise again than the one in which they groaned when it was corruptible?"[69]

According to Augustine, Porphyry's valid point is that it would indeed be a tragic thing for souls to return to the miserable condition of earthly embodiment. Thus, as Porphyry understood it, the dictum *corpus esse omne fugiendum* was correct inasmuch as he saw embodiment only in terms of the fallen human bodies we now have. But once one recognizes the possibility of an *incorruptible* human body, the main Platonic objections disappear. "Therefore Plato and Porphyry—or, rather, those of their admirers who are now alive—agree with us that even holy souls will return to bodies (as Plato says), but that they will not return to any evils (as Porphyry says). Now it follows from these premises that the soul will receive the kind of body in which it can live for ever in felicity, without any evil; which is what the Christian faith preaches."[70] Here Augustine

---

66. Augustine, *s.* 241.7. The same point is made in *civ. Dei* 10.29.

67. Augustine, *civ. Dei* 22.26. Also, Yudin, "Refutando a Porfirio mediante Platón." Yudin (251) thinks that Augustine misreads the *Timaeus*, taking Plato out of context and confusing the Demiurge with the One God. This does not change Augustine's point, however, since we have an instance of Plato approving of an eternal body.

68. Augustine, *s.* 241.7.

69. Augustine, *civ. Dei* 22.26.

70. Ibid., 22.28. He continues by suggesting that if we add Varro's teaching that the soul returns to the very same body, the whole question can be resolved simply by

is truly working his best rhetorical magic. In the face of two seemingly irreconcilable positions, he draws the extraordinary conclusion that Platonism, rather than contradicting the resurrection of the body, actually supports it.

Apologetics and Proclamation: Summary

Augustine, while admiring the Platonists and learning all he could from them, owed his primary allegiance to Christianity rather than Platonism. He recognized important truths in the philosophies that sprang from Plato, such as the existence of a single, all-powerful, Creator God, and the identification of the human end as union with God. In his disputes with the Platonists, Augustine's rhetoric and language were geared not toward mere polemical victory, but to a creative proclamation of the Gospel using the truths that the Platonists themselves already accepted. The basic presupposition of this is the potential compatibility of Christianity with Platonism, or at least elements thereof.

Augustine provides defenses of the resurrection's credibility based on the example of miracles (chiefly bodily healings) and on everyday wondrous events (like birth), which would be acclaimed as miracles were it not for their regularity. He points to God's omnipotence in order to dispose of the argument that resurrection is impossible. Since even the Platonists accept God's power, any out of hand dismissal of the resurrection is thereby disallowed.

The structure of Augustine's anti-Platonist rhetoric can be seen in *De Civitate Dei*. There, Augustine expresses his admiration for the thought of Platonists like Porphyry, who discovered the true goal of human existence. He then argues that since Platonism lacks a means of universal mediation between the human and the divine, its discovery of the human *telos* becomes frustrated by its impotence to attain that *telos*, which requires Christ who is both God and man.

Platonists like Porphyry reject the incarnation for the same reason they reject the resurrection of the body: they view the body as a weight on the soul and as incompatible with beatitude. Augustine, however, shows that incorruptible bodies—which the Platonists already acknowledge in the cases of the gods—are not a source of weight or misery. He plays Plato and Porphyry off each other, drawing the conclusion that we will indeed

---

recourse to the Platonists' own philosophers.

return to bodies (as Plato said), yet we will not return to corruptible bodies (as Porphyry said). In this way, he infers the doctrine of the resurrection from the Platonists' own teachings.

Augustine, then, not only utilizes elements of Platonic philosophy but actively employs that philosophy in his discussion with the Platonists. His goal, of course, is not only rhetorical victory but evangelization, since Christ who is the Truth fulfills all the longings of the philosophers: "If only you had known Him; if only you had entrusted yourself to Him for healing."[71]

Second Augustinian Characteristic

Anthropological Duality: Making Distinctions

The Charge of Dualism

In the twentieth century, the charge of dualism was leveled against Augustine on more than one occasion. Hans Küng has bemoaned the influence of what he calls "the Platonic-Augustinian-Cartesian body-soul dualism."[72] Karen Börresen recognizes that Augustine is no Gnostic, yet she still believes that his reading of Scripture is "impregnated by dualist anthropology,"[73] that his doctrine of original sin is derived from "a lingering Manichean dualism,"[74] and that his idea of a separated body and soul reuniting after death "is based on a dualist anthropology in the sense that it affirms that man consists of two radically opposed elements, one mortal and the other immortal."[75] Pietro Ferrisi, restricting his analysis to Augustine's very early work,[76] concludes (approvingly) that Augustine's

---

71. Ibid., 10.28.

72. Küng. *Eternal Life?*, 110. He also implicates Thomas Aquinas in this "Platonism" (219).

73. Börresen, "Augustin, interprète du dogme de la résurrection," 152. She states that Augustine's anthropology is "imprégnée d'anthropologie dualiste."

74. Ibid., 149. She blames "une réminiscence du dualisme manichéen."

75. Ibid., 154. Augustine's theology of resurrection "se fonde sur une anthropologie dualiste dans ce sense qu'elle affirme que l'homme consiste en deux éléments radicalement opposés, l'un mortel et l'autre immortel."

76. In this case, mainly Augustine's *De Fide et Symbolo*, written in 393.

eschatological ideas were based on those of Plato and Origen rather than the Hebrew world of the Old Testament.[77]

Gisbert Greshake suggests that Augustine's view of the soul is "Neoplatonically colored" and that "a certain body-soul dualism—a leftover of Manichean thought and the consequence of Neoplatonic influence—can hardly be overlooked in some of his formulations."[78] As is the case with Ferrisi, this conclusion appears to be based only on Augustine's early works.[79]

What are we to make of these statements, which represent what we might call the popular academic opinion on Augustine? Without responding to each directly, several observations are in order. First, there is no doubt—as we have already seen—that Augustine made use of Platonic ideas. Whether or not this is a problem is another question altogether. Second, Augustine's thought developed over the course of his life in a process of intellectual purification whereby, testing his philosophy against the truth of the Gospel and his own reason, he gradually rejected those elements that were found to be incompatible with Christian faith. It is therefore unhelpful to make sweeping statements about Augustine's view on a particular position based only on his early works, or without attention to his theological development.

Third, and most important for our investigation here, the accusations of dualism (whatever that word may mean in the minds of the accusers) unquestionably point to a real anthropological *duality* in Augustine's anthropology. Whether or not it is a dualism of the Platonic or Cartesian stripe, it is certainly not a monism. Augustine's theology of resurrection, like the rest of his thought, is predicated upon distinctions, the most fundamental being between body and soul. We will thus examine three key distinctions made by Augustine and observe how they serve to safeguard the reality of the resurrection.

---

77. Ferrisi, "La resurrezione della carne," 223.

78. Greshake, *Resurrectio Mortuorum*, 211–12. "Auf Grund seines neuplatonisch gefärbten Seelenverständnisses . . . Die Seele ist vielmehr nach Augustin rein geistig, leiblos und steht als solche dem Leib gegenüber. Ein gewisser Dualismus von Leib und Seele—Reste manichäischen Denkens und Folgen neuplatonischen Einflusses—läßt sich in manchen seiner Formulierungen kaum übersehen." Later in the same book, however, Greshake praises Augustine for his gradual rejection of the Platonic understanding of the soul's immortality (288–90).

79. Ibid., 212. He cites Augustine's *De quantitate animae* 13.22 to show that Augustine sees the soul as the pilot (German *Lenkerin*) of the body, and *De moribus ecclesiae* 1.27.52 to show that he also views the soul as something that uses the body.

The Distinction between Body and Soul

The most fundamental of the anthropological distinctions made by Augustine is that between body and soul. Following centuries of Greek thought, he accepts that there is something immaterial in man. Yet unlike Plato or his later followers, Augustine did not see the human being as soul alone, but always as a composite: "man is a rational substance consisting of soul and body."[80] Augustine emphasizes that while both make up the human being, they are not the same thing.[81]

The body represents the corporeal, or material, element, while the soul is incorporeal and immaterial. It is God "who brings about that wondrous combination and union of an incorporeal with a corporeal nature."[82] This union is the human being. Against those who would say that the "I" corresponds only to the soul, Augustine has strong words: "Anyone who would separate the body from human nature is an idiot."[83] "It's not a case, you see, of two opposed natures, but of one human being made from each nature; because it is by one God by whom humanity is made."[84]

Augustine's body-soul distinction (but not radical opposition) is a refusal of any anthropological monism. By locating both body and soul within human nature, he rejects materialism on the one hand, and Platonic spiritualism on the other. Although such spiritualism is often given the name dualism, it is ultimately a monism because it considers that the only thing of ultimate value in the human being is spirit. Augustine's anthropology cannot be called dualistic in the way that Plato's might, but it does contain two elements which, while closely related, are nonetheless distinguished. This distinction, naturally, raises the question of *how* these two elements are ordered to each other.

Soul-Body Hierarchy

While it is clear that for Augustine both body and soul are essential parts of the human being, it is also important that their relationship to each

---

80. Augustine, *Trin.* 15.11.
81. Augustine, *ep.* 238.2.12.
82. Augustine, *civ. Dei* 22.24.
83. Augustine, *an. et or.* 4.2.3. English translation from van Bavel, "Anthropology of Augustine," 38.
84. Augustine, *s.* 154.9. English translation from vol. III/5 of The Works of Saint Augustine.

other be characterized by a certain order or hierarchy. The soul is the body's life-giving principle,[85] to which the body is subject.[86] Augustine always maintained this hierarchy, yet as van Bavel points out, he eventually abandoned his early practice of speaking of the soul as "using" the body, probably due to its Platonic implications.[87]

Although the soul designates the incorporeal, life-giving principle in man, Augustine often uses the terms *spirit* (*spiritus*), *mind* (*mens*), and *animus* to indicate the location of intelligence and reason within the soul.[88] The three terms are sometimes used interchangeably, in which case they point simply to the rational element of man, in contrast to the basic life-principle which is the *anima*.[89]

In his early work *De Fide et Symbolo*, Augustine defines the human being in a tripartite way, although he acknowledges that this may also be done in a bipartite way (as we saw earlier):

> Because a human being is constituted of three elements, spirit [*spiritus*], soul [*anima*], and body [*corpus*], which at times are said to be two, since the soul is often included under spirit (for the reasonable part of that same entity, which animals lack, is called spirit), our principal element is the spirit. Next, the life by which we are joined to the body is called the soul. Finally, the body itself, because of its visible nature, comprises our third element.
>
> . . . This spirit [*spiritus*] is at times called mind [*mens*], and the apostle has this to say to it: *With my mind I obey the law of God* (Rom 7:25).[90]

This general anthropological structure remained relatively unchanged throughout Augustine's life. In *De Civitate Dei* 22.24, he states that "it is

---

85. Augustine, *Jo. ev. tr.* 23.6. English translation from *Tractates on the Gospel of John, 11–27*.

86. Augustine, *s.* 241.7 "If the soul is given honor by God, it must have something subject to it." Also, Augustine, *conf.* 8.9.21.

87. van Bavel, "Anthropology of Augustine," 39.

88. For a discussion of these terms, see Lawless, "Augustine and Human Embodiment," 168. Also Marrou, *Resurrection*, 15.

89. Lawless, "Augustine and Human Embodiment," 168.

90. Augustine, *f. et symb.* 10.23. English translation from "Faith and the Creed," in vol. I/8 of The Works of Saint Augustine. Thus, in Dyson's translation of *De Civitate Dei*, *animus* (being equivalent to *spiritus*) is translated as either "soul" or "mind" depending on the context.

God Who has given the human soul a mind."[91] It is this mind (or spirit) which commands the body.[92]

Augustine, however, was not rigorously systematic when it came to his vocabulary. Because of this, it is not surprising that he often finds it useful to lump *anima*, *animus*, *mens*, and *spiritus* under the general heading of *anima* (soul), when he is considering the incorporeal part of man in relation to the body.[93]

Even though Augustine can say—when using "soul" as a general term for the spiritual part of man—that the soul rules the body, he makes it clear that the soul is neither divine nor immutable, as some philosophers had asserted.[94] He insists that even if one equates God's breath in Gen 2:7 with the human soul,[95] that soul cannot be a particle or piece of God.[96] The soul, then, is not divine and does not derive its powers from any special participation in God's essence.

The Two Resurrections

Within this body-soul distinction, Augustine also distinguishes two types of resurrection: that of the soul, and that of the body. The first resurrection involves dying to one's old way of life and rising again through conversion.[97] "A man was drunken, now he is sober; he is dead to drunkenness, resurrected in sobriety. Thus when the soul falls away from all evil work it dies in a certain sense and it resurrects in doing good works."[98]

This resurrection of the soul was a doctrine also held by some Gnostics.[99] They, however, failed to recognize the second resurrection: that of

---

91. Augustine, *civ. Dei* 22.24. "Ipse itaque animae humanae mentem dedit."

92. Augustine, *conf.* 8.9.21. "Imperat animus corpori, et paretur statim." In this case, *animus* is used, but it is still the mind, or rational element, doing the commanding.

93. E.g., *civ. Dei* 8.5, where Augustine says that the faculty which judges beauty "is the mind of man [*mens hominis*] and the rational soul [*rationalis animae natura*]; and it certainly is not a body." Also, *civ. Dei* 13.8 which speaks of the separated soul (*anima*) awaiting the resurrection of its body. In this case, the soul stands for the whole spiritual component of the human being.

94. Augustine, *civ. Dei* 8.5.

95. Gen 2:7: "The LORD God formed man of dust from the ground, and breathed into his nostrils the breath of life; and man became a living being."

96. Augustine, *ep.* 205.4.19.

97. Augustine, *doc. Chr.* 1.19.18. Also, *civ. Dei* 20.6; *c. Faust.* 24.2.

98. Augustine, *s.* 362.21.23.

99. See Epiphanius, *Panarion* XL.2.5, where he speaks of the Archontics, who

the body. This second resurrection will happen at the end of the world, when those who have already experienced the first resurrection (that of the soul) will receive eternal life: "This first resurrection, however, is not the resurrection of the body, but of the soul.... For [it is] only those who take part in this first resurrection who are also to be blessed for all eternity. ... But after the second resurrection which is to come, the resurrection of the body, those who do not rise up in the first resurrection, the resurrection of souls, will be hurled into this death."[100]

This doctrine of two resurrections is based on the distinction of body and soul. This distinction supplies an anthropological structure within which Augustine can articulate the "already" and the "not yet" of resurrection. Through faith and baptism, we have already risen with Christ in our souls. By grace, our souls have been transformed and lifted up. We await the day when this will happen to our bodies as well. Augustine can thereby duly recognize that we are already risen with Christ without "demythologizing" the real resurrection of the *body*.

The Distinction between Death and Resurrection

To say that Augustine distinguishes between death and resurrection is another way of saying that he holds an intermediate state after death wherein the soul is separated from the body. The first thing to note, however, is that for Augustine, this separation of soul and body at death is a horrible event which produces "a sense of anguish, contrary to nature."[101] This *separation* of soul and body, unnatural as it is, is part of the horror and evil of death. The endurance of this painful event, however, "if it is undergone for the sake of godliness and righteousness... becomes the glory of those who are born again."[102] Death can thus be a redemptive experience, the suffering of which is due to the unnatural separation of body and soul which compose the one human being.

Beyond death, however, the souls of the blessed suffer no more anguish. In *De Civitate Dei*, Augustine states that "souls which have been

---

accepted only the resurrection of the soul but not of the flesh. Also, Hippolytus, *Refutatio* V.3 where he describes the Phrygians, who considered the earthly body to be a tomb so that "resurrection" meant leaving the body behind. Greshake (*Resurrectio Mortuorum*, 213–14) claims that no Father prior to Augustine taught the resurrection of the soul since they considered it a Gnostic doctrine.

100. Augustine, *civ. Dei* 20.6.

101. Ibid., 13.6. "Habet enim asperum sensum et contra naturam vis ipsa..."

102. Ibid.

Augustine on Resurrection

separated from the bodies of the godly are at rest, but those of the ungodly suffer punishment until their bodies rise again: those of the godly to eternal life, and those of the ungodly to the eternal death which is called the second death."[103] Elsewhere, in *Sermon* 240, he speaks of the reunion of soul and body that will happen at the resurrection: "so those who believe in the mediator, and live good lives in accordance with their faith, will indeed depart from the body and be at rest; but later on they will receive their bodies back, not as an embarrassment but as an embellishment, and they will live with God for ever. There will be nothing to delight them here to come back to, because they will have their bodies with them."[104] Here, Augustine is again arguing against the Platonists. The body will not be an embarrassment (vs. Porphyry), nor will the souls of the blessed yearn to return to another earthly body (vs. Plato) because they will already possess their own body.

But if the souls of the blessed are already "at rest" even before the resurrection, what does resurrection add to this? In *De Genesi ad Litteram*, Augustine explicates:

> There should, however, be no doubt that a man's mind, when it is carried out of the senses of the flesh in ecstasy, or when after death it has departed from the flesh, is unable to see the immutable essence of God just as the holy angels see it, even though it has passed beyond the likenesses of corporeal things. This may be because of some mysterious reason or simply because of the fact that it possesses a kind of natural appetite for managing the body. By reason of this appetite it is somehow hindered from going on with all its force to the highest heaven, so long as it is not joined with the body, for it is in managing the body that this appetite is satisfied.[105]

Here, he suggests that the separated soul cannot fully achieve the beatific vision until it is joined with its body.[106] Agostino Trapè has suggested that this actually puts Augustine at odds with the papal bull *Benedictus*

---

103. Ibid., 13.8.

104. Augustine, *s.* 240.5.

105. Augustine, *Gn. litt.* 12.35. English translation from vol. 42 of Ancient Christian Writers.

106. It might be added that although Augustine often speaks of the torment of both soul and body in hell (e.g., *s.* 362.20.23), it does not seem that, for Augustine, resurrection is necessary to sense the flames of punishment since he acknowledges that bodiless demons can also suffer from material flames, as the rich man in Jesus' parable (Luke 16:24) did even before the resurrection (*civ. Dei* 21.10).

Part One: Ratzinger the Augustinian

Deus,[107] although this "accusation" would seem somewhat anachronistic. Interestingly, Trapè finds some irony in the fact that the allegedly "Platonic" Augustine can speak of the serious difficulty for the beatitude of the separated soul, while Trapè asserts that some Aristotelians simply speak of an "accidental" increase in beatitude after the reunion of soul and body.[108]

Again, Augustine surprises us in his tendency to stress the unity of body and soul. We will conclude this section by considering an interesting passage:

> Moreover, the souls of the departed saints now have no grief over the death by which they were separated from their bodies, because their flesh rests in hope, no matter what injuries it may be seen to have suffered after all sensation has gone. They do not desire to forget their bodies, as Plato thought. Rather, because they remember what has been promised them by Him Who fails no one, and Who gave them an assurance that even the hairs of their head are safe, they look forward longingly and patiently to the resurrection of their bodies.[109]

Mamerto Alfeche suggests that Augustine's meaning is that "even after death the souls of the just still retain a certain kind of relationship with their bodies."[110] He also notes that it is the *flesh* of the departed that "rests in hope," rather than their souls.

Augustine's meaning may be more clearly educed when we consider that he is alluding to Ps 15:9 (LXX). The Douay-Rheims (translated from the Vulgate) reads, "Therefore my heart hath been glad, and my tongue hath rejoiced: moreover, my flesh also shall rest in hope. Because thou wilt not leave my soul in hell; nor wilt thou give thy holy one to see corruption."[111]

---

107. Trapè, "Escatologia e antiplatonismo," 241. *Benedictus Deus*, by Benedict XII, stated that the souls of the just (after any necessary purgation) ". . . even before the resumption of their bodies . . . have seen and see the divine essence by intuitive vision, and even face to face, with no mediating creature" (*Denzinger* 530).

108. Ibid., 241–42. He does not declare which Aristotelians he is speaking of.

109. Augustine, *civ. Dei* 13.20.

110. Alfeche, "Augustine's Discussions with Philosophers," 134.

111. Ps 15:9–10, Douay-Rheims version. Vulgate: "propterea laetatum est cor meum et exultavit gloria mea et caro mea habitavit confidenter non enim derelinques animam meam in inferno nec dabis sanctum tuum videre corruptionem ostendes mihi semitam vitae plenitudinem laetitiarum ante vultum tuum decores in dextera tua aeternos." The question of which Latin Bible translation Augustine was using is a difficult one. He originally used the Vetus Latina (Old Latin), but gradually adopted Jerome's Vulgate. The issue becomes complicated, however, by the fact that even after Augustine began using the Vulgate text, his citations from memory were sometimes from the

Augustine on Resurrection

Augustine is taking a passage applied by Peter (at Pentecost) to Jesus (Acts 2:26–27), and applying it to all the departed saints.

Those who have died, then, need not worry about the decomposition of their bodies because their flesh rests in hope, a hope grounded on God's faithfulness who will not in the end allow corruption to destroy his holy ones. This does not rule out the material disintegration of the body—Augustine clearly expects this to happen—but it is the assertion that the fleshly, material component of human existence will not be abandoned by God at the time of death and that God maintains a link between the souls of the dead and the bodies they have left behind. Although death is a profound dis-incarnation, that relationship between spirit and flesh is not severed absolutely.

The Soul's Immortality?

In some of his early works, Augustine attempts to rationally prove the immortality of the soul. In his *Soliloquies*, for example, he argues that since truth is eternal, then if the soul can contain truth (which it does) it must be immortal.[112] In his mature works, however, he does not assert an immortality of the soul on rationalistic bases. He acknowledges that the human soul does not cease to exist at death, but does not allow the human soul an immortality like God's. This is because of the infinite ontological gulf betweeen God and his creation.

Augustine thus cautiously affirms, "I do not at all doubt that the soul is immortal, not in the way God is, who alone has immortality, but in a certain way of its own. I do not doubt that it is a creature, not the substance of the creator."[113] He elsewhere states that the soul "is said to be immortal" because it has "in it a kind of permanent life, but changeable life."[114] The fact that the soul is mutable means that it cannot be the subject of any proof of immortality that would be grounded upon its supposedly perfect

---

Vetus Latina. For a discussion of all this, see Houghton, "Augustine's Adoption of the Vulgate Gospels."

112. Augustine, *sol.* 2.18. English translation from *The Soliloquies of Augustine*, 103. "For God and the soul remain, which two if true, are so because the Truth is in them; but no man doubts concerning the immortality of God. Also, the mind is believed to be immortal, if Truth, which cannot perish, is really proved to be in it."

113. Augustine, *ep.* 143.7. The metaphysical fact that the soul is not made of the same substance as God (as the Manicheans supposed) means that human souls cannot have immortality like God's.

114. Augustine, *Jo. ev. tr.* 23.9.

simplicity or immutability. The soul's immortality is the result of the gift of God's life rather than any inherent power of its own: "The life of your flesh is your soul; the life of your soul is your God. As the flesh dies when its soul, which is its life, has been lost, so the soul does when God, who is its life, has been lost."[115] This does not mean that sinful souls cease to exist, but that they cannot possess *life*, which is found only in God. True immortality demands more than mere existence; it demands *life*.

The soul, then, may be called immortal only in an equivocal sense. It is true that it neither ceases to exist nor decomposes after death. But full immortality requires something more than we currently possess: resurrection. "Only a spiritual being is immortal by virtue of the fact that it cannot possibly die; and this condition is promised to us in the resurrection."[116] Immortality is a gift to be given to the blessed; it is not something naturally possessed.

The Distinction between the Body and Corruption

We have already seen how Augustine distinguishes between the corruptibility of earthly bodies, and bodies as such. This distinction is pivotal in his argument for the resurrection, because it allows Augustine to dissociate those negative qualities often associated with the body—corruption and a tendency toward sinfulness—from the idea of risen embodiment. Augustine argues, therefore, that matter and the body are neither evil (as the Manicheans thought), nor inherently corruptible (as the Platonists thought) but that the problems associated with the body are the consequence of sin.

The Source of Evil: Sin, Not Embodiment

Although Augustine holds the body-soul distinction, he does not follow the Manichaeans in equating the human body and matter with evil. He shares this position with the Platonists, who saw matter and the body as being a problem (even a prison), but not intrinsically evil: "The Platonists are not, indeed, so foolish as the Manichaeans; for they do not detest

---

115. Ibid., 47.8. See also *f. et symb.* 10.23; *Jo. ev. tr.* 23.9—Augustine here connects this with Christ's words that we should fear him who can kill body and soul in Gehenna (Matt 10:28). The death of the soul, then, becomes absolute in hell where the soul is not annihilated but loses all "life" (relationship to God).

116. Augustine, *Gn. litt.* 6.25.

earthly bodies as the natural substance of evil."[117] Augustine, however, goes further than the Platonists, stating that it is neither matter nor embodiment that is a problem for the human soul; it is only the disorder and corruptibility brought about by sin that make the body (and the material world) into a difficulty.

Thus, the evils that plague the human body "didn't come about through our natural condition"[118] but rather from human sin. Thomas Clarke, in his study of Augustine's understanding of sin and man's relationship to creation, notes that in the beginning man was like God in that he possessed reason.[119] He was thus set above the rest of creation. With sin, however, man chose the lower over the higher, and the mutable over the immutable, thus inverting the natural order of creation. This "sets off a chain reaction which reaches to the lowest levels of creation."[120] Man loses both his likeness to God, and his dominion over creation. Thus, in Augustine's view, the natural world punishes man, not because of vengeful spite but because man has broken his harmony with that world.

Further, sin disrupts not only man's relationship with the world, but with himself as well, so that the body no longer obeys the soul. Augustine declares, "For it certainly was not just that obedience should be rendered by his servant, that is, by his body, to him, who did not obey his own Lord."[121] We thus experience inner conflict in this life: "'The flesh lusteth against the Spirit, and the Spirit against the flesh' unceasingly, so that we cannot do the things that we would, and rid ourselves entirely of evil desires. Rather, we can only subdue such desires by withholding our consent from them as far as we can, with God's help."[122] But it is *sin* that has made the body appear to be a hindrance to the soul, and not the body itself. For those accustomed to seeing Augustine as a crypto-Manichaean somaphobe, his real view comes

---

117. Augustine, *civ. Dei* 14.5.

118. Augustine, *s.* 242A.3.

119. This, and the following comments in the same paragraph, are taken from Clarke, "Cosmic Redemption," 155–56.

120. Ibid., 155.

121. Augustine, *nupt. et conc.* 1.6.7. English tranlation here from Alfeche, "*Corpus Spirituale* according to St. Augustine," 264–65. Also, *civ. Dei* 13.13: "Because it [the soul] had of its own free will forsaken its superior Lord, it no longer held its own inferior servant in obedience to its will. Nor could it in any way keep the flesh in subjection, as it would always have been able to do if it had itself remained subject to God."

122. Augustine, *civ. Dei* 22.23. Augustine is refering to Gal 5:17, "For the desires of the flesh are against the Spirit, and the desires of the Spirit are against the flesh," as well as Rom 7:19, "For I do not do the good I want, but the evil I do not want is what I do."

as something of a shock: "it was not the corruptible flesh that made the soul sinful; it was the sinful soul that made the flesh corruptible."[123] John Hugo suggests that it was actually Augustine's Platonism that led him in this direction, since in Platonism only the soul—not the body—can sense anything on its own. In such a system, he argues, the body could never be held to account for sin since all sensory ability and agency belongs to the soul.[124] This position is not only an exoneration of the flesh, but also a rejection of biological determinism.

The fact is, however, that man has sinned and cannot save himself. This sin has passed to all humanity since "we were all in that one man [Adam]."[125] Because of this, "the whole mass of the human race is condemned."[126] This does not mean, however, that humanity is now inherently evil, as Augustine's concept of *privatio boni* shows.[127] He can therefore say that sin has not destroyed human nature but is simply like blindness to an eye.[128] Sin, in fact, "is itself the evidence which proves that the nature was created good; for if it had not itself been a great good, albeit not equal to the Creator, then, clearly, its falling away from God as from its light could not have been an evil to it."[129] In other words, the fact that sin is so bad proves that human nature is so good.

Because our nature is wounded and does not function as it should, Augustine can maintain that "the body is such that the management of it is difficult and burdensome, as is the case with this corruptible flesh, which is a load upon the soul (coming as it does from a fallen race)."[130] This bur-

---

123. Ibid., 14.3. Earlier, in *Gn. litt.* 10.12, Augustine expressed the view that both body and soul are equally culpable for sin: "I think that all the learned as well as the unlearned will not doubt that the flesh without the soul can't lust for something. For this reason the cause of carnal concupiscence itself is not only in the soul, but much less is it in the flesh alone. It arises from both in relation with each other; from the soul, because without it no pleasure can be felt; from the flesh, in its turn, because without it no carnal pleasure can be felt." Augustine's placing of the blame squarely on the soul in the later work *civ. Dei* may be due to a development in his thought, or more likely the rhetorical situation.

124. Hugo, *St. Augustine on Nature, Sex, and Marriage*, 34.

125. Augustine, *civ. Dei* 13.14. Augustine's unintentional use of a mistranslation of Rom 5:12 ("... in quo omnes peccaverunt ...") is well known and need not be discussed here.

126. Ibid., 21.12. "Hinc est universa generis humani massa damnata."

127. The concept of evil as *privatio boni* was adopted from Plotinus.

128. Augustine, *civ. Dei* 22.1.

129. Ibid., 22.1.

130. Augustine, *Gn. litt.* 12.35. Here, Augustine is essentially following Wis 9:15,

den, however, is not due to embodiment as such, but to the corruption of the body by sin. Against a Platonic interpretation, which would see the body as a burden simply because it is a body, Augustine insists that "it is not the body, but the body's corruptibility, which is a burden to the soul."[131]

The Body-Flesh Distinction and the Later Distinction between Flesh as Substance and Flesh as Immorality or Corruption

One of the most difficult Scripture passages Augustine had to wrestle with in his understanding of the resurrection was 1 Cor 15:50: "flesh and blood cannot inherit the kingdom of God, nor does the perishable inherit the imperishable." The challenge, of course, was how to take Paul seriously while still maintaining the resurrection of a real body. Ultimately, Augustine's solution lay in distinguishing what was wrong with the flesh—corruptibility and a tendency toward immorality—from the flesh itself. In this way, he was able to differentiate the substance of the flesh from the effects of sin upon it. Yet this solution did not come to Augustine immediately.

During his early years as a Catholic, Augustine did not distinguish between flesh as substance and flesh as corruption, seeing flesh as inherently and incurably corruptible.[132] Thus, he held that in the resurrection the substance of the flesh will be transformed into body, and will no longer be flesh.[133] This view is present in such early works as *De Fide et Symbolo* (written 393),[134] *Contra Adimantum* (written 393),[135] and *De Agone*

"for a perishable body weighs down the soul."

131. Augustine, *civ. Dei* 13.16.

132. It is clear, as we will show, that Augustine's understanding of the resurrection developed over his life. Although Van Fleteren may go too far when he claims that Augustine began his Catholic life being unaware of the Church's teaching on the resurrection ("Augustine and the Resurrection," 14), Augustine certainly did move in a direction that laid greater emphasis on the resurrection's materiality.

133. Although Augustine maintains the *resurrectio carnis* as early as 388 (Augustine, *quant.* 33.76), he gives no explanation there of how he understands the term *carnis*. It should thus be interpreted according to his other statements close to that time, which are cited below.

134. Augustine, *f. et symb.* 10.23–24.

135. Augustine, *c. Adim.* 12.

Cristiano (written 396).¹³⁶ We also see this view in *Sermon* 264, although there is dispute over its date of composition.¹³⁷

During this time, Augustine held that "all flesh is of necessity corporeal, but not every body is flesh."¹³⁸ As for the human body, "at that moment of angelic transformation it will no longer be flesh and blood but only a body."¹³⁹ In the *Retractationes*, however, a more mature Augustine corrected this statement: "this is not to be interpreted as if the substance of the flesh will no longer exist [in the resurrection]; but, by the term flesh and blood, we are to understand that the Apostle meant the corruption itself of flesh and blood."¹⁴⁰ Probably because he realized the seriousness of his previous error, Augustine later made many attempts to explain that the resurrected body would not be without flesh.¹⁴¹

Mamerto Alfeche has argued that from 393–396, Augustine uses "flesh and blood" only "of the corruptible substance of human beings and of human sinfulness, but not of the incorruptible substance of the resurrection-life bodies."¹⁴² Augustine therefore only used *corpus* (and never *caro*) to describe the risen body. This is particularly evident when, in several early works, Augustine cites Luke 24:39, where the post-paschal Jesus tells his disciples that "a spirit has not flesh and bones as you see that I have." Augustine, however, so intent on excluding the flesh from the resurrection, changes the passage to read "a spirit has no bones and *nerves*, just as you can see that I have."¹⁴³ He removes the Latin "*carnem*," and in-

---

136. Augustine, *agon.* 32.34.

137. Alfeche holds that it must have been written between 393 and 396. Alfeche, "Rising of the Dead," 79.

138. Augustine, *f. et symb.* 10.24.

139. Ibid. Also, *agon.* 32.34: "the body will no longer be flesh and blood, but a heavenly body . . . flesh and blood, therefore, will be changed, and the body will become heavenly and angelic." English translation from *The Christian Combat*.

140. Augustine, *retr.* 2.3. English translation from *The Retractations*.

141. E.g., Augustine, *ep.* 205.2.16; *civ. Dei* 13.20.

142. Alfeche, "Rising of the Dead," 72–73.

143. E.g., Augustine, *agon.* 24.26. "Palpate, et videte, quoniam spiritus ossa et nervos non habet, sicut me videtis habere." Also, *s.* 264.6, which is why Alfeche dates it before 396. He acknowledges that his view on the date for *Sermon* 264 is not shared by others, namely, Anne-Marie La Bonnardière and A. Kunzelmann. La Bonnardière, however, tends to simply follow Kunzelmann on sermon dates, and Kunzelmann's dating rationale is often tenuous at best. This is partly due to his method of grouping Augustine's sermons according to which heresy they were directed against. He considers *Sermon* 264 to be against the Arians, and thus dates it between 413–20. The following is the entirety of his argument for this dating: "Augustine certainly does not name any heretics

serts "*nervos*."¹⁴⁴ In his later works, however, Augustine ceased modifying the passage and let *carnem* stand.¹⁴⁵

One might wonder whether Augustine's initial reticence to allow flesh and blood into the resurrected body was truly dictated by his reading of Paul, or whether it might be the vestige of a certain mistrust of materiality—what Börresen might call "une réminiscence du dualisme manichéen."¹⁴⁶ The distinction made between body and flesh seems to point in this direction.¹⁴⁷ What is most compelling, however, is that Augustine moved beyond this view to a more integral anthropology that saw the flesh as a necessary part of human nature. Even his supposed Platonic foundations did not hold him back from ultimately rejecting this dualistic view as incompatible with Christian revelation.

The mature Augustine was able to read 1 Cor 15:50 as referring only to the corruption belonging to sinful flesh, rather than the flesh itself: "For 'flesh' in the sense of its substance, in accordance with the words, *A spirit does not have flesh and blood, as you see that I have* (Luke 24:39), will possess the kingdom of God, but 'flesh' when understood in the sense of its corruption will not possess it."¹⁴⁸

---

here, however it is striking that he speaks of the mystery of the Trinity on the feast of Christ's Ascension and at the conclusion urgently exhorts his hearers to hold fast to the Catholic faith in the Trinity. This allows us to reason that the sermon was given at a time when the doctrine of the Trinity was in danger, which was often the case in these years [410–20]." German: "Hier nennt Augustin zwar keine Irrlehrer, es ist aber auffallend, dass er am Feste Christi Himmelfahrt über das Geheimnis der Trinität spricht und zudem am Schluss seine Zuhörer eindringlich ermahnt, sie möchten am katholischen Glauben über die Trinität festhalten. Das lässt schliessen, dass der Sermo zu einer Zeit gehalten ist, wo der Trinitätslehre Gefahr drohte, was in den angegebenen Jahren öfters der Fall war." Kunzelmann, "Die Chronologie der Sermones des Hl. Augustinus," 484. One need not be a scholar to recognize how conjectural this reasoning is. In this case, Alfeche's more focused textual research would be a better guide in establishing a date for *Sermon* 264.

144. The word *carnem* (and not *nervos*) is found in both the Vetus Latina and the Vulgate translations of Luke 24:39, so there is little question that Augustine was allowing himself a somewhat adventurous paraphrase.

145. E.g., Augustine, *ep.* 205.2.16. "Spiritus ossa et carnem non habet, sicut me videtis habere."

146. Börresen, "Augustin, interprète du dogme de la résurrection," 149.

147. In fact, Ferrisi ("La resurrezione della carne," 223) sees it as Origenist and praises Augustine for it.

148. Augustine, *ep.* 205.2.16. This was composed about 419 or 420. Notice that Augustine now uses "flesh" in his reading of Luke 24:39 rather than "nerves." See also Augustine, *c. Jul.* 6.40 (written 421).

The important distinction made by Augustine is one of separating ontology from phenomenology. Simply because the body is always experienced as a decaying burden does not mean this experience belongs inherently to all possible bodies. Augustine instructs his parishioners, "if we were saying that the flesh is going to rise again in order to be hungry, thirsty, sick, to be in difficulties and subject to decay, then you would be absolutely right not to believe."[149] But the risen flesh will be incorruptible with no trace of weakness. Again, Augustine queries his congregation, "What is it about the body that you don't like? I will tell you; it's the body's liability to decay, its mortality. But the things you like will be there [in the resurrection]; the things you don't like won't."[150] The flesh is *not* inseparably bound up with corruptibility, and in the resurrection, this link will be severed. This distinction is possibly Augustine's most profound insight into the nature of the risen body.

The Question of the Spiritual Body in 1 Cor 15:44

Still, some of Augustine's opponents considered that the flesh's ultimate glory would be to be transformed into spirit in the resurrection.[151] Responding to this, Augustine grants that "the flesh will then be spiritual, and subject to the spirit; but it will still be flesh and not spirit, just as the spirit, even when carnal and subject to the flesh, is still spirit and not flesh."[152]

This raises the issue of another set of distinctions which Augustine borrows from St. Paul in 1 Cor 15:44:[153] the difference between the *corpus animale* and the *corpus spiritale*. The former was the kind possessed by Adam, and still possessed by us. This *corpus animale* is enlivened by the soul, but is not completely subject to the *spiritus*.[154] It therefore experi-

---

149. Augustine, *s.* 240.3.

150. Ibid., 242A.3.

151. In *civ. Dei* 13.30, Augustine states that the flesh which serves the spirit is called spiritual "not because flesh will be converted into spirit, which is what some have inferred from what is written: 'It is sown a natural body, it is raised a spiritual body.'" He does not identify who these people are, however.

152. Augustine, *civ. Dei* 22.21. Also, *civ. Dei* 13.20. By "spirit," Augustine means the human *spiritus*, not the Holy Spirit.

153. "σπείρεται σῶμα ψυχικόν, ἐγείρεται σῶμα πνευματικόν. Εἰ ἔστιν σῶμα ψυχικόν, ἔστιν σῶμα πνευματικόν." RSV: "It is sown a physical body; it is raised a spiritual body. If there is a physical body, there is also a spiritual body."

154. Augustine, *ep.* 205.2.9. A natural body is similar to that of animals—it needs food and is subject to decay. "But a body is called spiritual because it is now immortal with its spirit [*cum spiritu*]."

Augustine on Resurrection

ences various physical limitations. Augustine suggested that had Adam and Eve remained faithful, their bodies might have been transformed by God into spiritual bodies without the intervention of death.[155]

Fallen humanity still retains the *corpus animale*, with the added complication of concupiscence (something Adam and Eve were free of before sin).[156] Before his resurrection, Christ possessed a *corpus animale*, yet was without sin.[157] The problem with the *corpus animale*, however, is that it is susceptible to all kinds of weakness, and with the entry of sin, moral weakness and corruption have contaminated it like a chronic disease.[158]

We have already spoken of the disruption of the order between body and soul that occurred with sin. True beatitude and peace can only come about when the disorder resultant from sin is overcome. "The peace of all things lies in the tranquility of order; and order is the disposition of equal and unequal things in such a way as to give to each its proper place."[159] The proper place of the soul is to govern the body, but this order has been destroyed by man's disobedience. We therefore experience concupiscence and death, and our being is in inner turmoil.

But in heaven, Augustine declares, "there will no longer be any conflicts or trespasses."[160] There will be harmony between flesh and spirit so that "nothing within us will fight against us, but just as we shall have no external enemies, so we shall not have to suffer ourselves as our own inner enemies."[161] "The body will be subject in every way to the spirit without

---

155. Augustine, *Gen. litt.* 6.23.

156. E.g., Augustine, *civ. Dei* 14.11. "The choice of the will, then, is truly free only when it is not the slave of vices and sins. God gave to the will such freedom, and, now that it has been lost through its own fault, it cannot be restored save by Him Who could bestow it."

157. Augustine, *ep.* 205.2.9. Christ's body "was a natural body, because it was taken from Adam, [but] it is now spiritual since it has been inseparably united to the spirit" (et quod erat corpus animale, quoniam ex Adam sumptum est, nunc esse spiritale, quoniam spiritui iam inseparabiliter copulatum est).

158. Alfeche ("Rising of the Dead," 67) explains it thus: "The soul in an animal body lives in the body but does not vivify it to the extent that it takes away from its corruptibility; whereas the soul in the spiritual body vivifies the body and makes it spiritual by taking away all corruption. Moreover, a human being with the spiritual body is in perfect union with the Risen Lord and His Spirit (cf. 1 Cor. 6,17)."

159. Augustine, *civ. Dei* 19.13.

160. Ibid., 22.23. Also, *ep.* 143.6: "And so, then the soul will rule a spiritual body in every way as it chooses, but now it does not rule the body in every way but as the laws of the universe allow."

161. Augustine, *ench.* 23.91. English translation from vol. I/8 of The Works of Saint

any corruption or death,"[162] and "with a supreme and marvelous readiness to obey."[163] This subjection to the spirit is why the risen body is called a *corpus spiritale*.[164]

This perfect ordering of body and spirit will be such that the body will no longer be constrained in many of the ways it is now. Augustine raises the example of travel: in this life one may desire to be with a friend somewhere far away, but the body feels like a weight, slowing one down so that one can never get there fast enough. In the resurrection, the body will be able to go anywhere one wants without any hesitation.[165]

The transformation of the relationship between body and soul will thus be a reordering on two levels: the ontological and the moral. On the ontological level, the risen body will be incorruptible, immortal, and possessed of supernatural characteristics.[166] On the moral level, there will be no conflict between spirit and flesh, body and soul, so that whatever the spirit desires, the body will do.[167] The internal revolt described by Paul in Romans 7 will be perfectly overcome.

Anthropological Duality: Summary

Augustine's theology—while not rigidly systematic—makes use of important distinctions. The stress placed on the difference between body and soul has led some critics to accuse Augustine of Platonic dualism, but a careful reading of Augustine's theology leads in a different direction. While certainly characterized by duality, Augustine's anthropology attempts to

---

Augustine. Unless otherwise noted, all quotations from the *Enchiridion* are from this edition.

162. Augustine, *c. Adim.* 12.4.

163. Augustine, *civ. Dei* 22.20.

164. Augustine, *Gen. litt.* 12.35. "Accordingly, when the soul is made equal to the angels and receives again this body, no longer a natural body but a spiritual one because of the transformation that is to be, it will have the perfect measure of its being, obeying and commanding, vivified and vivifying with such a wonderful ease that what was once its burden will be its glory."

165. Augustine, *s.* 277.7.

166. For example, the body "will then not be earthly, but heavenly . . . [it is] the spiritual body, which Christ himself, as our Head, already has; and this is the kind of body which His members will have at the final resurrection of the dead" (Augustine, *civ. Dei* 13.23).

167. For discussions of this, see Mourant, *Augustine on Immortality*, 47; Alfeche, "*Corpus Spirituale* according to St. Augustine," 254.

unite rather than to divide the human being. His insistence that both body and soul are essential components of human nature contrasts sharply with the Platonic and Manichean views.

Although Augustine allows for an intermediate state whereby the soul is separated from the body after death, the soul does not achieve full beatitude until it is reunited with its body, the separation from which is against nature. Augustine also distinguishes between the evil brought about by sin, and the human body. Rather than accusing the body or the flesh as the source of sin (as the Platonists and Manicheans did), he actually blames the soul for sin's origin. This allows Augustine to further distinguish between the corruptibility of the flesh as we know it, and the flesh itself. He can therefore hold in an uncompromising way the *resurrectio carnis*, allowing the work of the incarnation to bear its full fruit. "Thus, the good and true Mediator showed that it is sin which is evil, and not the substance or nature of flesh. He showed that a body of flesh and a human soul could be assumed and retained without sin, and laid aside at death, and changed into something better by resurrection."[168]

Augustine's theology would be better described as "dual" or "distinguishing" than "dualistic." There are no elements in humanity that are radically opposed to each other (as with dualism). The union of soul and body, in fact, is part of human nature. If sin means the distortion of this nature and thus of the body-soul union, then the resurrection will mean the elevation and healing of this nature so that body and soul will be united in a way far surpassing their current arrangement. The distinction between body and soul, then, serves as the foundation for Augustine's other distinctions. It allows him to differentiate between the "already" (the resurrection of the soul) and the "not yet" (the resurrection of the body) of resurrection. The delay of the resurrection of the body thus ensures that that resurrection will be truly material and bodily, since it will involve the matter of *this* world. Further, Augustine's recognition of the body-soul distinction allows him to distinguish between the body, and the source of human corruption (which is actually the soul and its decision to sin). This balanced maintenance of a certain duality allows him to sidestep the radical anti-somatism of the Manicheans.

The only real dualism in Augustine's system is between sin and grace. Yet even there, the evil present in human nature is ultimately only the absence of good, whose presence attests to the goodness of that nature as God created it. Augustine's eschatological worldview, then, is not one of

168. Augustine, *civ. Dei* 10.24.

two forces in combat. It is one in which the one God will ultimately fill his creation with himself, until it is complete.

Third Augustinian Characteristic

Matter: Discerning Continuities

Unlike the Platonists and the Manicheans, Augustine gave a high value to the body and matter. We will now observe that Augustine's view of resurrection and beatitude means not the bypassing or annulling, but rather the elevation of the matter of this world. Therefore, the risen body will truly be composed of the same matter as the earthly body, and this very world will be changed for the better. We will consider how Augustine sees the risen body as an indicator of continuity with the life of this world, and show how his belief in a bodily vision of God represents a truly remarkable exaltation of matter. Matter is therefore not merely a matrix in which spirit expresses itself but is truly part of God's creation and therefore fully capable of salvation.

The Material Identity of the Risen Body

We have already seen that Augustine's anthropology posits the existence of a soul that lives on after death, providing personal continuity. At first glance, this fact suggests a certain kinship with Plato's idea of the immortality of the soul. Yet when we examine Augustine's testimony on the resurrection body, we discover that his position is far from the spiritual and disembodied view of the Platonists. It is interesting, then, that Augustine's theology is sometimes criticized on the one hand for being too Platonic and disembodied, and on the other for being too physicalist and placing too much emphasis on matter.

Augustine's view on the nature of the resurrected body is in many ways a response to the devaluation of the body and of matter present in Platonism and Manicheism.[169] One of the perennial difficulties in the theology of resurrection is the relationship between the earthly and the

---

169. O'Meara suggests it is the result of a vendetta he had against Porphyry ("Parting from Porphyry," 359). There are, of course, significant differences between Platonism and Manicheism, but they are both opposed by Augustine inasmuch as they both assert that a material body is an obstacle to the soul's beatitude.

risen body. Augustine's solution is to posit a numerical, material identity between them.

> Nor does the earthly material from which mortal flesh is created perish in the sight of God, but whatever dust or ashes it may dissolve into, whatever vapors or winds it may vanish into, whatever other bodies or even elements it may be turned into, by whatever animals or even men it may have been eaten as food and so turned into flesh, in an instant of time it returns to the human soul that first gave it life so that it might become human, grow, and live.[170]

Augustine is certain that we will receive back our whole body, no matter where the parts have been dispersed.[171]

He holds this strong material view of the resurrection for various reasons, among them his understanding of the incarnation and his critical stance toward the Platonic notion of beatitude. But equally important for Augustine is the continuity provided by having the same body. Thus, against the Manicheans he asserts that it is not true that "what will be buried would not rise but that it would be set aside like one tunic and that another better one would be put on, [but rather] he [Christ] wanted to explain most clearly that this very body [*hoc ipsum*] will be changed for the better, just as Christ's clothes were not set aside and others donned on the mountain, but the very clothes that were there were transformed for the better in brightness."[172] Like Christ's transfigured clothes, our bodies will not be discarded in favor of better ones. They will be changed (*in melius commutabitur*).

Christ's body was not discarded at death, but it was raised and transformed. "So what was lifted up into heaven, if not what had been taken from earth?"[173] In this case, Augustine is refering to the foundational principle of the incarnation: Christ assumed flesh so that it could be saved. And what was saved was not a spiritual analogue to his earthly flesh, but

---

170. Augustine, *ench.* 23.88.

171. Augustine, *civ. Dei* 22.20. "Even if the body has been completely ground to powder in some dreadful accident, or by the ferocity of enemies; even if it has been so entirely scattered to the winds or into the water that there is nothing whatever left of it: still it cannot be in any way withdrawn from the omnipotence of the Creator; rather, not a hair of its head shall perish."

172. Augustine, *c. Faust.* 11.3. English translation from vol. I/20 of The Works of Saint Augustine. Unless otherwise noted, all quotations from *Contra Faustum* are from this edition.

173. Augustine, *s.* 242.6.

the very flesh he took from the earth. Likewise, our real bodies will be raised with Christ, will be transformed, and will dwell with him in heaven.

Augustine's insistence on material identity is so strong that he sometimes seems to hold that *all* the matter that belonged to one's earthly body will be returned to the risen body. When considering the problem of what to do with body parts that constantly grow and fall off, like hair and nails, he provides the image of a statue molded from pieces of bronze that will be melted down and recast: every part will be restored, but not necessarily to the same place.[174] What is important is that God will "remake our flesh with wonderful and indescribable speed from all the material that constituted it."[175]

After expressing opinions on the age and physical proportions of the risen body, however, Augustine acknowledges that in this regard a number of views are possible, "provided, however, that there is to be no deformity, no infirmity, no heaviness, no corruption—nothing of any kind unfit for that kingdom in which the sons of the resurrection and of the promise are to be equal to the angels of God, if not in body and age, then certainly in felicity."[176]

Augustine's criterion here is primarily an aesthetic one. The particular details of the body are less important than the fact that it will be glorious and free of all the burdens of this earthly existence. Elsewhere, after speculating on how God might restore the flesh of a man eaten by cannibals (he holds that the one who had the flesh first will lay claim to it in the resurrection), he adds that even

> if it [flesh] has perished entirely, so that no part of its substance remained in any hidden place of nature, the Almighty could still restore it by such means as He willed [*unde vellet, eam repararet Omnipotens*]. For the Truth has said, "Not a hair of your head shall perish"; and, in view of this saying, it would be absurd if we were to suppose that, though no hair of a man's head can perish, large pieces of his flesh can perish because eaten and consumed by the starving.[177]

Thus, while Augustine insists on material identity, he is open to miraculous intervention by God (whose power is enough argument for the

---

174. Augustine, *civ. Dei* 22.19. He bases this on Christ's words that "not a hair of your head shall perish" (Luke 21:18).

175. Augustine, *ench.* 23.88. Here, he is also discussing the statue analogy.

176. Augustine, *civ. Dei* 22.20.

177. Ibid.

resurrection) in order to ensure bodily continuity even in awkward situations like that of cannibalism.

Some Criticisms

John O'Meara describes how Scotus Eriugena was "staggered, amazed, and horror-stricken" at how materialist and un-Platonic Augustine's view of resurrection was.[178] Gisbert Greshake is also concerned by Augustine's "massive visual realism" wherein it is "this visible, earthly body which—although in a transfigured form—rises in absolute, direct, physical identity."[179]

Caroline Walker Bynum ridicules Augustine's materialism, calling it "the salvation of bits."[180] In her view, Augustine was so distrustful of the material world that he viewed all change as putrefaction and decay. Thus, for him, resurrection had to be a perfect restoration to stasis and non-change.[181] Bynum's problem is chiefly with Augustine's departure from Origen's metaphor of the "Pauline seed."[182] She appears sympathetic to Eriugena's view of resurrection,[183] and so it is not surprising that she is unimpressed by Augustine's materialism, asking rhetorically, "why bring heaven so close to earth?"[184]

Gerald O'Collins also is concerned that "Augustine's attention to physical detail risks reducing our risen state to that of the kind of improved earthly bodies which people heaven in much Christian art."[185] He does not, however, explain why this would be a bad thing.

---

178. O'Meara, "Parting from Porphyry," 357–58. O'Meara refers to Joannis Scoti, *De Divisione Naturae* V, 991C–992A, although the quoted passage is actually from 986B, where Eriugena describes the notion of a resurrection involving real body parts, whereupon he comments, "Sed dum talia in libris sanctorum Patrum lego, stupefactus haesito maximoque horrore concussus titubo."

179. Greshake, *Resurrectio Mortuorum*, 213. "Doch ingesamt herrscht ein massiver anschaulicher Realismus: Es ist dieser sichtbare irdische Leib, der—wenn auch in verklärter Gestalt—in absoluter, geradezu physizistischer Identität aufersteht." Here, Greshake cites *civ. Dei* 22.12.

180. Bynum, *Resurrection of the Body*, 105.

181. Ibid., 101–4.

182. Ibid., 101, 104.

183. Ibid., 142–46, 155.

184. Ibid., 109. Perhaps the most obvious response to this question would be that in the incarnation God has already done so.

185. O'Collins, "Augustine on the Resurrection," 72.

As N. D. O'Donoghue points out, however, Augustine uses such materialistic images because of his resistance to "the strong gravitational pull of Platonism."[186] While it seems unlikely that Augustine's materialism could be attributed solely to anti-Platonism (his understanding of the incarnation and Christ's risen body led him in a similar direction), it is possible that the graphic nature of his descriptions—what Greshake calls his "massive visual realism"—may be enhanced by his anti-Platonism.

One of the chief reasons, in any case, for positing a numerical material identity between the earthly and risen bodies is one of personal continuity. Against Porphyry, Augustine says,

> What is required to ensure the soul's blessedness, then, is not an escape from any kind of body whatsoever but the acquisition of an incorruptible body. And what incorruptible body could be better adapted to the joy of those who rise again than the one in which they groaned when it was corruptible? . . . they will possess it in such a way as never to lose it again, nor to be parted from it for even the briefest moment by any death.[187]

According to Henri Marrou, the knowledge that we will possess the same body "gives us the assurance of being reunited to the former companion of our joys and sorrows, that body which has fought and suffered" and provides the security of personal continuity.[188]

When discussing the resurrection, Augustine starts with established premises and then draws conclusions from them. He begins with the belief that because of the incarnation and resurrection of Christ, matter will not be annihilated but elevated.[189] The human body will not be replaced, but restored. Having decided to take matter seriously, he then draws out what he sees as necessary implications. This is the source of his devotion to what Bynum calls "the salvation of bits." Augustine believes that these bits have value because they belong to a human being. To save someone without saving those "bits" would be a spiritualistic, Manichean kind of salvation.

---

186. O'Donoghue, "Awakening of the Dead," 54. O'Donoghue points out that this is especially apparent in *De Civitate Dei*.

187. Augustine, *civ. Dei* 22.26.

188. Marrou, *Resurrection*, 28.

189. Augustine, *civ. Dei* 10.24. "Thus, the good and true Mediator showed that it is sin which is evil, and not the substance or nature of flesh. He showed that a body of flesh and a human soul could be assumed and retained without sin, and laid aside at death, and changed into something better by resurrection."

Yet how can dispersed, decomposed matter be gathered together and reformed into a human being? Augustine responds with his own rhetorical question: "how can anything either lie hidden from Him Who perceives all things, or irrevocably escape Him Who moves all things?"[190] Thus the human body, even after death, retains a certain connection to God; it is not lost from his sight. Although the parts may seem to us to be dispersed and decomposed, to God's mind they are eternally present. In this case, the apparent "dispersion" of the matter is illusory, for even if a body is utterly decomposed, "all things in their entirety are before the eyes of the Creator, even when they are not evident to mortal senses."[191] If the souls of the blessed are truly with their God, who sees and animates all things, then it is not surprising that "their flesh rests in hope."[192]

The Transformation of the Body and the Material World

We have already discussed the body's transformation at the resurrection from *corpus animale* to *corpus spiritale*. Seen from the point of view of this polarity, what changes is the completeness or perfection of the vivification (i.e., spiritualization) of the body and not its materiality. But what happens to the matter itself that composes the body? And what of the matter composing the rest of the material world? Our response to these questions owes much to the work done by Thomas Clarke.[193]

The New Qualities of Matter

Clarke claims that Augustine does not believe in a cosmic *redemption* since the cosmos does not stand in need of one. Thus, Augustine did not hold a fiery destruction of the world.[194] He did, however, following 1 Cor 7:31 ("For the form of this world is passing away"),[195] anticipate an escha-

---

190. Ibid., 22.20.
191. Augustine, *s.* 361.12.12.
192. Augustine, *civ. Dei* 13.20.
193. Clarke has two works on this topic: "St. Augustine and Cosmic Redemption" and *Eschatological Transformation*, which was his doctoral dissertation.
194. Clarke, "Cosmic Redemption," 159. In his dissertation, Clarke suggests that a major reason for Augustine's rejection of cosmic redemption was his mistrust of Manicheism and its obsession with the liberation of light particles thought to be trapped in matter.
195. Augustine's Latin (*civ. Dei* 20.16): "figura huius mundi . . . praeteribit." The

tological fire. This fire, however, will not touch the substance (*substantia*) of the material world, but only its figure or qualities (*qualitates*).

> The figure of this world will pass away in a conflagration of all the fires of the universe, just as it was of old drowned by the inundation of all the waters of the universe. By that conflagration, as I call it, the qualities of the corruptible elements which were fitted to our corruptible bodies will wholly perish in the burning. Then, by a miraculous transformation, our very substance will take on the qualities which belong to immortal bodies; and the purpose of this will be to equip the world, now made new and better, with a fitting population of men who are themselves renewed and made better even in their flesh.[196]

Earlier on in *De Civitate Dei*, Augustine makes the same point, albeit more briefly, when he indicates that the risen body "will have been made fit to dwell in heaven: not by losing its nature [*natura*], but by changing its quality [*qualitate*]."[197]

Here we see Augustine maintaining his position on the material identity of the earthly and risen bodies, while simultaneously allowing for a real change. He locates this change not in the *substantia* of the material body—which provides the continuity—but in its *qualitates*. Yet this continuity is not restricted to the human body. The world itself will perdure and be transformed for the better. Augustine's language in *De Civitate Dei* 20.16 draws a parallel between the transformations that will occur in the flesh of the human body (*in melius innovatis*) and in the material world (*in melius innovatus*). We will be resurrected not to live in an ethereal heaven, but in a new and transformed material world.

In commenting on this passage, Henri Marrou asserts that what is annihilated is only "evil, that non-being; corruptibility, that aptitude to diminution, that exposure to nothingness."[198] He points out that the notion of *corruptio*, which Augustine repeatedly insists will not be pres-

---

Vulgate reads "praeterit enim figura huius mundi."

196. Augustine, *civ. Dei* 20.16. Emphasis added. ". . . figura huius mundi mundanorum ignium conflagratione praeteribit, sicut factum est mundanarum aquarum inundatione diluvium. Illa itaque, ut dixi, conflagratione mundana elementorum corruptibilium qualitates, quae corporibus nostris corruptibilibus congruebant, ardendo penitus interibunt, atque ipsa substantia eas qualitates habebit, quae corporibus immortalibus mirabili mutatione conveniant; ut scilicet mundus in melius innovatus apte accommodetur hominibus etiam carne in melius innovatis."

197. Ibid., 13.23.

198. Marrou, *Resurrection*, 31.

ent in heaven, is only comprehensible in light of the doctrine of "the non-substantive nature of evil."[199] Therefore, in the resurrection, matter's tendency toward non-being will be erased. Nothing good will be lost. The removal of corruption, then, is not a change as much as it is a filling-in of the ontological gaps in fallen, created being. In this way, no "thing" is lost, but every*thing* (i.e., that which is good) is retained and elevated. In Augustine's understanding of resurrectional transformation we already have a concrete example of Thomas Aquinas' dictum that "grace does not destroy nature but perfects it."[200]

The Completion of the Body

We can observe Augustine illustrating the principle that the eradication of corruption is not the subtraction of a positive sort of evil but a completion of being when he states that even aborted fetuses and other babies who have died will be raised as adults.[201] This is not a question of the imposition of a radically new form. On the contrary, these infants will "receive as a gift what would have come to them with time."[202] The resurrection "will supply anything the fetus lacks in form."[203] The same is true for children with congenital deformities: they will have "their nature healed and rectified."[204]

In *De Civitate Dei* Augustine states that these children, while lacking "full stature," nonetheless already possess it "potentially, even though not yet in their actual size."[205] In this case, the mature stature is present even in the immature form. Augustine continues: "Every material substance, then, seems to contain within itself what one might call a pattern of everything which does not yet exist—or, rather, which is as yet latent—but which in the course of time will come into existence, or, rather, into sight."[206]

Augustine is certainly affirming that the adult form of the body is contained, in germ as it were, in each fetus. But is he also suggesting

199. Ibid., 22.
200. Thomas Aquinas, *Summa Theologiae* I,1.8 ad. 2.
201. Augustine, *s.* 242.4; *ench.* 23.85; *civ. Dei* 22.14.
202. Augustine, *s.* 242.4.
203. Augustine, *ench.* 23.85.
204. Ibid., 23.87.
205. Augustine, *civ. Dei* 22.14. Augustine continues to explain that this potentiality is the same as the way a body is latent in a seed (he is presumably speaking here of human *semen*).
206. Ibid.

that the risen form of the body is somehow contained within our mortal bodies? The fact that he sometimes describes the resurrection using the metaphor of the seed sown in the ground would support such an idea.[207] However, Augustine is always insistent that this transformation will be the result of an infusion of grace, and not merely an automatic development from nature. Therefore, if Augustine does mean to say that the glory of the risen body is in some way latent in the earthly body then this latency must be understood not in a naturalistic way but as a sort of *potentia obedientialis* for the grace God gives in the resurrection.

Divinization

For Augustine, we are not resurrected simply to have better bodies than we did before. Rather, in the resurrection we fully share in God's life. We will fully bear the image of God, since our bodies will be like Christ's body.[208] We will also be clothed with Christ's "heavenly immortality" just as the angels are.[209] The eternal God will make us share in his eternity: "The Word exists before time, and through him all time was made; he was born in time, though he is eternal life; he calls temporal creatures, and makes them eternal."[210]

Elsewhere, Augustine is even more blunt about the glorious destiny of the blessed: "it is in order not to be a man that you have been called by the one who became man for your sake . . . God, you see, wants to make you a god [*Deus enim deum te vult facere*]; not by nature of course, like the one whom he begot; but by his gift and by adoption. For just as he through being humbled came to share your mortality; so through lifting you up he brings you to share his immortality."[211] In this very Athanasian understanding of redemption, divinization is the natural outcome of sal-

---

207. See, e.g., Augustine, *s.* 242A.2; 361.9.9. Incidentally, this is the very metaphor that Bynum believes Augustine rejects in favor of more static images.

208. Augustine, *Trin.* 14.24. "From this it is clear that the image of God will achieve its full likeness of him when it attains to the full vision of him—though this text from the apostle John might also appear to be referring to the immortality of the body. In this respect too we will be like God, but only like the Son, who alone in the triad took a body in which he died and rose again, carrying it up to the heavenly regions."

209. Augustine, *civ. Dei* 13.23; 13.24; 22.1.

210. Augustine, *en. Ps.* 101.2.10. English translation from vol. III/19 of The Works of Saint Augustine.

211. Augustine, *s.* 166.4. Also, *civ. Dei* 21.15: "For there is only one Son of God by nature, Who in His compassion became the Son of man for our sakes, that we, being by nature sons of men, might become sons of God by grace through Him."

vation. For Augustine, divine properties like immortality and eternity will be communicated to us by grace.

The Risen Body and Historical Continuity

We have already discussed how material identity can function as a vehicle of personal continuity. Yet the body's particular characteristics also function for Augustine as a means of maintaining one's identity after death. This is because the human body is the locus of our interaction with the world. In a sense, it bears the imprints and echoes of our life experiences and personal history. Gerald O'Collins explains his understanding of Augustine on this point: "Through our bodiliness we freely create and develop a whole web of relationships with other people, the world, and God. Our history comes from our body being in relationship. As bodies we have our history—from conception right through to death . . . That human, bodily history which makes up the story of each person will be brought to new life."[212] As Johannes van Bavel stresses, for Augustine "man's personal history becomes very important; indeed, it even receives eternal value."[213] And the preservation of this personal history is manifested concretely in the risen body.

The Wounds of the Martyrs

Perhaps the clearest revelation of personal history is found in the wounds that remain in risen bodies. Against Faustus, the Manichean, Augustine maintains that the scars in Christ's risen body were real and not an illusion.[214] They indicated that the risen Christ was the same as the earthly Christ, thus allowing his disciples to recognize him.[215] Yet the persistence of wounds is not restricted to Christ alone, but extends to those who have suffered and died for him: "I do not know why this is so, but the love we bear for the blessed martyrs makes us desire to see in the kingdom of

---

212. O'Collins, "Augustine on the Resurrection," 72–73. Also cf. Marrou, *Resurrection*, 28. O'Collins, however, is somewhat hesitant to embrace the corresponding material continuity espoused by Augustine. He thus suggests modifying Augustine's dictum that all will rise "with the same body," saying instead, "in the resurrection all will rise with the same embodied history."

213. van Bavel, "Anthropology of Augustine," 42.

214. Augustine, *c. Faust.* 11.3

215. Augustine, *civ. Dei* 22.19.

heaven the marks of the wounds which they received for Christ's name; and it may be that we shall indeed see them. For this will not be a deformity, but a badge of honour, and the beauty of their virtue—a beauty which is in the body, but not of the body—will shine forth in it."[216] If any limbs have been hacked off, they will be restored. The scars will remain, but we are "not to deem these marks of virtue blemishes, or call them such"[217] because these marks are outward manifestations of the suffering love endured by Christians for Christ. Just as Jesus' wounds remain in his body as a sign of his identity as our Savior, so the wounds of Christian witnesses will remain as signs of their christoformity.[218]

These "marks of virtue" will thus be retained, even though the risen bodies of the martyrs will be free of every defect. Evils such as deformities will be perfectly remedied, but wounds suffered for Christ will endure as signs of virtue, honor, and sanctity. The body is the bearer of these marks of glory which signify the concretization and permanent preservation of the history of one's salvation.

The Persistence of Gender

Another important area in which bodily history is manifested in the resurrection—in contradistinction to many other church fathers—is the continuity of gender. Unlike some of his contemporaries, Augustine held that women would remain women in the resurrection. Others had held that they would be changed into men or that all would return to a primal, sexless state.[219]

In fact, there is a close relationship here between protology and eschatology, with the former coloring the latter. If one holds (as Gregory of

216. Ibid.

217. Ibid.

218. For a discussion of this, see Jones, *Marks of His Wounds*, which discusses Augustine's Christocentric reinterpretation of bodily woundedness and suffering.

219. See, e.g., Gregory of Nyssa, *On the Making of Man* 17.4 where he suggests that sexual difference was designed by God, who in his foreknowledge knew that humans would sin (and thus die) and therefore need a means of propagation. Also, in 17.2 Gregory states that eternal life is essentially a return to the original state, in which we have an asexual life like the angels. Jerome also seems to have held something like this, e.g., his *Apology Against Rufinus* 1.29. On the other hand, Tertullian (in *De Resurrectione Carnis,* chap. 60) had previously stated that sexual difference as well as sexual organs would remain in the resurrection. It is likely that Augustine read Tertullian (a fellow North African), although it is beyond the scope of our study to determine what Tertullian's influence might have been on Augustine's thought in this regard.

Augustine on Resurrection

Nyssa did) that gender is a consequence of sin (or, God's foreknowledge of human sin) then it cannot be present in the eschaton. Augustine, however, underwent a considerable development in his thought on the topic, modifying his view over his lifetime from one which posited a sexless original creation, to one which held that both the sexes and sexual intercourse were part of God's original plan.[220] It would be interesting to explore the extent to which Augustine's development reflected a move away from a Platonism fixated on unity toward a more Trinitarian anthropology that valued difference, although this is not the place for such a study. In any case, once the existence of the sexes is seen as part of (good) human nature rather than as the sign of a fall from grace, their presence in the resurrection follows as a matter of course. This is because, as we have already pointed out, Augustine is working under the basic premise which was later systematized by Thomas Aquinas: that grace does not destroy nature, but elevates and perfects it.[221]

In *De Civitate Dei*, Augustine spends two chapters of Book XXII refuting arguments from other Christians against the existence of women in the resurrection. Against the argument that a woman's body incites lust, and would therefore be unfit for resurrection, Augustine responds: "For then [in the resurrection] there will be no lust, which is now the cause of confusion. For before they sinned, the man and the woman were naked, and were not ashamed. Vice will be taken away from those bodies, therefore, and nature preserved. And the sex of a woman is not a vice, but nature ... He, then, who instituted two sexes will restore them both."[222] Responding to another argument, he continues, "the Lord denied that there would be marriages in the resurrection, not women."[223] He also rejects the argument, based on Eph 4:13 (regarding coming to the perfection of the "perfect man"), which held that women must become men.[224]

The core of Augustine's argument, of course, is the notion that the sexes belong to human nature. Since they are created by God, and are therefore not a sign of *corruptio*, they will not be obliterated but rather

---

220. For a thorough summary of the development of Augustine's thought on this issue, see Roberts, *Creation and Covenant*, 39–72.

221. Thomas Aquinas, *Summa Theologiae* I,1,8, ad2.

222. Augustine, *civ. Dei* 22.17.

223. Ibid. Here, Augustine is responding to an interpretation—used by Gregory of Nyssa and others—of Matt 22:23–33 (and parallels).

224. Ibid., 22.18. Augustine indicates that in this case (and many others), "man" includes both sexes.

perfected. Augustine thus states that the sexual organs will be present but will have a new beauty and a new use.[225] Like the rest of the body, sexuality will be transformed, yet retained.

Sexuality is therefore another part of personal continuity. Lawrence Welch explains that "if risen bodies were asexual they would not be the resurrection of *our* bodies, the bodies that God made in the good creation."[226] Christopher Roberts argues that Augustine's teaching accurately mirrors his understanding of sexuality's power in the realm of human sinfulness: "if sexual difference bears the scars of disobedience, then we can also expect it to be healed in redemption."[227]

One final reason that Augustine insists on the presence of the sexes in heaven is the nuptial imagery with which he envisions the Christ-Church relationship.[228] If marriage can be a sacrament—at least in the sense that it can symbolize and make present something as great as the Christ-Church relationship—then it cannot be something ephemeral and inconsequential in the grand scheme of human salvation.[229]

There are thus two reasons why sexuality must be present in the eschaton. First, it is part of human nature and therefore a necessary component of one's personal identity. What is from nature will not be destroyed, but rather "He . . . who instituted two sexes will restore them both."[230] Second, human sexuality is a means chosen by God to reflect the Christ-Church relationship. In this sense, it is sacramental and possesses enduring value.

The Body: Locus of the Communal Visio Dei

We have seen how, for Augustine, continuity between the earthly and risen body is maintained by the preservation of the material of the body itself,

---

225. Ibid., 22.17.

226. Welch, "Augustinian Foundations," 366. Also Roberts, *Creation and Covenant*, 71: "Maleness or femaleness is an important part of a person that must be retained for the sake of continuity with mortal identity."

227. Roberts, *Creation and Covenant*, 71.

228. For a detailed discussion, see Welch, "Augustinian Foundations." For some examples of this imagery in Augustine's works, see *s.* 264.4; 362.14.16; *doc. Chr.* 1.16.15; *civ. Dei* 22.17.

229. Welch, "Augustinian Foundations," 373. "Augustine knew that the masculinity and femininity of created humanity is a redeemed reality and ultimately an eschatological reality because its exemplar, its archetype is Christ, the Bridegroom, and the Church, his Bride."

230. Augustine, *civ. Dei* 22.17.

and by the body's characteristics such as scars and gender. We will now examine the pinnacle of honor bestowed upon matter: the risen body's vision and contemplation of God.

For Augustine, as for much of the Latin tradition after him, the climax of beatitude is the *visio Dei*.[231] Here again, Augustine's thought developed over time. Early on, he maintained that the vision of God would be only a spiritual one. In *Letter* 92 (written before 408), Augustine rejected what he considered the foolishness of those "drunk with carnal thoughts" who supposed that God could be seen with the eyes of the risen body since God, as pure Spirit, could only be seen in spirit.[232] This reasoning follows from the Platonic notion that like understands like.[233] Several years later, however, Augustine still doubted that God could be seen by bodily eyes but had considerably cooled his invective against those who held the affirmative position, allowing that it was at least a possibility.[234]

---

231. This finds its foundation in, *inter alia*, 1 Cor 13:12a: "For now we see in a mirror dimly, but then face to face."

232. Augustine, *ep.* 92 (written before 408). There, he decries some who teach that "we now see God by the mind, but will then see him with the body ... Christ granted to his own flesh that it might see God with the eyes of the body; then they added that all the saints would see God in the same way, once they received their bodies back in the resurrection" (*ep.* 92.4). Augustine rejects this view as foolish nonsense, responding, "Let the flesh drunk with carnal thoughts hear this: *God is spirit, and for this reason those who worship God must worship him in spirit and in truth* (Jn 4:24). If they must worship him in spirit and truth, how much more must they see him in spirit and in truth!" (*ep.* 92.5) English translation from vol. II/1 of The Works of Saint Augustine.

233. In *civ. Dei* 20.29 Augustine lays out this line of reasoning without subscribing to it: "Now the reasoning of the philosophers asserts that intelligible things are perceived by the vision of the mind and sensible things—that is, corporeal things—by the body's senses, whereas the mind cannot observe intelligible things by means of the body, nor corporeal things simply by its own activity. If we could establish this reasoning as entirely certain, then it would clearly follow that God could not be seen by the eye even of a spiritual body."

234. Augustine, *ep.* 147 (written 413 or 414). This letter is entirely on the topic of seeing God. Here, Augustine appeals to Jerome and Ambrose to support the "spiritual vision," but no longer condemns the opposing view. He acknowledges that "if there will be bodies [in the resurrection], there will be something that bodily eyes can see ... But, with regard to the spiritual body, if God gives us help, we will see whether we can discuss it in some other work" (*ep.* 147.54; this is the conclusion of the letter). English translation from vol. II/2 of The Works of Saint Augustine. Also, in *ep.* 148 (written 413 or 414) Augustine writes to the bishop Fortunatian and admits that it is possible that the eyes of the risen body may see God, although this must not be taken to mean that we will therefore not see God interiorly as well (*ep.* 148.17). Additionally, in *Sermon* 277 (given in 413), Augustine cautions that God is not a body and cannot be seen as if he occupied physical space (*s.* 277.13–14). At the end of the sermon, however, he allows the possibility of fleshly eyes seeing God: "God cannot be seen in a place,

Part One: Ratzinger the Augustinian

By the time he finished *De Civitate Dei*, however, he had come to a new appreciation of the value of the body in human existence. His about-face is in this regard foreshadowed in Book X, where he states that God's substance "remains ever invisible to corruptible eyes,"[235] the important qualifier here being "corruptible." We have already seen how Augustine distinguishes between the body and corruption. We thus have the possibility of *incorruptible* eyes seeing God's substance.

In Book XXII, chapter 29, Augustine takes up the question explicitly: "And so the saints will see God in the body [*in ipso corpore*]; but whether they will see Him by means of the body's eyes, as we now see the sun, moon, stars, sea and earth and all the things on earth: that is no small question."[236] Augustine first considers the prophetic gift of seeing far-off things in one's heart, and acknowledges that this form of vision will be present.[237] Yet the question remains: even if other forms of vision are possible, what are the eyes for? Will they simply become useless appendages, giving way to spiritual sight?

Here, Augustine explodes the dictum that had hindered the Platonists, that is, that only like comprehends like.[238] He declares that in heaven, "our eyes will have the power of seeing incorporeal things."[239] Since the prophets saw corporeal things by the spirit, "why, then, should there not by the same token be a power in a spiritual body to enable even spirit to be perceived by such a body? For 'God is a Spirit.'"[240] Here we have the completion of an earlier intuition of Augustine's, when in *De Genesi ad Litteram* 12.35 he had claimed that the separated soul cannot see God's

---

because he is not a body; because he is everywhere, because he is not less in one part, and more in another. Let us hold on to this with the utmost firmness. But if that flesh undergoes such a change that by it can be seen what cannot be seen in a place; fine, let it be so. But we have to inquire what is taught. And if it isn't taught, it shouldn't yet be denied; but certainly it must at least be doubted" (*s.* 277.18). English translation from vol. III/8 of The Works of Saint Augustine.

235. Augustine, *civ. Dei* 10.15. Also, *civ. Dei* 22.29: "God forbid, therefore, that we should say that the saints in the life to come will not see God when they close their eyes; for they will always see Him in the Spirit [*spiritu*]." The rendering of the ablative *spiritu* is given here by Dyson as "in the Spirit," by Walsh as "in their spirits," and by Dods as "with their spirit." In any case, we are dealing with a case of spiritual vision that does not require the eyes of the body.

236. Ibid., 22.29.

237. Ibid.

238. Ibid.

239. Ibid.

240. Ibid.

substance fully until it rejoins its body. If we join up these two insights of Augustine's, we can say that the *visio Dei* is complete when God is seen simultaneously by the interior, spiritual eyes and by the physical eyes of the glorified *corpus spiritale*. By the end of *De Civitate Dei*, Augustine's view of the risen body has developed to the point that it is *capax visionis Dei*. We thus have a case of matter—earthly matter—being so elevated by its incorporation into a risen, human body, that it participates in seeing God, who is pure Spirit. This probably represents the greatest exaltation of matter in Augustine's theology.

The Communal Nature of the *Visio*

Augustine's understanding of the *visio Dei*, like his notion of the *opera Dei*, involves others.[241] He holds that seeing God will not be a solitary event, but a communal one:

> It may well be, then—indeed, this is entirely credible—that, in the world to come, we shall see the bodily forms of the new heaven and the new earth in such a way as to perceive God with total clarity and distinctness, everywhere present and governing all things, both material and spiritual. In this life, we understand the invisible things of God by the things which are made, and we see Him darkly and in part, as in a glass, and by faith rather than by perceiving corporeal appearances with our bodily eyes. In the life to come, however, it may be that we shall see Him by means of the bodies which we shall then wear, and wherever we shall turn our eyes. In this life, after all, as soon as we become aware of the men among whom we live, we do not merely believe that they are alive and displaying vital motions: we see it, beyond any doubt, by means of our bodies, though we are not able to see their life without their bodies. By the same token, in the world to come, wherever we shall look with the spiritual eyes of our bodies, we shall then, by means of our bodies, behold the incorporeal God ruling all things.[242]

The new heavens and earth will be so perfectly permeated with God's being, and so utterly ordered by him, that by perceiving these things which he has both made and elevated, we will perceive God himself. It is the

---

241. The relationship between these two is discussed by van Bavel, "Anthropology of Augustine," 45–46.

242. Augustine, *civ. Dei* 22.29.

eschatological perfection of the principle of Romans 1:20.[243] In this case, however, the perfect transparency of the being of redeemed creation makes this vision complete rather than partial.

Augustine has again gone far beyond where Platonists dare to tread, for not only is the eye of the body used to see God, but it is used to see God *in the bodies of others*. For "God will then be known to us and visible to us in such a way that we shall see Him by the spirit in ourselves, in one another, in Himself, in the new heavens and the new earth, and in every created thing which shall then exist; and also by the body we shall see Him in every body to which the keen vision of the eye of the spiritual body shall extend."[244] It is rather surprising that Augustine nowhere (to my knowledge) states that we will behold God in the *souls* of the blessed. This honor is reserved for bodies. Just as we perceive the life of a person through his body, so in heaven we will perceive God, who will be the life of all, through the bodies of all. It would appear to be a testament to Augustine's understanding of the incarnation and to his surpassing of Platonic hindrances that he ended up with an eschatology that so exalts matter and the body.

The nature of the *visio* is thus not only bodily but also communal.[245] There, as in this world, God will manifest himself to us through others in an incarnate way. Our union with him will be bound up with our union with others.[246] And this union is no disembodied unity but involves *both* soul and body.

---

243. "... his invisible nature, namely, his eternal power and deity, has been clearly perceived in the things that have been made."

244. Augustine, *civ. Dei* 22.29.

245. Marrou (*Resurrection*, 33) comments on this social dimension of Augustine's view of beatitude: "For life in the heavenly city is a social life. Nothing could be more foreign to the Augustinian concept than to imagine each soul bound, so to say, exclusively, by direct line to God, and leaving others out of account. We must not forget that we are and shall remain members one of another, forming the same body, that of Christ in his plenitude."

246. In *s.* 24.5 Augustine declares regarding the other blessed whom we have never before met: "You will know them all. Those who are there won't recognize each other just because they have faces; mutual recognition will come from a greater kind of knowledge. They will see each other, but much more perfectly, in the same way as prophets are accustomed to see things here. They will see in a divine manner, since they will be full of God. And there will be nothing to give offense, nothing to be hidden from people's knowledge."

Matter: Summary

Rather than positing a radical split between matter and spirit, as the Platonists (and especially the Manicheans) did, Augustine sees the body and the matter that composes it as possessing enduring value. He posits a numerical identity between the earthly body and the risen one, maintaining what Bynum disparages as "the salvation of bits." Yet it is central to Augustine's thesis that these "bits" are valuable because they are the bits of a human body. In the resurrection, earthly matter will be retained, but its *qualitates* will be changed and all corruptibility will disappear. Our bodies will be changed and renewed, as will the rest of the material world. Human beings will share in God's divinity.

In Augustine, the risen body also functions as a bearer of one's personal history. Therefore, it bears the marks of wounds suffered for Christ, as well as the particular characteristics associated with gender. Yet most striking of all is Augustine's assertion that we will be able to see God not only with our hearts, but with our bodily eyes. The spiritual body (which is still body and not spirit) will have the ability to perceive spirit and will see God's life active in the bodies of the other blessed. The *visio Dei* will thus be communal in two senses: (1) we will be together when we see God, and (2) we will see God in each other.

Some Concluding Remarks on Nature and Grace

Considering that Augustine is known as the Doctor of Grace—mainly for his anti-Pelagian writings—one might expect a similar emphasis in his doctrine of resurrection. Yet what one finds is strikingly different. Although Augustine does not downplay the miraculous transformation that will occur at the eschaton, one is struck by how much emphasis he lays on *nature*. It is the same matter that will be saved, it is the same body—complete with sex and scars—that will exist forever. And it is with this same body that we will see our God.

On the topic of resurrection, Augustine might rather be known as the *Doctor naturae*, for against all those who claimed a radical discontinuity with this present life—whether in the form of a rejection of the body, as with the Platonists, or in the form of wild cosmological mythology, as with the Manicheans—Augustine held that the body and soul with which we serve God in this life will be the body and soul that will be glorified and divinized in the next. The danger here, of course, is the same danger present in the Pelagian controversy, for if nature is given too much latitude then man saves himself. But allow grace to eclipse nature, and there is no "man" left to be saved.

Perhaps the reason that to us Augustine's account sounds so skewed to the side of nature is simply the theological atmosphere of the last century. By modern standards, Augustine seems to exaggerate the continuity with the present life. But it may be that we have allowed "grace" to overshadow nature to the point that we have obscured the human being who is saved.

Fourth Augustinian Characteristic

The Beauty of the Body

The final characteristic of Augustine's theology of resurrection that we will consider is an often overlooked one. When speaking of the human body—even this earthly body—Augustine is often in awe and wonder at its *beauty*. George Lawless holds that "in all of Patristic literature, I dare say, no Father of the Church has written so admiringly of the human body."[247] This aesthetic element has gone largely unnoticed, however,[248] or has been dismissed as trivial.[249] It will thus be necessary to make several observations on the role of beauty in Augustine's theology of resurrection.

The Body Beautiful: Harmony

In the ancient world, the body was honored in art for its form and beauty. At the same time, it was often denigrated by philosophers for its tendency to mutability and decay. As we have already seen, Augustine makes the distinction between the body itself, and its corruptibility. He is therefore free to speak of the body's beauty without glorifying decay. Against

---

247. Lawless, "Augustine and Human Embodiment," 180. Marrou ("Anthropology of Augustine," 23) is also surprised by how often Augustine praises bodily beauty.

248. Ibid., 185. "Augustine's assessment of the human body has so far failed to receive the attention it deserves." Van Bavel ("Anthropology of Augustine," 39) also notes that no one has yet studied how Augustine uses biology and anatomy in his anthropology.

249. Bynum, *Resurrection of the Body*, 99. She dismisses Augustine's emphasis on beauty because of its "Neoplatonic emphasis on structure and harmony." But might this reflect a *positive* aspect of Neoplatonism, rather than grounds for dismissing Augustine out of hand?

Porphyry, he declares that "our faith, instructed by God, praises the body; because even the body which we have now . . . even this body has its own beauty and advantages, in the arrangement of its limbs, the distinction of the senses, its upright posture, and many other things which amaze those who consider it carefully."[250]

What Augustine finds most beautiful about the body is not any organ in particular, but the harmonious working together of the whole:

> Which of us, after all, knows how these parts [internal organs] are linked with each other, and in what proportions they are fitted together? That's what harmony means, a word taken from music; where we can certainly see the sinews, the strings, stretched on the guitar . . . Anybody who has learned the intelligent art of this kind that is to be found in the parts of the human body is so amazed, so delighted, that this art, this harmony, this proportion is preferred by those who understand it to all visible beauty.[251]

In heaven, the inner workings of the body will be made manifest, and "all those elements of the body's harmony . . . will be hidden no longer . . . the delight which their rational beauty gives us will kindle our rational minds to the praise of so great an Artist."[252] From this statement, two important points arise. First, the beauty of the risen body is *rational*, and second, its purpose is to direct our minds to praise God. The fact that this beauty is rational is important for Augustine, for it is in being rational that the body can incite the rational mind to praise its Creator. For Augustine, praise of the Creator cannot be wild and ecstatic at the expense of rationality. God, who is Reason, is properly praised and worshiped *reasonably*.[253]

The body's harmony consists of the perfect ordering of its parts. But in the resurrection, these parts will be transformed and raised up to a new level. Every bodily organ will be present, while many will be given new uses. Even the sexual organs, which "are here private or shameful . . . won't

---

250. Augustine, *s.* 241.7.

251. Ibid., 243.4. Also, *civ. Dei* 22.24 where Augustine states that if we could see the beautiful harmony of the internal organs, it "would so delight the mind, which makes use of the eyes, with their rational beauty that we should prefer that beauty more than the merely visible beauty which pleases the eye alone."

252. Augustine, *civ. Dei* 22.30.

253. This is not to say that worship must be a purely cerebral exercise, but only that for Augustine praise or worship that circumvented reason would not be genuine. This is the general idea expressed by Paul in 1 Cor 14:33: "For God is not a God of confusion but of peace."

be shameful or private there," because there will be no lust.[254] They will be given a new beauty and a new use.[255]

But we now come to a decisive point in Augustine's aesthetic of resurrection: he holds that many parts of the body will have no use at all, but will be present exclusively for their beauty. He points out how various parts of the body (a man's nipples, for example) do not provide any function, yet contribute to personal beauty.[256] He even goes so far as to say that "I think . . . when the body was created, dignity took precedence over necessity. After all, necessity is a transitory thing; whereas the time is coming when we shall enjoy each other's beauty without any lust: an enjoyment which will specially redound to the praise of the Creator, Who, as it is said in the psalm, has 'put on praise and comeliness.'"[257]

We have seen how for Augustine, the *visio Dei* is actually mediated by the bodies of the other blessed. Yet this mediation happens—at least in part—through the perception of beauty. Here, Augustine has moved beyond a utilitarian view of the body to an aesthetic one. It is now not so much a question of what the risen body can *do*, as how beautiful it will be. This is because of the intimate connection between beauty and contemplation. By contemplating the glorified bodies of others, we will see God (who is Reason) acting and vivifying those bodies by their harmonious integration. The risen body will not only offer itself in praise of its Creator,[258] but will be so transparent that those who gaze upon its beauty will gaze upon the beauty of their Lord.

The Beauty of the Body: Summary

For Augustine, the human body is not only a valuable and indispensable part of human nature. It is beautiful. By making use of the concept of *harmonia*, Augustine illustrates how the body's beauty lies in the perfect ordering of its parts. This bodily harmony, which will be perfected in

---

254. Augutsine, s. 243.7.

255. Augustine, *civ. Dei* 22.17.

256. Augustine, s. 243.6; *civ. Dei* 22.24.

257. Augustine, *civ. Dei* 22.24.

258. Ibid., 22.30. "When the body is made incorruptible, all the members and inward parts which we now see assigned to their various necessary offices will join together in praising God; for there will then be no necessity, but only full, certain, secure and everlasting felicity."

heaven, reflects the perfect harmony between body and soul which will also reach perfection in the eschaton.

Every part of the risen body will serve in praise of its Creator. This will happen in part through the transparency of the risen body, so that perceiving it is perceiving God. In this way, the beauty of the risen body lifts the mind to praise and worship its Creator. Because Augustine can distinguish between bodiliness and corruptibility, he can recognize the limitations and difficulties associated with this earthly body without losing sight of its beauty. He can even view the risen body as the means by which we will see God, and therefore as truly *imago Dei*.

Ratzinger's Theology of Resurrection in View of Augustine's

Having determined and examined four key characteristics of Augustine's theology of resurrection, we will now use these characteristics to consider and evaluate Joseph Ratzinger's theology of the resurrection of the body. Our goal here is not simply an exposition of Ratzinger's theology but rather an examination and evaluation of it from the perspective of our Augustinian characteristics. We will therefore consider that theology under the headings of our four Augustinian characteristics, beginning with the first: apologetics and proclamation.

2

Apologetics and Proclamation in Ratzinger's Theology of Resurrection

In this chapter, we will observe how the relationship between Ratzinger's theology of resurrection and his understanding of Platonism developed in a direction inverse to Augustine's own development: Ratzinger began as a suspicious "anti-Platonist," but gradually came to embrace the contributions of Greek philosophy to a Christian understanding of resurrection, whereas Augustine began as a Platonist and gradually rejected elements of that philosophy. It will also be demonstrated that a concern for proclamation (which Ratzinger shares with Augustine) has strongly shaped Ratzinger's theology of resurrection and that this concern has transformed itself over the course of his life, as he came to have less and less regard for the "modern worldview" and its exclusion of the miraculous. In this way, Ratzinger's apologetic approach has shifted toward the mature position of Augustine.

Apologetics and Proclamation in Ratzinger's Theology of Resurrection

The Movement Away from Anti-Platonism

We will begin by examining how Ratzinger began as a self-confessed "anti-Platonist" who believed that Hellenist anthropology was not a complement but a competitor to Christianity. Ratzinger was particularly suspicious of the Greek body-soul schema, fearing it to be dualistic. We will see how Ratzinger came to believe that the philosophy of Plato (and the body-soul schema as well) was not as dualistic as he at first feared, and that the modern "anti-Platonic" position he once held was in fact the real dualistic culprit. This move towards a more dual and "Platonic" anthropology (in the sense that it allows a real distinction between two elements, body and soul) signifies a rapprochement with Augustine's theology of resurrection.

Ratzinger's Early Position: Christianity Corrupted by Platonism

In the Patristic period of which Augustine is a part, the complex process of the synthesis of Christian and Greek thought was still underway. We have seen how Augustine was critical of tendencies within Platonism that he considered to be at odds with the kerygma (e.g., his critiques of reincarnation, of the existence of spiritual intermediaries between man and God, of any denial of the incarnation and of the resurrection's materiality, and of the devaluation of the human body). When looking back over history, however, many twentieth-century theologians came to the conclusion that the synthesis of Christian and Platonic thought represented more a corruption than an innovative synthesis.

Oscar Cullmann famously laments that most Christians understand salvation not as resurrection but rather as the Greek concept of the "immortality of the soul." His best-known accusation in this regard is that in Christianity "1 Corinthians 15 has been sacrificed for the *Phaedo*."[1] For Cullmann, the two concepts—immortality of the soul, and resurrection of the dead—are incompatible:

> The fact that later Christianity effected a link between the two beliefs and that today the ordinary Christian simply confuses them has not persuaded me to be silent about what I, in common with most exegetes, regard as true; and all the more so,

---

1. Cullmann, *Immortality of the Soul*, 8. This was given in English as the Ingersoll Lecture on the Immortality of Man at Harvard University in 1955.

since the link established between the expectation of the "resurrection of the dead" and the belief in the "immortality of the soul" is not in fact a link at all but renunciation of one in favour of the other.²

Preceding Cullmann in this "incompatibility" view was his fellow Lutheran Paul Althaus (1888–1966), who in his 1922 work *Die letzten Dinge* held the incommensurability of the ideas of resurrection and immortality.³ Although Althaus modified his position in his 1950 article "Retraktationen zur Eschatologie"⁴ so that both "resurrection" and "immortality of the soul" were valid concepts, by that point his earlier idea had already taken firm root in the Protestant theological community, particularly in Germany, and was not to be uprooted: resurrection was the Christian, biblical image, while immortality was a Greek intrusion. The idea was not without effect on the young theologian Joseph Ratzinger, as he later described: "I had begun boldly with those theses which, uncommon at the time, have become almost universally accepted even in the Catholic world: that is, I had tried to construct a 'de-Platonized' eschatology. But the longer I dealt with the questions and the more I immersed myself in the sources, the more the antitheses I had built up collapsed in my hands and the more the inner logic of the Church's tradition revealed itself."⁵

This "de-Platonizing" tendency is evident in Ratzinger's early writings, particularly from 1957–1968. In his 1957 encyclopedia entry "Auferstehung des Fleisches,"⁶ Ratzinger had not yet fully developed the anti-Greek sentiment that would later manifest itself, yet he nonetheless

2. Ibid., 7–8.

3. Althaus, *Die letzten Dinge*, 114.

4. Althaus, "Retraktationen zur Eschatologie." Althaus nonetheless did not hold that the sayings about resurrection and immortality could be *combined*, but that they could be held next to each other (257).

5. Ratzinger, *Eschatologie*, 15 (*Eschatology*, xxv). Unless otherwise noted, all translations from *Eschatologie* are my own. I will also provide references to the current 2nd English edition, even though that translation has a significant number of problems. "Ich hatte kühn mit jenen Thesen begonnen, die—damals noch ungewohnt—sich heute auch im katholischen Raum fast allgemein durchgesetzt haben, d.h. ich hatte versucht, eine 'entplatonisierte' Eschatologie zu konstruieren. Je länger ich aber mit den Fragen umging, je mehr ich mich in die Quellen vertiefte, desto mehr zerfielen mir die aufgebauten Antithesen unter der Hand und desto mehr enthüllte sich die innere Logik der kirchlichen Überlieferung." As previously mentioned, the 6th German edition of 2007 uses different pagination from the original, 1990 version of the 6th edition. To make things even more confusing, both of these differ from the first edition, which has been cited by most of the relevant secondary literature up to this point.

6. Ratzinger, "Auferstehung des Fleisches" (1957).

warned that "any portrayal of the Christian doctrine of salvation which relies far too much on the immortality of the individual soul is in danger of falsifying the overall picture of the Christian message."[7] He also hinted at the difference between his understanding of the Greek idea of immortality, and Christian resurrection: "Thus, Christian faith in immortality is essentially hope in the resurrection. Only in this way does it actually become clear that the ultimate salvation of man comes not from the self-contained power of human nature, but from God's power alone which has revealed itself in Jesus Christ."[8] In this early work, Ratzinger exemplifies a common line of reasoning used to reject the Greek understanding of the immortality of the soul: if a soul, *by its own power or substance*, were incapable of death then the Christian understanding of salvation by God's grace would be thereby undermined. Such a *substantialistic* formulation of immortality is always (rightly) to be rejected.

Ratzinger's critique of the Greek concept of the immortality of the soul reached its highest intensity in his 1968 *Einführung in das Christentum (Introduction to Christianity)*. In the section of the book dealing with resurrection (much of which is simply adapted from a 1967 encyclopedia entry),[9] Ratzinger holds that there is no complementarity at all between the Greek and biblical understandings of immortality: "The Greek conception is based on the idea that man is composed of two mutually foreign substances, one of which (the body [*Körper*]) perishes, while the other (the soul) is in itself imperishable and therefore goes on existing in its own right independent of any other beings ... The biblical train of thought, on the other hand, presupposes the undivided unity of man."[10] Ratzinger then goes on to attack the idea of the soul's reunion with a physical body: "the real heart of faith in resurrection does not consist in the idea of the restoration of bodies [*Körper*], to which we have reduced it in our thinking;

---

7. Ibid., 1049. "In der Tat ist jede Darstellung der christl. Heilslehre, die allzu ausschließl. die Unsterblichkeit der Einzelseele betont, in Gefahr, das Gesamtbild der christl. Botschaft zu verfälschen."

8. Ibid., 1051. "So ist christl. Unsterblichkeitsglaube wesentl. A.s-hoffnung. Nur so wird auch wirklich deutlich, daß das Endheil des Menschen nicht aus der Eigenmacht der menschl. Natur, sondern allein aus der Macht Gottes kommt, die sich in Christus Jesus geoffenbart hat."

9. Ratzinger, "Auferstehung des Fleisches" (1967). This should not be confused with his 1957 encyclopedia entry by the same name. This entry appears in English as "Resurrection: Theological," in vol. 5 of *Sacramentum Mundi*.

10. Ratzinger, *Introduction to Christianity*, 349. Originally published 1968. Hereafter cited as *Intro*. All German citations of this work are from the 9th edition of *Einführung in das Christentum* (Munich: Kösel-Verlag, 2007). Hereafter cited as *Einführung*.

such is the case even though this is the pictorial image used throughout the Bible."¹¹ Rather, the true content of resurrection faith is "an immortality of the 'person,' of the *one* creation 'man.'"¹²

Such an assessment raises a genuine dilemma for Ratzinger's theology, however. If the main problem with Platonism is its devaluation of materiality and the body, then why would a "de-Platonized eschatology" be reticent to speak of resurrection as the restoration of bodies? In a later work, Ratzinger explained that this anti-Platonic movement is based on setting a supposedly biblical view of man in opposition to a philosophical, or Greek one. In such a biblical view, "man is seen in his undivided totality and unity as God's creature and cannot be split apart into body and soul."¹³ The reason, then, that the resurrection cannot be a "restoration of bodies" is that such a "restoration" would presuppose the separation of soul and body, a concept supposedly foreign to biblical thought.¹⁴

Although by the time of his 1980 article "Zwischen Tod und Auferstehung"¹⁵ Ratzinger had long rejected attempts at "de-Platonization" and already asserted the value of Greek thought, his discussion there reveals what he believes to be the roots of modern anti-Platonism. There, he laments that the discovery of the so-called biblical view has led many to reject anything which appeared to be the result of Greek influence, describing this condition as "an intensified recurrence of anti-Hellenic emotion."¹⁶ He contends that this fear of all things Greek is fueled by two factors: (1) *Skepticism about ontology and any talk of being.* "In theology, ontological thought was readily denounced as static and placed in opposition to the historical-dynamic approach of the Bible; the ontological was opposed to the dialogical and the personal."¹⁷ (2) *The fear of being accused of dualism.*

11. Ratzinger, *Intro.*, 349 (*Einführung*, 331).

12. Ibid., 350.

13. Ratzinger, *Eschatologie*, 68 (*Eschatology*, 74). "Denn hier werde ganz im Gegenteil der Mensch in seiner ungeteilten Ganzheit und Einheit als Gottes Geschöpf angesehen, das sich nicht in Leib und Seele auseinanderteilen lasse."

14. E.g., Ratzinger, *Intro.*, 349.

15. Ratzinger, "Zwischen Tod und Auferstehung." The article is also included as the second appendix of the 6th German edition of *Eschatologie* (207–23). Unless otherwise noted, I will provide my own translations and supply page numbers from *Eschatologie*. The article is also available in English as the first appendix of *Eschatology* (241–60; endnotes 286–88).

16. Ibid. (*Eschatologie*, 213; *Eschatology*, 250). "einer verstärkten Wiederkehr des antihellenischen Affekts."

17. Ibid. (*Eschatologie*, 213; *Eschatology*, 250). "In der Theologie wurde gerne dem

Apologetics and Proclamation in Ratzinger's Theology of Resurrection

"Viewing man as a being composed of body and soul and believing in an ongoing survival of the soul between the death of the body and its resurrection . . . would be a fall from the biblical idea of creation into Greek dualism, which splits the world into spirit and matter."[18] Ratzinger admits that he indulged in this anti-Platonism in his early years, and it seems likely that the reasons for this are the ones he provides above.

Ratzinger's Later Thought: A Reevaluation of Plato

Ratzinger's turn away from anti-Platonizing began even before the writing of *Eschatologie*. One first finds a transformed appreciation for Platonism and the notion of the immortality of the soul in Ratzinger's article "Jenseits des Todes" (1972).[19] Although Ratzinger does not articulate here a comprehensive understanding of the importance of Greek thought in the history of Christianity, he does espouse a new valuation of Plato's anthropology. Following Ulrich Duchrow's 1970 historical study *Christenheit und Weltverantwortung*,[20] Ratzinger states that regarding the current resurrection polemic and the notion of Platonic dualism, "Platonism has sunk here to a mere catchword that has no longer anything to do with the historical reality of Platonic philosophy."[21]

In *Eschatologie* (1977), Ratzinger further develops the notion that Plato's own teachings were often different from the dualistic doctrines popularly attributed to him. Here again, Ratzinger follows Duchrow closely, developing further Duchrow's basic thesis. He argues that while Plato made use of the Orphic tradition, he "philosophically refashioned

---

als statisch denunzierten ontologischen Denken die geschichtlich-dynamische Einstellung der Bibel entgegenhalten; auch wurde das Ontologische als sachhaft dem Dialogischen und Personalen entgegengesetzt."

18. Ibid. (*Eschatologie*, 213; *Eschatology*, 250). "Dem Menschen als Wesen aus Leib und Seele anzusehen, an ein Fortleben der Seele zwischen dem Tod des Leibes und seiner Auferstehung zu glauben . . . galt zusehends als Absturz aus dem biblischen Schöpfungsgedanken in den griechischen Dualismus, der die Welt in Geist und Materie teilt."

19. Ratzinger, "Jenseits des Todes." An English translation appeared simultaneously in *Communio* as "Beyond Death." Unless otherwise noted, I will refer to the English version..

20. Duchrow, *Christenheit und Weltverantwortung*. Although only a small portion of this work is dedicated to Plato, that portion is widely cited by German theologians writing on resurrection.

21. Ratzinger, "Beyond Death," 158 n. 4.

this religious tradition and related it to his fundamental theme, justice."²² Plato was attempting to respond to a political and spiritual crisis that plagued ancient Hellas, not to establish an individualistic understanding of immortality. Ratzinger therefore wishes to show

> the untenability of the common caricature of Platonism upon which so many theological clichés depend. The true target of Plato's thought is completely misunderstood when he is classified as an individualistic, dualistic thinker who negates the earthly and counsels a flight into the hereafter. The particular point upon which his thought is built is in reality the rejuvenation of the *polis*, establishing politics anew. His philosophy, which revolves around justice, develops in political crisis and out of the awareness that the *polis* cannot endure if justice is not reality and truth.²³

Ratzinger believes that the Platonic primacy of the political is evinced in Plato's anthropology of the soul, in which three parts exist, corresponding to the three levels of Greek society.²⁴ In this case, the soul is a microcosm of the Polis. Plato placed his idea of immortality at the service of his political thought, so that the inherent dualistic elements "lose their dualistic edge."²⁵ Further, he claimed no absolute certainty about the nature of the body-soul relationship, so that even in the *Phaedo* Plato is careful to state that his account of the soul may not be completely accurate.²⁶ The

---

22. Ratzinger, *Eschatologie*, 118 (*Eschatology*, 141). "Ebenso sicher ist aber dies, . . . daß Platon diese religiöse Überlieferung philosophisch umgestaltet und seinem Grundthema, der Gerechtigkeit, zugeordnet hat." Ratzinger also states that the Orphic tradition cannot be equated with all that is Greek.

23. Ibid., 72 (*Eschatology*, 78–79). "Diese scheinbar von unserem theologischen Problem weit abführenden Überlegungen sind nötig, weil sie das Unhaltbare der geläufigen Platonismus-Schematik zeigen, auf der so viele theologische Klischeevorstellungen beruhen. Die wahre Zielrichtung von Platons Denken wird völlig verkannt, wo er als individualistischer und dualistischer Denker eingestuft wird, der das Irdische verneint und die Menschen zur Flucht ins Jenseits anleitet. Sein eigentlicher Konstruktionspunkt ist in Wirklichkeit gerade die Wiederermöglichung der Polis, die Neugründung der Politik. Seine um die Gerechtigkeit kreisende Philosophie entwickelt sich in der Krise des Politischen und aus der Erkenntnis heraus, daß die Polis nicht Bestand haben kann, wenn Gerechtigkeit nicht Wirklichkeit, Wahrheit ist."

24. Ibid., 118 (*Eschatology*, 142). Ratzinger is again following Duchrow, *Weltverantwortung*, 61. Also, see Plato's *Republic* 589a 7.

25. Ibid., 119 (*Eschatology*, 143). "Dualistische Überlieferungsstücke . . . verlieren so ihre dualistische Pointe."

26. Ibid., 119 (*Eschatology*, 143). Ratzinger refers to *Phaedo* 114d. "No sensible man would insist that these things are as I have described them, but I think it is fitting for

result is that "Plato knows no dualism with regard to the soul's powers—his goal is the inner unity of man, the gathering-together and purification of all those powers in 'justice.'"[27] This means that, in opposition to the views of many modern theologians, Plato did not leave behind "a 'Greek schema' lying on the street simply to be picked up and used,"[28] and that "the doctrine—found in all the newer theological works—of the Greek-Platonic dualism of body and soul, together with the associated doctrine of the immortality of the latter, is a fantasy created by theologians with no correspondence to reality."[29]

Whether or not the overarching direction of Plato's philosophy is "dualistic," however, it is clear that Joseph Ratzinger, probably by 1972 (certainly by 1977, and definitively by 1980) had undergone something of a conversion with respect to the role of Greek, and more specifically, Platonic, thought in theological anthropology. Whereas in 1968 he explicitly placed the Greek body-soul distinction in opposition to the biblical and unified view of man, within a decade Ratzinger had overhauled his theology so that Greek thought was now evaluated more positively. We will now consider briefly the role that Ratzinger grants to Greek thought in the drama of Christian theology.

Greek Thought and the Christian Tradition

First of all, we should note that although Ratzinger, in his 1967 article "Auferstehung des Fleisches" (which also appeared, with some additions, in *Einführung*), holds that resurrection and immortality are non-complementary and mutually opposed, he does not thereby reject absolutely the concept of immortality. Even if at this time he believed that the doctrine

---

a man to risk the belief—for the risk is a noble one—that this, or something like this, is true about our souls and their dwelling places, since the soul is evidently immortal." Translation from *Plato: Five Dialogues*, trans. G. M. A. Grube, 152.

27. Ibid., 118 (*Eschatology*, 142). "Platon zunächst keinen Dualismus hinsichtlich der seelischen Kräfte des Menschen kennt—sein Ziel ist ja gerade die innere Einheit des Menschen, die Sammlung und Reinigung aller Kräfte in der 'Gerechtigkeit.'"

28. Ibid., 119 (*Eschatology*, 143–44). "So hinterließ er [Platon] . . . gar nicht ein 'griechisches Schema', das nun auf der Straße gelegen hätte und nur hätte übernommen werden brauchen oder können."

29. Ibid., 120 (*Eschatology*, 145). "Diese wenigen Andeutungen mögen genügen, um zu zeigen, daß die durch alle neueren theologischen Traktate geisternde Lehre von dem griechisch-platonischen Dualismus zwischen Leib und Seele samt der dazugehörigen Lehre von der Unsterblichkeit der letzteren eine Phantasie von Theologen ohne Entsprechung in der Wirklichkeit ist."

of immortality had an "originally dualistic intention," he was willing to grudgingly concede its use. For, since "'soul' is the key-word for the personal unity of man as a supra-material being, one can and must speak of the 'natural immortality' of the spirit-person, and hence that of the 'soul.'"[30] Yet in this case, Ratzinger does not see soul and body as being separable or distinct entities. Rather, the two terms correspond to man's "intrinsic differentiation by virtue of a spiritual and a material *principle* of being."[31] Here, body and soul are essentially different ways of speaking of the whole.

The impression given here differs from the Church's more traditional formulations. By the writing of *Eschatologie*, however, Ratzinger was more concerned to develop a theology that was clearly congruent with the Catholic tradition. Looking back in 2006, this is how he described that effort: "I had attempted [in *Eschatologie*] to show that the development of an anthropological conceptuality that used the expressions 'body' and 'soul,' as it took place in the tradition and had been formulated at the Council of Vienne (*DH* 902), was a thoroughly proper development of the guidelines of biblical anthropology."[32] Ratzinger thus does not see the patristic period as being a capitulation to a hostile Hellenism. He asserts that "the ancient Church remained extremely conservative in the realm of eschatological imagery; there was no changeover from 'Semitic' to 'Hellenistic' but rather the Church remained completely in the Semitic canon of images as the art of the catacombs, the liturgy, and theology combine to show."[33] Several years earlier, Ratzinger had stated that Jewish ideas of the afterlife "even in Augustine were still exercising more influence than Plato's schemata."[34]

30. Ratzinger, "Resurrection," 342.

31. Ibid.

32. Ratzinger, *Vorwort zur Neuausgabe* (*Eschatologie*, 12; *Eschatology*, xix). "Ich hatte darzustellen versucht, daß die Entfaltung einer anthropologischen Begrifflichkeit mit den Ausdrücken Leib und Seele, wie sie in der Tradition erfolgt ist und in Konzil von Vienne formuliert wurde (*DH* 902), durchaus sachgemäß die Vorgaben der biblischen Anthropologie weiterentwickelt." Decree 1 of the Council of Vienne (1311–1312) states, "In order that all may know the truth of the faith in its purity and all error may be excluded, we define that anyone who presumes henceforth to assert, defend or hold stubbornly that the rational or intellectual soul is not the form of the human body of itself and essentially, is to be considered a heretic." *Decrees of the Ecumenical Councils*, 1:361.

33. Ratzinger, *Eschatologie*, 110 (*Eschatology*, 130). "Wir werden sehen, daß die alte Kirche gerade im Bereich der eschatologischen Vorstellungen äußerst konservativ geblieben ist, keinen Wechsel von 'semitisch' zu 'hellenistisch' vollzogen hat, sondern vollständig im semitischen Bilderkanon verblieb, wie Katakombenkunst, Liturgie und Theologie einheitlich zeigen."

34. Ratzinger, "Beyond Death," 161. This was in 1972. Ratzinger does not give any

Apologetics and Proclamation in Ratzinger's Theology of Resurrection

One of the central arguments of *Eschatologie* is that Greek anthropology—which includes concepts like immortality, and the body-soul distinction—is not opposed to, but rather fully consonant with, the message of the Bible. Biblical resurrection faith, Ratzinger claims, follows from the very concept of God. It is thus based not on a particular anthropology, but on a *theology*.[35] "In this respect one can expect it to be capable of adopting various anthropologies and of expressing itself in them."[36]

This faith was already expressing itself through Hellenistic terms in the Old Testament, as evidenced by the wisdom literature and the production of the Septuagint.[37] Looking back over the Church's history, Ratzinger sees this dialogue with Hellenism as highly providential. As the controversies of the early Councils show, "pure Biblicism gets us nowhere."[38] The particular virtue of Greek philosophy, however, was that it was not content with images and myths but rather "it put the question about truth."[39] In this way, Greek thought remains an essential part of the Christian tradition whose anthropological insights cannot be dispensed with: "Even as philosophy progresses, Plato, Aristotle and Thomas do not become 'prehistory' but rather remain original examples of an enduring approach to the ground of things."[40]

From the above, we can state that with respect to his willingness to utilize the truths of Platonism, Ratzinger is fully within the Augustinian program. Augustine praised the Platonists for their discovery of truth. Ratzinger believes that this attention to the *truth* which Platonic thought brings has been an indispensable gift to the Church's tradition.

---

examples to back up this claim.

35. Ratzinger, *Eschatologie*, 102 (*Eschatology*, 119).

36. Ibid., 101 (*Eschatology*, 118–19). "Insofern kann man erwarten, daß er imstande ist, sich verschiedene Anthropologien anzueignen und sich in ihnen auszudrücken."

37. Ratzinger, *Truth and Tolerance*, 91. Originally appeared as *Glaube—Wahrheit—Toleranz* (2003).

38. Ratzinger, *Eschatologie*, 93 (*Eschatology*, 106). "So ist sehr schnell sichtbar geworden, daß der pure Biblizismus hier nicht weiterführt."

39. Ratzinger, *Truth and Tolerance*, 95.

40. Ratzinger, *Eschatologie*, 33 (*Eschatology*, 24). "Platon, Aristoteles, Thomas werden auch im Fortgehen des Philosophierens nicht zu 'Vorgeschichte', sondern bleiben originäre Gestalten eines beständigen Zugehens auf den Grund der Dinge."

Part One: Ratzinger the Augustinian

Anti-Platonism and Dematerialization

As we have already seen, Augustine's chief objection to the Platonism of his day was its devaluation of the body and of materiality. Ironically, the anti-Platonism of the twentieth century—at least as concerns resurrection—has developed into a view that Ratzinger believes dematerializes the resurrection and devalues the body. This anti-Platonic view is most clearly articulated in the theory known as "resurrection in death," whose most eloquent and well-known exponent has also been Ratzinger's chief antagonist on the issue of resurrection: Gisbert Greshake.[41] Without at this point discussing this view in great detail, it will be nonetheless helpful to note that the idea of "resurrection in death" is based on the assertion that a "disembodied soul" is impossible.[42] Since Christian faith concerns resurrection (and not the immortality of the soul), it thus follows that the resurrection of the whole person happens at the moment of death. In this way, even in death human nature remains undivided along the fault-lines of a supposedly dualistic Greek anthropology.

As we will later discuss in greater detail, Ratzinger attacks the idea of "resurrection in death" as dangerously spiritualistic since it ultimately denies any connection between the earthly physical body and the risen body, claiming resurrection for a man whose body still lies in the grave. Here we have an interesting—and surprising—parallel with Augustine. Just as Augustine attacked Porphyry and the Platonists for spiritualizing beatitude, so Ratzinger attacks recent anti-Platonists for doing the same thing. The difference is that modern anti-Platonists believe they are arguing for embodiment against Platonic spiritualizing, whereas Ratzinger contends that they are doing just the opposite. His is a mirror image of Augustine's argument, but it arrives at the same conclusion. It is interesting, however, that Ratzinger considers the traditional view, with its separation of body and soul at death, to be better capable of assuring a real, physical resurrection.

---

41. The view was first articulated by Greshake in his doctoral dissertation, later published in 1969 as *Auferstehung der Toten*. He has reiterated it in numerous publications since then.

42. Greshake, "Leib-Seele-Problematik," 163, 168. On 168, Greshake declares the three principal aims of his theology of resurrection. The third is "the elimination of a self-contradictory state of a disembodied soul" (die Eliminierung eines in sich widersprüchlichen Zustandes einer leiblosen Seele). Also, Greshake, *Tod und Auferstehung*, 118.

Augustinian Evaluation

In order to evaluate Ratzinger's Augustinianism in the area of his departure from "anti-Platonism," we naturally need to distinguish between his early and later writings. It has sometimes been suggested that 1968 marked a turning point in Ratzinger's theology.[43] Such a delineation appears to hold for his theology of resurrection. In his works up to and including that year, we note an interesting situation: Ratzinger is attempting to construct a "de-Platonized" eschatology which has no need of a body-soul distinction, yet it is not clear that this eschatology includes the resurrection of real human bodies. Ratzinger's early eschatology is thus decidedly non-Augustinian in a double respect: it not only tries to avoid the Platonic dual anthropology of body and soul which Augustine made use of in explaining the resurrection, but it replaces the resurrection of real bodies with "the immortality of the person."[44] One could say that Ratzinger rejects some of those elements of Platonic anthropology that Augustine accepts (e.g., the body-soul schema), and even appears close to accepting the immateriality of beatitude (a Platonic idea rejected by Augustine).[45]

It is clear from Ratzinger's discussion in *Einführung* that his understanding of Platonic anthropology in that work has little in common with Augustine's understanding of it. For Augustine, the existence of a body and a soul need not automatically lead to the notion that the body is the soul's prison. Augustine freely used these concepts, and distinguished them in order to unite them in the resurrection. Ratzinger's early treatment of Platonic thought and his dismissal of Greek anthropology is less

---

43. For a discussion of this, see Rowland, *Ratzinger's Faith*, 12–13.

44. Ratzinger, *Intro.*, 350.

45. Thus, Kasper ("Das Wesen des Christlichen") claims that Ratzinger's *Einführung* contains a "latent dualism" which manifests itself in several of Ratzinger's positions, including the primacy of Logos over mere matter, and of spirit over bios (185). Kasper asserts that "the latent idealism and secularism in Ratzinger's *Einführung* is ultimately grounded in his Platonizing starting point, through which—against the repeatedly declared better intentions of the author and in spite of his continual stress on the positivity of what is Christian (30ff, 62f., 153f., 199ff., 219f., 267f.)—the intrinsically Christian scandal of the '*Logos sarx egeneto*' (Jn 1:14) repeatedly falls under the dominion and dictates of that conception of reality held by Greek philosophy" (185). [Der latente Idealismus und Säkularismus in R.s Einführung ist letztlich in seinem platonisierenden Ausgangspunkt begründet, durch den das eigentliche christliche Skandalum des '*Logos sarx egeneto*' (Joh 1,14) gegen den immer wieder erklärten besseren Willen des Autors und trotz seiner ständigen Betonung der Positivität des Christlichen (30ff., 62f., 153f., 199ff., 219f., 267f.) doch immer wieder unter die Vorherrschaft und unter die Gesetzlichkeiten des Wirklichkeitsbegriffs der griechischen Philosophie gerät.]

nuanced and rigorous than Augustine's careful acceptance of certain elements of Platonic philosophy.

Ratzinger's later work on resurrection, however, deserves a different evaluation. By 1972, it appears that Ratzinger had begun to undergo the same process that Augustine experienced after his conversion: he began to examine Platonic anthropology and to distinguish those aspects of it that could lead to a deepening of the understanding of Christian faith. He found the body-soul distinction to be one of those elements worth retaining. He also began to lay greater emphasis on the resurrection's materiality. We can therefore say that Ratzinger's later work is Augustinian in that it deals critically with Plato rather than dismissing him offhand as a dualist with nothing useful to say to Christianity.

When we observe together Ratzinger's earlier and later works, we can observe a certain trajectory vis-à-vis Platonism which can be compared to Augustine's own path. Augustine began as an avowed Platonist and gradually recognized that certain elements of Platonism could not be harmonized with the truth of the Gospel. In this sense, his trajectory is *away from* a pure and thorough Platonism. Ratzinger, however, began with an anthropological position that was ostensibly anti-Platonic (concerning the body-soul distinction) yet simultaneously (in a sense) Platonic (concerning materiality in the resurrection).[46] As regards the body-soul distinction and a more general acceptance of the value of Greek thought, Ratzinger's trajectory is opposite to that of Augustine (i.e., he moved toward a greater acceptance of Platonism), and we might say that their trajectories converge upon a "golden mean" wherein Platonic thought is properly valued for its unique contributions to anthropology. Regarding materiality, however, Ratzinger (as we will soon see in more detail) is on the same trajectory as Augustine; both thinkers began with an understanding of resurrection that devalued matter and subsequently asserted a greater resurrectional materiality in their later works.

Polemics and Proclamation

Like Augustine, Ratzinger has a great passion for proclaiming the resurrection. We will now observe how this passion is manifested in Ratzinger's polemical controversies with his opponents, showing that Ratzinger's chief concern is to make the resurrection credible and proclaim-able to the world of today. The way that Ratzinger has gone about doing this,

---

46. Again, cf. Kasper, "Das Wesen des Christlichen," 185.

Apologetics and Proclamation in Ratzinger's Theology of Resurrection

however, has changed over time in proportion to the esteem he has granted to the "modern worldview." As he has become more suspicious of the universal claims of modernity and natural science, he has correspondingly become more traditional in his proclamation of the resurrection. In this regard, his apologetic approach has become more Augustinian: he does not modify his proclamation to fit the modern worldview, but rather seeks to find support in the modern world for his proclamation of resurrection.

Ratzinger and Polemics

Although Ratzinger is not the rhetorician that Augustine was, he harbors a similar penchant for polemics.[47] His argument over the resurrection with Greshake (as well as with Greshake's sometime coauthor, Gerhard Lohfink) began with *Eschatologie* in 1977, although even in "Jenseits des Todes" (1972) Ratzinger had attacked the idea of "resurrection in death" without naming it directly. But by 1977 Ratzinger confronted Greshake head-on, citing passages from his works.

Although generally avoiding *ad hominem* arguments, Ratzinger is remorseless in exposing his opponents' ideas to ridicule. He suggests that Lohfink's concept of the *aevum* "performs a hypostatization of history which lags behind Plato's doctrine of the Ideas mainly for its want of logical consistency,"[48] thus directly criticizing the anti-Platonist Lohfink as merely a logically incoherent Platonist, rather than an effective critic. Ratzinger's most dismissive polemic, however, is reserved for Greshake's

---

47. Consider the foreword to the 1977 edition of *Eschatologie*: "So the result of two decades' work presented here still stands against the prevailing opinion, but in an opposite way to that of my first attempts. This is not out of love of controversy, but because of the exigencies of the matter in question" (*Eschatologie*, 15; *Eschatology*, xxv). [So steht das hier vorliegende Ergebnis zweier Jahrzehnte nun in umgekehrter Weise quer zur herrschenden Meinung als meine ersten Versuche es damals taten—nicht aus Lust am Widerspruch, sondern vom Zwang der Sache her.] While it may be true that "the exigencies of the matter" led Ratzinger to change his mind over Platonism and Christian thought, anyone who has read large amounts of Ratzinger will find it hard to take seriously the idea that he does not love controversy. Ratzinger's well-known love of conflict is evident in virtually all his works, which are frequently directed against persons or ideas.

48. Ratzinger, *Eschatologie*, 96 (*Eschatology*, 112). "Im übrigen muß man hier wiederum in doppelter Hinsicht einen verschärften Platonismus anprangern: . . . zum anderen wird mit dem Aevum eine Hypostasierung der Geschichte vollführt, die hinter Platons Ideenlehre vor allem durch ihren Mangel an logischer Konsequenz zurückbleibt." Lohfink responds to Ratzinger's accusation in "Das Zeitproblem und die Vollendung der Welt." Lohfink claims that Ratzinger misunderstands his position.

Part One: Ratzinger the Augustinian

formulation of "resurrection in death." Ratzinger states of Greshake's position that "theology and preaching cannot long work with such a dodgy hermeneutical patchwork, full of logical flaws and cracks. As soon as possible we should bid farewell to this idea that strikes preaching dumb and thereby disqualifies itself as a way of understanding."[49] This statement understandably offended Greshake, who decried Ratzinger's "persistently polemical tone,"[50] retorting "I find such and similar statements outrageous, especially since on closer inspection the basis given for them melts away into nothing, and the particular difficulties which are necessarily present in every eschatological conception are either ignored or carefully papered over."[51]

Greshake generated his own share of polemical heat, with the result being a fiery debate that raged throughout the 1980s.[52] During this period, both accused the other of "Platonism."[53] Thus, Ratzinger can say that "resurrection in death" must be denounced as "an aggravated Platonism" because "in such models the body is definitively deleted from the hope of salvation."[54] He also states that the false antithesis which "resurrection in death" creates between physical time and eternity results in "a shoddy

---

49. Ratzinger, *Eschatologie*, 97 (*Eschatology*, 112). "Mit einem so vertrackten hermeneutischen Flickwerk, das voller logischer Risse und Sprünge ist, können Theologie und Verkündigung auf Dauer nicht arbeiten. Man sollte danach trachten, möglichst schnell ein Denken zu verabschieden, das die Verkündigung sprachlos macht und sich damit als Weise des Verstehens selbst aufhebt." Although not strictly *ad hominem*, this type of rhetoric relies on ridiculing the opposing view.

50. Greshake, "Leib-Seele-Problematik," 180 n. 58. "Der durchgehend polemische Ton Ratzingers wurde schon an manchen Beispielen deutlich gemacht."

51. Ibid. "Ich finde solche und ähnliche Äußerungen empörend, zumal die dafür gegebene Begründung, sieht man näher zu, ins Nichts zerrinnt und die eigenen Aporien, in die—vermutlich notwendig—jede eschatologische Konzeption gerät, entweder nicht reflektiert oder mühsam verkleistert werden."

52. Writing in 1990, Ratzinger notes that "in the entire dispute of the last decade I have been constantly surprised by the extreme polemical oversimplification of my ideas, in which I have often been unable to recognize my actual assertions." Ratzinger, *Nachwort zur 6. Auflage* (*Eschatologie*, 191). [Im ganzen Disput des letzen Jahrzehnts ist mir immer wieder neu die extreme polemische Vergröberung meiner Gedanken aufgefallen, in der ich meine wirklichen Aussagen häufig nicht wiedererkennen konnte.]

53. For a detailed portrayal of Ratzinger's and Greshake's mutual accusations of "Platonism," see Nachtwei, *Dialogische Unsterblichkeit*, 164–68. This covers the period up to 1985.

54. Ratzinger, *Eschatologie*, 96 (*Eschatology*, 112). "Im übrigens muß man hier wiederum in doppelter Hinsicht eine verschärften Platonismus anprangern. Zum einen wird in solchen Modellen der Leib definitiv aus der Hoffnung des Heils gestrichen."

'Platonism' such as Plato and the Platonists never knew."[55] But perhaps most effective (and aggressive) from a rhetorical point of view is his attempt to associate "resurrection in death" with Valentinian Gnosticism.

In *Eschatologie*, Ratzinger suggests that the Gnostic leader Valentinus (c. 100–c. 160) taught that a man must see himself as already "risen," basing this idea on the principle that it is "timelessness which reigns beyond the sphere of historical change."[56] The example of Valentinus shows us that "through the acceptance of a calculated catena of biblical texts and their combination with a time-eternity philosophy, the formula 'resurrection of the flesh' can be maintained on the one hand while simultaneously effecting the total spiritualization of Christian hope."[57] No one wants to be seen as Valentinus's heir, and the rhetorical force of aligning "resurrection in death" with Gnosticism is clear.

The Imprecision of the Word *Platonism*

Nachtwei notes that when Ratzinger condemns Greshake and Lohfink, he sometimes uses *Platonism* as a catchword to indicate features like Gnosticism and spiritualism.[58] For Greshake's part, he sees Ratzinger's insistence on duality (body *and* soul) as evidence of Platonic dualism. The result is a confusing semantic muddle in which *Platonism* means different things at different times, even when used by the same people. Nachtwei wisely points out that "one should certainly not leave this concept in a linguistic and conceptual grey area in which anybody can make it mean whatever he wants."[59] Nachtwei's study, however, was completed twenty-five years

---

55. Ratzinger, "Beyond Death," 161.

56. Ratzinger, *Eschatologie*, 140 (*Eschatology*, 174). "Diese überraschende Wendung wird bei Valentin nicht nur biblizistisch begründet, sondern auch systematisch untermauert: mit der Zeitlosigkeit, die jenseits des geschichtlichen Wandels herrsche."

57. Ibid., 141 (*Eschatology*, 174). "So kann durch die Aufnahme eines bestimmten Strangs biblischer Texte und ihre Kombination mit einer Zeit-Ewigkeits-Philosophie einerseits die Formel von der 'Auferstehung des Fleisches' festgehalten und gleichzeitig die völlige Spiritualisierung der christlichen Hoffnung durchgeführt werden."
Interestingly, in *Current Questions* 4.2 (a document of the International Theological Commission, of which Ratzinger was president) the same connection is made. It notes that there were second-century Gnostics who called the resurrection "the mere survival of a soul endowed with a kind of corporeity." This rejected position is similar to the phenomenological anthropology adopted by Greshake in *Resurrectio Mortuorum*.

58. Nachtwei, *Dialogische Unsterblichkeit*, 166.

59. Ibid., 168. "Man sollte wohl doch, damit dieser Begriff nicht in einer sprachlichen und begrifflichen Grauzone verbleibt, in die jede hineindeuten kann, was er will,

ago and it should be noted that Ratzinger has since refrained from using *Platonism* as a polemical catchword (*Schlagwort*). Whether this is due to a greater awareness on his part or simply to the end of the debate with Greshake is difficult to say.

Ratzinger's Polemical "Victory"

Although the dispute with Greshake was originally about the body-soul distinction and the intermediate state, Greshake has since modified his position. In *Resurrectio Mortuorum* (1986) he admits the use of the term *soul*, even calling it an *Urwort*.[60] Josef Wohlmuth has recently pointed out that Greshake and Lohfink rejected an intermediate state in order that resurrection might happen in death.[61] But Greshake has, since 1980, held the existence of a type of intermediate state, although he does not admit that a soul awaits the resurrection of its body but only that the already-risen individual awaits the fulfillment of all history.[62] For this reason, Greshake's claim to hold an "intermediate state" is somewhat misleading since his view has little in common with the ordinary understanding of the term.

Ratzinger's Concern for Proclamation

As we have seen, Augustine's polemic against the Platonists had as its goal not refutation but evangelization. In Ratzinger, we find a similar kerygmatic concern. However, whereas Augustine shows genuine concern for the salvation of his chief opponent (Porphyry), Ratzinger's care is devoted to preserving the kerygmatic *nature* and *language* of resurrection theology rather than on the evangelization of his opponent, Greshake. There are obvious differences here: Porphyry was long-dead before Augustine wrote against him, and it would be interesting (although impossible here) to compare Augustine's polemical style used against Porphyry with that used by him against living, contemporary heretics. Greshake, of course, is

---

jeweils vorher klar sagen, was man mit Platonismus meint."

60. Greshake, *Resurrectio Mortuorum*, 274. Calls the soul an *Urwort* suggests that it is part of the verbal patrimony of Christianity.

61. Wohlmuth, *Mysterium der Verwandlung*, 165.

62. Greshake, "Leib-Seele-Problematik," 178; *Tod und Auferstehung*, 119. Interestingly, Greshake claims that he has never changed his position in this regard.

Apologetics and Proclamation in Ratzinger's Theology of Resurrection

a Catholic whose views on resurrection (while considered dangerous by Ratzinger) are not on the same level as Porphyry's.[63]

While both Ratzinger and Greshake affirm partial truths in their opponents' theologies,[64] both are concerned with making the proclamation of the Gospel believable today. In 1987, looking back on the debate, Ratzinger states that it is "ultimately not a philosophical dispute, but a dispute on the one hand about faith's ability to be proclaimed and on the other about the resurrection."[65] For Ratzinger, proclamation always has primacy. "The kerygma is both point of origin and endpoint for theology. If the kerygma disintegrates in the course of theological reflection then it is not the kerygma that collapses, but theology."[66] Ratzinger's chief objection to "resurrection in death" is that it wrests the language of faith from its traditional locus, giving to words meanings that do not belong to the common sense of the faithful.

Ratzinger illustrates this concern with an example:

> Proclamation has lost its language. For, in the end one can certainly teach the believer that there is no immortality of the soul, but no language of proclamation will make it clear to him that

---

63. Concerning the issue of whether Ratzinger thought Greshake's view was heretical or not, it is interesting to note that in the original published version of "Zwischen Tod und Auferstehung," *Internationale katholische Zeitschrift Communio* 9 (1980) 209–26, note 14 (concerning the danger of applying "resurrection in death" to Jesus) concludes by stating, "Thus the theological work of, for example, Greshake and Lohfink should in no way be considered to be close to heresy. Even if I cannot follow the logic of their thought, I have never contested the seriousness and compellingness of their ideas." [Damit soll in keiner Weise die theologische Arbeit etwa von Greshake und Lohfink in die Nähe der Häresie gerückt werden. Auch wenn ich der Logik ihres Denkens nicht folgen kann, habe ich den Ernst und das Vorwärtstreibende ihrer Gedanken nie bestritten.] Yet in all following publications of the article (as an appendix in the English and German editions of *Eschatologie*) this sentence no longer appears.

64. Ratzinger, "Zwischen Tod und Auferstehung" (*Eschatologie*, 219; *Eschatology*, 258).

65. Ratzinger, *Nachwort zur 6. Auflage* (*Eschatologie*, 198; *Eschatology*, 269). "Für mich als Theologen ist dies letztlich kein philosophischer Streit, sondern ein Streit zum einen um die Verkündigungsfähigkeit des Glaubens, zum anderen ein Disput um die Auferstehung." Ratzinger goes on to say that "the eschatological question is at the same time actually the question about the essence of Christianity." (*Eschatologie*, 200; *Eschatology*, 272). "Für mich ist . . . die eschatologische Frage zugleich die Frage nach dem Wesen des Christentums überhaupt."

66. Ratzinger, *Eschatologie*, 198 (*Eschatology*, 268). "Es ist vielmehr umgekehrt so, daß das Kerygma Ausgangspunkt und Zielpunkt der Theologie ist. Wenn sich auf dem Weg ihrer Reflexion das Kerygma selbst auflöst, dann ist nicht das Kerygma gescheitert, sondern die Theologie."

his dead friend has just risen from the dead. This is because such a use of "resurrection" is a classic case of *lingua docta*, the language of historicist scholars, but is no expression of the common, and commonly understood, faith. Apart from the fact that the hermeneutical contortions which are the necessary background to the formula's comprehensibility could never become part of proclamation, the theologian *qua* scholar has thus retreated into a theological linguistic- and intellectual-ghetto in which no one communicates with him either linguistically or intellectually.[67]

Since the language of faith is the common inheritance of all believers, it cannot be experimented upon by theologians. In Ratzinger's view, theology must be subservient to the common language of faith rather than the other way around.

This concern for proclamation was present in Ratzinger's theology even before *Eschatologie*. In *Einführung* (1968), he attacks attempts to utterly reconceive the resurrection in moral or political terms as being "dishonest" to the Christian message and insincere in dealing with the questions of non-Christians.[68] And more recently (in 2004), he forcefully defends the physical resurrection of Jesus' body because "what is really in question is the core of the image of God and the realism of God's historical action . . . and so it is a question of whether we can entrust ourselves to the

---

67. Ratzinger, "Zwischen Tod und Auferstehung" (*Eschatologie*, 216; *Eschatology*, 254). "Dafür hat die Verkündigung ihre Sprache verloren. Denn man kann dem Gläubigen zwar schließlich beibringen, daß es eine Unsterblichkeit der Seele nicht gebe. Daß aber sein toter Freund soeben auferstandenen sei, das kann ihm keine Sprache der Verkündigung einsichtig machen, weil diese Verwendung von 'Auferstehung' typische *lingua docta*, historistische Gelehrtensprache, aber kein möglicher Ausdruck gemeinsamen und gemeinsam verstandenen Glaubens ist. Abgesehen davon, daß die hermeneutischen Windungen, die als Hintergrund zur Verständlichkeit der Formel nötig sind, niemals in die Verkündigung eingehen können, begibt sich der Theologe damit auch als Gelehrter in ein theologisches Sprach- und Denkgetto, in dem niemand mit ihm sprachlich und denkerisch kommuniziert." Written in 1980, this was before Greshake changed his position to allow for the use of the word *soul*. The exact argument cited here is used against resurrection in death by the International Theological Commission in *Current Questions* 2.1.

68. Ratzinger, *Intro.*, 56. "When some theologian explains that 'the resurrection of the dead' simply means that one must cheerfully set about the work of the future afresh every day, offense is certainly avoided. But are we then really still being honest? Is there not serious dishonesty in seeking to maintain Christianity as a viable proposition by such artifices of interpretation? Have we not much rather the duty, when we feel forced to take refuge in solutions of this sort, to admit that we have reached the end of the road? . . . An 'interpreted' Christianity of this kind that has lost all contact with reality implies a lack of sincerity in dealing with the questions of the non-Christian."

word of faith, whether we trust God and whether we can live and die on the ground of faith."[69]

In *Spe Salvi* (2007), Benedict XVI notes the necessity of proper proclamation of our hope in the resurrection. He suggests that "perhaps many people reject the faith today simply because they do not find the prospect of eternal life attractive . . . To continue living for ever —endlessly—appears more like a curse than a gift. Death, admittedly, one would wish to postpone for as long as possible. But to live always, without end—this, all things considered, can only be monotonous and ultimately unbearable."[70] This is reminiscent of Augustine's *Sermon* 242A in which he reminds his congregation that those things which make earthly life painful will not be present in heaven. In both cases, theology is to be placed at the service of the kerygma in order to instill faith in, and hope for the resurrection.

It is with this in mind that Ratzinger concludes the afterword to the 6th German edition of *Eschatologie*. Although he has completed his eschatology, "it is clear that the dispute over it must go on, because here it is a question about the heart of Christianity—of whether it is still good news today, whether it still 'has power to save our souls' (Jas 1:21)."[71]

Proclamation and the "Modern Worldview"

The Adaptation of Proclamation to the Modern Worldview

Augustine took pains to ensure that his proclamation of the resurrection would resonate in the dominant worldview of his time, which was permeated by Platonism. Yet he was not content simply to adapt his message to fit within the constrained ideological framework of Platonists like

---

69. Ratzinger, "Jungfrauengeburt und leeres Grab" (2004). The nineteen-hundred-word text lacks paragraph and page numbers, although it was later published as *Skandalöser Realismus*. All English translations of this document are my own, as it has never appeared in English. "So wird sichtbar . . . dass vielmehr der Kern des Gottesbildes und der Realismus von Gottes geschichtlichem Handeln in Frage steht . . . Und so geht es darum, ob wir uns dem Wort des Glaubens anvertrauen können, ob wir Gott trauen und ob wir auf dem Grund des Glaubens leben und sterben können."

70. Benedict XVI, Encyclical *Spe Salvi* (2007) §10.

71. Ratzinger, *Nachwort zur 6. Auflage* (*Eschatologie*, 203). "Aber es ist klar, daß der Disput darüber weitergehen muß, denn hier handelt es sich um die Mitte des Christentums—darum, ob es auch heute Evangelium ist, ob es auch heute 'die Macht hat, unser Seelen zu retten' (Jak 1,21)."

Part One: Ratzinger the Augustinian

Porphyry. When the worldview of Augustine's contemporaries was wrong, it was the worldview that needed to be changed rather than the Gospel. I will attempt to show that, whether consciously or not, this method was not always employed by Ratzinger. In fact, the relationship between his theology of resurrection and the so-called modern worldview has undergone a considerable development.

By the mid-twentieth century, there was a movement in Catholic theology that sought to bring this theology fully into conversation with modern science. The spirit of this movement is evidenced by comments like this one from Pierre Teilhard de Chardin: "There is a lack of proportion between the insignificant mankind still presented by our catechisms, and the massive mankind which science tells us about."[72] This trend also reveals itself in the tendency for theologians to attempt to situate whatever they are doing within an "evolutionary" framework.[73]

In his early encyclopedia entry "Auferstehung des Fleisches" (1957), Ratzinger notes the problem that the resurrection poses to the modern worldview: "The chief difficulty that modern man has with the resurrection is the world's view of nature: The resurrection appears to presume the 'mythological worldview,' while the 'scientific worldview' of today has not only dismantled heaven and hell as geographical places, but has also discovered a unified structure of matter which appears to exclude a transfigured state of the world and an unchanging embodiment."[74] Ratzinger then goes on to state that, as far as possible, we must rethink the worldview of antiquity, while retaining the *"Faktum"* intended by those seemingly mythological images.[75] But what might it mean to rethink this worldview? A decade later, Ratzinger begins to explore this in *Einführung*.

In that work, Ratzinger still holds the incommensurability of Greek and biblical thought (at least with respect to the immortality of the soul and the resurrection of the body). After acknowledging problems with the

---

72. Teilhard de Chardin, "Christ the Evolver," 142. Article originally published in 1942.

73. A classic example would be Rahner's "Christianity within an Evolutionary View of the World."

74. Ratzinger, "Auferstehung des Fleisches" (1957), 1050. "Die Hauptschwierigkeit des modernen Menschen gg. die A. ist weltbildl. Natur: Die A. scheint das 'myth. Weltbild' vorauszusetzen, während das 'wiss. Weltbild' v. heute nicht nur Himmel u. Hölle als geograph. Orte abgebaut, sondern auch eine einheitl. Struktur der Materie entdeckt hat, die einen verklärten Weltzustand u. eine werdelose Leiblichkeit auszuschließen scheint."

75. Ibid.

Apologetics and Proclamation in Ratzinger's Theology of Resurrection

Greek concept of immortality, Ratzinger goes on to show how difficult is the traditional concept of resurrection:

> The unity of man, fine, but who can imagine, on the basis of our present-day image of the world [*heutigen Weltbild*], a resurrection of the body [*Leibes*]? This resurrection would also imply— or so it seems, at any rate—a new heaven and a new earth; it would require immortal bodies [*Körper*] needing no sustenance and a completely different condition of matter. But is this not all completely absurd, quite contrary to our understanding of matter and its modes of behavior, and therefore hopelessly mythological?[76]

At this point, a twenty-first-century reader of Ratzinger would expect him to respond with a *sed contra*, vigorously asserting the reality of the resurrected body. But instead, he attempts to solve the dilemma by explaining that we have got our understanding all wrong; we have attempted to fuse two incompatible ideas (i.e., immortality and resurrection) together.[77] He then states that "the real heart of the faith in resurrection does not consist at all in the idea of the restoration of bodies [*Körper*], to which we have reduced it in our thinking; such is the case even though this is the pictorial image used throughout the Bible."[78] He subsequently asserts that resurrection simply concerns the "person" (and not only the physical body).[79]

In this case, Ratzinger's theology of resurrection corresponds well with modern ideas about science: since modern man, imbued by the scientific worldview, apparently cannot believe in such "immortal bodies," Ratzinger assures us that the resurrection is not "the restoration of bodies." His kerygmatic intent is to eliminate obstacles to faith which might be

---

76. Ratzinger, *Intro.*, 347–48 (*Einführung*, 329–30). Ratzinger is not univocally claiming that the resurrection of the body is "hopelessly mythological," but he *is* claiming that any view of resurrection that includes "immortal bodies" and the transformation of matter cannot be believed by modern people and is in fact based on a false assumption.

77. Ibid., 349 (*Einführung*, 331). "We must grasp the fact that originally it was not a question of two complementary ideas; on the contrary, we are confronted with two different outlooks, which cannot simply be added together: the image of man, of God, and of the future is in each case quite different, and thus at bottom each of the two views can only be understood as an attempt at a total answer to the question of human fate."

78. Ibid., 349 (*Einführung*, 331).

79. Ibid., 349 (*Einführung*, 331). "The awakening of the dead (not of bodies!) of which Scripture speaks is thus concerned with the salvation of the *one*, undivided man, not just with the fate of one (perhaps secondary) half of man." Ratzinger then states that the Bible teaches that resurrection means "an immortality of the 'person,' of the *one* creation, man" (*Intro.*, 350; *Einführung*, 332).

posed by science. One might ask, however (especially in light of his later theology) whether such a decision necessarily does justice to that faith, or whether this might be a case of Bultmannian demythologization. Walter Kasper, in his review of *Einführung*, argued that it was the latter: "What Ratzinger writes in the chapters on the descent to hell, the resurrection, the ascension, and Christ's return, as well as on the resurrection of the flesh, is not outdone in the least by any theology of demythologization, and one has to ask why Ratzinger so polemically dismisses the demythologization program on so many occasions (29f., 242, 257; cf. however, in a somewhat different sense 104, 177)."[80]

There can be no question that Ratzinger—even in *Einführung*—is not intentionally indulging in demythologization à la Bultmann. His descriptions of the resurrection, however, suggest that he is engaging in a reinterpretation of the classical resurrection schema. Inasmuch as this is done in order to adapt the resurrection to a scientific worldview, it must be seen as contrasting sharply with Augustine's approach, which in the dominant worldview seeks confirmations of the resurrection rather than tailoring the resurrection to the dominant worldview.

Proclamation in Spite of the Modern Worldview

By 1977, however, one can detect in Ratzinger's eschatological writings a distinct posture of defiance toward the modern worldview.[81] In the Introduction to *Eschatologie* he notes that the current trend in eschatology has been to focus on the "creation of a new world" while the traditional Last Things have been pushed to the backburner. He then counters that "we must keep the question of the present before us, but it cannot become the criterion of our statements. We must rather attempt to integrate the

---

80. Kasper, "Das Wesen des Christlichen," 183. "Was R. in den Kapiteln über die Höllenfahrt, Auferstehung, Himmelfahrt, Wiederkunft Christi, sowie über die Auferstehung des Fleisches schreibt, steht keiner Entmythologisierungstheologie auch nur im Geringsten nach, und man fragt sich, weshalb er das Programm der Entmythologisierung mehrfach so einseitig polemisch abtut (29f, 242, 257; vgl. jedoch in einem etwas anderen Sinn 104, 177)." Kasper's page references are to the 1st edition of *Einführung*, which differ from those of the current (9th) edition.

81. In *Die Tochter Zion*, Ratzinger directly attacks the modern worldview and its rejection of the biological nature of Jesus' virginal conception (also admitting his own error in *Einführung* when he discussed that article of faith). In this work, however, he does not connect his critique of the modern worldview with the question of resurrection. That connection was not made explicit until 2004 (in "Jungfrauengeburt und leeres Grab," which repeats many of the arguments made in *Die Tochter Zion* but applies them to Jesus' bodily resurrection as well).

opposing criteria on the basis of the Christian center, to find the proper balance and to understand the actual promise of the faith more deeply."[82] Even if an emphasis on the traditional Last Things may seem "outdated [unaktuell]," these things "involve what is specific to the Christian view of what is to come and its presence here and now."[83] For this reason, they must not be omitted in accommodation to the *Zeitgeist*.

In a 1992 lecture given to the Christian Academy in Prague, Ratzinger asserts that there is a lack of concern for "eternal life" and a general disbelief in miracles because of the prevalence of the notion that the world is a closed, scientific system.[84] This worldview, he argues, means that "even the birth of Jesus from the Virgin and the genuine Resurrection of Jesus, which snatched his body from decay, are at best relegated to the status of insignificant and marginal questions: it seems to make us feel uncomfortable that God should have intervened in biological or physical processes."[85]

In 2004, Ratzinger again points out the danger of the modern worldview in regard to the resurrection. Once again defending the biological nature of Jesus' resurrection, Ratzinger attacks the critics thus:

> In opposition to all these statements, but particularly against the articles of faith on the virginal conception of Jesus and the saving of his body from decay, that is, the transformation of his body into the new mode of existence of the resurrection, an interjection arises today: But this is all excluded by the "modern worldview"! In view of such a supposed certainty concerning the implications of the modern worldview, it must first of all be asked: What, in fact, is the "modern worldview"? Who defines

---

82. Ratzinger, *Eschatologie*, 27 (*Eschatology*, 15). "Die Anfrage der Gegenwart muß uns vor Augen stehen. Aber sie kann nicht zum Maßstab unserer Aussagen werden. Wir müssen vielmehr versuchen, von der Mitte des Christlichen her die gegenläufigen Faktoren zu integrieren, die Gewichte richtig zu setzen und die tatsächliche Zusage des Glaubens tiefer verstehen zu lernen."

83. Ibid., 20 (*Eschatology*, 4). "Obwohl in der Tat die Frage nach Zukunft und Gegenwart und mit ihr der ganze Themenkreis Hoffnung und Praxis der Hoffnung in den Bereich der eschatologischen Thematik gehört, kann ein Grundriß der katholischen Dogmatik sich einer solchen Verschiebung der Perspektiven nicht anschließen, und zwar nicht bloß aus dem äußeren Grund, weil man von einem Lehrbuch Information über die klassischen Inhalte eines Faches verlangen muß, sondern auch aus dem inneren Grund, weil diese Fragen selbst das Spezifische der christlichen Sicht auf das Kommende und auf seine Gegenwart einschließen und dem Menschen so nötig sind, wie ihm das Christliche nötig ist, auch wenn es ihm aus mancherlei Gründen in seiner Glaubensgestalt als unaktuell erscheinen mag."

84. Ratzinger, "My Joy," 131. Published in German as "Mein Glück."

85. Ibid.

Part One: Ratzinger the Augustinian

it? How far does its certainty go? Competent scholars, the Jewish philosopher Hans Jonas for example, have now pointed out the limits of the myth of the modern worldview and have dispelled the unquestioning false certainty derived from it.[86]

Throughout the article "Jungfrauengeburt und leeres Grab," Ratzinger's argument is that God acts in ways that are scandalous to our modern sensibilities. He acts on matter; he intervenes in the bodily, biological world.[87] To deny this would be to deny God's power, so that "faith would become Gnosis: it would no longer be able to relate to history but would be reduced to the sphere of the spiritual. It would be denatured."[88] The problem of God acting in history in audacious ways, then, becomes more than a debate about matter or miracles: "It is a question . . . of whether God is God" and "whether we can live and die on the ground of faith."[89] For a God who cannot act on matter "is no God at all but only a product of psychology and wishful thinking."[90] Here, Ratzinger's *apologia* for the reality of Jesus' resurrection closely parallels Paul's argument in 1 Cor 15:12–19.[91] Rather

---

86. Ratzinger, "Jungfrauengeburt und leeres Grab." "Gegenüber allen diesen Aussagen, besonders aber gegenüber den Glaubensartikeln von der jungfräulichen Empfängnis Jesu und seiner Rettung vor der Verwesung, das heißt der Umwandlung seines Leibes in die neue Weise des Seins der Auferstehung hinein, erhebt sich heute der Einwurf: Aber dies alles ist doch durch das „moderne Weltbild" ausgeschlossen. Angesichts einer solchen Scheingewissheit über die Implikationen des modernen Weltbildes ist zuallererst zu fragen: Was ist denn das eigentlich, das „moderne Weltbild"? Wer definiert es? Wie weit reichen seine Gewissheiten? Kompetente Gelehrte, zum Beispiel der jüdische Philosoph Hans Jonas, haben den Mythos des modernen Weltbildes inzwischen in seine Grenzen verwiesen und die daraus abgeleiteten unbefragten Scheingewissheiten aufgelöst."

87. Ibid. "God's Spirit can bring about something new and can intervene in the real world, in the world of the body." "Gottes Geist kann Neues schaffen, in der leibhaftigen Welt, in die Welt des Leibes eingreifen." This article will be discussed in greater detail when we consider the materiality of the resurrection.

88. Ibid. "Aus Glaube würde „Gnosis": Der Glaube könnte sich nicht mehr auf die Geschichte beziehen, sondern wäre auf die Sphäre des Spirituellen beschränkt. Er wäre denaturiert."

89. Ibid. "Es geht darum, ob Gott Gott ist . . . und ob wir auf dem Grund des Glaubens leben und sterben können."

90. Ibid. "Ein solcher Gott ist jedoch kein Gott, sondern nur noch ein Element der Psychologie und der Vertröstung."

91. "Now if Christ is preached as raised from the dead, how can some of you say that there is no resurrection of the dead? But if there is no resurrection of the dead, then Christ has not been raised; if Christ has not been raised, then our preaching is in vain and your faith is in vain. We are even found to be misrepresenting God, because we testified of God that he raised Christ, whom he did not raise if it is true that the dead

than *proving* the resurrection, he shows that when miracles like the resurrection are excluded *a priori*, Christian faith becomes futile and pitiful.

The Use of Natural Science in Apologetics

We have already seen how Augustine provided examples from the natural world—what today we might call natural science—to illustrate the plausibility of an incorruptible, risen body. This strategy is also carried out by Ratzinger. In "Zwischen Tod und Auferstehung" (1980), he cites the work of John Eccles and Karl Popper on brain and consciousness, which suggests a certain "dualism" in man.[92] Both of these writers would normally be considered positivists and are by no means religious apologists. Ratzinger, however, includes them in his discussion of the body-soul question in order to show that the Church's faith is rational and supported by objective science.

Later, in the afterword to the English edition (1987), Ratzinger cites further work by Eccles,[93] which he claims shows that "there are no compelling grounds for accepting a reductive materialism. Rather are there more pressing reasons for accepting the immateriality and survival of mind, and especially of the personal soul after the death of the body."[94]

Ratzinger's concern here is to show that the idea expressed by the word *soul* is more than a counterfeit Greek term; it actually corresponds to reality. His point is that the Church's language (i.e., *soul*) is a better fit with the scientific data than is an anthropological vocabulary which jettisons that language. Writing in 1980 (before Greshake's acceptance of the word *soul*), Ratzinger states, "With the theory of 'resurrection in death,' however, the theologian demolishes the bridges of intellectual common-ground connecting him to philosophy and to the history of Christian thought."[95]

---

are not raised."

92. Ratzinger, "Zwischen Tod und Auferstehung" (*Eschatologie*, 216–17; *Eschatology*, 255). Here, Ratzinger cites two works: Eccles, "Hirn und Bewusstsein," and Popper and Eccles, *The Self and Its Brain*. For discussions of Ratzinger's use of Popper and Eccles, see Nachtwei, *Dialogische Unsterblichkeit*, 147–53, who also discusses Ratzinger's use of Josef Seifert. Also, Sonnemans, *Seele*, 493–97.

93. Eccles and Robinson, *The Wonder of Being Human*.

94. Ratzinger, "Afterword to the English Edition," *Eschatology*, 264. Ratzinger discusses Eccles and Robinson again in the *Nachwort zur 6. Auflage* (*Eschatologie*, 195), but the passage cited here is unique to the English afterword.

95. Ratzinger, "Zwischen Tod und Auferstehung" (*Eschatologie*, 217; *Eschatology*, 256). "Mit der Theorie von der Auferstehung im Tode bricht er [der Theologe] hingegen die Brücken der Gemeinsamkeit des Denkens zur Philosophie hin ab, so wie er sie

Body-soul anthropology, then, provides a better point of common ground with science than a reductive materialism which denies the existence of a soul.

Augustinian Evaluation

As we have seen, Ratzinger has undergone a significant change in his eschatology. When Augustine explained the resurrection in *De Civitate Dei*, he used Platonic philosophy familiar to his contemporaries to support the Christian view, and drew support from examples of natural phenomena accepted by all. Yet in Ratzinger's *Einführung* (1968), we see the reverse: the modification of the classical Christian view in favor of one more palatable to a contemporary, scientific view. In this way, Ratzinger's apologetic approach to the resurrection of the body in *Einführung* is different from the way Augustine approached the dominant worldview of his time.

Moving forward, however, we observe a steady shift whereby the relative weight given to the authority of natural science diminishes,[96] and Ratzinger connects himself more closely to the traditional ecclesial formulations. In this respect, a very Augustinian flavor is present in *Eschatologie*, although at times one still detects there a certain esteem for the modern worldview. In his later writings on resurrection, however, we see a sharpening of his critique of the modern worldview to the point that its applicability to the resurrection is explicitly dismissed. Both Ratzinger and Augustine have a deep desire to proclaim the Gospel in a way that is credible to their contemporaries. Ratzinger, however, came to see that many aspects of the modern worldview were in fact incompatible with Christian faith (e.g., the materialistic denial of the miraculous) and had to be rejected rather than incorporated into theology.

Yet he rejects dogmatic materialism and not science as such. He can therefore, like Augustine, cite examples from modern science to support the existence of a soul that survives the death of the body. In his later works, this transformed attitude toward the modern worldview becomes most clear since Ratzinger now uses science as a support for the doctrine of the resurrection rather than suggesting that the traditional doctrine of

---

zur Geschichte des christlichen Denkens abbricht." Interestingly, this seems to be one of the reasons Greshake eventually accepted the term *soul*.

96. For example, Ratzinger became more aware of and critical of both Neo-Darwinism and Teilhard de Chardin. For the former, see Benedict XVI, *Schöpfung und Evolution*, 151. For the latter, see Ratzinger, "End of Time," 14–15.

the resurrection is utterly mythological from the point of view of science, as he does in *Einführung*. This unashamed approach to science exhibited by Ratzinger beginning around 1977–80 closely parallels Augustine's use of examples from the natural world to show the reasonableness of the resurrection of the body. Both men are able to find in nature support for faith.

Looking at Ratzinger's Augustinianism, then, we see a clear development. During his life as a theologian, Ratzinger has moved farther away from a theology that would be acceptable to many moderns, and closer to what could be called a more realist or physicalist view having more in common with Augustine's theology. This shift did not occur because Ratzinger came to view proclamation as less important, but was in part due to his recognition of the strictures that the modern worldview places upon theology. Ratzinger does not want theology to be dictated by the prejudices and presuppositions of modern natural science.

Conclusion

We have now considered Ratzinger's theology of resurrection from the perspective of Augustine's insistence on apologetics, marked as it is by proclamation. We have found that ultimately, both thinkers made critical use of Platonic anthropology, although Augustine began his Christian life as a Platonist for whom a certain purgative process was necessary in order to expunge those elements of Platonism incompatible with Christian faith, whereas Ratzinger began in conscious opposition to Platonism and gradually recognized the valuable contribution that Platonic and Greek thought could make to a Christian eschatology.

Both Ratzinger and Augustine consider that the kerygma is of primary importance. Their theologies of resurrection are therefore both concerned with making resurrection faith credible to their contemporaries. But whereas Augustine found support for the resurrection in the dominant Platonic worldview of his time, Ratzinger only approached such a posture by stages. In attempting to forge a modern doctrine of the resurrection that can be believed today (or, in the 1960s), Ratzinger's early works grant to the modern worldview a certain normativity, whereas in his more recent writings, the authority of the modern worldview is explicitly rejected and the Church's faith in the resurrection is the standard by which modern thoughts and ideas must be judged. In this way, Ratzinger's apologetic approach to the resurrection has become more Augustinian.

Part Two

Crucial Distinctions in Ratzinger's
Theology of Resurrection

3

The Body-Soul Distinction

We will begin our exploration of the body-soul distinction in Ratzinger's theology by examining the body-soul duality, noting how his theology has gradually developed to embrace this distinction which is so fundamental to Augustinian anthropology. We will then observe Ratzinger's assessment of Thomas Aquinas' teaching that the soul is the body's form. The problems that Ratzinger raises against this teaching suggest that his preference is for a more Augustinian, dual schema (as opposed to a highly unitary, strictly hylomorphic one). We will then examine and evaluate an idea Ratzinger offers as an apparent solution to these problems: the concept (influenced by Rahner and Teilhard de Chardin) that the soul becomes all-cosmic in death. I will suggest, however, that this idea is not Augustinian and creates more problems than it solves. Finally, we will consider Ratzinger's *dialogical* understanding of the soul, noting its Augustinian roots.

Part Two: Crucial Distinctions in Ratzinger's Theology of Resurrection

The Development of the Body-Soul Distinction in Ratzinger's Theology

Ratzinger's Early Theology

As Ratzinger became less and less wary of the supposedly dangerous dualism of Greek thought, he became more and more open to using the body-soul distinction in eschatology. Although it does not appear that Ratzinger from the very beginning of his education subscribed to the theory that Platonism had corrupted Christian theology—in his doctoral dissertation, for example, he had seen in Augustine's early use of Plato that there can be such a thing as "a Christian dualism"[1]—it is clear that by the time of *Einführung* (1968), he was highly cautious about what he saw as Hellenistic dualism and therefore made virtually no distinction between soul and body. He did, however, concede a certain theological validity for the term *soul*, since "'having a spiritual soul' means precisely being willed, known, and loved by God in a special way; it means being a creature called by God to an eternal dialogue and therefore capable for its own part of knowing God and of replying to him. What we call in substantialist language 'having a soul' we will describe in a more historical, actual language as 'being God's partner in a dialogue.'"[2]

This definition of the soul in terms of *relationship* to God will be discussed later when we consider Ratzinger's concept of dialogical immortality. In this case, however, "soul" is not presented as a counterpart to the body but as a way of expressing the whole person's relatedness to God. Thus, it is consonant with Ratzinger's other comments in *Einführung*

---

1. Ratzinger, *Volk und Haus Gottes*, 16. "Thus the discovery of Neoplatonism is actually understood as Augustine's great breakthrough experience. He himself apparently believed he had discovered the uniquely Christian dimension in the *mundus intelligibilis*. Let us not simply say that this was a mistake! There is a Christian dualism, and the man who without knowing it had always read Plato with Christian eyes is in this moment not so far from that Christian dualism as it may at first appear to us." My translation. [Von hierher versteht sich die Entdeckung des Neuplatonismus tatsächlich als das große Durchbruchserlebnis Augustins. Er selbst glaubte offenbar, mit dem *mundus intelligibilis* die eigentliche christliche Dimension entdeckt zu haben. Sagen wir nicht so einfachhin, dies sei ein Irrtum gewesen! Es gibt einen christlichen Dualismus, und der Mann, der auch Platon immer schon, ohne es zu wissen, mit christlichen Augen las, ist in diesem Augenblick nicht so weit davon, wie es uns aufs erste vielleicht scheinen möchte.]

2. Ratzinger, *Intro.*, 355 (*Einführung*, 337).

The Body-Soul Distinction

which deny the notion of a separation of body and soul in death.[3] We have already discussed these comments in chapter 2. Thus, we can say that while *Einführung* does employ the terms *body* and *soul*, it does not see them as separate realities but rather as different ways of viewing the human being.

A Turning Point: Soul Distinguished from Body

Only four years later, however (in "Jenseits des Todes," 1972), Ratzinger's fear that the body-soul distinction was dualistic showed signs of abating. He considered that even if the term *soul* has a dualistic origin, this "says something about the danger but nothing about the impossibility of using it."[4] He believed the dualistic dangers inherent in the term had in fact been largely purified by medieval theology.[5] Ratzinger continued, "It seems to me that it is high time theology set about rehabilitating the taboo concepts of 'immortality' and the 'soul.'"[6] Despite the different tack in "Jenseits des Todes," however, what we see is only a change of course and not yet a full defense of the body-soul distinction. This would not come until *Eschatologie* (1977).

In that work and in those immediately following it, Ratzinger finds himself in something of a new position: defending the traditional Christian (and Greek) distinction of body and soul against the new theology of "resurrection in death." Some of Ratzinger's uneasiness with traditional formulations remains in *Eschatologie*, but a clear movement is evident toward an anthropology that posits a clear *distinction* between body and soul.

---

3. Ibid., 349–50 (*Einführung*, 331–32). "The Greek conception is based on the idea that man is composed of two mutually foreign substances, one of which (the body) perishes, while the other (the soul) is in itself imperishable and goes on existing in its own right independent of any other beings. Indeed, it is only in the separation from the body, which is essentially foreign to it, so they thought, that the soul came fully into its own. The biblical train of thought, on the other hand, presupposes the undivided unity of man; for example, Scripture contains no word denoting only the body (separated and distinguished from the soul), while conversely in the vast majority of cases the word *soul*, too, means the whole corporeally existing man." Such ideas are part of what Ratzinger later described as his earlier attempts to construct a "de-Platonized eschatology" (cf. *Eschatologie*, 15; *Eschatology*, xxv).

4. Ratzinger, "Beyond Death," 162.

5. Ibid.

6. Ibid., 163.

Part Two: Crucial Distinctions in Ratzinger's Theology of Resurrection

Part of the shift seems due to Ratzinger's new view that the idea of the immortality of the soul that had developed in the early Church owed more to the Jewish tradition than to Greek philosophy: "the ancient Church remained extremely conservative in the realm of eschatological imagery; there was no changeover from 'Semitic' to 'Hellenistic' but rather the Church remained completely in the Semitic canon of images as the art of the catacombs, the liturgy, and theology combine to show."[7] Ratzinger also considers the classical Christian idea of the soul to be unique to Christianity and not a simple borrowing from Greek thought: "*The concept of the soul as employed in liturgy and theology up to the Second Vatican Council has as little to do with antiquity as the idea of resurrection. It is a strictly Christian concept.*"[8] He thereby rejects the idea that the notion of "soul" current in theology was a foreign concept introduced via Hellenism.

In *Eschatologie*, Ratzinger not only defends the Christian concept of soul from the derogatory accusation of "Hellenism," but he also argues that the soul-concept is necessary simply to understand the human being. Since the physical constitution of the body is changing constantly throughout one's life, "in this respect a duality which distinguishes the constant from the variable is necessarily required simply by the logic of the question. *For this reason, the distinction between soul and body is essential.*"[9] In this case, the concept of the soul is necessary to indicate personal identity. But does holding such an immaterial principle mean a lapse into dualism?

Regarding this fear, Ratzinger notes that the accusation of "dualism" is inappropriate when directed toward the Christian concept of the soul.[10] For, although one ought to avoid a "substantialistic" theory of immortality grounded "upon the indivisibility of spiritual substance" rather than upon a relation to God,[11] Ratzinger asserts that "nowhere in the great theolo-

---

7. Ratzinger, *Eschatologie*, 110 (*Eschatology*, 130). "Wir werden sehen, daß die alte Kirche gerade im Bereich der eschatologischen Vorstellungen äußerst konservativ geblieben ist, keinen Wechsel von 'semitisch' zu 'hellenistisch' vollzogen hat, sondern vollständig im semitischen Bilderkanon verblieb, wie Katakombenkunst, Liturgie und Theologie einheitlich zeigen."

8. Ibid., 124 (*Eschatology*, 150). "*Der Begriff der Seele, wie ihn Liturgie und Theologie bis zum 2. Vaticanum verwendet haben, hat mit der Antike so wenig zu tun wie der Auferstehungsgedanke. Er ist ein streng christlicher Begriff.*" Italics in original.

9. Ibid., 130 (*Eschatology*, 158). "Insofern ist eine Dualität, die die Konstante von den Variablen unterscheidet, unerläßlich und einfach von der Logik der Sache her gefordert. *Die Unterscheidung zwischen Leib und Seele ist aus diesem Grund unverzichtbar.*" (italics in original)

10. Ibid., 124 (*Eschatology*, 151).

11. Ibid., 124 (*Eschatology*, 151). "Der Vorwurf des 'Dualismus' . . . wird so

The Body-Soul Distinction

gians have I found a purely 'substantialistic' grounding of the doctrine of immortality. Not even Plato suggests this."[12]

Thus, in *Eschatologie* Ratzinger maintains that the Christian concept of "soul" was not slavishly imported from Greek philosophy but is closely connected to the Jewish tradition. He considers that even Thomas' use of Aristotle's hylomorphism involved a profound transformation, making the resultant concept a uniquely Christian one. Finally, Ratzinger argues that the Christian soul-concept is not dualistic since its immortality has never been based on any built-in, inherent power of the soul's substance, even if an accusation is often made to that effect.

The Soul: Separable from the Body?

We have thus far seen Ratzinger argue that the soul must be *distinguished* from the body. But can it be *separated* from it? That Ratzinger answers in the affirmative is suggested in his attack on "resurrection in death": "In this model the body is given up to death and at the same time the man's survival is claimed. This finger-wagging at the concept of the soul thereby loses all comprehensibility, because now one has to secretly reassert a distinct reality of the person separated from the body. The concept of the soul was meant to express nothing other than this."[13]

Here, Ratzinger's intent is to discredit Greshake's claim that one can deny the existence of a soul and simultaneously hold that the person attains fulfillment (resurrection) immediately after death. Since the argument is intended to show the necessity of the soul-concept, we must assume that when Ratzinger says the idea of the soul meant to convey nothing other than "the continuing authentic reality of the person in separation from his or her body," he actually approves of such a view. Ratzinger's position here

---

unterstützt durch die Auffassung, wo von Seele geredet werde, werde 'Unsterblichkeit' substanzialistisch, aus der Unteilbarkeit der geistigen Substanz, und damit theologisch unangemessen begründet."

12. Ibid., 124 (*Eschatology*, 151). "Aber bei den großen theologischen Lehrern habe ich nirgends eine rein 'substanzialistische' Unsterblichkeitsbegründung gefunden, die übrigens auch Platon nicht gibt." Greshake agrees with Ratzinger that such a substantialistic idea of immortality was not held by Plato himself. Greshake believes it was not introduced until High Scholasticism (*Resurrectio Mortuorum*, 290).

13. Ratzinger, *Eschatologie*, 94 (*Eschatology*, 109). "Jedenfalls wird auch in diesem Modell der Leib dem Tod überlassen und gleichzeitig ein Fortleben des Menschen behauptet. Die Schelte auf den Begriff der Seele verlierte damit ihre Verständlichkeit, denn im stillen muß man ja nun doch wieder eine vom Leib abgetrennte Eigenwirklichkeit der Person behaupten—nichts anderes aber hatte der Seelenbegriff sagen wollen."

Part Two: Crucial Distinctions in Ratzinger's Theology of Resurrection

appears to be identical to the classical one (held by Augustine) that the soul leaves the body at death.

Three years after *Eschatologie*, in "Zwischen Tod und Auferstehung," Ratzinger makes essentially the same argument against "resurrection in death," arguing that distinctions must be made in order to safeguard the reality of the resurrection and personal identity after death:

> According to these considerations [i.e., "resurrection in death"], man is absolutely indivisible; without the body there is no man: this is what drives people to seek out this way of thinking. But it cannot be doubted that after death, man's *body* remains in space and time. It does not rise, but is laid in the tomb. So this de-temporalization which reigns beyond death does not hold good for the body. But what, then, does it hold good for, if nothing in man is separable from the body? Or is there still something which, amid the spatio-temporal disintegration of the body, endures and is distinguishable from the body, which steps outside of time, which now finally takes the body completely into its possession? But if there is such a something, why should it not properly be called a soul? And how can it properly be called a body, since it clearly has nothing to do with man's historical body and its materiality? And how is there in fact now no dualism if a second, post-death body is posited (and how could it be otherwise?) whose origin and mode of existence remain obscure?[14]

Again, Ratzinger considers the notion that "nothing in man is separable from the body" to be ultimately inconsistent with the fundamental intention of "resurrection in death," namely to hold a fulfilled state for the individual immediately after death. This is because of the empirical fact that in death, the body is left to decay.

---

14. Ratzinger,"Zwischen Tod und Auferstehung" (*Eschatologie*, 214-15; *Eschatology*, 252-53). "Aber nun steht die Frage auf. Der Mensch ist nach diesen Überlegungen schlechthin unteilbar; ohne den Leib gibt es nicht: Deswegen mußte man ja diesen Denkweg suchen. Nun bleibt aber nach dem Tod der *Leib* des Menschen unzweifelhaft in der Zeit und im Raum. Er steht nicht auf, sondern wird ins Grab gelegt. Für den Leib gilt also die Entzeitlichung nicht, die jenseits des Todes herrscht. Aber für wen gilt sie dann, wenn nichts am Menschen vom Leib abtrennbar ist? Oder gibt es da doch etwas, was im zeiträumlichen Zersetzwerden des Leibes von ihm unterscheidbar besteht und aus der Zeit heraustritt, die ihn nun erst vollends in Besitz nimmt? Wenn es aber ein solches Etwas gibt, warum darf man es dann eigentlich nicht Seele nennen? Und mit welchem Recht kann man es eigentlich Leib nennen, da es doch mit dem geschichtlichem Leib des Menschen und seiner Materialität offenkundig nichts zu tun hat? Wieso ist es nun eigentlich kein Dualismus, wenn man nach dem Tod einen zweiten Leib postuliert (das muß man doch wohl?), dessen Herkunft und Existenzart dunkel bleiben?"

The Body-Soul Distinction

We need to be clear, however, that in the above passage Ratzinger is not articulating his own position but rather showing that even the theology of "resurrection in death" cannot get by without the concept of a soul. Thus, Ratzinger is *not* arguing that at the moment of death there is something "which steps outside of time" and "takes the body completely into its possession."[15]

In any case, the argument is intended to prove the internal coherency of the idea of a "soul" which is separable from the body and to show the utter *in*coherence of a view of resurrection which denies that anything is separable from the body. Ratzinger thus emphasizes not only the body-soul distinction, but the necessity of allowing their separation at death in order to safeguard the continuity of the person. If this separation were disallowed, we would be left with two unsavory options: either a postmortem total re-creation (*ex nihilo*!)[16] or the decay of the whole person in the grave.

Dualism and Monism

We have seen that Augustine's anthropology makes distinctions in order to maintain unity. His use of the body-soul distinction is intended to safeguard the salvation of the whole man against Gnostic and Porphyrian objections that only the soul is saved. In Augustine, this distinction allows him to assert a final reunion of soul and body, guaranteeing the salvation of both spirit and matter and precluding a spiritual monism. Ratzinger appears to have come eventually to a similar conclusion. Beginning in 1980, and repeatedly after that, he has voiced his disapproval of what he sees as a dangerous monism in contemporary theologies of resurrection.

Ratzinger therefore warns against the danger of rejecting the body-soul distinction, for "a Christian (and any thinker for that matter) should

15. Ratzinger, "Zwischen Tod und Auferstehung" (*Eschatologie*, 215; *Eschatology*, 253).

16. At this point in the debate, Ratzinger still has not yet fully grasped Greshake's position. Greshake does not argue for a postmortem second body (as in the *Ganztod* theory), because he sees "resurrection" as the endurance of *Leiblichkeit* (bodiliness), which is *not* spatio-temporal at all. See Greshake, "Verhältnis 'Unsterblichkeit der Seele' und 'Auferstehung des Leibes,'" 116–17, where Greshake states that "bodiliness is thus forever inscribed in the subject, even if the self-actualizing spatio-temporal bondage known as 'physical corporeality' finds an end in death." [Die Leiblichkeit ist somit für immer im Subjekt eingeschrieben, auch wenn die als 'Körperhaftigkeit' sich realisierende Raum-Zeit-Gebundenheit im Tod ein Ende findet.] Ratzinger's argument, however, is predicated upon the idea that the resurrection will be *material*, something he seems to assume (at this point in the debate) that Greshake would also naturally hold.

Part Two: Crucial Distinctions in Ratzinger's Theology of Resurrection

not view monism as less dangerous and fatal than dualism."[17] He later cautions that because of fear of a "false physicalism . . . there is now a great danger of pulling the faith completely out of material reality and thereby ending up in a new Docetism which begins in Christology and ends in eschatology."[18] Not long after this statement, when reviewing recent German works on the resurrection, Ratzinger laments that "on the whole, the above cited German-language works [by Hans Küng,[19] Herbert Vorgrimler,[20] Franz-Josef Nocke,[21] Johann Auer,[22] and Medard Kehl[23]], although with different variations in their explanations, all feel obliged to hold a 'monistic' solution."[24]

Monism, of course, is not Ratzinger's solution (nor in all fairness would the above authors be likely to label themselves monists). He believes that in order to maintain a doctrine of resurrection that is ultimately coherent, some type of duality must be maintained. This is because a spirit-monism ultimately denies the salvation of matter. Ratzinger now sees a real danger in that tendency in modern theology to spiritualize salvation and separate God from the material world, characterizing it as a "new Docetism"[25] and later dubbing it "a subtle new Gnosticism."[26] In other words, monism is actually a sort of reincarnation of all those undesirable elements that are so rightly rejected in Platonic dualism.

17. Ratzinger,"Zwischen Tod und Auferstehung" (*Eschatologie*, 218–19; *Eschatology*, 258). "Im übrigen sollte ein Christ (und ein Denker überhaupt) den Monismus nicht für weniger gefährlich und fatal ansehen als den Dualismus."

18. Ratzinger, *Nachwort zur 6. Auflage* (*Eschatologie*, 201). "Wohl niemand verkennt heute mehr, wie wichtig es ist, sich vor falschem Physizismus zu hüten und die Grenze einer wesentlich religiösen Aussage einzuhalten. Aber damit ist die Gefahr groß geworden, den Glauben völlig aus der materiellen Wirklichkeit zurückziehen und so in einem neuen Doketismus zu landen, der bei Christologie beginnt und bei der Eschatologie endet." This passage also appears on p. 273 of the English edition of *Eschatology*, but the translation there is problematic and results in an unclear meaning.

19. Küng, *Ewiges Leben* (1982). Published in English as *Eternal Life*.

20. Vorgrimler, *Hoffnung auf Vollendung* (1980).

21. Nocke, *Eschatologie* (1982).

22. Auer, *Der Glaube an die Vollendung der Welt* (1984).

23. Kehl, *Eschatologie* (1986).

24. Ratzinger, *Nachwort zur 6. Auflage* (*Eschatologie*, 190). "Im großen und ganzen glauben die vorgenannten deutschsprachigen Werke mit verschiedenen Variationen in der näheren Erklärung an einer 'monistischen' Lösung festhalten zu müssen."

25. Ibid (*Eschatologie*, 201). The statement dates from 1987, as mentioned above.

26. Ratzinger,"Jungfrauengeburt und leeres Grab." The accusation is leveled against those who seek to deny the physical reality of Jesus' bodily resurrection.

Ratzinger and the anima forma corporis Doctrine of Thomas Aquinas: A Crucial Development

We have seen how Ratzinger developed his understanding of the necessity of the body-soul distinction. Yet how does he understand the nature of the body-soul *relationship*? Particularly valuable to our study are *Eschatologie* and "Zwischen Tod und Auferstehung," where Ratzinger attempts to develop the insights of Thomas Aquinas in his struggle to articulate an anthropology of soul and body which does justice to faith in the resurrection. As we will see, however, he finds the Thomistic doctrine to be problematic in certain respects.

The Origins of the Christian Soul

For Ratzinger, Thomas Aquinas' development of the doctrine of the soul as the substantial form of the body (*anima forma corporis*) goes "beyond monism and dualism. It should be counted among the indispensable, fundamental elements of anthropological insight."[27] Ratzinger articulates this idea in *Eschatologie* by giving a simplified historical account of the origins of the Christian idea of the soul.

He explains that the somewhat mythical explanation of the soul given by Plato was purified by Aristotle, in whom the soul was an organic principle, bound as form to matter and perishable along with that matter.[28] For Aristotle, the truly spiritual element was not the soul, but the *nous* (mind). What Christian theology needed, however, was an anthropology that recognized that the whole man was God's creation, while simultaneously recognizing the difference between a perishable and abiding element. "Such an anthropology would thus have to fuse together Plato and Aristotle precisely where they stand mutually opposed."[29] What was needed was Aristotle's insistence on the inseparable unity of body and soul, combined with Plato's emphasis on the soul's spiritual nature.[30]

---

27. Ratzinger, "Zwischen Tod und Auferstehung" (*Eschatologie*, 218; *Eschatology*, 258). "Hier ist vom Schöpfungsglauben und der ihm korrespondierenden christlichen Hoffnung her eine Position jenseits von Monismus und Dualismus erreicht worden, die zu den unverlierbaren Grundelementen anthropologischer Einsicht gezählt werden sollte."

28. Ratzinger, *Eschatologie*, 119 (*Eschatology*, 144).

29. Ibid., 122 (*Eschatology*, 148). "Eine derartige Anthropologie hatte folglich genau das zu verschmelzen, worin Platons und Aristoteles gegeneinanderstehen."

30. Ibid., 122 (*Eschatology*, 148).

Part Two: Crucial Distinctions in Ratzinger's Theology of Resurrection

Although Thomas followed Aristotle in defining the soul as *forma corporis*, this definition was really "a complete transformation of Aristotelianism"[31] since for Thomas the soul was not only the form of matter but also something personal and spiritual.[32] As such, Ratzinger contends that this understanding would have been unthinkable for Aristotelianism.[33] In Thomas' new view, the *nous* is subsumed under the heading "soul," and body and soul are mutually determinative; not identical, yet one, constituting the single human being.[34]

Ratzinger notes that "the material elements which compose the physical human body receive their quality as 'body' only through the fact that they are organized and thoroughly impressed by the soul's expressive power."[35] The identity of one's embodiment, then, depends on the soul. Ratzinger makes this clear in a passage from *Eschatologie*:

> The individual atoms and molecules as such are not "the man" and the identity of embodiment does not depend upon them. Rather, it depends much more on the fact that matter comes under the soul's power of expression. So just as the soul is now on the one hand defined by matter, so on the other the body is completely defined by the soul: body, and certainly the identical body, is that which the soul builds as its physical-corporeal expression. Precisely because embodiment now belongs so inseparably to human existence, the identity of embodiment is not determined by matter but by the soul.[36]

---

31. Ibid., 123–24 (*Eschatology*, 148). "Wenn Thomas mit Aristoteles die Frage nach dem Wesen der 'Seele' mit der Formel klärt 'anima forma corporis' (die Seele ist die 'Form' des Leibes), so liegt darin eine vollständige Umwandlung des Aristotelismus."

32. Ibid., 123 (*Eschatology*, 149).

33. Ibid., 123 (*Eschatology*, 149). Sonnemans, however, has doubts as to "whether the Christian concept of soul is as fully new as Ratzinger claims," although he does not provide any supporting evidence (Sonnemans, *Seele*, 451). "Es bleibt aber fraglich, ob der christliche Seelenbegriff so *völlig* neu ist, wie Ratzinger annimmt." Italics in original.

34. Ibid., 144 (*Eschatology*, 179).

35. Ibid., 144 (*Eschatology*, 179). "Auf der anderen Seite aber bedeutet dies auch, daß die materiellen Elemente, die den menschlichen Körper aufbauen, ihre Qualität als 'Leib' nur dadurch empfangen, daß sie von der Ausdruckskraft der Seele organisiert und durchprägt werden."

36. Ibid., 144–45 (*Eschatology*, 179). "Nicht die einzelnen Atome und Moleküle als solche sind 'der Mensch' und nicht an ihnen hängt daher die Identität der 'Leiblichkeit'; sie hängt vielmehr daran, daß Materie unter die Ausdruckskraft der Seele tritt. So wie die Seele sich nun einerseits von Materie her definiert, so ist umgekehrt der Leib ganz von der Seele definiert: Leib, und zwar identischer Leib, ist das, was die Seele sich als ihren körperlichen Ausdruck baut. Gerade weil die Leiblichkeit nun so unlösbar zum

This appears quite close to the Thomistic conception, in which the body is the physical manifestation of the spiritual soul so that in effect, seeing the body is seeing the soul. In this view, the soul is thus not 'in' the body, but is itself the reality which the body reveals to us.

Difficulties with Thomistic Hylomorphism

Ratzinger, however, does not accept the Thomistic formula without reservation, noting certain difficulties in it. Although he was already aware of some of these issues in 1957,[37] his critique of this formula in *Eschatologie* owes much to Theodor Schneider's 1972 book *Die Einheit des Menschen*.[38]

The heart of the problem concerns prime matter (*materia prima*). Since in both Aristotle and Thomas, matter without form is simply *materia prima* (i.e., pure potency and not really "matter" at all in the common sense of the word), a grave difficulty arises when we consider the departure of the soul from the body. If the human soul is the body's only substantial form, then at the moment of death, a human body ceases to be a human body, and "between the living body and the corpse lies the chasm of *materia prima*."[39] With the soul's departure, then, new forms take the place that the soul once held, the result being a corpse which is not at all identical to the body which was previously informed by the soul. Understood thus, however, this idea denies the identity of the dead body of Jesus with the body that was crucified, to say nothing of the identity of the risen body with the body that once lived: "in this respect the Thomistic

---

Menschsein gehört, wird die Identität der Leiblichkeit nicht von der Materie, sondern von der Seele her bestimmt." The published English translation (*Eschatology*, 179) initially translates *Leiblichkeit* as "bodiliness," and then for the rest of the page translates it as "living body." It also translates *Leib* as "living body."

37. Ratzinger, "Auferstehungsleib," 1052. "Even he [Aquinas] teaches it to be indeed fundamental that the same material parts which once composed the earthly body will be reanimated. His doctrine of the soul as the unique form of the body, however, requires the conception that the body without its soul reverts somewhere close to the border of *materia prima*." [Auch er lehrt grundsätzlich, daß in der Auferstehung dieselben Materieteile wiederbelebt werden, die einst den irdischen Leib bildeten. Seine Lehre v. der Seele als einziger Körperform bedingt jedoch die Auffassung, daß der entseelte Leib nahe an die Grenze der materia prima zurückkehrt.]

38. Schneider, *Die Einheit des Menschen*. On 199–200, Schneider discusses the problem of the identity of the dead body of Jesus.

39. Ratzinger, *Eschatologie*, 145 (*Eschatology*, 180). "Zwischen dem lebendigen Leib und dem Leichnam liegt der Graben der materia prima."

Part Two: Crucial Distinctions in Ratzinger's Theology of Resurrection

doctrine, strictly applied, cannot maintain any identity at all between the body before and after death."[40]

Ratzinger raises another question: "the question of conception, of true parenthood, also arises if the body does not get its identity from matter but only from the soul, which is not inherited."[41] In this case, we would have immense problems, for if Jesus' human identity is not derived from Mary's body but only from his own soul (which was created by God at his conception) then he is not truly Son of Mary, nor did he take flesh from her.[42] Further questions arise concerning the validity of the veneration of relics and the possibility of the presence of Christ in the Eucharist.[43]

The problem here is that if the only principle providing continuity between a living and a dead body, between a fertilized egg and a human being, is *materia prima* (which is not really any*thing*), then the soul's entry into, and exit from, the world of matter always implies a radical break and discontinuity within that world. The purpose of viewing the soul as *forma corporis* was to maintain the unity between body and soul. But now it appears to be endangering important doctrines.

What, then, was Thomas Aquinas' response to these problems? Although Ratzinger does not provide us with this information, we will pause to consider it briefly. Thomas was in fact aware of these objections, and responds to some of them in his *Quaestiones Quodlibetales*. At this point we will limit ourselves to consideration of the important question of the numerical identity of the dead body of Christ, which Thomas discusses in *Quodl.* IV, q. 5, and later in *Summa* III, q. 50. In both of these works, Thomas bases the identity of Jesus' dead body on the hypostasis of the Word (since his soul had departed at the moment of his death). In the *Summa* (III, q. 50) he states that *numerical identity* is supplied by the *suppositum*, while *specific identity* is provided by the form.[44] So, Jesus' identity

---

40. Ibid., 145 (*Eschatology*, 180). "Insofern kann die thomistische Lehre, streng durchgeführt, überhaupt keine Identität zwischen dem Leib vor und nach dem Tod festhalten." See also Schneider, *Die Einheit des Menschen*, 61–62.

41. Ibid., 145 (*Eschatology*, 180). ". . . aber auch die Frage der Empfängnis, der wirklichen Elternschaft stellt sich, wenn der Leib seine Identität in gar keiner Weise aus der Materie, sondern nur von der nicht-vererbten Seele bekommt." See also Schneider, *Die Einheit des Menschen*, 60, 206ff.

42. Schneider, *Die Einheit des Menschen*, 61.

43. Ibid., 60. For a discussion of the problem of eucharistic presence, see 61, 205–6.

44. Thomas Aquinas, *Summa Theologiae* III, q. 50, a. 5, ad 2. "Numerical identity follows upon the supposit; specific identity follows from the form. Whenever a supposit subsists in one single nature, it necessarily follows that when the specific unity is

The Body-Soul Distinction

as a divine person allows for the numerical identity of his body before and after death. This does not hold for the rest of us, however: "The dead body of any other man does not remain united to a permanent hypostasis, as Christ's dead body did. Hence the dead body of any ordinary man is not the same simply but only in some respect, inasmuch as it remains the same matter, but has not the same form. Christ's body, however, remained the same simply because of the identity of the supposit, as was said."[45] Since this appears to imply that Christ's body is an exception to hylomorphic anthropology, Aquinas has been accused of not fully and consistently maintaining the Chalcedonian doctrine that Christ's humanity is identical to ours.[46]

It is noteworthy that this problem did not exist before Thomas. Those "Augustinian" medieval theologians (i.e., those who considered themselves to be in the tradition of Augustine) like Peter Lombard (1100–1160),[47] Bonaventure (1221–1274),[48] and Duns Scotus (1265–1308),[49] had maintained a *forma corporeitas* which existed in man alongside the soul. In this view, man consisted of two substantial forms. This allowed for the resumption of a real, identical body in the resurrection, since a dead body still possessed the *forma corporeitas*. As Schneider points out, however, a key point of Thomas' theory was the explicit rejection of the "Augustinian" *forma corporeitas* in favor of a vision in which the soul was the unique

---

destroyed, the numerical unity likewise ceases. But the hypostasis of the Word of God subsists in two natures. Hence, although in Christ the body does not remain the same according to its specific human nature, numerically it remains the same body by reason of the supposit of the Word of God."

45. *Summa* III, q. 50, a. 5, ad 1.

46. For a recent example, see Moisuc, "Aristotélisme et christologie," 149–50.

47. Peter Lombard, *IV Sent.* d. 31, 5. In dealing with the question of whether a fetus is alive, he states, "Sed iam formato corpori anima datur" (the soul is given to an already formed body). In *PL* 192:920.

48. Bonaventure, *II Sent.* d. 17, a. 1, q. 2. In Quaracchi 1885, 413–16. This is a discussion of whether the rational soul is possessed of spiritual matter. Bonaventure asserts that even the soul has a form, and that "the physical body is a composite of matter and form, yet still has an appetite to receive the soul." My translation. [. . . sicut corpus organicum ex materia et forma compositum est, et tamen habet appetitum ad suscipiendam animam (416)].

49. Duns Scotus, *Lib IV Sent.*, d. 11, q. 3. Here, Duns Scotus is discussing the presence of Christ in the Eucharist.

Part Two: Crucial Distinctions in Ratzinger's Theology of Resurrection

substantial form.[50] This elegant solution eliminated a certain dualism, but resulted in a serious problem of material identity.

Concerning this particular point, Ratzinger in *Eschatologie* appears rather ambivalent with respect to Thomas. Although, on the one hand, he claims that the *anima forma corporis* doctrine was a great innovation, he also considers that the difficulties considered above are insuperable within Thomas' system, suggesting that "this was the reason why Thomas himself shrank back from the consequences of his theory and, in the question of the resurrection, extensively fenced it in with supplementary constructions. Durandus of Saint-Pourçain (c. 1275–1334) was the first to dare to rigorously carry through Aquinas' starting point with all its consequences and thereby to ground the identity of the risen body exclusively on the identity of the soul."[51] Durandus' view, however, is unacceptable to Ratzinger. "The Aristotelian-Thomistic concept of matter and form at the foundation of Durandus' thesis can simply no longer be held by us today in its original form. In this respect, a slavish repristinization of a strict Thomism is certainly no way to proceed."[52]

Here, Ratzinger's belief becomes clear that Thomas' hylomorphism cannot deal with the objections raised without completely dispensing with material continuity. Although he does not discuss it, it is evident that Ratzinger considers Thomas' own solution to these problems to be unconvincing.[53] His treatment of the question here is similar to his con-

50. Schneider, *Die Einheit des Menschen*, 43–48. This section is titled "Thomas und der 'Augustinismus.'" In *Summa* I, q. 76, a.4 ("Whether in man there is another form besides the intellectual soul?") Thomas responds that there is no other substantial form in the human body but the intellectual soul.

51. Ratzinger, *Eschatologie*, 145–46 (*Eschatology*, 180–81). "Dies war der Grund, weshalb Thomas selbst vor den Konsequenzen seiner These zurückschreckte und sie für die Auferstehungsfrage durch ergänzende Konstruktionen wieder weitgehend einschränkte. Erst Durandus von San Porciano (ca. 1275–1334) wagte es, den Ansatz des Aquinaten mit allen seinen Folgerungen streng durchzuführen und damit die Identität des Auferstehungsleibes ausschließlich auf die Identität der Seele zu gründen."

52. Ibid., 146 (*Eschatology*, 181). "Nun ist uns das aristotelisch-thomistische Konzept von Materie und Form, das der These des Durandus zugrunde liegt, heute in seiner ursprünglichen Gestalt einfach nicht mehr vollziehbar; insofern ist eine schlichte Repristinierung eines konsequenten Thomismus sicher kein Weg."

53. As we have noted already, Thomas responded to several of the issues raised above in his *Quaestiones Quodlibetales*. For example, in *Quodl.* IV, q. 5 a. 1 (whether the body of Christ that was nailed to the cross was numerically the same body as that laid in the tomb), Thomas argues that although there is a real difference between a living and a dead body, there is a stronger numerical identity in the case of Christ "because the hypostasis of the Word of God was never separated from its body" (quia hypostasis Verbi Dei nunquam separata est abeius corpore). For this reason, we can speak of

The Body-Soul Distinction

sideration of it in 1957, where he considered the position of Durandus to be a "decisive radicalization of these [i.e., Thomas'] starting points"[54] yet nonetheless considered the successors of Durandus as the true heirs of the *anima forma corporis* concept.[55] The key difference in *Eschatologie* is that here, Ratzinger does not approve of the Durandian solution whereas he appears to do so in "Auferstehungsleib."

In any case, Ratzinger feels that although Thomas had a valuable insight, his great synthesis "must today be carried out anew."[56]

> Thomas certainly does not provide a recipe to be conveniently copied out, but his central idea endures as a sign pointing the way forward. This idea lies in the created body-soul unity, which on the one hand implies the soul's irrevocable orientation to matter, and on the other hand means that the identity of the body is not to be thought of in terms of matter, but rather in terms of the person, of the soul. The physical frame becomes

---

numerical identity. Given that such a solution is based on the person (hypostasis), it is surprising that Ratzinger—given his interest in relation over substance—does not delve into it further.

54. Ratzinger, "Auferstehungsleib," 1052. "Die entscheidende Radikalisierung dieser Ansätze erfolgt jedoch erst bei *Durandus v. S. Porciano*."

55. Ibid., 1053. "As concerns the question of the *identity* of the risen body, the reasoning of Durandus' followers is primarily based on a strict thinking-through of the Thomistic doctrine of the individuality of the substantial form. That means that every formation calls for *materia prima*, and also that even after death the physical body [*Körper*] is not simply left behind as a sort of abandoned casing for the soul, but rather that something new arises in a new-formation out of *materia prima*. From here on, all identity between physical bodies can only be identity on the ground of the assumed-being of the one, individual *materia prima*. The resultant body [*Nachfolgekörper*] (=corpse) of the once animated body [*Leibes*] certainly maintains a particular relation to the risen body, but without being absolutely identical with it. So, it is 'convenient' but not 'necessary' that the resurrection be connected to the corpse (Hugueny)." [Was die Frage der *Identität* des A. angeht, so beruht die Argumentation der Anhänger des Durandus vorzügl. auf einer konsequenten Durchdenkung der thomist. Lehre v. der Einzigkeit der substanziellen Form. Das bedeutet, daß jede Formung an der materia prima ansetzt, daß also auch nach dem Tod nicht einfach der Körper gleichsam als verlassenes Gehäuse der Seele zurückbleibt, sondern daß in einer Neuformung aus der materia prima Neues entsteht. Alle Identität unter Körpern könnte v. hier aus nur Identität auf Grund des Genommenseins v. der einen, einzigen materia prima sein. Der Nachfolgekörper (=Leichnam) des ehemals belebten Leibes behält zu diesem zwar eine besondere Beziehung, ohne jedoch mit ihm schlechterdings identisch zu sein. So ist es 'konvenient', aber nicht 'notwendig', daß die Auferstehung an ihn anknüpft (Hugueny).]

56. Ratzinger, *Eschatologie*, 146 (*Eschatology*, 181). "Die Synthese, die Thomas unter den Bedingungen seines Jahrhunderts auf geniale Weise formuliert hat, muß heute neu vollzogen werden."

Part Two: Crucial Distinctions in Ratzinger's Theology of Resurrection

the body by means of the person; bodiliness is something other than a sum of physiological parts.[57]

The above citation presents us with several difficult issues. First of all, Ratzinger has already made clear that Durandus' thesis—that the identity of the risen body is based only on the soul and in no way on matter—is not tenable. We have already noted that he believes Durandus to be a (brutally) faithful interpreter of Thomas' concept of matter and form. It is thus puzzling that Ratzinger sees Thomas' valuable "central idea" as indicating that the body's identity is not determined by matter but by the soul.

The obvious question is: if "the Aristotelian-Thomistic concept of matter and form" which Durandus developed "can simply no longer be held by us today in its original form,"[58] then in what way can Thomas' "central idea" be a signpost for us today? Or, put differently: if Thomas' central idea (i.e., his *anima forma corporis* theory) inevitably leads directly to Durandus, then is this a road we want to travel down? In this instance, it appears that Ratzinger has not fully reconciled his own thoughts toward Thomas, or at least not made them clear. Throughout *Eschatologie* and in his other writings, it is evident that he holds great respect for Aquinas. Yet here Ratzinger appears unsure as to how to evaluate Thomas' hylomorphism.

In any case, we are still left with the problem of Durandus and the difficulties that have been raised with the *anima forma corporis* theory. If the soul retains an "irrevocable ordination to matter" which might endure beyond death, and if we suppose that the person subsists in the soul, then might we be close to the solution to the problem of the identity of the dead body of Jesus which was given by Thomas himself—namely, that bodily identity was maintained by the *person* of the Word of God?[59] Or, put differently: might the *soul*, by its "irrevocable orientation to matter" even after death, be capable of ensuring bodily identity without requiring a

---

57. Ibid., 146 (*Eschatology*, 181). "So bietet Thomas gewiß kein bequem zu kopierendes Rezept, aber sein zentraler Gedanke bleibt als Wegweisung bestehen: Er liegt in der schöpfungsmäßigen Einheit von Leib und Seele, die einerseits die unlösbare Zuordnung der Seele auf die Materie in sich schließt, zum anderen aber bedeutet, daß die Identität des Leibes nicht von der Materie, sondern von der Person, von der Seele her zu denken ist. Der Körper wird zum 'Leib' von der Personmitte her; Leiblichkeit ist etwas anderes als eine Summe von Körpern."

58. Ibid., 146 (*Eschatology*, 181). "Nun ist uns das aristotelisch-thomistische Konzept von Materie und Form, das der These des Durandus zugrunde liegt, heute in seiner ursprünglichen Gestalt einfach nicht mehr vollziehbar."

59. Thomas Aquinas, *Quodl* IV, q. 5, a. 1.

new embodiment out of *materia prima*? Such a notion would not itself be strictly Thomistic, but would find support in Augustine's thought. At this point, however, Ratzinger does not take up again the difficulties raised in the beginning and instead breaks off the discussion abruptly.[60]

The Soul's Post-death Relation to Matter

As we have observed, in *Eschatologie* Ratzinger raises some problems that arise from Thomas' *anima forma corporis* theory while simultaneously approving of the central idea of that theory. He then enters into a discussion (which we will examine shortly) of post-death time and the relationship between eschatological fulfillment and history, stressing the interrelatedness of all human beings. It is then that he returns to the question of the materiality of the risen body, and the question of what happens to the soul after death.

The All-Cosmic Soul

This three-page subsection, titled "On the question of the bodiliness of the resurrection,"[61] begins thus and is worth quoting at length:

> A short while ago we left the question of the resurrection's materiality at the place to which Thomas Aquinas had brought it. The fundamental insight which started with Thomas was given a new twist by Karl Rahner when he noted that in death, the soul does not become acosmic but all-cosmic (*Theologie des Todes*, 22). That means that on the basis of its essence, the soul retains its orientation to the material world, even if this is no longer in the mode of the entelechial formation of an organism but now in an orientation to this world as such and as a whole. This idea can easily be combined with insights formulated by Teilhard de Chardin. We might roughly say: relation to the cosmos is necessarily also relation to the temporality of the universe, because the universe, matter, is as such temporally composed, it is a process of becoming. This temporality of the universe, which only knows being in the form of becoming, nonetheless has a

---

60. Ratzinger, *Eschatologie*, 146 (*Eschatology*, 181).

61. Ratzinger, "Zur Frage nach der Leibhaftigkeit der Auferstehung" (*Eschatologie*, 154; *Eschatology*, 191). Although "leibhaftig" means "bodily," it also has the connotation of something that is real, concrete, and not imaginary.

direction, which emerges in the gradual construction of the biosphere and noosphere out of and beyond the physical moment. It is above all an advance toward ever more complex unities and thereby cries out for total complexity, for a unity which encompasses all previous unities. The appearance of each individual spirit in the world of matter is, cosmically considered, a moment in this history of the complexification of matter and spirit. This is because, strangely enough, matter's demand for unity is fulfilled precisely by the non-material, by spirit. Spirit is thus not the scattering of the actually united into the dual, but rather the necessary, and necessarily qualitatively new force of the unification of that which has fallen into disintegration and disunity.

"The Last Day," "The End of the World," and "The Resurrection of the Flesh" would then be figures for the coming-to-an-end of this process. This coming-to-an-end can only happen from without, through the qualitatively new and other, and therein corresponds to the innermost "drift" of cosmic being.[62]

Regarding this Rahnerian-Teilhardian schema of eschatological fulfillment, we have several things to say. First of all, Ratzinger had already held a similar position in 1957 when he stated that "the soul, which in

62. Ratzinger, *Eschatologie*, 154 (*Eschatology*, 191–92). "Wir haben die Frage nach der Materialität der Auferstehung vorhin an der Stelle liegengelassen, an die Thomas von Aquin sie gebracht hat. Der Grundeinsicht, die bei Thomas aufgebrochen ist, hat Karl Rahner eine neue Wendung gegeben, wenn er bemerkt, im Tode werde die Seele nicht akosmisch sondern allkosmisch (Theologie des Todes 22). Das bedeutet, daß ihr von Wesen her die Zuordnung auf die materielle Welt bleibt, wenn auch nicht mehr in der Weise der entelechialen Formung eines Organismus, so doch nun in einer Zuordnung zu dieser Welt als solcher und ganzer. Dieser Gedanke läßt sich unschwer mit Einsichten verbinden, die Teilhard de Chardin formuliert hat. Wir können etwa sagen: Beziehung auf den Kosmos ist notwendig auch Beziehung auf die Zeitlichkeit des Alls, denn das All, die Materie ist als solches zeitlich verfaßt, ein Prozeß des Werdens. Diese Zeitlichkeit des Alls, die Sein nur in der Form des Werdens kennt, hat aber eine Richtung, die sich in dem allmählichen Aufbau der Biosphäre und der Noosphäre aus und über den physikalischen Momenten abzeichnet. Sie ist vor allem ein Voranschreiten zu immer komplexeren Einheiten und ruft damit nach der totalen Komplexität, nach einer Einheit, die alle bisherigen Einheiten übergreift. Das Auftreten jedes einzelnen Geistes in der Welt der Materie ist, kosmisch betrachtet, ein Moment an dieser Geschichte der Komplexion von Materie und Geist; denn merkwürdig genug—das Postulat der Materie nach Einheit erfüllt sich gerade vom Nicht-Materiellen, vom Geist her, der so nicht die Zersprengung des eigentlich Einigen ins Duale ist, sondern die notwendige und notwendig qualitativ neue Kraft der Vereinigung des aus sich Zerfallenen und Uneinigen.

'"Jüngster Tag,' 'Ende der Welt,' 'Auferstehung des Fleisches' wären dann Chiffren für das Zu-Ende-Kommen dieses Prozesses, das wieder nur von außen her, durch das qualitativ Neue und andere geschehen kann und doch darin der innersten 'Drift' des kosmischen Seins entspricht."

earthly existence is essentially bound to the body, maintains also in the intermediate state between death and resurrection its orientation to the world and to the body."[63] At that time, however, Ratzinger did not develop the idea along the lines he does in *Eschatologie*.

Here, however, Ratzinger unites Rahner's idea of the all-cosmic soul (which Rahner himself later abandoned in favor of "resurrection in death")[64] with Teilhard's theology of the ascending process of the unification of matter and spirit. In this case, the risen "body" is a way of expressing the outcome of this process. But this is no automatic process whose final conclusion is built-in from the start; its completion (which is resurrection) can only come about by means of "the qualitatively new and other." This power is Christ, who is "not merely something external, but rather the unique point of origin of all created being, who therefore, coming 'from without' can fulfil the innermost being of the cosmos."[65]

In this vision (as in Teilhard's theology), resurrection is seen more in terms of cosmic than of individual fulfillment. Thus, the appearance of new human beings is seen as "a moment in this history of the complexification of matter and spirit." Ratzinger declares that "that all-cosmic existence inaugurated by death would lead to universal interchange, universal openness, and so to the overcoming of all alienation: only when such is the unity of creation can it be true that God is 'all in all' (1 Cor 15:28)."[66]

It is interesting, however, that in the above instance, resurrection is seen not as an unexpected, sudden event but as the completion of a *process* which corresponds to the inner tendency of all cosmic being toward greater spiritualization and unity. In this regard, Nachtwei claims that Ratzinger's use of the notion of the all-cosmic soul serves a distinctly different purpose than it does in Rahner:

---

63. Ratzinger, "Auferstehung des Fleisches" (1957), 1051. "Sie [die Seele], die im irdischen Dasein wesentl. leibgebunden ist, behält auch im Zwischenzustand zwischen Tod u. A. ihren Welt- u. Leibbezug."

64. Rahner, "Über den Zwischenzustand," 461–65. The article appears in English as "The Intermediate State."

65. Ratzinger, *Eschatologie*, 156 (*Eschatology*, 193). "Allerdings sieht der Glaube in Christus dennoch nichts einfach Äußerliches, sondern den eigenen Ausgangspunkt alles geschaffenen Seins, der daher 'von außen' kommend das Innerste des Kosmos erfüllen kann."

66. Ibid., 154–55 (*Eschatology*, 192). "jenes Allkosmisch-Sein, welches der Tod eröffnet, würde dann zu universalem Austausch, universaler Offenheit und so zur Überwindung aller Entfremdung führen: Erst wo solche Einheit der Schöpfung ist, kann gelten, daß 'Gott alles in allem' ist (1 Kor 15,28)."

Rahner had developed this thesis in order to avoid the difficulty of a bodiless soul in the intermediate state between death and resurrection. He defended it for his whole life, but he has now notably given it up because, since the hypothesis of resurrection in death has earned larger acceptance in modern theology, the difficulty can be better solved in this way . . . For Ratzinger, the all-cosmic becoming of the spirit is not a postulate of the intermediate-state. It is the dynamic event of the final state itself, which begins in death. This is fulfilled in an exchange of love between God, man, world.[67]

It should be noted that Ratzinger's notion of the soul's ongoing relation to "the temporality of the universe" is connected to his thesis of post-death time wherein individual souls retain a relationship to continuing history. But it still must be asked: what sort of *embodiment* is an all-cosmic existence? And what similarity would such an existence have to resurrection? If Nachtwei is correct in his assessment—namely, that for Ratzinger the final state itself begins in death—then we are faced with something of an inconsistency when we compare such a view to the arguments employed by Ratzinger in his polemic with Greshake. For in the latter case, Ratzinger consistently argues that resurrection cannot be said to occur as long as the corpse lies in the ground. But in this more Teilhardian vision of resurrection as the completion of a cosmic process we appear to have a discordant view. For, if resurrection is the fulfillment of a process that already begins in death, then by what right can Ratzinger reject "resurrection in death"?

The Dialogical Immortality of the Soul

In Augustine, the soul's immortality is not grounded in its own substance. Against the Manicheans, he held that the soul is not made of any piece of the divine substance, for God alone possesses true immortality. What gives life to the soul is not in fact anything from its own substance, but

---

67. Nachtwei, *Dialogische Unsterblichkeit*, 173–74. "*Rahner* hatte diese These entwickelt, um der Schwierigkeit einer leibfreien Seele im Zwischenzustand zwischen Tod und Auferstehung ausweichen zu können. Er hat sie ein Leben lang verteidigt, gibt sie aber jetzt bezeichnenderweise auf, weil, seit in der modernen Theologie die Hypothese von der Auferstehung im Tode breiteren Raum gewonnen hat, die Schwierigkeit sich so besser lösen läßt . . . Für *Ratzinger* ist das Allkosmischwerden des Geistes nicht Postulat des Zwischenzustandes. Es ist das dynamische Geschehen des im Tod beginnenden Vollendungszustandes selbst. Dies erfüllt sich in einem Austausch der Liebe zwischen Gott, Mensch, Welt."

rather *God*.⁶⁸ The soul's likeness to God allows it to know him who is its life. And while this likeness is not itself immortality, it provides a foothold for it. In this sense, Ratzinger's idea of "dialogical immortality"—that we live forever not because of any inherent power, but by our relatedness to God—exhibits a certain kinship with Augustine's thought.

The History of the Idea

Since Nachtwei has already exhaustively traced the historical development of this idea of dialogical immortality, only the highlights will be noted here.⁶⁹ First of all, Ratzinger appears to have derived his original inspiration for the idea from Paul Althaus' *Die letzten Dinge*, which suggested that what is immortal is not a separable soul but rather our relationship to God which touches man in his body-soul totality.⁷⁰ The particular twist Ratzinger brings is the idea that we live forever because we are inscribed in God's memory: "What the theological concept of soul tries to outline is nothing other than the fact that man is known and loved by God in a different way from all other beings under him—known, in order to know in return, loved, in order to love in return. This way of standing in God's memory is what makes man live eternally—because God's memory never ends."⁷¹

In his 1967 encyclopedia entry "Auferstehung des Fleisches," and in *Einführung* (which includes and expands upon this), Ratzinger develops this thesis further. He cites Song of Songs 8:6 ("Love is strong as death"), drawing from this the idea that love desires infinity and indestructability.⁷² Being loved by God, then, entails immortality: "It is a question of a

68. Augustine, *Jo. ev. tr.* 47.8.

69. Nachtwei, *Dialogische Unsterblichkeit*, particularly 7–22, which provide a chronology of the development.

70. This is discussed by Nachtwei (*Dialogische Unsterblichkeit*, 13). Ratzinger apparently read the 1956 edition. See, e.g., Althaus, *Die letzten Dinge*, 110: "We know nothing of an immortality of the 'soul,' but only an immortality of our relationship to God." "Wir wissen nichts von einer Unsterblichkeit der 'Seele', aber von der Unsterblichkeit unseres Gottesverhältnisses."

71. Ratzinger, *Sakramentale Begründung*, 16. The text is taken from a lecture given in 1965. "Was die Theologie mit dem Begriff 'Seele' zu umschreiben sucht, ist ja gar nichts anderes als die Tatsache, daß der Mensch in anderer Weise von Gott gekannt und geliebt ist als alle anderen Wesen unter ihm—gekannt, um wieder zu erkennen, geliebt, um wieder zu lieben. Diese Art von Stehen im Gedächtnis Gottes ist das, was den Menschen ewig leben macht—denn Gottes Gedächtnis endet nie."

72. Ratzinger, *Intro.*, 302.

Part Two: Crucial Distinctions in Ratzinger's Theology of Resurrection

'dialogical' immortality (= being *raised* up); that is, immortality does not result simply from the inherent inability of the indivisible to die but rather from the saving act of the Lover who has the power to bring it about. Therefore, because man is known and loved by God, he can no longer totally perish. If all love wants eternity, then God's love not only wants it, but brings it about and *is* eternity."[73]

As we can see here—and as we have already noted—Ratzinger is attempting to develop a way of speaking of immortality that is not grounded upon a substantialistic theory of the immortality of the soul. He does this by describing the soul and its immortality not in terms of *substance* but rather *relation*.

Relation and Person

We have already noted that in 1968, Ratzinger (in *Einführung*) prefers speaking of "being God's partner in a dialogue" to the "substantialist language [of] 'having a soul.'"[74] By 1977, however, he had already spent several years working on rehabilitating the soul-concept. In doing so, Ratzinger is careful to outline a notion of "soul" that is clearly not "substantialistic." This is clearest in his formulation in "Zwischen Tod und Auferstehung": "Immortality is not embedded in man himself; it is based on a relation, on a relationship to what is eternal and to what makes eternity meaningful. This link, which can give life and fulfil it, is Truth. It is Love. Man can thus live eternally because he is capable of a relationship to that which gives eternity. 'Soul' is that whereby this relationship finds a basis in man. Soul is nothing other than man's ability for relation to Truth, to eternal Love."[75]

---

73. My translation of Ratzinger, *Einführung*, 332. "Es handelt sich um eine 'dialogische' Unsterblichkeit (= Auf*erweckung*!); das heißt, Unsterblichkeit ergibt sich nicht einfach aus der Selbstverständlichkeit des Nicht-sterben-Könnens des Unteilbaren, sondern aus der rettenden Tat des Liebenden, der die Macht dazu hat: Der Mensch kann deshalb nicht mehr total untergehen, weil er von Gott gekannt und geliebt ist. Wenn alle Liebe Ewigkeit will—Gottes Liebe will sie nicht nur, sondern wirkt und ist sie." Foster's translation of this passage in *Intro.*, 350, is not as clear as it could be. The main problem is his repeated translation (here and in following passages) of Auferweckung as "awakening." It is problematic because Ratzinger is attempting to stress the active element (on God's part) of drawing us upwards into relationship with him. Thus, "being raised up" expresses more faithfully what Ratzinger is getting at.

74. Ratzinger, *Intro.*, 355.

75. Ratzinger, "Zwischen Tod und Auferstehung" (*Eschatologie*, 219; *Eschatology*, 259). "Unsterblichkeit steckt nicht im Menschen selbst; sie beruht auf einer Relation, auf der Beziehung zu dem, was ewig ist und was Ewigkeit sinnvoll macht. Diese Beständige, das Leben geben und erfüllen kann, ist die Wahrheit, die Liebe. Der Mensch kann

This emphasis on the dialogical, on relation, is a central component of Ratzinger's theology. It is interesting that Ratzinger sometimes comes close to equating the soul with the person,[76] as his dialogical understanding of the soul is closely connected to that understanding of "person" evinced in his 1973 article "Zum Personverständnis in der Theologie."[77] There, he cites the Fathers (particularly Augustine) to remind the reader that "the three persons that exist in God are in their nature relations. They are, therefore, not substances that stand next to each other, but they are real existing relations, and nothing besides. . . . Relation, being related, is not something superadded to the person, but *is* the person itself."[78] The human person, too, is constituted by relation to the other. "Man is a being of relativity. The more totally and resolutely that that relativity reaches

---

deswegen ewig leben, weil er der Beziehung zu dem fähig ist, was Ewigkeit gibt. Das, woran diese Beziehung im Menschen einen Anhalt findet, nennen wir 'Seele.' Seele ist nichts anderes als die Beziehungsfähigkeit des Menschen zur Wahrheit, zur ewigen Liebe." Ratzinger cites this passage in the 2006 foreword to the latest version of *Eschatologie*, indicating that it continues to express his thoughts on the matter.

76. Ratzinger, *Eschatologie*, 146 (*Eschatology*, 181). Here, he mentions that the identity of the body must be thought of "on the basis of the person, of the soul." "Die Schöpfungsmäßigen Einheit von Leib und Seele . . . bedeutet, daß die Identität des Leibes nicht von der Materie, sondern von der Person, von der Seele her zu denken ist."

77. English translation found in Ratzinger, "Concerning the Notion of Person in Theology." Originally published as the chapter "Zum Personverständnis in der Theologie," in *Dogma und Verkündigung* (1973). Hereafter cited as "Personverständnis." Some elements of the article, however, are derived from an earlier article, "Zum Personverständnis der Dogmatik" (1966).

78. Ratzinger, "Person in Theology," 444 ("Personverständnis," 211). Although toward the end of the article Ratzinger accuses Augustine's psychological analogy of the Trinity of restricting the divine persons to the intra-divine realm (the immanent Trinity) while reducing God to a mere "I" in relation to man and thus losing the "we" dimension, he corrects this opinion in a footnote: "I must admit that today I would not judge as harshly as I did in this paper, because for Augustine the 'psychological doctrine of the Trinity' remains an *attempt* at an understanding, in which the factors of the tradition hold the balance. The more incisive turn came when Thomas carried out his separation between the philosophical one-God-doctrine and the theological doctrine of the Trinity: it led Thomas to consider legitimate that formula which had been considered heretical in the early Church, namely that God is *una persona* (Summa III, q3, a3, ad 1)." [My translation. "Ich würde heute freilich nicht mehr so hart urteilen, wie es in diesem Referat geschehen, weil für *Augustinus* die 'psychologische Trinitätslehre' ein Verstehenversuch bleibt, dem die Faktoren der Überlieferung die Balance halten. Einschneidender war die Wende, die *Thomas* durch seine Trennung zwischen der philosophischen Ein-Gott-Lehre und der theologischen Trinitätslehre vollzog: Sie führte *Thomas* dahin, die in der alten Kirche für häretisch geltende Formel, Gott sei una persona, für legitim anzusehen (S theol III q 3 a 3 ad 1)."]

Part Two: Crucial Distinctions in Ratzinger's Theology of Resurrection

toward its final goal, toward transcendence, the more he is himself."[79] Thus, Ratzinger rejects Boethius' definiton of person as *naturae rationalis individua substantia*[80] as "an expression that remained stuck on the level of the substantialistic thinking of the Greek mind."[81] This is not the place to engage in a detailed discussion of Ratzinger's understanding of the human person. It should be evident from the above citations, however, that Ratzinger wants to emphasize relation over substance.

In *Eschatologie*, relatedness to God "constitutes what is deepest in man's being: it is precisely what we call 'soul.'"[82] Ratzinger also connects this with the Platonic idea (employed by Augustine in his early years) that relation to truth (which is eternal) brings immortality.[83] Since Christ is himself the Truth, this Platonic idea is superfulfilled in him:

> Plato had recognized that immortality can only come from what is immortal, from the truth, and that man's hope of eternal life is grounded in his relation to the truth. But the truth remains ultimately an abstraction. When he who could say of himself "I am the truth" (Jn 14:6) came into the world, the meaning of this statement was radically altered. The formula that "truth gives immortality" could remain intact but it was now fused together with another formula: "I am the resurrection and the life. Whoever believes in me will live, even if he has already died ..."

---

79. Ratzinger, "Personverständnis," 220 ("Person in Theology," 452). "Der Mensch ist das Wesen der Relativität. Er ist um so mehr er selbst, je totaler und zielstrebiger die Relativität auf ihr letztes Zeil hin, auf die Transzendenz hin, reicht." My translation. This passage is echoed in *Eschatologie*, 127 (*Eschatology*, 155).

80. Boethius, *Liber de Persona et Duabus Naturis* 3. In *PL* 64: 1343. "Quocirca si persona in solis substantiis est, atque in his rationalibus, substantiaque omnis natura est, nec in universalibus, sed in individuis constat, reperta personae est igitur definitio: Persona est naturae rationalis individua substantia."

81. "Personverständnis," 216–17 ("Person in Theology," 448). My translation. "Man sieht, der Personbegriff steht gänzlich auf der Substanzebene; das kann weder bie der Trinität noch bei der Christologie etwas klären; es ist eine Aussage, die auf der Ebene des substantialistisch denkenden griechischen Geistes verharrt."

82. Ratzinger, *Eschatologie*, 127 (*Eschatology*, 155). "Wenn wir also vorhin zu der Einsicht kamen, daß nicht ein beziehungsloses Selbersein den Menschen unsterblich macht, sondern gerade seine Bezogenheit, die Beziehungsfähigkeit auf Gott hin, dann müssen wir jetzt hinzufügen, daß diese Geöffnetheit der Existenz nicht eine Zutat zu einem etwa auch unabhängig davon bestehenden Sein ist, sondern das Tiefste des menschlichen Wesens ausmacht: Sie ist gerade das, was wir 'Seele' nennen."

83. Augustine, *sol.* 2.19.

The Body-Soul Distinction

(Jn 11:25). The formula had become a path: in a relationship with Christ the truth can be loved.[84]

This dialogical notion of immortality has also been employed by Benedict XVI in the encyclical *Spe Salvi*: "Life in its true sense is not something we have exclusively in or from ourselves: it is a relationship. And life in its totality is a relationship with him who is the source of life. If we are in relation with him who does not die, who is Life itself and Love itself, then we are in life. Then we 'live.'"[85] Even more recently, Benedict XVI stated that "faith tells us that the true immortality to which we aspire is not an idea, a concept, but rather a relationship of full communion with the living God: it means abiding in His hands, in His love, and in Him becoming at one with all our brothers and sisters whom He created and redeemed."[86]

Before proceeding, however, we should make it clear that Ratzinger does not simply equate person and soul. While he does see person as relation—and nothing besides—the soul is that which allows for this relation. Although Ratzinger clearly declares that person is not a substance, he does not say the same for the soul.[87] One might say that for Ratzinger, our personhood is essentially our relation to the other, while this personhood presupposes a basis for this relation, which is the soul.

---

84. Ratzinger, "Zwischen Tod und Auferstehung" (*Eschatologie*, 220; *Eschatology*, 259). "Platon hatte erkannt, daß die Unsterblichkeit nur von dem kommen kann, was unsterblich *ist*, von der Wahrheit, und daß für den Menschen daher die Hoffnung des ewigen Lebens in seiner Beziehung zur Wahrheit gründet. Aber die Wahrheit blieb letztlich ein Abstraktum. Als dann derjenige in die Welt trat, der von sich sagen konnte 'Ich vin die Wahrheit' (Joh 14,6), war auch die Bedeutung dieser Aussagen von Grund auf verändert. Die Formel, daß die Wahrheit Unsterblichkeit gibt, konnte ungeschmälert aufrecht erhalten werden, aber sie war nun zusammengeschmolzen mit der anderen Formel: 'Ich bin die Auferstehung und das Leben. Wer an mich glaubt, wird leben, auch wenn er schon gestorben ist . . .' (Joh 11,25). Die Formel war zu einem Weg geworden: In der Beziehung zu Christus kann die Wahrheit geliebt werden." Also, cf. *Eschatologie*, 125–26 (*Eschatology*, 152).

85. Benedict XVI, *Spe Salvi* 27.

86. Benedict XVI, Homily, November 3, 2012.

87. It should be admitted, however, that in *Einführung* this is not at all clear. Thus, in Ratzinger's discussion of body and soul in *Intro.*, 355 (*Einführung*, 337), it is not clear that the soul is anything more than a way of expressing relatedness to God. This is in contradistinction to "Zwischen Tod und Auferstehung," where he makes clear that the soul is the *basis* of that relation.

Part Two: Crucial Distinctions in Ratzinger's Theology of Resurrection

The Soul as Relation and the Question of Duality

Ratzinger does not describe the soul as an isolated substance *unto itself* but rather sees it dialogically, as the basis for relation to God. But if, as Sonnemans supposes, Ratzinger's concept of "soul" includes the entire human being (since God does not relate only to the spiritual part of man but to his body as well),[88] why not simply use the term *person* or *man*? Nachtwei suggests that Ratzinger holds on to the term *soul* for three reasons: (1) the fact that *soul* is a *Glaubensbegriff* (a term belonging to the faith), (2) the fact that *soul* is part of the philosophical and theological tradition of the West and not to be discarded, and (3) the fact that even natural science now recognizes the existence of mind, or at least something beyond the body.[89]

From the above, however, it should be apparent that there are in fact two different emphases in Ratzinger's theology of the soul. On the one hand, *soul* can stand for man's capacity for relatedness to God. In this case, it might refer to the whole man, undivided, as Sonnemans suggests. Yet we have already noted that Ratzinger recognizes the necessity of "a duality which distinguishes the constant from the variable factors,"[90] a duality which grounds the (necessary, according to him) body-soul distinction.

Thus, when Ratzinger says that the soul is "nothing other than" the capacity for relatedness to God, we must remember that on the one hand, Ratzinger does not want to deny that the body is related to God, yet on the other, he does recognize the existence of a spiritual part of man, distinguishable from his body. Are these two emphases reconcilable? They are if we interpret them in a traditional way. If the soul is a spiritual substance (although not an isolated substance unrelated to God) which allows the human being to be related to God, then we can say on the one hand that the body is (by means of the soul) related to God, while on the other hand we can maintain that the soul is distinguishable from the body inasmuch as it is spirit. Sonnemans' assertion, then, that for Ratzinger the soul includes the entire man is overly simplistic and does not do justice to his thought as a whole.

---

88. This is discussed by Sonnemans (*Seele*, 455–59).

89. Nachtwei, *Dialogische Unsterblichkeit*, 140–41.

90. Ratzinger, *Eschatologie*, 130 (*Eschatology*, 158). "Insofern ist eine Dualität, die die Konstante von den Variablen unterschiedet, unerläßlich und einfach von der Logik der Sache her gefordert. *Die Unterscheidung zwischen Seele und Leib ist aus diesem Grund unverzichtbar.*" Italics in original.

The immortality of the soul, then, derives from its relation to its Creator. But what of the body? If the body shares in the dialogue of the person with his Creator, what implications might this have for the resurrection of the body *as* body? Could one's body be related to God by means of the soul, so that that body might attain to everlasting life in the resurrection? We have already considered Ratzinger's idea that the soul retains an ongoing relationship to all of the world's matter after death. At the end of this book we will consider, with the help of Augustine, alternate ways of developing Ratzinger's theology with respect to the soul's ongoing orientation to matter.

Augustinian Evaluation

Concerning the body-soul distinction, Ratzinger's theology appears to be on an Augustinian trajectory when viewed over time. His gradual acceptance of that distinction—a distinction taken for granted by Augustine—is certainly a move in the direction of the bishop of Hippo. Yet there is nothing specifically Augustinian about holding the existence of a spiritual soul. What is interesting is the way that Ratzinger views that soul, and its relation to the body.

Dualism and Monism

Many of the positions that Augustine fought against can be considered monistic in that they teach that only the spirit has ultimate value. The Platonic-Porphyrian doctrine that true human beatitude requires perfect disembodiment falls into the category of eschatological monism. It is interesting, however, that Ratzinger places many twentieth-century German Catholic theologians in the monist camp as well. Ratzinger believes that "resurrection in death" and its variants ultimately mean a spiritualistic vision of resurrection where there is no room for the body and matter. Rather than bringing about a dualism which devalues the body, the traditional body-soul distinction actually preserves the resurrection of the body: "As the debate goes on it becomes clearer and clearer that the particular function of the idea of the immortality of the soul is to keep hold of a real resurrection of the flesh."[91]

91. Ratzinger, *Nachwort zur 6. Auflage* (*Eschatologie*, 194; *Eschatology*, 267). "Im Fortgang der Debatte wird immer deutlicher, daß die eigentliche Funktion des Gedankens der Unsterblichkeit der Seele das Festhalten wirklicher Auferstehung des Fleisches ist."

Part Two: Crucial Distinctions in Ratzinger's Theology of Resurrection

This duality is absolutely necessary because of the event of *death*, as Ratzinger so clearly emphasizes. Since the material body clearly does not rise at the moment of death, there must be something separable from it which endures. And, if that body is to rise again, then there must be some form of ongoing human existence to which that body can again be united. Thus, the duality of the Augustinian body-soul anthropology preserves both the ongoing existence of the person after death, and the real, material character of the final resurrection.

Thomism and Augustinianism

"Augustinianism" can be viewed not only as the theology of Augustine of Hippo, but as a stream of theology in the Church, distinct from Thomism. In this respect, Ratzinger's doctrine of the soul appears at first to be something of a mixed bag. He wants to retain Thomas' *anima forma corporis* theory and considers it to be an anthropological breakthrough, yet he simultaneously criticizes that very theory for what he considers to be insoluble problems. What is interesting is that the problems that Ratzinger identifies are the result of the rejection of the "Augustinian" anthropology that reigned until the time of Thomas Aquinas. The denial of the *forma corporeitas* and the subsequent assertion that the intellectual soul informs *materia prima* directly results in a far closer correspondence and unity between body and soul than is found in Augustine's or Plato's anthropology. The drawback however, as Ratzinger rightly observes, is that this excising of what might be called Augustinian-Platonic duality results in a certain monistic tendency so that the body now has no being apart from the soul. There can therefore be no "body" to be raised at the end of time (or even in Jesus' tomb for that matter).

Although many theologians have no problem with the soul alone functioning as the principle of the identity of risen embodiment, Ratzinger rejects Durandus' thesis. This rejection appears to be the manifestation of what is at bottom an Augustinian intuition, namely that the failure to properly acknowledge soul and body as distinct realities ultimately means the devaluation of the latter.

Augustine and the All-Cosmic Soul

Ratzinger's notion (derived from Rahner) that the soul becomes all-cosmic at the point of death makes for an interesting comparison with Augustine's theology. It is true that in some of Augustine's early writings we find the

The Body-Soul Distinction

Platonic concept of a world-soul,[92] of which all souls form a part. Augustine, however, later rejected this idea in the *Retractationes*, noting that "all this was said in an utterly rash manner."[93] In Augustine's case, then, the world-soul was one of those Platonic elements that was gradually filtered out of his theology. The concept simply does not factor into his later writings, in which the individual souls of the faithful departed are at rest until the event of the resurrection when they are reunited with their bodies.

The Rahnerian-Teilhardian notion of the soul's becoming all-cosmic at death is certainly not identical to the Platonic idea of the world-soul. It is hypothesized for a different set of reasons, particularly the desire to avoid a spirit-matter dualism. There is, however, a striking similarity when we consider that part of Ratzinger's reason for supposing an all-cosmic soul is to ensure an ongoing relation of the soul to the temporality of the universe (and thus to maintain post-death time). Roland Teske has suggested that the idea of the Platonic world-soul would have given greater coherence to Augustine's own notion of *memoria*-time.[94] If this is true, there may be a closer correspondence between Ratzinger's all-cosmic soul and Plato's world-soul than appears at first glance, since in Ratzinger the all-cosmic soul serves as a support for the idea (derived from Augustine) of post-death *memoria*-time.

Although Augustine later abandoned the idea of the world-soul, he did posit a kind of ongoing relationship of the soul to the dead body.[95] Yet

92. E.g., Augustine, *imm. an.* 15.24; *mus.* 6.14.44.

93. Augustine, *retr.* 1.5.3. English translation from *The Retractations*. This statement is in reference to *imm. an.* 15.24, where Augustine had suggested that there is a soul that universally animates the world, as well as souls that animate individual things within that world. Also, in *retr.* 1.10.4 Augustine refers to statements he made in *mus.* 6.14.44: "But that this world is an animate being, as Plato and numerous other philosophers thought, I have not been able to investigate by solid reasoning [*ratione certa*], nor have I found that I accept this idea on the authority of the sacred Scriptures. Hence, something said by me, too, in the book *On the Immortality of the Soul* [i.e., that God transmits the form to the body through the soul], which can be interpreted in this way, I have noted was said too rashly—not because I maintain that this is false, but because I do not understand that it is true that the world is an animate being."

94. Teske, "Soul," 811 suggests that the idea of a world-soul, with which individual souls are somehow one, may help explain Augustine's understanding of time as a distension of the soul in *conf.* 11.26.33. "For, if all individual souls are somehow one with the universal soul which forms the sensible world, the distension of an individual soul forms a part of the whole of time." The idea of *memoria* time derived from *Confessions* is integral to Ratzinger's explanation of the intermediate state. Ratzinger does not connect it to a world-soul, although he does appear to connect it to an all-cosmic state of the soul after death.

95. Augustine, *civ. Dei* 13.20.

Part Two: Crucial Distinctions in Ratzinger's Theology of Resurrection

his mature theology does not appear to warrant an orientation of the soul to the cosmos as such and as a whole. In Augustine's discussion of risen embodiment, he clearly distinguishes between individual and cosmic fulfillment. He holds both, but does not mingle them. Risen men and women maintain real (albeit glorified) bodies; they will not be embodied in the entire cosmos. Augustine's emphasis on the separated soul's orientation to the matter of its *own* body (and not the whole world) is consistent with this division.

Ratzinger's use of the all-cosmic soul becomes further complicated by the fact that in *Eschatologie*, ostensibly at least, Ratzinger sees this idea as building upon the insights of Thomas, and necessitated by the problems within Thomas' system. But does an all-cosmic soul bring us closer to a solution? If the post-death soul's orientation to the material world is "no longer in the mode of the entelechial formation of an organism but now in an orientation to this world as such and as a whole,"[96] then what is retained of the Thomistic *anima forma corporis* doctrine? In Thomas, the soul is united to matter precisely as the body's substantial form. A more ambiguous post-death relationship to the whole of matter in general, in which the soul does not act as the matter's form but is associated with it in a more general way, cannot be dismissed out of hand. But it is difficult to see how such an idea builds upon either Thomistic or Augustinian anthropology.

Ratzinger's use of the all-cosmic post-death soul, then, cannot be considered to be an Augustinian innovation. In this regard it would be more accurate simply to label the idea Rahnerian or Teilhardian. Although Augustine says little about the world-orientation of the soul after death, what he does say indicates that those souls maintain a relationship to their own bodies and not to the whole cosmos. It should be noted, however, that Ratzinger has not employed this concept since 1977. It is therefore unclear whether it is still an idea held by him today.[97]

---

96. Ratzinger, *Eschatologie*, 154 (*Eschatology*, 191).

97. Consider a comment by Ratzinger in the foreword to the 6th German edition: "The bodiliness of Christ, who retains a body in eternity, means the taking seriously of history and matter; I tried to show this on pages 156–60." [Die Leibhaftigkeit Christi, der in Ewigkeit Leib behält, bedeutet das Ernstnehmen der Geschichte und der Materie; ich habe das auf den Seiten 156–60 darzustellen versucht] (*Eschatologie*, 14; *Eschatology*, xxi). The page numbers cited by Ratzinger do not point to any discrete section of the book. In the German text, one finds on pp. 156–60 a discussion of the biblical sayings about Christ's eschatological return. In the English edition, on pp. 184–89 (the numbers given in the CUA Press translation) one finds a discussion of *memoria* time and the concept of finding one's "place in the whole" at the end of history. Neither

Augustine and Dialogical Immortality

As we have noted, Augustine did not ground the soul's immortality on its own substance, but on God. Ratzinger's dialogical understanding of the soul as the foothold for relationship to God is thus consonant with Augustine's view as long as we are careful to consider the soul as the *basis* of the man-God relation and not the relation itself (which, in Ratzinger's anthropology, is the person). In other words, if "soul" becomes a catch-all for relatedness to God then it loses its meaning and becomes synonymous with the human being itself. If, however, it is maintained that the soul is spirit, and that the whole man is drawn into relationship with God by the soul, then we are close to Augustine's understanding. Although Ratzinger does not say as much, it appears that he agrees with Augustine that the soul must have a certain primacy over the body. Only in this way can the soul be "man's ability for relation to Truth, to eternal Love"[98] and simultaneously distinguishable from the body.

---

of these passages deals with matter. What is most likely, however, is that Ratzinger is referring to the rather "Teilhardian" section on the union of spirit and matter (titled "Zur Frage nach der Leibhaftigkeit der Auferstehung"), which is found on pp. 157–60 of the 1st German edition, which Ratzinger would likely have been consulting. Given Ratzinger's somewhat apologetic tone throughout the foreword (e.g., "I am very conscious of the limitation of what I attempted in 1977" [Diese Grenze meines Versuchs von 1977 ist mir sehr bewußt] *Eschatologie*, 14; *Eschatology*, xxii), it is possible that Ratzinger is here attempting to distinguish between his *intention* (i.e., what he "tried to show") and the way he attempted to realize it (i.e., by a Teilhardian schema).

98. Ratzinger, "Zwischen Tod und Auferstehung" (*Eschatologie*, 219; *Eschatology*, 259). "Seele ist nichts anderes als die Beziehungsfähigkeit des Menschen zur Wahrheit, zur ewigen Liebe."

4

The Distinction between Death and Resurrection

The Intermediate State

We will now take up the Augustinian distinction between death and resurrection, or the assertion of an "intermediate state" after death in which the soul awaits reunion with its body. Augustine clearly distinguished between the event of death and the event of rising again. For him, there is an intermediate period wherein the soul—lacking its body—waits for the resurrection, unable until then to attain the fullest glory of the *visio Dei*.[1] This distinction entails two elements. On the one hand, there is the fact of an *interval* between the moment of death and the resurrection of the dead at the end of time. On the other, there is the notion that the human being who awaits this resurrection during this interval lacks his body.

In this chapter, we will consider these two issues: (1) the question of a soul existing apart from a body, and (2) the question of post-death time. With respect to the first issue, we will consider theological objections to the notion of a so-called *anima separata* and examine how and why Ratzinger came to accept such an idea, also noting the importance in the debate of the 1979 document from the Congregation for the Doctrine

---

1. Augustine, *Gn. litt.* 12.35.

The Distinction between Death and Resurrection

of the Faith *Epistula de Quibusdam Quaestionibus ad Eschatologiam Spectantibus*. With respect to the second issue, we will consider Ratzinger's understanding of the individual's connectedness to others and to history, which makes itself felt in his discussion of purgatory. We will then examine his use of Augustine's concept of *memoria*-time and his critique of the concept of time he perceives in "resurrection in death" theology.

The Question of the Anima Separata

As we have already noted, Ratzinger argues against Greshake that in order to make sense of post-death fulfillment there must exist a soul, separable from the body. Greshake, however, as we will see, believes that such a concept is nonsensical. We will thus begin our considerations by examining Greshake's theological objections to the idea before considering Ratzinger's view. Greshake objects that in the idea of the *anima separata* "a potent dualism shines through. This is also one of the reasons why very many theologians today accept the concept that the resurrection of the one, entire man already happens in death and that at the end of life what returns to God is not a bodiless soul but rather the man in his body-soul unity (admittedly with an embodiment which is not that of the corpse lying in the grave, but rather a 'transfigured embodiment')."[2] Greshake also argues that since bodies are part of the way we communicate with others, the saints in heaven must have bodies. Otherwise their capacity for communion would be lessened.[3] His chief objection, however, lies in his assessment that based on Thomistic anthropology, a soul without its body is simply self-contradictory: "Ratzinger and other theological critics propose an intermediate state of a soul which is still awaiting the fulfillment of its body—for me the concept of a bodiless soul is a non-concept."[4]

---

2. Greshake, "Seelenwanderung," 238. "Nun schimmert in der Tat in diesen Vorstellungen ein kräftiger Dualismus durch. Dies ist auch einer der Gründe, warum heute sehr viele Theologen der Auffassung zuneigen, daß schon im Tod Auferstehung des einen und ganzen Menschen geschieht, daß also am Lebensende nicht eine leibfreie Seele zu Gott heimkehrt, sondern der Mensch in seiner leib-seelischen Einheit (freilich mit einer Leiblichkeit, die nicht den im Grab verbleibenden Leichnam meint, sondern 'verklärte Leiblichkeit')."

3. Greshake, "Leib-Seele-Problematik," 180.

4. Ibid. "Für Ratzinger und andere theologische Kritiker gibt es den Zwischenzustand einer Seele, die noch auf die Vollendung ihres Leibes wartet—für mich ist der Begriff einer leibfreien Seele ein Un-Begriff."

Part Two: Crucial Distinctions in Ratzinger's Theology of Resurrection

For, Greshake explains, even in the "traditional conception," one would have to say that the soul is co-constituted through its relation to the body.[5] Thus, as long as it is not united to its body, it remains (to use Thomas' words) only a fragment, a part of a man, and not the man himself.[6] In this way, even the traditional view does not allow one to speak of a fulfilled existence for the disembodied soul. This is why Greshake speaks of the self-contradiction of the idea of a bodiless soul coming to fulfillment.[7]

One source of Greshake's difficulty is the papal bull *Benedictus Deus* (1336), which taught that the souls of the blessed do not wait in an intermediate place after death but "have seen and see the divine essence by intuitive vision, and even face to face, with no mediating creature."[8] This difficulty is seemingly exacerbated by the bull *Apostolici Regiminis* of Lateran V (1513), which taught that the intellectual soul is not mortal.[9]

Ratzinger and the Not-Totally-Separated *Anima Separata*

Having examined the important objections against the *anima separata* as articulated by Greshake, we will now consider how Ratzinger approaches this question. In *Eschatologie* he argues that "even according to *Benedictus Deus* there is an element of provisionality as long as the *resumptio corporum*—the reunion with the body—and the general judgment are still to come."[10] It is thus not a question of a perfected, final state. Ratzinger

---

5. Greshake, "Seelenwanderung," 238. "Doch auch wenn man diese neuere Auffassung nicht teilt, ist zur rechten Interpretation der Vorstellung einer im Tod zu Gott heimkehrenden 'leibfreien Seele' zu bemerken, daß diese—nach traditioneller Auffassung—wesenhaft auf den Leib verwiesen bleibt, ja, daß sie geradezu (mit-)konstituiert ist durch ihre Relation zum Leib."

6. Ibid. "Darüber hinaus gilt, daß, solange sie nicht wiederum mit dem Leib wesenhaft vereint ist, sie in ihrer Leiblosigkeit—wie Thomas v. Aquin bemerkt—ein 'Krüppelwesen', 'Fragment', 'Teil des Menschen', nicht der Mensch selbst ist." Greshake does not provide references to Thomas here, although he may be thinking of *Quaestiones Disputatae de Anima* 2,239; An. 9c where Thomas notes that a human eye can only equivocally be called an eye once the soul has departed.

7. Greshake, "Leib-Seele-Problematik," 173.

8. Benedict XII, *Benedictus Deus*, in *Denzinger* 530.

9. Leo X, *Apostolici Regiminis*, in *Denzinger* 738. "We condemn and reject all who assert that the intellectual soul is mortal, or is one in all men."

10. Ratzinger, *Eschatologie*, 116 (*Eschatology*, 139). "Auch nach 'Benedictus Deus' gibt es noch das Moment der Ausständigkeit, sofern die resumptio corporum—die Weidervereinigung mit dem Leib—und das allgemeine Gericht noch ausstehen."

The Distinction between Death and Resurrection

is not arguing for the perfect fulfillment of the *anima separata* since he acknowledges that this soul lacks its body and is not yet risen. This was the notion eventually expressed by the International Theological Commission in 1992, when it defended the *anima separata* from accusations that it dispensed with the necessity for resurrection by positing a perfectly fulfilled bodiless state after death. For, since "the state of the survival of the soul after death is neither definitive nor ontologically supreme, but 'intermediate' and transitory and ultimately ordered to the resurrection, Christian anthropology has characteristics proper to itself and quite different from the anthropology of the Platonic philosophers."[11]

Part of the difficulty in responding to the idea of a bodiless soul—an *anima separata*—is apparent ambiguity over *what* the soul is separated from. This ambiguity is perpetuated in *Einführung* where Ratzinger writes that "where the 'communion of saints' is an article of faith, the idea of the *anima separata* (the 'separated soul' of Scholastic theology) has in the last analysis become obsolete."[12] Because Ratzinger understands the person as defined by relation rather than substance, the possibility of being separated from others (and thus from history) is naturally an impossibility. But is such an isolation the primary referent of the term *anima separata*?[13]

Again in *Eschatologie*, Ratzinger can say that "wherever man steps into the 'I' of Christ, he has already entered into the space of definitive life. The question of an intermediate state between death and resurrection, a kind of interruption of that life, does not emerge at all [in the Gospels], because quite simply the 'I' of Jesus *is* the resurrection."[14] What we have here is essentially Augustine's teaching on the resurrection of the *soul* expressed in another way. In Augustine, however, such a "resurrection" does

---

11. International Theological Commission, *Current Questions* 5.1.

12. Ratzinger, *Intro.*, 351.

13. In his article "Auferstehung und ewiges Leben," 313 (originally published in *Tod und Leben*, 92–103 [1959]), Ratzinger had already recognized that *anima separata* can be understood in two ways: "Thus de Lubac can correctly say that the *anima separata* undergoes a double separation: from its own body, and from the full communion of the body of Christ." [My translation. "So kann Lubac mit Recht sagen, daß die anima separata einer zweifachen Trennung unterliegt: derjenigen vom eigenen Leib und derjenigen von der vollen Gemeinschaft des Leibes Christi."] Yet in *Einführung* at least, Ratzinger tends to consider the term mainly according to the second type of separation enunciated by de Lubac.

14. Ratzinger, *Eschatologie*, 100 (*Eschatology*, 117). "Überall, wo der Mensch in das Ich Christi eintritt, ist er jetzt schon in den Raum des endgültigen Lebens eingetreten. Die Frage eines Zwischenzustandes zwischen Tod und Auferstehung, etwa einer Unterbrechung des Lebens, kommt gar nicht auf, weil eben das Ich Jesu die Auferstehung *ist*."

Part Two: Crucial Distinctions in Ratzinger's Theology of Resurrection

not preclude the possibility of actually dying and undergoing the separation of soul and body, whose only solution is the second resurrection (that of the body).

In the 2006 foreword to the 6th edition of *Eschatologie*, Ratzinger comments on the ideas he expressed in the book, and connects our resurrection to our membership in Christ's body: "Belonging to the body of Christ, we are united to the body of the Risen One, to his resurrection . . . Beginning with baptism we belong to the body of the Risen One and are in this sense already fastened to our future, never to be completely 'bodiless'—a naked *anima separata*—even if our pilgrimage cannot be at an end as long as history continues."[15] Thus, being part of Christ's body means not being dis-embodied. But again, the original meaning of the term *anima separata* was meant to convey nothing other than the idea that the souls of the dead are separated from, and await the resurrection of, their bodies—which will not happen until the end of time. It did not designate the absolute rupture of every relationship, nor even an isolation from the other blessed. Ratzinger here appears to be using "*anima separata*" in a different sense. On the one hand, he wants to maintain the post-death existence of the souls of human beings who await fulfillment at the end of history in a state that cannot be termed "resurrection." On the other, however, he wants to emphasize strongly that this existence is not a lonely, isolated existence wherein the soul huddles naked, waiting to be finally clothed. We could also express this in more Augustinian terms: those who have already experienced the first resurrection (of the soul) are not isolated but are at rest and in communion with Christ's body (the whole Church) as they await the second resurrection—that of their own bodies.[16]

---

15. Ratzinger, *Vorwort Papst Benedikts XVI. zur Neuausgabe* (*Eschatologie*, 13–14; *Eschatology*, xxi). "Dem Leib Christi zugehörend, sind wir dem Leib des Auferstandenen, seiner Auferstehung geeint . . . Von der Taufe an gehören wir dem Leib des Auferstandenen zu und sind in diesem Sinn schon an unsere Zukunft festgemacht, nie mehr ganz 'leiblos'—bloße anima separata—auch wenn unsere Pilgerschaft noch nicht zu Ende sein kann, solange die Geschichte unterwegs ist." Also, consider this 1992 statement from "My Joy," 147–48: "If we set aside the word 'soul,' then we inevitably fall into a materialistic conception in which the body [*Leib*] is not exalted but robbed of its dignity. When many people say that a disembodied soul [*leiblose Seele*], between death and resurrection, is an absurdity, then obviously they have not listened carefully enough to Holy Scripture. For since the Ascension of Christ the problem of the soul's being disembodied no longer exists: the Body of Christ is the new heaven, which is no longer closed. If we ourselves have become members of the body of Christ, then our souls are safely held within this body, which has become *their* body, and thus they await the final resurrection, in which God will be all in all."

16. For example, Augustine, *civ. Dei* 20.6: "Thus, there are two regenerations

The 1979 Document of the Congregation for the Doctrine of the Faith and Its History

Two years after the publication of *Eschatologie*, the Congregation for the Doctrine of the Faith published its "Letter on Certain Questions Regarding Eschatology." The letter has been discussed extensively by, among others, Ratzinger,[17] Greshake,[18] and Sonnemans.[19] This document is of immense importance to discussions of the *anima separata* since it affirms the validity of the term *soul* to designate a spiritual element that survives beyond death, and describes the extent of this soul's embodiment.

The letter from the Congregation, addressed to the bishops of the world, was dated May 17, 1979. The second paragraph states that the resurrection involves the entire person, yet it is the third paragraph that is most interesting:

> The Church affirms that a spiritual element survives and subsists after death, an element endowed with consciousness and will, so that the "human self" subsists. To designate this element, the Church uses the word "soul," the accepted term in the usage of Scripture and Tradition. Although not unaware that this term has various meanings in the Bible, the Church thinks that there is no valid reason for rejecting it; moreover, she considers that the use of some word as a vehicle is absolutely indispensable in order to support the faith of Christians.[20]

This certainly supports Ratzinger's contention that *soul*, being a central part of the Church's proclamation, cannot be rejected. It also appears to affirm a real duality, since the soul is "a spiritual element" that "subsists after death" and possesses "consciousness and will" in which subsists "the human self [*ego humanum*]." This is a clear repudiation of an anti-Hellenic emphasis on unity at the expense of duality.

... The first, which 'now is,' is the resurrection of the soul, which is here and now, and prevents us from coming to the second death; and the second, which is not yet, is that which is to come at the end of the world. This second resurrection is not of the soul but of the body; and, at the last judgment, it will send many to the second death, and bring others to the life in which there is no death."

17. Ratzinger, "Zwischen Tod und Auferstehung" (*Eschatologie*, 207–10; *Eschatology*, 241–45).

18. Greshake, "Römischen Lehrschreiben."

19. Sonnemans' rather critical evaluation can be found in *Seele*, 458–65.

20. "Letter on Certain Questions," 3. English text taken from *L'Osservatore Romano* (English Edition), July 23, 1979, 7.

Part Two: Crucial Distinctions in Ratzinger's Theology of Resurrection

Yet even this wording was not deemed strong enough by the Congregation, for prior to its August publication in *Acta Apostolicae Sedis*, an extra clause was added which states that the soul lacks full embodiment. This was apparently to exclude the position that the post-death soul already possesses complete bodiliness and thus is already risen.[21] Below are given the texts of the original letter, and the revised version in *AAS*.

Original Version	*Final, Official Version*
Ecclesia affirmat continuationem et subsistentiam, post mortem, elementi spiritualis, conscientia et voluntate praediti, ita ut ipsum "ego humanum" subsistat. Ad huiusmodi elementum designandum Ecclesia utitur voce "anima."[22]	Ecclesia affirmat continuationem et subsistentiam, post mortem, elementi spiritualis, conscientia et voluntate praediti, ita ut ipsum "ego humanum," *interim tamen complemento sui corporis carens,* subsistat. Ad huiusmodi elementum designandum Ecclesia utitur voce "anima."[23]

It appears that the addition was done in a rather uncoordinated fashion, since the new wording was included in the July 16–17 Italian edition of *L'Osservatore Romano*,[24] yet omitted from the English version (July 23)[25] and the French version (July 24).[26] In the English literature there has been no theological commentary on the implications of this clause.

The added clause was well known among German-speaking theologians, however, with Greshake immediately questioning the authority of

---

21. Looking back in 1998, Greshake ("Parteiischer Rückblick," 542 n. 16) states that the clause was added because "resurrection in death" was not condemned strongly enough in the first version. Because of this addition, he calls the document "verunglückten" (basically, a disaster, a fatal accident).

22. Congregation for the Doctrine of the Faith, "Epistula de Quibusdam Quaestionibus ad Eschatologiam Spectantibus" (Vatican City State, 1979). Original letter accessed from the archives of the Archdiocese of Ottawa, Canada.

23. Congregation for the Doctrine of the Faith, "Epistula de Quibusdam Quaestionibus ad Eschatologiam Spectantibus," *Acta Apostolicae Sedis* 71 (1979) 941, par. 3. I have emphasized the added clause.

24. *L'Osservatore Romano* (Italian Edition), July 16–17, 1979, 2. This includes a side-by-side 2-column layout with both Latin and Italian texts.

25. *L'Osservatore Romano* (English Edition), July 23, 1979, 7.

26. *L'Osservatore Romano* (French Edition), July 24, 1979, 2.

the addition.²⁷ What is surprising, however, is that when Ratzinger cites paragraph 3 of the letter in his 1980 article "Zwischen Tod und Auferstehung," he cites it *without* the added clause.²⁸ He also uses a German wording different from that published by the German Bishops' Conference.²⁹

It is possible that Ratzinger completed work on the article before the new clause was added. In this case, he could have prepared his own translation from the original Latin version he would have received as Archbishop of Munich. This would explain both the translation differences and the omission of the clause. The translation difference, however, could also be attributed to the fact that Ratzinger judged that parts of the "official" German translation were faulty.³⁰ The omission of the clause is mysterious, however, since Ratzinger's *Communio* article contained (as an appendix) his commentary on the new translation (with the clause). Given that the clause would have strengthened Ratzinger's argument against Greshake, its omission in "Zwischen" remains an enigma.

In any case, the German version of the text is interesting, since the Latin "interim tamen complemento sui corporis carens" is rendered "wobei es freilich in der Zwischenzeit seiner vollen Körperlichkeit entbehrt." The Latin *corpus* covers the semantic range of both *Leib* and *Körper* in German, so it is interesting that the official German translation opted for

---

27. Greshake, "Römischen Lehrschreiben," 190. He speaks of "such after-the-fact entries (whose official character is disputable since, in the first place, the version of a letter which is in force is the one you actually receive)." [Solche nachträgliche Eintragungen (über deren offiziellen Charakter man streiten kann, insofern zunächst einmal *die* Fassung eines Briefes rechtskräftig ist, die jemanden tatsächlich erreicht hat).] He repeats this argument in "Rückblick," 542 n. 16. Greshake goes on to suggest that the adding of the clause is evidence of contradictory opinions within the Congregation itself ("Römischen Lehrschreiben," 190).

28. Ratzinger, "Zwischen Tod und Auferstehung" (*Eschatologie*, 209; *Eschatology*, 245).

29. "Schreiben der Kongregation für die Glaubenslehre zu einigen Fragen der Eschatologie," edited by Sekretariat der Deutschen Bischofskonferenz (*Verlautbarungen des Apostolischen Stuhls* 11: 1979), 5. Ratzinger's citation is found in "Zwischen Tod und Auferstehung," *Eschatologie*, 209.

30. The German text of the Letter is published as an appendix to "Zwischen Tod und Auferstehung" in *International katholische Zeitschrift Communio* 9 (1980) 223–26. The text there includes the new clause. There is also a footnote in which Ratzinger writes that the German translation is faulty when it states, "daß es keinen stichhaltigen Grund dafür gibt, ihn abzulehnen, zumal ja irgendein sprachlicher Ausdruck zur Stütze des Glaubens der Christen einfach notwendig ist." He has no comments on the added clause, however, suggesting that he may not have known about it.

Part Two: Crucial Distinctions in Ratzinger's Theology of Resurrection

Körper, with its more physical implications.[31] Given that the clause was added *after* the publication of the document, there can be no question that the leadership of the Congregation would have discussed it extensively. And, given that the debate on the resurrection was chiefly a German one, it is difficult to imagine that the Congregation simply left the translation of *corpus* to others.

This is the belief of Sonnemans, who claims that by choosing *Körperlichkeit* (physical embodiment), the Congregation is indicating something more than *Leiblichkeit* (embodiment, bodiliness) and has materiality in mind.[32] And this, Sonnemans suggests, is actually close to what Ratzinger was getting at in *Eschatologie* and "Zwischen Tod und Auferstehung."[33]

If it was truly the Congregation's intent to imply that "resurrection" consists in *more than* the enduring "bodiliness" (*Leiblichkeit*) of a soul that has been imprinted by its interaction with matter during its life, then the statement that the soul now lacks full "physical bodiliness" (*Körperlichkeit*) could be an indication that this physicality will one day be restored and that the resurrection will be a *material* fulfillment.

Sonnemans suggests that since a *vollen Körperlichkeit* is spoken of, this can only mean that the post-death soul does possess a certain bodiliness, even if it is not yet *full*.[34] This indicates that theologians may speak of bodiliness as belonging to the postmortem soul as long as this does not lead to the assertion that the fulfillment of the cosmos occurs already

---

31. The Prefect of the Congregation was Franjo Cardinal Seper, a Croatian, while the secretary was Jérome Hamer, a Belgian who had taught at the bilingual (German and French) University of Fribourg. Greshake, however, objects to this translation: "Here... the official German translation shows an imprecision: '*corpus*' cannot here be translated with 'Körper' or 'Körperlichkeit,' if one differentiates—as is current in modern anthropology—between Körper and Leib" ("Römischen Lehrschreiben," 191 n. 86). [Hier liegt... in der offiziellen deutschen Übersetzung eine Ungenauigkeit vor: 'corpus' kann hier nicht mit Körper bzw. Körperlichkeit übersetzt werden, differenziert man— wie dies in der modernen Anthropologie geläufig ist—zwischen Körper und Leib.]

32. Sonnemans, *Seele*, 461. "Der Intention nach wird von der Glaubenskongregation die *individuelle, nicht volle 'Körperlichkeit'* betont, was schon auf *mehr als 'Leiblichkeit'* zeilt und die 'Materialität' anvisiert, welche Ratzinger ansprach." Italics in original.

33. Ibid.

34. Ibid., 460. He cites Ratzinger as agreeing with this when Ratzinger says in "Zwischen Tod und Auferstehung" (*Eschatologie*, 219; *Eschatology*, 258) that "the soul, which endures, holds interiorly within itself the matter of its life." [die Seele, die fortbesteht, hält verinnerlicht die Materie ihres Lebens in sich.]

in death.[35] Wohlmuth rightly suspects that the added clause was directed against the theology of "resurrection in death," but adds that it does not explicitly condemn the idea by name.[36] Few condemned positions, however, are mentioned by name in Roman documents. In spite of this, Greshake has since stated that the added clause was ultimately ineffective: "Even this subordinate clause didn't mean much, because it left open the question of what exactly was meant by *complementum corporis*."[37]

The Soul and the Human "I"

The problem of the *anima separata* concept, as we have seen, is that it can appear dualistic since it posits a human existence apart from the body. Thus, controversy has arisen over the document's statement that the soul, which is the "spiritual element" that subsists after death, seems to be equated with the "*ego humanum*" (the human self or "I"). Basing his critique on Thomas Aquinas, Sonnemans has criticized this, since in Thomas the soul without the body cannot be the human *ego*.[38] This criticism touches Ratzinger's theology as well since for him the soul is the basis for the relation which is the person, the "I".

During Ratzinger's tenure as Prefect of the Congregation for the Doctrine of the Faith, the International Theological Commission addressed this concern in its 1992 document on eschatology. After noting the oft-cited assertion of Thomas that the soul, since incomplete due to the lack of its body, cannot properly be called a person, it asserts that one may nonetheless say that the "human 'I'" *subsists in* the separated soul because that subsistent soul is the bearer of continuity between the person who lived on earth and the person who will be raised.[39] The separated soul is "on the one hand, an ontologically incomplete reality and, on the other hand, is conscious."[40] The *anima separata*, then, cannot be *equated with*

---

35. Sonnemans, *Seele*, 461. Greshake eventually admitted this distinction in *Tod und Auferstehung*, 119.

36. Wohlmuth, *Mysterium der Verwandlung*, 177.

37. Greshake, "Parteiische Rückblick," 542 n. 16. "Aber auch dieser Nebensatz besagt nicht viel, weil hier offen bleibt, was eigentlich complementum corporis bedeutet."

38. Sonnemans, *Seele*, 458, 464. See Thomas Aquinas, *In Epistolam I ad Corinthios*, chap. 15, lectio 2: "anima autem, cum sit pars corporis homini, non est totus homo, et anima mea non est ego; unde, licet anima consequatur salutem in alia vita, non tamen ego vel quilibet homo."

39. International Theological Commission, *Current Questions*, 5.4

40. Ibid.

the person or the "I," yet the person subsists in the soul which is the bearer of continuity. Thus, Thomas is interpreted by the Commission in a way thoroughly along the lines of Ratzinger's thought.

Post-Death Time and History

Having considered the question of the *anima separata*, we now turn to the question of post-death time. In Augustine, there is an intermediate state simply because the history of the world has not yet come to an end. Until the full number of the City of God is made up, history continues. This is essentially also the case with Ratzinger, although he develops the idea differently. Ratzinger's position on a temporal intermediate state is unclear in *Einführung*,[41] but by 1977 he refuses to speak of a final fulfillment occuring in death because of the unbreakable link that the individual has, even after death, with ongoing history.

We have already seen how for Ratzinger, the person is defined by relationship. Likewise, in the intermediate state one does not become disconnected from history, for "every individual life has an impact that is woven in its own way into the whole of the rest of history."[42] Thus,

> the man who dies steps outside of history—for him it is (temporarily!) concluded; but he does not lose his relation to history because the network of human relationality belongs to his very essence. The idea of resurrection in death deprives history of its seriousness: for all intents and purposes, when considered from another standpoint, history is already concluded. But the reality-character of ongoing history and the temporal index of life after death is of fundamental significance for the Christian concept of God as presented in Christology, and thus in God's care for time in the midst of time.[43]

41. Ratzinger, *Intro.*, 352–53 (*Einführung*, 334–35). Ratzinger states that being related to God is life and resurrection, and this relationship includes other human beings. He goes on: "This also clarifies the question, much discussed in the patristic period and again since Luther, of the 'intermediate state' between death and resurrection: the existence with Christ inaugurated by faith is the start of resurrected life and therefore outlasts death (see Phil 1:23; 2 Cor 5:8; 1 Thess 5:10). The dialogue of faith is itself already life, which can no longer be shattered by death. The idea of the sleep of death that has been continually discussed by Lutheran theologians . . . is therefore untenable." Here it is not clear whether Ratzinger is rejecting absolutely an intermediate state, or simply the "sleep of death" theory proposed by Luther.

42. Ratzinger, "End of Time," 6.

43. Ratzinger, *Eschatologie*, 148 (*Eschatology*, 184–85). "Der Mensch, der stirbt,

The Distinction between Death and Resurrection

Because Christ assumed a real body and raised it up, neither Christology nor eschatology can be conceived without any relation to history and time.

But why must the dead "wait" for the end of history? Ratzinger explains that it is because they are themselves implicated in the lives of those others who still live:

> Thus, the coming-to-an-end of history in the real interdependence of all men and of the whole creation is for no man something merely extrinsic which would no longer intrinsically affect him. The doctrine of the body of Christ here expresses—only with that final consistency made possible by Christology—what anthropology on its own could only anticipate: every man exists in himself and outside himself; everyone exists simultaneously in other people, and what happens in the individual affects the totality of humanity; what happens in humanity happens to the individual. The body of Christ, then, means that all human beings are one organism and that therefore the fate of the whole is everyone's own fate.[44]

We are therefore judged at the moment of death (individual judgment), but the general judgment cannot take place until each person's place in the whole has been determined by the working out of history.[45] "Although the final truth of this man is fixed in death, something new comes about when all the world's guilt has been expurgated and when finally—after all the

---

tritt selbst aus der Geschichte heraus—sie ist für ihn (vorläufig!) abgeschlossen; aber er verliert nicht die Beziehung auf die Geschichte, weil das Netz der menschlichen Relationalität zu seinem Wesen selber gehört. Die Vorstellung von der Auferstehung im Tode nimmt auch der Geschichte ihren Ernst: Im Grund ist ja dann, von einem anderen Standpunkt her gesehen, die Geschichte eigentlich schon abgeschlossen. Der Realitätscharakter der weitergehenden Geschichte und so der zeitliche Index des Lebens nach dem Tod ist aber für den christlichen Gottesbegriff, der sich in der Christologie und so in Gottes Sorge für die Zeit inmitten der Zeit darstellt, von grundlegender Bedeutung."

44. Ibid., 153 (*Eschatology*, 190). "Demnach ist aber as Zu-Ende-Kommen der Geschichte bei der realen Interdependenz aller Menschen und der ganzen Schöpfung für keinen Menschen etwas bloß Äußeres, das ihn selbst eigentlich nicht mehr beträfe. Die Lehre vom Leibe Christi formuliert hier nur mit jener letzten Konsequenz, die die Christologie ermöglicht, was an sich von der Anthropologie her zu erwarten ist: Jeder Mensch existiert in sich und außer sich; jeder existiert zugleich in den anderen, und was im einzelnen geschieht, wirkt auf das Ganze der Menschheit; was in der Menschheit geschieht, geschieht an ihm. Leib Christi heißt dann, daß alle Menschen ein Organismus sind und daß daher das Schicksal des Ganzen eines jeden eigenes Schicksal ist."

45. Ibid., 153 (*Eschatology*, 190).

Part Two: Crucial Distinctions in Ratzinger's Theology of Resurrection

actions that originated from him have been, so to speak, assimilated and established—his place in the whole is finally determined."[46]

Greshake contests Ratzinger's view and maintains that we need not wait for the end of history to find our place in the whole, since "in the resurrection of Jesus, the 'whole' is already there, there is thus nothing qualitatively new to wait for, [and] our resurrection is inclusion into his risen body. Thus, the individual already *has* his place in the whole."[47] Greshake goes on to argue that if resurrection is not truly 'resurrection' until the Last Day, then neither is Jesus truly risen.[48]

Elsewhere, however, Greshake appears to hold a position very close to Ratzinger's when he asserts that in the intermediate state (which is for him already a resurrection-state), the individual waits for "his 'whole body,' that is, the *universality of his relations to history*, a history which has not yet gone through the rupture of death, to find ultimate fulfillment."[49] The notable difference here between Greshake and Ratzinger is that Ratzinger assumes there will be a bodily resurrection at the end of time. Thus, the "waiting" of the intermediate state culminates in both resurrection *and* judgment. Greshake, however, assumes a resurrection in death, and so the "body" which is received at the end of history is simply a metaphor for the fulfillment of all the individual's relations to that history. Both believe that there can be no ultimate fulfillment as long as history goes on (although it is unclear whether by "history" Greshake means the same thing as Ratzinger),[50] but for Ratzinger the resurrection at the end of time is a discrete event rather than a metaphor for that end.

---

46. Ibid., 166 (*Eschatology*, 207). "Obgleich mit dem Tod die endgültige Wahrheit dieses Menschen feststeht, wird es etwas Neues sein, wenn alle Schuld der Welt ausgelitten ist und damit auch erst endgültig, sozusagen nach dem Verbrauch und der Bewahrung aller von ihm ausgegangenen Wirkungen, sein Platz im Ganzen entschieden ist."

47. Greshake, "Leib-Seele-Problematik," 179. "Aber dagegen ist doch zu halten, daß in der Auferstehung Jesu das 'Ganze' schon gegeben ist, daß mithin nichts qualitativ Neues mehr zu erwarten und unsere Auferstehung je die Einbeziehung in seinen Auferstehungsleib ist. Somit *hat* der einzelne auch schon seinen Platz im Ganzen."

48. Ibid., 181.

49. Greshake, *Tod und Auferstehung*, 119. "die einzelne schon auferstandene Person sozusagen darauf 'wartet', daß ihr 'ganzer Leib', d.h. aber die *Universalität ihrer Bezüge zur* (noch nicht durch den Bruch des Todes gegangenen) *Geschichte*, endgültige Vollendung findet." Italics in original.

50. Because of the fact that in *Auferstehung der Toten*, Greshake seems to hold a basically open view of earthly history, it is unclear whether in the above cited passage he means the end of history as a whole, or simply the end of the relationships the individual developed with the world during his life.

Post-Death Time: Ratzinger's Use of the Augustinian Concept of Memoria

We have seen that Ratzinger asserts a post-death waiting period necessitated by the individual's ongoing connection to history. But what sort of time is this? How might it be experienced by the individual? In order to illustrate this, Ratzinger believes that distinctions must be made. He criticizes the "resurrection in death" theory for what he considers to be an overly simplistic view of time which only allows for two possibilities: physical-earthly time, and eternity. For Ratzinger, however, time is a fundamental characteristic of human existence. He draws this insight from Augustine's *Confessions*, Book XI.[51]

Already in "Jenseits des Todes" (1972), Ratzinger had criticized the dualistic nature of time as he perceived it in the "resurrection in death" theory. There, he suggested that a solution to this dualism might be found in Augustine's "considerations of human memory" consisting in "the distinction he draws between physical time and time as humanly experienced."[52] Let us pause momentarily to consider what Augustine says in this regard.

In *Confessions* Book XI, Augustine asks: since the past no longer exists, since the future does not yet exist, and "the present's only claim to be called 'time' is that it is slipping away into the past," how can we possibly say that time exists at all?[53] He responds that what we *can* say is that past, present, and future are all *present* in the mind.[54] The measuring of time consists in the mind's measuring of the distance between these events etched into the memory. "What I measure is the impression which passing phenomena leave in you [my mind], which abides after they have passed by: that is what I measure as a present reality, not the things that passed by so that the impression could be formed. The impression itself is what I measure when I measure intervals of time. Hence either time is this impression, or what I measure is not time."[55] Time, then, is not strictly speaking something external but is a human psychological condition or experience. "Thus, it appears that time is nothing other than tension, but

---

51. In *Eschatologie*, 147 (*Eschatology*, 182), Ratzinger claims he is deriving the notion from *Confessions* Book X, but all the ideas he draws on are from Book XI.

52. Ratzinger, "Beyond Death," 160.

53. Augustine, *conf.* 11.14.17.

54. Ibid., 11.20.26.

55. Ibid., 11.27.36.

Part Two: Crucial Distinctions in Ratzinger's Theology of Resurrection

tension of what I do not know. It would be surprising if it is not a tension of the mind itself."[56]

In *Eschatologie*, Ratzinger develops this idea further. He points out that "man, as long as he is a physical body, shares in physical time which is measured with parameters based on the rotational velocity of bodies."[57] But man is also spirit. Because of the body-soul unity, "his belonging to the physical-corporeal world also affects the manner of his spiritual realization."[58] And while participation in this physical-corporeal time shapes our conscious awareness, our temporality is even spiritually deeper than that.[59]

Ratzinger explains: "Man has time not only physically, but anthropologically. Following Augustine, let us call this 'human time' *memoria*-time; we can then add that this *memoria*-time is imprinted by man's relation to the physical-corporeal world but is not entirely bound to it nor can it be entirely dissolved into it. This means, then, that when man steps out of the world of *bios*, *memoria*-time is detached from physical time and remains as pure *memoria*-time but does not become 'eternity.'"[60] While on the surface, this theory of *memoria*-time appears designed to explain the "waiting" period of the intermediate state, its permanent anthropological character suggests that it would hold true even for the fulfillment that will occur after the resurrection. Thus, in 1998 Ratzinger asks, "can we come up with some idea of time gathered up into a final definitive state, a state in which it is not revoked but finds the valid way for it to continue to exist? I

---

56. Ibid., 11.26.33. My translation. "Inde mihi visum est nihil esse aliud tempus quam distentionem: sed cuius rei, nescio, et mirum, si non ipsius animi."

57. Ratzinger, *Eschatologie*, 147 (*Eschatology*, 183). "der Mensch, sofern er Körper ist, an der physikalischen Zeit teilhat, die nach der Umdrehungsgeschwindigkeit von Körpern mit Parametern gemessen wird." Presumably Ratzinger is thinking of the movements of the heavenly bodies.

58. Ibid., 147 (*Eschatology*, 183). "Da beides [i.e., Körper und Geist] in ihm untrennbar ist, wirkt seine Zugehörigkeit zur körperlichen Welt auch in die Weise seines geistigen Vollzuges hinein."

59. Ibid., 147 (*Eschatology*, 183).

60. Ibid., 148 (*Eschatology*, 184). "Der Mensch hat Zeit nicht nur physikalisch, sondern anthropologisch. Nennen wir diese 'menschliche Zeit' im Anschluß an Augustin Memoria-Zeit; wir können dann noch hinzufügen, daß diese Memoria-Zeit von der Beziehung des Menschen auf die körperliche Welt geprägt, aber nicht gänzlich an sie gebunden und auch nicht gänzlich in sie auflösbar ist. Das bedeutet dann, daß sich beim Heraustreten des Menschen aus der Welt des Bios die Memoria-Zeit von der physikalischen Zeit löst und dann als reine Memoria-Zeit bleibt, aber nicht zu 'Ewigkeit' wird."

The Distinction between Death and Resurrection

think that our reason can derive some help from the concept of *memory*."[61] He suggests that as we interiorize time as it passes by, that time receives a continuing existence "on a new level in which, on the one hand, it ceases as a time that passes, but yet, on the other hand, is given a continuing existence, a sort of eternity."[62]

Ratzinger is thus grappling with two questions. On the one hand there is the issue of time in the intermediate state, and on the other, the question of how human beings (temporal as they are) might experience eternity. On the first count, Ratzinger sees *memoria*-time as binding us to the history of the world because of our relatedness to others. Man's "particular mode of temporality results from his relationality—from the fact that he only becomes himself in being-with-others for others."[63] On the second, Ratzinger wants to envisage an eschatological state in which time is not canceled out, but preserved and drawn into eternity. In this way, eternity is not simply non-time. It is "rather the power of the present in all time . . . it is not timelessness but dominion over time."[64]

Ratzinger's Critique of the Concept of Time in "Resurrection in Death"

The Problem of Detemporalization and Dematerialization

Ratzinger believes that one of the problems with "resurrection in death" is its failure to take seriously the distinction between non-time and eternity.[65]

61. Ratzinger, "End of Time," 24.

62. Ibid. Ratzinger continues: "The way that love internalizes time and is embraced by eternity can give us some sense of God's relationship to time and sovereignty over time."

63. Ratzinger, *Eschatologie*, 148 (*Eschatology*, 183–84). "Nicht zuletzt resultiert seine besondere Weise der Zeitlichkeit aus seiner Relationalität—daraus, daß er er selber nur wird im Sein-mit-anderen zu anderen hin."

64. Ratzinger, *Intro.*, 317. Here, Ratzinger sees the incarnation as the ultimate manifestation of God's dominion over time: "with us Jesus is time, and with God he is eternity."

65. Ratzinger, "Afterword to the English Edition," *Eschatology*, 263. "What had hampered the earlier discussion was not least a lack of philosophical seriousness. The simplemindedness with which the concepts of time and eternity were handled showed an absence of awareness of that quite fundamental reflection which the Fathers and the Middle Ages had dedicated to this question. Hypotheses can only be questionable

Part Two: Crucial Distinctions in Ratzinger's Theology of Resurrection

For Ratzinger, it is not a case of only two options: bodily time and eternity. As we have just seen, Ratzinger also posits a *memoria*-time, a time which is anthropological but not bound to physicality and bodiliness. The chief problem with "resurrection in death," according to Ratzinger, is that it makes the assumption that time is connected to bodiliness. He explains this assumption thus:

> A broad cross section of theologies advocates the opinion that temporality is connected to bodiliness, and that as a consequence the movement of human beings from life into death is at the same time a movement out of time and into non-time—an idea, of course, that could have never arisen in the Aristotelian system. Thus, whoever leaves physically/biologically determined bodiliness behind could not enter into an interim phase of the expectation of the end of time. She would find herself completely outside of time and in eternity, which is non-time ... Being there, where God is, in the non-time of eternity, one has arrived at the already-perfected world of the resurrection beyond history, since with God as wholly untemporal, everything is already everlastingly present there. In this way history as time could placidly keep on going while on the other side, history is always already fulfilled. The suffering that is endured on the one side is on the other always overcome in the definitive victory of God.[66]

The problem here is rather simple. If we are faced with the two contrary possibilities of time and eternity, if time is associated with the body and matter, and if eternity is timelessness, then eternity must necessarily be not only atemporal, but also bodiless and immaterial. Ratzinger notes that the detemporalization of time in "resurrection in death" "implied a dematerialization, for it is obvious that in the moment of his death man's physical body does not rise."[67] This "gives rise to a dualism of two worlds in which it seems to me that history loses all its seriousness."[68] We will

---

when they rest on such insecure foundations as the asumption that dying means an exit from time to non-time, or that the nontemporal is straightforwardly identifiable with eternity." This passage is only extant in the English version cited above.

66. Ratzinger, "End of Time," 9. A similar (but less developed) passage is found in *Eschatologie*, 93 (*Eschatology*, 107). Some elements of this explanation evoke passages from Greshake, e.g., *Auferstehung der Toten*, 406.

67. Ratzinger, *Eschatologie*, 134 (*Eschatology*, 165). "diese Entzeitlichung hatte eine Entmaterialisierung zur Folge, denn daß der Mensch im Augenblick seines Todes nicht körperlich aufersteht, liegt auf der Hand."

68. Ratzinger, "End of Time," 9. Ratzinger goes on: "I must confess that I continue

The Distinction between Death and Resurrection

return to the question of matter later, but will conclude our current consideration of the time-matter connection with one of Ratzinger's incisive critiques of "resurrection in death": "Of course, two questions arise here. The first is: Isn't this a covert re-establishment of the doctrine of immortality, philosophically based on rather adventurous presuppositions? Because now, resurrection is being enlisted for the man still lying on his deathbed, or even being carried to the grave. The man's indivisibility and his bond to the embodiment he has only just lost—which was after all the starting point of the construction—now suddenly appears to no longer have any role to play."[69]

Ratzinger's central argument against "resurrection in death"—that its detemporalization tends towards dematerialization of the resurrection—echoes a critique by Candido Pozo from 1970.[70] Interestingly, Pozo went on to become the head of the subcommittee of the International Theological Commission which, under Ratzinger's prefecture (as head of the Congregation for the Doctrine of the Faith) produced a 1992 document which criticized "resurrection in death."

The Problem of Eternity

Another problem Ratzinger raises concerns the possibility of a man, to whom temporality belongs by nature, simply being transposed into sheer

---

to find this dualism unintelligible, however broadly it is being accepted today with the talk of resurrection in death" ("End of Time," 10). This was in 1998, long after his debate with Greshake had subsided.

69. Ratzinger, *Eschatologie*, 94 (*Eschatology*, 108). "Hier entstehen freilich zwei Fragen. Die erste lautet: Handelt es sich hier nicht um eine kaschierte Wiederherstellung der Unsterblichkeitslehre, die philosophisch auf etwas abenteuerlicheren Voraussetzungen beruht? Denn nun wird Auferstehung für den in Anspruch genommen, der noch auf dem Sterbebette liegt bzw. eben zu Grabe getragen wird. Die Unteilbarkeit des Menschen und seine Bindung an die eben erloschene Leiblichkeit, die doch Ausgangspunkt der Konstruktion war, scheint nun plötzlich keine Rolle mehr zu spielen."

70. Pozo, "Problemática," 521. The following text is part of the (English) summary at the end of the article: "The new tendency to place the Resurrection at the moment of death loses this aspect of bodily continuity. The paradox is that, while it begins by affirming man's indissoluble unity, it goes on to propose the profound division inherent in the person's definitive abandonment of the body. Furthermore, if the Resurrection is placed at the moment of death, it becomes spiritualized. In other words, in the effort to eliminate the eschatology of souls by explaining the next life in terms of Resurrection, what is really endangered is the true Christian idea of Resurrection, which is replaced with a mere continuation of the 'ego.'"

Part Two: Crucial Distinctions in Ratzinger's Theology of Resurrection

eternity.[71] Ratzinger rejects the possibility that an eternity with a beginning could really be eternity,[72] for otherwise "one would have to posit man in the realm of eternity as always already risen and would thus abolish serious anthropology, effectively falling into that caricatured Platonism which was supposed to be combated at all costs."[73] Eternity should only be predicated of God himself, not the time of the world to come.[74]

The key problem with "resurrection in death" (specifically in this case, Gerhard Lohfink's concept of time) is that "the relation remains absolutely obscure between on the one hand, every new beginning of human life in history, both *present* and *future*, and on the other, that which supposedly already reigns beyond death: the not merely individual, but *historical perfect*."[75] For if in dying one enters into the fulfillment of history, then history can be said to be already complete. But if this is so, this world in which we now live loses all seriousness. This is why Ratzinger so aggressively attacks Greshake's assertion that "ongoing history is on the one hand open, its future is not determined, nothing is decided; but for God it is nothing but a victory procession."[76] Ratzinger wants to hold an ongoing connection between the afterlife and history, and thus retorts that

---

71. Ratzinger, *Eschatologie*, 95 (*Eschatology*, 109).

72. Ibid., 95, 146 (*Eschatology*, 109, 182).

73. Ibid., 95 (*Eschatology*, 109–10). "Würde man es leugnen [i.e., daß die Auferstehung des Menschen einen Beginn hat] . . . dann müßte man den Menschen im Bereich der Ewigkeit als anfangslos schon auferstanden unterstellen, womit man jede ernsthafte Anthropologie aufheben würde und tatsächlich in jenen karikierten Platonismus verfiele, der doch vor allem bekämpft werden soll."

74. Ratzinger, "Zwischen Tod und Auferstehung" (*Eschatologie*, 215; *Eschatology*, 253).

75. Ratzinger, *Eschatologie*, 96 (*Eschatology*, 111). "Der Bezug zwischen den je neuen Anfängen menschlichen Lebens in der Geschichte, zwischen ihrem Präsens und Futur einerseits und dem angeblich jenseits des Todes schon herrschenden nicht bloß individuellen, sondern geschichtlichen Perfekt bleibt schlechthin ungeklärt." My italics. Here, Ratzinger is making a grammatical pun. The German words he uses for present, future, and perfect are all grammatical terms indicating verb tense. The term "historical perfect" thus implies that what lies beyond death has already been fully achieved.

76. Greshake, *Auferstehung der Toten*, 406. Greshake continues, "This term 'victory procession' demonstrates fittingly the meaning of unbounded, ongoing history: for God the *victory* is not delayed, but only the victory *procession*." [So verstanden, ist die weitergehende Geschichte einerseits offen, ihre Zukunft liegt nicht fest, nichts ist entschieden; für Gott aber ist sie ein einziger Siegeszug. Gerade dieses Wort 'Siegeszug' veranschaulicht (!) treffend den Sinn der unbegrenzt weiterlaufenden Geschichte: Für Gott ist nicht der Sieg ausständig, sondern der Siegeszug.]

The Distinction between Death and Resurrection

"such a divine victory procession would have something cruel and misanthropic about it."[77]

Greshake has objected to being misunderstood and denies that he equates non-time with eternity.[78] In this case, his clarity in articulating his position might be questioned since he admits to having been misunderstood by a plethora of theologians including Anton Ziegenaus, Hermann Wohlgschaft, Herbert Vorgrimler, Sebastian Greiner, Gerhard Nachtwei, Dieter Hattrup, Markus Knapp, and Christoph Schönborn (not to mention Ratzinger).[79] Although it is not unusual for numerous theologians to disagree with a particular position, it is remarkable for so many to misunderstand such a position.

While it is true that Ratzinger (as in the above) does tend to cite Greshake in the most damning way possible, there are other statements in Greshake's writing that support Ratzinger's reading. For example, shortly before the above citation by Ratzinger (from *Auferstehung der Toten*, 406), Greshake claims that through man's sin, history

> has been turned back into a futile nothingness, it has been given over to the powers and principalities of death. Considered thus, the question is reformulated: does not the death and decay of the Old Age have as a consequence its ultimate annihilation? Because—so one could argue—for God to be "all in all" requires the ultimate annihilation of everything that is against God, an ultimate victory of God over this history which is now still determined by the vicissitudes of power. And this is just what happens at the end of the world, in the resurrection on the Last Day.[80]

77. Ratzinger, *Eschatologie*, 152 (*Eschatology*, 188). "Ein solcher Siegeszug Gottes hätte etwas Grausames und Menschenverächterisches an sich."

78. Greshake, "Leib-Seele-Problematik," 161. He states that it is "completely inaccurate [völlig unzutreffende]" that he holds that death is an entry into atemporal eternity (unzeitliche Ewigkeit). He insists that his position is rather that "death means the entry into a not-yet-closed-off process of fulfillment" (der Tod bedeutet das Hineintreten in einen noch unabgeschlossenen Prozeß der Vollendung, 162).

79. Regarding Ziegenaus, see Greshake, "Leib-Seele-Problematik," 162 n. 12; regarding Wohlgschaft, see "Leib-Seele-Problematik," 178 n. 56; regarding Vorgrimler, Greiner, Nachtwei, Hattrup, Knapp, and Schönborn, see "Parteiische Rückblick," 543–44.

80. Greshake, *Auferstehung der Toten*, 405. "durch die Schuld des Menschen ist sie [die Geschichte] verkehrt in eitle Nichtigkeit; sie hat sich hingegeben an die Mächte und Gewalten des Todes. Bedenkt man dies, so stellt sich die Frage neu; Folgt aus der Todes-Verfallenheit des alten Äons nicht seine endgültige Vernichtung? Denn—so könnte man argumentieren—'Gott alles in allem': das erfordert die endgültige Vernichtung

Part Two: Crucial Distinctions in Ratzinger's Theology of Resurrection

This passage gives the impression that human history has been perverted and thus must be annihilated rather than redeemed. Greshake, however, often makes statements that appear to contradict the accusations of Ratzinger (and others), as when he says, "God cannot fail history,"[81] but such statements are difficult to reconcile with other assertions Greshake makes. Thus, even Wohlmuth, who is generally sympathetic to Greshake, can state that "in Greshake there is a danger of blurring the borders of time and eternity, God and the world."[82] Although Greshake must be taken at his word when he states that he does not hold a fulfillment of all history at the moment of death, the controversy over this issue in his theology indicates at the very least a serious ambiguity or inconsistency in his theological expression.

Is There Memoria-*Time in Purgatory?*

One of the forces behind Ratzinger's formulation of the notion of *memoria*-time was the need to explain how souls could "wait" in the intermediate state. Ratzinger's concept of *memoria*-time holds even for a soul without its body, since this kind of time is not bound to physicality. It would thus appear that being dead does not mean a release from temporality. Yet when Ratzinger speaks of purgatory, he is reticent to speak of any temporality at all.

Of purgatory, Ratzinger affirms that "the transforming 'moment' of this encounter eludes earthly measurements of time—it is not eternal, but is a transition, although trying to qualify it as short or long based on temporal measurements derived from physics would be naïve."[83] Even in *Spe Salvi*, Benedict XVI asserts that "there is no need to convert earthly time into God's time: in the communion of souls simple terrestrial time is superseded. It is never too late to touch the heart of another, nor is it ever

---

alles Widergöttlichen, einen endgültigen Sieg Gottes über diese Geschichte, die jetzt noch vom Zueinander und Widereinander der Mächte bestimmt ist. Und eben dies geschieht am Ende der Welt, bei der Auferstehung am Jüngsten Tag."

81. Ibid. "Gott kann an der Geschichte nicht scheitern."

82. Wohlmuth, *Mysterium der Verwandlung*, 171 n. 112. "Bei Greshake drohen die Grenzen von Zeit und Ewigkeit, Gott und Welt zu verschwimmen."

83. Ratzinger, *Eschatologie*, 183 (*Eschatology*, 230). "Der verwandelnde 'Augenblick' dieser Begegnung entzieht sich irdischen Zeitmaßen—er ist nicht ewig, sondern Übergang, aber ihn als ganz kurz oder als lang nach den aus der Physik übernommenen Zeitmaßen qualifizieren zu wollen, wäre gleich naiv."

The Distinction between Death and Resurrection

in vain."[84] Because of this, Peter Phan has decried Ratzinger's formulation of *memoria*-time in *Eschatologie* as "a clear instance of trying to have one's cake and eat it too."[85] Phan also accuses Ratzinger of not thinking through the difference between *memoria*-time before and after death.[86]

While it is true that Ratzinger carefully avoids speaking of purgatory and indulgences in terms of earthly time, he nowhere states that purgatory is atemporal. Since, as he argues elsewhere, time belongs to man as man, how could purgatory be a genuinely *human* experience if it were atemporal? Although Ratzinger does not directly connect his concept of purgatory with *memoria*-time, this is a case of Ratzinger leaving incomplete the task of incorporating the two ideas into a greater synthesis. He makes it clear that purgatory does not proceed based on *earthly* time. He does not, however, claim that it is timeless. Thus, his theology of purgatory ought to be read in light of his view of *memoria*-time.

Phan's second objection—that Ratzinger has not considered the difference between *memoria*-time before and after death—is essentially correct. Ratzinger has nowhere developed the *memoria*-time thesis beyond *ad hoc* use in explaining post-death time. This does not impact the coherence of his idea, however. It appears that he is simply leaving the task of its systematic development to others.[87]

Augustinian Evaluation

The *Anima Separata*

We have seen that like Augustine, Ratzinger holds the existence of a spiritual soul that survives the death of the body and waits for the resurrection, which will occur at the end of time. Ratzinger essentially accepts the doctrine of the *anima separata* but lays stress on the soul's inclusion in Christ's body and its relation to the *communio sanctorum* rather than on the fact of its "separation." Ratzinger's intent is to assure the believer that post-death existence is not a "separated" sort of existence, except in the sense that one still awaits the resurrection of one's body.

---

84. Benedict XVI, *Spe Salvi* 48.
85. Phan, "Current Theology," 520 n. 49.
86. Ibid.
87. For example, Ratzinger, "End of Time," 24.

Part Two: Crucial Distinctions in Ratzinger's Theology of Resurrection

It is interesting that Ratzinger rejects Greshake's assertion (which Greshake claims derives from Thomas) that a separated soul is an impossibility. Although this is not the place to consider whether Thomas' doctrine of the soul and person is internally coherent (Greshake believes it is not),[88] we should recall that Ratzinger believes Thomas' hylomorphism cannot be strictly maintained. Ratzinger's insistence on a soul which survives the death of the body, then, cannot be considered to be strictly Thomistic (to use Ratzinger's own terminology) but would seem rather to belong to that more dual schema articulated by Augustine. To be sure, Thomas himself considered that the soul could exist after death apart from its body, but given that there are tensions within Thomas' hylomorphism on this matter (as we have already discussed), we might consider Aquinas' final position to fall on the "Augustinian" side of things rather than on the purely Aristotelian. We could thus say that Ratzinger's formulation is an affirmation of the Augustinian side of the tension already present in the theology of Thomas Aquinas.

Post-Death Time

As regards post-death time in Augustine, a "waiting" period is simply assumed since the end has not yet come. Ratzinger, however, goes further and explains this waiting on the basis of his relational understanding of the person. Since each person is co-constituted by his relation to others, he cannot be complete until he finds his place in the whole, which cannot be determined until history has worked itself out definitively.

What Ratzinger intends by a "place in the whole" is in a way similar to what is expressed by Augustine visually when he speaks of the wounds retained by the risen martyrs. For Augustine, one's Christological *history* can be permanently expressed in the risen body. The risen body becomes the vehicle of the manifestation of the eternal fixity and permanence that is achieved by one's personal history as it concerns salvation. Ratzinger does not express this idea using bodily imagery but instead speaks of one's place in the corporate whole of Christ's body.

While both conceptions articulate how a risen person retains a relationship to history, Augustine's use of risen "wounds" emphasizes one's *individual* history, while Ratzinger's idea of a final "place in the whole" stresses one's location within *communal* history. Augustine speaks of

---

88. Greshake, "Parteiische Rückblick," 554–55. Greshake believes that in Thomas there are two irreconcilable concepts of *persona* at play.

The Distinction between Death and Resurrection

individual bodies, whereas Ratzinger only speaks of the individual within the corporate body. Augustine, however, does speak extensively of communion in heaven, stating that we will see and know everyone.[89] Ratzinger, however, does not say anything concrete (apart from those very early statements in "Auferstehungsleib")[90] about the individual risen body. His insistence on viewing relatedness to history in its communal aspect, however, is consistent with his understanding of the individual person as constituted by relationship with others. Since the individual is only individual inasmuch as he is related to others, finding one's "place in the whole" is not a dissolving of the individual into the communal, but rather means the determination and fulfillment of the individual *qua* individual, as well as of the community.

At this point it might be noted that in all of Ratzinger's theology of resurrection, his only explicit appeal to Augustine is not to *De Civitate Dei* but to the concept of *memoria* found in *Confessions*, a concept which plays no role at all in Augustine's own theology of resurrection. If we grant the coherence of Augustine's thought (while of course taking into account genuine developments), can one rightly call Ratzinger's use of *memoria*-time Augustinian?

First of all, it must be admitted that in much of Ratzinger's work, what is commonly recognized as "Augustinian" content is often either the Augustinian emphasis on interiority or man's need for grace. One might thus speak of Ratzinger's reliance on the Augustine of the *Confessions*. The voice of the mature Augustine found in *De Civitate Dei* Book XXII, however, is hard to find in Ratzinger's theology.[91] This raises a difficult question concerning any sort of attempt at an "Augustinian evaluation," namely, what counts as "Augustinian"? Since Augustine's theology developed throughout his Christian life, and since he treated so many different topics and used a variety of styles, the term *Augustinian* risks becoming

---

89. Augustine, *s.* 24.5.

90. Ratzinger, "Auferstehungsleib," 1054. "In spite of the fundamental transformation it undergoes, the risen body remains a real human body, even retaining sexual difference." [Der auferstandene Leib bleibt trotz der grundlegenden Verwandlung, die er erfährt, ein wahrer Menschenleib, auch der Unterschied der Geschlechter bleibt bestehen.]

91. The only instance I am aware of where Ratzinger mentions *De Civitate Dei* XXII is his citation of the passage on the eternal rest from *civ. Dei* 22.30 (the conclusion of the entire *De Civitate Dei*) at the very end of his doctoral dissertation (*Volk und Haus Gottes*, 327–28).

Part Two: Crucial Distinctions in Ratzinger's Theology of Resurrection

empty and nebulous. This problem makes itself felt particularly when considering Ratzinger's use of *memoria*.

We may begin to find a way out, however, since our Augustinian reference point is Augustine's *mature* thought on the resurrection. This only gets us halfway out, however, for while it is true that Augustine does not use the concept of *memoria*-time in any of his discussions of post-death existence, it is also true that he never rejected the idea in his later thought. This raises the double question of whether that concept is compatible with an understanding of post-death time and, if so, why Augustine did not make this connection himself.

As regards the first, since Augustine did not declare the intermediate state to be atemporal there would seem to be no reason that his psychological understanding of time would not hold after death. Regarding the second, his failure to connect explicitly his concept of time from *Confessions* with his understanding of the post-death period is more than likely due to the lack of an appropriate occasion which would have prompted him to defend post-death time. Ratzinger, however, *was* faced with such a controversy, and so his use of Augustine's concept of *memoria*-time can be seen as an authentic development of Augustine's thought, even if Augustine himself did not apply the idea to his own theology of resurrection.

5

The Body and the Flesh?

The Leib-Körper *Distinction*

Augustinian Background

We have seen how Augustine for a time maintained a distinction between *corpus* (body) and *caro* (flesh) in the resurrection, based largely on his reading of 1 Cor 15:50 ("flesh and blood cannot inherit the kingdom of God"). In this rather Origenistic view, the "spiritual body" (*sōma pneumatikōn, corpus spiritale*; 1 Cor 15:44) is understood to be purely spiritual and lacking matter and flesh. Thus, the resurrection can be said to be bodily, but not material or fleshly. Augustine, however, soon rejected this distinction, as evidenced in his later writings on resurrection. In his mature theology, the resurrection is truly a *resurrectio carnis*: "For 'flesh' in the sense of its substance, in accordance with the words, *A spirit does not have flesh and blood, as you see that I have* (Lk 24:39), will possess the kingdom of God, but 'flesh' when understood in the sense of its corruption will not possess it."[1] The "spiritual body" is now no longer seen as immaterial, for

---

1. Augustine, *ep.* 205.2.16. See also *c. Jul.* 6.40.

Part Two: Crucial Distinctions in Ratzinger's Theology of Resurrection

just as the spirit is not improperly called carnal when it serves the flesh, so shall the flesh rightly be called spiritual when it serves the spirit. This is not because flesh will be converted into spirit, which is what some have inferred from what is written: "It is sown a natural body, it is raised a spiritual body" [1 Cor 15:44]. Rather, it is because it will be subject to the spirit with a supreme and marvellous readiness to obey, and will fulfil its will in the most assured knowledge of indestructible immortality, with all distress, all corruptibility and all reluctance gone.[2]

When Augustine began to distinguish between flesh as substance and flesh as corruption, he was free to acknowledge 1 Cor 15:50 while simultaneously allowing for the resurrection of the material substance of the human body. He effectively transformed the flesh-body distinction into a distinction between two ways of considering flesh. This conceptual move is the condition for Augustine's material understanding of the resurrection.

The Origin of the *Leib-Körper* Distinction

Something analogous to Augustine's early distinction between *corpus* and *caro* has developed in the German language. The words *Leib* and *Körper* can both be translated into English as "body" and possess only slightly different senses in everyday speech. *Leib*, etymologically related to the English word *life*, is the word used in German translations of Scripture for one's body. *Leib* has traditionally intended the full semantic range of the Latin *corpus*. It can even denote physicality, as in the Hail Mary ("gebenedeit ist die Frucht deines Leibes, Jesus!"), where it stands in for the Latin *ventris*. Generally, however, it covers the same semantic range as the English *body*. *Körper*, etymologically related to *corpus*, is in many ways synonymous with *Leib*, but it possesses the additional signification of any three-dimensional object in space and is thus used in geometry and physics.[3] In virtually all traditional theological usage, however (e.g., in speaking of the body of Christ), *Leib* is used.

With the phenomenology of Edmund Husserl, however, a clearer distinction was introduced between *Leib* and *Körper* wherein *Körper* stands for the physical, objective body and *Leib* stands for the lived or

---

2. Augustine, *civ. Dei* 13.20. Also, *civ. Dei* 22.21.

3. E.g., "Körper," in *Wörterbuch der deutschen Gegenwartssprache*, 2201. Conversely, the same dictionary's first definition for *Leib* is *Körper*.

experienced body.⁴ Because of the linguistic particularities of this distinction, special care must be taken when dealing with translations.⁵

The *Leib-Körper* distinction arose in phenomenology in order to allow reflection on the body from the point of view of human experience. In its original, Husserlian context, it had nothing to do with resurrection or eschatology. Greshake, however, suggests that the distinction actually has metaphysical roots in the theology of Thomas Aquinas, who stated that a body (*Leib*) separated from its soul is only equivocally called a body.⁶ In this way, one could say (using Husserl's terminology) that what was formerly an animated body (*Leib*) becomes a mere *Körper* when no longer inhabited by the subject or soul.

It is not difficult to see that the transposition of this distinction into the theology of resurrection will have consequences for the resurrection's materiality, inasmuch as *Körper* is identified with materiality and physiology, while *Leib* is associated with subjectivity and inner experience.

---

4. Husserl, *Cartesianische Meditationen*. The *Leib-Körper* disctinction is employed throughout the Fifth Meditation. Something of a definition is found on 128. I provide the German text since the available English translation is highly paraphrastic. "Unter den eigenheitlich gefaßten Körpern dieser *Natur* finde ich dann in einziger Auszeichnung meinen Leib, nämlich als den einzigen, der nicht bloßer Körper ist, sondern eben Leib, das einzige Objekt innerhalb meiner abstraktiven Weltschicht, dem ich erfahrungsgemäß Empfindungsfelder zurechne, obschon in verschiedenen Zugehörigkeitsweisen (tastempfindungsfeld, Wärme-Kälte-Feld usw.), das einzige, *in dem ich unmittelbar schalte und walte*, und insonderheit walte in jedem seiner *Organe–*." Also, cf. Ricoeur's discussion of Husserl's Fifth Cartesian Meditation: "the owned body (*corps propre* or *Leib*), the body which I move, with which I perceive, by which I express myself. This body serves as reference pole for all physical bodies (*Körper*)" (Ricoeur, *Husserl*, 121).

5. For example, considerable confusion can arise when reading English translations of phenomenological works, as the French tradition, following Merleau-Ponty, uses the word *chair* (flesh) as roughly equivalent to *Leib*, while *corps* (body), the French cognate of *Körper*, connotes physicality and objectivity. This can result in confusing English translations of French works, as evidenced in Ricoeur's apparent (to the English reader!) statement that Husserl utilized "the distinction between flesh and body" (Ricoeur, *Oneself as Another*). In this case the distinction sounds exactly like Augustine's flesh-body (*caro-corpus*) distinction, but the meanings are actually reversed. Additionally, the published English translation of *Eschatology* generally renders both *leiblich* and *körperlich* as "corporeal," eliding the important distinction.

6. Greshake, "Leib-Seele-Problematik," 163 n. 16. He cites Aquinas' *Quaestiones Disputatae de Anima* 2,239; An. 9c. What Thomas actually says is that an organ like an eye can only equivocally be called an eye when the soul has departed. The general meaning holds, however.

Part Two: Crucial Distinctions in Ratzinger's Theology of Resurrection

Ratzinger's Early Theology: Leib *and* Körper *Distinguished*

In Ratzinger's early works, right up to and including *Eschatologie* (1977), he utilizes the *Leib-Körper* distinction. The first evidence of this is his 1957 encyclopedia entry "Auferstehungsleib," in which he speaks of "der Nachfolgekörper (=Leichnam) des ehemals belebten Leibes."[7] He also approvingly cites Hengstenberg's distinction between *Körperlichkeit*, which passes away, and *Leiblichkeit*, which endures, the latter of which is based on Origen's *eidos to karakterizon* (characteristic form).[8]

Einführung in das Christentum: Resurrection of the *Leib*, Not the *Körper*

In Ratzinger's rather dismissive discussion of Greek anthropology in *Einführung*, he repeatedly places the *Körper* (rather than the *Leib*) as the counterpart to the soul.[9] This linguistic setting of the stage allows him to state that, in contradistinction to Greek thought, Scripture speaks of "the raising of the dead (not of physical bodies [*der Körper*]!)"[10] and that "the real core of resurrection faith in no way consists in the idea of the restoration of physical bodies [*der Körper*]."[11] He asserts this most clearly when he claims that according to both John 6:63 and 1 Cor 15:50, "the 'resurrection of the flesh,' the 'resurrection of *bodies*' [*der Leiber*] is not a 'resurrection of *physical bodies*' [*der Körper*]."[12] Here, the *Körper* is definitely excluded from the resurrection.

---

7. Ratzinger, "Auferstehungsleib," 1053. Because this section is focused on the German language, passages that involve the terms *Leib* and *Körper* may when necessary be left untranslated except in footnotes. Here, Ratzinger is speaking of "the physical successor (= corpse) of the once animated body."

8. Ibid. Although Ratzinger provides no reference, he appears to have in mind Hengstenberg, *Der Leib und die letzten Dinge*, particularly 195ff. There, Hengstenberg is attempting to develop the *Leib-Körper* distinction along the lines of Scheler's phenomenology.

9. Ratzinger, *Einführung*, 331.

10. Ibid. "die Auferweckung der Toten (nicht der Körper!)"

11. Ibid. "der eigentliche Kern des Auferstehungsglaubens gar nicht in der Idee der Rückgabe der Körper besteht."

12. Ibid., 339. Italics in original. "Die 'Auferstehung des Fleisches', die 'Auferstehung der *Leiber*' nicht eine 'Auferstehung der *Körper* ist." Ratzinger's interpretation here of John 6:63 ("It is the spirit that gives life, the flesh is of no avail; the words that I have spoken to you are spirit and life") is puzzling, since the context—Jesus' repeated calls to eat his flesh (e.g., John 6:51, 53, 54, 55, 56)—requires a distinction between two senses

The Body and the Flesh?

Eschatologie: A More Ambiguous *Leib-Körper* Distinction

In *Eschatologie*, the *Leib-Körper* distinction is still employed, but it is no longer used in a way that excludes the *Körper* from the resurrection. For example, at one point Ratzinger makes a distinction between *Körper* (physical body) and *Leiblichkeit* (embodiment, bodiliness), yet in this case he argues (against Greshake, who at this point denied the soul) that it is the soul that makes this distinction possible: "The material elements which compose the human *Körper* receive their quality as '*Leib*' only through the fact that they are organized and thoroughly impressed by the soul's expressive power. A distinction between '*Körper*' and 'embodiment' [*Leiblichkeit*] is thus possible, which Origen had already attempted with his idea of characteristic form but which he could not yet formulate with the conceptual tools he had available."[13] It is thus the soul that makes the material components of the *Körper* into a *Leib*. Ratzinger explains this further: "Just as the soul, on the one hand, is now defined by matter, so conversely the *Leib* is defined completely by the soul: *Leib*, and precisely the identical *Leib*, is that which the soul builds as its physical-corporeal [*körperlichen*] expression. Precisely because embodiment now belongs so inseparably to human existence, the identity of embodiment [*Leiblichkeit*]

---

of flesh: one that gives eternal life, and one that does not. It is the latter that Jesus declares to be useless. Ratzinger, however, seems to be taking it as a metaphysical injunction against materiality. This is particularly evident when he repeats his interpretation of Paul (*Einführung*, 340): "Let us say this once more: Paul teaches not the resurrection of the physical body, but the resurrection of persons. This is not at all the return of the 'body of flesh,' that is, of the biological structure, which Paul explicitly designates as impossible ('the perishable cannot become imperishable'), but rather the otherness of the life of the resurrection, as it was modeled in the risen Lord." [Paulus lehrt, um es noch einmal zu sagen, nicht die Auferstehung der Körper, sondern der Personen, und dies gerade nicht in der Wiederkehr der 'Fleischesleiber,' das heißt der biologischen Gebilde, die er ausdrücklich als unmöglich bezeichnet ('das Vergängliche kann nicht unvergänglich werden'), sondern in der Andersartigkeit des Lebens der Auferstehung, wie es im auferstandenen Herrn vorgebildet ist.]

13. Ratzinger, *Eschatologie*, 144 (*Eschatology*, 179). "Die materiellen Elemente, die den menschlichen Körper aufbauen, ihre Qualität als 'Leib' nur dadurch empfangen, daß sie von der Ausdruckskraft der Seele organisiert und durchprägt werden. Es wird eine Unterscheidung zwischen 'Körper' und 'Leiblichkeit' möglich, die Origenes mit seinem Gedanken der charakteristischen Gestalt schon gesucht hatte, aber mit seinen Denkmitteln noch nicht formulieren konnte." In 1990, however, Ratzinger clearly stated that Hengstenberg's distinction between Körper and Leiblichkeit was useful but did not itself amount to a resurrection (*Nachwort zur 6. Auflage, Eschatologie*, 192).

is not determined by matter but by the soul."[14] In this case, the *Leib* is the physical-corporeal expression of the soul, and *Leiblichkeit* (embodiment) is not determined by matter, but by the soul. This is stated most neatly when Ratzinger clarifies, "Der Körper wird zum 'Leib' von der Person-mitte her; Leiblichkeit ist etwas anderes als eine Summe von Körpern."[15] In none of the above statements from *Eschatologie*, however, do we find that notion that was expressed in *Einführung*: that the *Leib* can exist apart from the *Körper*. Ratzinger still draws a distinction between *Leib* and *Körper*, but he does not explicitly exclude the *Körper* from salvation as he does in *Einführung*.

1 Corinthians 15:50: A New Interpretation in *Eschatologie*

Since 1 Cor 15:50 is the focal point of Augustine's body-flesh distinction, it is interesting to consider Ratzinger's treatment of this passage. His early interpretation closely follows Augustine's early theology in that the physical body—the *Körper*—is excluded from salvation. We have already seen how he expresses this in *Einführung*,[16] where he states that verse 50 is "a sort of key to the whole"[17] of 1 Cor 15. For this statement he was scathingly criticized by his later ally, Candido Pozo, who singled out Ratzinger as the leading representative of a "new tendency" to spiritualize the resurrection. According to Pozo, Ratzinger's exegesis in *Einführung* is discordant with the theology of the second-century Fathers and "reproduce[s] an extraordinarily spiritualizing and Platonic tone."[18]

---

14. Ibid., 145 (*Eschatology*, 179). "So wie die Seele sich nun einerseits von Materie her definiert, so ist umgekehrt der Leib ganz von der Seele definiert: Leib, und zwar identischer Leib, ist das, was die Seele sich als ihren körperlichen Ausdruck baut. Gerade weil die Leiblichkeit nun so unlösbar zum Menschsein gehört, wird die Identität der Leiblichkeit nicht von der Materie, sondern von der Seele her bestimmt."

15. Ibid., 146 (*Eschatology*, 181). "The physiological body becomes a living body by means of the person; bodiliness is more than a sum of physiological parts."

16. Ratzinger, *Intro.*, 356–58 (*Einführung*, 338–40). This is discussed above, in chapter 4.

17. Ibid., 356 (*Einführung*, 338).

18. Pozo, "Problemática," 516–18. Pozo declares that Ratzinger's claim that verse 50 is the "key to the whole" is surprising for anyone who knows the history of this verse in the controversies of the second century. He also takes issue with Ratzinger's claim that *soma* can mean both *sarx* and *pneuma*. He claims that Ratzinger's explanations "sound very far off from the ecclesiastical realism of the resurrection and reproduce an extraordinarily spiritualizing and Platonic tone." [suenan muy lejos del realismo eclesiastico de

The Body and the Flesh?

In *Eschatologie*, however, Ratzinger's reading of 1 Cor 15:50 undergoes a noticeable shift. "Here, every naturalistic or physicalistic view of the resurrection is emphatically cut off. All speculations which might conceive of how the perishable might become imperishable are rendered superfluous: according to Paul, this will just not happen. But the absoluteness with which Paul opposes naturalistic conceptions does prevent him from speaking even further of the resurrection of the *body* [*Leibes*], which is something other than a return of the 'physical body' [*Körper*] according to the manner of this world."[19] In this case, Ratzinger does not claim that 1 Cor 15:50 proves there is *no* "Auferstehung der Körper"[20] but rather that it indicates that the resurrection is *something other than* receiving again one's earthly *Körper* as it exists in the present world. Here, the *Leib-Körper* distinction is employed, but not in the exclusionary way that it is used in *Einführung*. In both works Ratzinger is concerned to guard against an extreme physicalism, but in *Eschatologie* his rhetoric is more careful so as not to exclude physicality utterly from the resurrection.

He goes on to explain Paul's understanding of body, this time avoiding that exegesis from *Einführung* that had been criticized by Pozo:

> For Paul, contradicting naturalism does not mean abandoning the resurrection but rather allows it to be seen correctly. Paul conceives of "body" not only in the Adamic sense of the "ensouled body" but also in the christological sense modeled on the resurrection of Jesus Christ, as embodiment on the basis of the Holy Spirit. What is opposed to a physicalist realism is not a spiritualism, but a pneumatic realism. With this dialectic, the Pauline text does not merely evoke all the Evangelists' accounts of the Lord's resurrection (Mussner 101–106), but also the inner tension which is stamped upon the eucharistic chapter of John's Gospel (ch. 6). Here, against the spiritualistic evaporation

---

la resurreccion y reproducen un tono extrañamente espiritualizante y platonico.] Pozo speaks of "the new tendency" to spiritualize the resurrection, and cites Ratzinger as the primary (and only) representative of this new tendency.

19. Ratzinger, *Eschatologie*, 137 (*Eschatology*, 169). Emphasis in original. "Jede naturalistische und physizistische Sicht der Auferstehung ist hier mit Nachdruck abgeschnitten. Damit sind auch Spekulationen überflüssig gemacht, die ersinnen sollen, wie das Vergängliche doch unvergänglich werden könne: Eben dies wird nach Paulus nicht geschehen. Aber die Unbedingtheit, mit der Paulus hier naturalistische Konzeptionen entgegentritt, hindert ihn doch nicht daran, auch weiterhin von Auferstehung des *Leibes* zu sprechen, die etwas anderes ist als Wiederkehr der 'Körper' nach der Weise dieser Welt."

20. Ratzinger, *Einführung*, 339.

Part Two: Crucial Distinctions in Ratzinger's Theology of Resurrection

> of faith, Church, and sacrament, stands the hard realism of the sayings: "My flesh is true food, and my blood is true drink. Whoever eats my flesh and drinks my blood remains in me and I in him" (v. 55f.). On the other hand, against a naturalistic conception of the Risen One and of his presence in the Church's liturgy stands the stark saying, which seems to directly wipe out what was said previously but in reality first shows us its true meaning: "It is the Spirit that gives life, the flesh is useless" (v. 63). The "flesh" of Christ is "Spirit," but the Spirit of Christ is "flesh": only within this tension can we see through all naturalisms and spiritualisms to the unique, new realism of the Risen One.[21]

This is a clear shift with respect to *Einführung*. Here, Ratzinger does not deny the "fleshliness" of the risen body, but places the concept of flesh within a spirit-flesh dialectic based on 1 Cor 15:44 and John 6.

In this new understanding of 1 Cor 15:50, Ratzinger now emphatically rejects spiritualism but still remains uncertain as to the degree of the resurrection's materiality. He thus concludes that "as regards the materiality of this resurrection, virtually everything remains open. The total otherness of the resurrection is strikingly asserted. What is positively meant by the resurrection's pneumatic realism, which is opposed to spiritualization, cannot be immediately determined."[22]

---

21. Ratzinger, *Eschatologie*, 137–38 (*Eschatology*, 169–70). "Die Bestreitung des Naturalismus bedeutet für ihn nicht die Preisgabe der Auferstehung, sondern erst deren richtiges Sichtbarwerden. Leib gibt es für ihn nicht nur in der adamischen Weise des 'seelenhaften Leibes', sondern auch in der von der Auferstehung Jesu Christi her vorgebildeten christologischen Weise, als Leibhaftigkeit vom Heiligen Geist her. Dem physizistischen Realismus wird nicht ein Spiritualismus, sondern ein pneumatischer Realismus entgegengestellt. Mit dieser Dialektik erinnert der paulinische Text nicht bloß an alle Berichte der Evangelisten über die Auferstehung des Herrn (Mußner 101–6), sondern auch an die innere Spannung, die das eucharistische Kapitel des Johannes Evangeliums (Kap. 6) prägt. Gegen die spiritualistische Verflüchtigung von Glaube, Kirche und Sakrament steht hier der harte Realismus der Sätze: 'Mein Fleisch ist eine wahre Speise, und mein Blut ein wahrer Trank. Wer mein Fleisch ißt und mein Blut trinkt, der bleibt in mir und ich in ihm' (Vers 55f.). Gegen eine naturalistische Fassung des Auferstandenen und seiner Präsenz im Gottesdienst der Kirche steht aber umgekehrt der schroffe Satz, der das Vorige geradezu auszustreichen scheint, es in Wahrheit aber erst in seiner wirklichen Bedeutung zu sehen lehrt: 'Der Geist ist's, der Leben schafft; das Fleisch nützt nichts' (Vers 63). Das 'Fleisch' Christi ist 'Geist', aber der Geist Christi ist 'Fleisch': Nur in dieser Spannung wird der besondere und neue Realismus des Auferstandenen durch alle Naturalismen und Spiritualismen hindurch sichtbar." Here, the published English translation unfortunately omits the sentence "The 'flesh' of Christ is 'Spirit,' but the Spirit of Christ is 'flesh.'"

22. Ibid., 139 (*Eschatology*, 172). "Hinsichtlich der Materialität dieser Auferstehung

The Body and the Flesh?

Greshake, unsurprisingly, considers all this to be "illegitimate exegesis."[23] In his view, Paul does not expect a spiritual *body*, but a *person* filled with God's Spirit.[24] In any case, Ratzinger seems to be moving closer to the realism of Augustine's mature view that in the resurrection, the flesh will be spiritualized without becoming spirit and ceasing to be flesh.[25]

Ratzinger's Later Theology: The Material Leib

In *Eschatologie*, Ratzinger lays out an anthropology wherein the material *Körper* becomes *Leib* through the soul's power. It is very interesting to note, however, that when attacking Greshake and his theory of "resurrection in death," Ratzinger always abandons the *Leib-Körper* distinction altogether and instead associates the *Leib* with materiality. In this way, there are two different currents of thought in *Eschatologie* regarding the *Leib-Körper* distinction.

Eschatologie: The Dead *Leib* and Augustinianism

Against Greshake, Ratzinger asks, "with what right can one speak of '*Leiblichkeit*' if any connection to matter is explicitly denied?"[26] He rejects "resurrection in death" because in this theory "the *Leib* is definitively deleted

---

bleibt nahezu alles offen. Ihr Ganz-anders wird eindringlich behauptet. Was ihr pneumatischer Realismus, der den Spiritualisierungen entgegengehalten wird, positiv bedeutet, ist zunächst nicht auszumachen."

23. Greshake, "Leib-Seele-Problematik," 175. "According to Ratzinger, 1 Cor 15 is supposed to provide evidence that Paul, in spite of rejecting that naturalistic and physicalistic view of the *Anastasis*, still held a resurrection of the *body*. That appears to me to be illegitimate exegesis!" [Nach Ratzinger soll 1 Kor 15 dafür den Beweis abgeben, daß Paulus trotz Ablehnung jeder naturalistischen und phyzistischen Sicht der Anastasis dennoch eine Auferstehung des *Leibes* vertritt. Aber das scheint mir eine unzulässige Exegese zu sein!]

24. Ibid., 176.

25. Augustine, *civ. Dei* 22.21. "The flesh will then be spiritual, and subject to the spirit; but it will still be flesh and not spirit."

26. Ratzinger, *Eschatologie*, 94 (*Eschatology*, 109). "Solche Gedanken mögen sinnvoll sein; es fragt sich nur, mit welchem Recht man dann noch von 'Leiblichkeit' sprechen kann, wenn ausdrücklich jede Beziehung zur Materie bestritten ist."

Part Two: Crucial Distinctions in Ratzinger's Theology of Resurrection

from the hope of salvation"[27] and is "given up to death."[28] He further argues that "resurrection in death" detemporalizes the resurrection, and "this detemporalization implied a dematerialization, since it is obvious that in the moment of death man does not rise physically [*körperlich*]."[29] Here, Ratzinger's rhetoric implies that resurrection ought to be material.

Concerning the above statements, Sonnemans believes Ratzinger has made his discussion with Greshake more difficult "through a terminologically inappropriate portrayal of the problem."[30] He alleges that Ratzinger fails to recognize that "it is not just a question of the physical-corporeal [*körperliche*], but rather of the *bodily* [*leibhafte*] resurrection."[31] Sonnemans notes that "Ratzinger seems to associate *Leiblichkeit* with the corpse; and thereby introduces a new theme which has the totality of the *material* in view, while Greshake exludes this aspect at the outset."[32]

Sonnemans suggests that Ratzinger's argument against Greshake's supposed dematerialization of the resurrection is invalid because Greshake's theory can allow for the resurrection of a man who has just died, "as long as one properly holds the distinction between *Körper* and *Leib*."[33] Sonnemans flatly contradicts Ratzinger's accusation that in "resurrection in death" the *Leib* is given up to death, claiming that what is really

---

27. Ibid., 96 (*Eschatology*, 112). "Zum einen wird in solchen Modellen der Leib definitiv aus der Hoffnung des Heils gestrichen."

28. Ibid., 94 (*Eschatology*, 109). "Jedenfalls wird auch in diesem Modell der Leib dem Tod überlassen und gleichzeitig ein Fortleben des Menschen behauptet."

29. Ibid., 134 (*Eschatology*, 165). "diese Entzeitlichung hatte eine Entmaterialisierung zur Folge, denn daß der Mensch im Augenblick des Todes nicht körperlich aufersteht, liegt auf der Hand."

30. Sonnemans, *Seele*, 432. "Dabei erschwert Ratzinger die Auseinandersetzung durch eine terminologisch nicht angemessene Darstellung des Problems."

31. Ibid. "es geht aber eben nicht um die körperliche, sondern um die *leibhafte* Auferstehung."

32. Ibid. "Ratzinger scheint die *Leiblichkeit* mit dem Leichnam in Verbindung zu setzen: damit schneidet er aber ein neues Thema an, das die Gesamt-Aspekt des *Materiellen* im Auge hat, während Greshake diesen Aspekt zunächst ausklammert." Italics in original. Sonnemans goes on to note that thanks to the Leib-Körper distinction, Greshake holds a new kind of Leiblichkeit that is not based on the earthly Körper (left behind as a corpse). He also notes that this is essentially a preservation of Ratzinger's early theology (i.e., in *Einführung*).

33. Ibid., 441. "Allerdings scheint die empirische Feststellung, daß der Mensch im Tode *nicht körperlich* aufersteht, kein Argument gegen den Ansatz Greshakes zu sein, der für den eben Verstorbenen die Auferstehung fordert, solange man den Unterschied von Körper und Leib aufrechterhält." Italics in original.

The Body and the Flesh?

given up is only the *Leichnam* (corpse) and not the *Leib*.[34] Sonnemans, however, does not see this as a shift in Ratzinger's thought so much as an inconsistency. He can thus say, "therefore one cannot claim as Ratzinger does that the '*Leib*' has been deleted from the salvific economy. Because what stays behind is not at all the *Leib* but rather the 'dead *Leib*', the 'dead *Körper*', the 'corpse'. The identity of the risen body is not bound up with that of the earthly *Körper*. If Ratzinger wanted to claim an identity of the risen body with the earthly *Körper*, his position would have to be significantly modified."[35] We will note two things here. First, as Sonnemans admits, Ratzinger's argument here fails *only if* one maintains the *Leib-Körper* distinction. It is thus interesting that in the ongoing argument, Ratzinger has abandoned that distinction (something which was not yet evident to Sonnemans in 1985). Second, Sonnemans rightly observes that up to that point (i.e., the writing of *Eschatologie*), Ratzinger's theology had in many ways incorporated a distinction between *Leib* and *Körper*, so that a rejection of the distinction would require a reworked (or at least, a reinterpreted) position.

While there is no question that in *Eschatologie*, Ratzinger uses *Leib-Körper* terminology, it is also clear that he does not use it in the same way Greshake does. Greshake would certainly agree with Ratzinger that "The *Körper* becomes a '*Leib*' by means of the person,"[36] and that in the *Leib*, "matter comes under the soul's power of expression."[37] A *Körper* can thus become a *Leib* by means of the person or soul, a concept for which Greshake finds support in Thomistic hylomorphism. But the real issue is: what happens when the soul (or, to use Greshake's earlier terminology, the "subjectivity") leaves the *Leib*? According to Greshake, it immediately reverts to a *Körper*, a corpse. For him, the effects of "the soul's power of expression" cease immediately at the point of death. In this sense, Greshake is following closely what Ratzinger considers a "strict Thomism." But we have already seen that because of this problem of *materia prima* and the

34. Ibid. He is referring to *Eschatologie*, 94 (cited above).

35. Ibid., 441–42. "Deshalb kann man nicht wie Ratzinger behaupten, daß der 'Leib' aus der Heilsordnung gestrichen werde. Denn was bleibt, ist ja nicht der 'Leib', sondern der 'tote Leib', der 'tote Körper', der 'Leichnam'. Die Identität des Auferstehungsleibes ist aber nicht an die mit dem irdischen Körper gebunden. Wenn Ratzinger doch eine Identität des Auferstehungsleibes mit dem irdischen Körper fordern wollte, dann hätte sich seine Position wohl verändert."

36. Ratzinger, *Eschatologie*, 146 (*Eschatology*, 181). "Der Körper wird zum 'Leib' von der Personmitte her."

37. Ibid., 144–45 (*Eschatology*, 179).

Part Two: Crucial Distinctions in Ratzinger's Theology of Resurrection

seemingly insoluble issues it poses, Ratzinger believes that such a "strict Thomism is certainly no way to proceed."[38]

Since in *Eschatologie* Ratzinger can speak of a dead *Leib*—a concept that would be an oxymoron for Greshake—it appears that Ratzinger is either (as Sonnemans suggests) simply using inappropriate terminology, or beginning to articulate a new position. Might he in fact be arguing for something like the medieval Augustinian notion of the *forma corporeitas*, by which a dead body remains a real body? In any case, the question cannot be resolved by recourse to *Eschatologie* alone. We will have to look further.

1980 to the Present: The Conspicuous Absence of the *Körper*

Within *Eschatologie*, there seem at first to be two opposing approaches to the *Leib-Körper* distinction. This seeming contradiction has been noted by both Sonnemans and Greshake.[39] It is remarkable, however, that after *Eschatologie*, Ratzinger never again uses the word *Körper* when describing the resurrection, preferring instead to speak only of the *Leib*.[40] This is the case even when materiality is at issue. We thus have a *Leib* which now appears to cover the entire semantic range of *Leib* and *Körper* in Ratzinger's earlier theology.

---

38. Ibid., 146 (*Eschatology*, 181).

39. Greshake, "Leib-Seele-Problematik," 163. Here, Greshake defends himself from Ratzinger's criticisms, noting that even Ratzinger recognizes that "Es wird eine Unterscheidung zwischen 'Körper' und 'Leiblichkeit' möglich." (*Eschatologie*, 144).

40. While it is difficult to prove a universal negative, it is true that in every post-1977 Ratzinger text cited in this work, neither the word *Körper* nor any of its variants is used when describing the dead or risen body. When commenting on a popular trend in modern theology, however, Ratzinger very recently observed that "most commentators . . . conclude that the question of the empty tomb is immaterial and can therefore be ignored, which tends also to mean that it probably was not empty anyway, so at least a dispute with modern science over the possibility of a bodily [*körperlich*] resurrection can be avoided." Ratzinger, *Jesus of Nazareth II*, 253–54. German text in Ratzinger, *Jesus von Nazareth II*, 279. In this case, however, Ratzinger is not using the *Leib-Körper* distinction but rather simply describing (disapprovingly) how many modern theologians find a physical bodily resurrection impossible. Later on the same page, he declares that the empty tomb "is nevertheless a necessary condition for Resurrection faith, which was specifically concerned with the body [*Leib*] and, consequently, with the whole of the person."

The Body and the Flesh?

Thus, in "Zwischen Tod und Auferstehung" (1980), Ratzinger is now consistent when he speaks only of the *Leib* in condemning Greshake's idea of "resurrection in death":

> But now, however, a question arises. According to these considerations, man is absolutely indivisible; without the body there is no man: this is what drives people to seek out this way of thinking. But it cannot be doubted that after death, man's *body* remains in space and time. It does not rise, but is laid in the tomb. So this detemporalization which reigns beyond death does not hold good for the body. But what, then, does it hold good for, if nothing in man is separable from the body? Or is there still something which, amid the spatio-temporal disintegration of the body, endures and is distinguishable from the body, which steps outside of time, which now finally takes the body completely into its possession? But if there is such a something, why should it not properly be called a soul? And how can it properly be called a body, since it clearly has nothing to do with man's historical body and its materiality? And how is there in fact now no dualism if a second, post-death body is posited (and how could it be otherwise?) whose origin and mode of existence remain obscure?[41]

As we noted previously, this passage is part of a *reductio ad absurdum* in which Ratzinger attempts to illustrate the incoherence of "resurrection in death." We should therefore clarify that Ratzinger does *not* hold that (1) there is a detemporalization beyond death, (2) nothing in man is separable from the body, (3) the soul steps outside of time at death, or (4) in death the soul takes the body completely into its possession. These are all theses Ratzinger attributes to Greshake (although Greshake would deny that he holds the first and third).

41. Ratzinger, "Zwischen Tod und Auferstehung" (*Eschatologie*, 214–15; *Eschatology*, 252–53). "Aber nun steht die Frage auf. Der Mensch ist nach diesen Überlegungen schlechthin unteilbar; ohne den Leib gibt es ihn nicht: Deswegen mußte man ja diesen Denkweg suchen. Nun bleibt aber nach dem Tod der *Leib* des Menschen unzweifelhaft in der Zeit und im Raum. Er steht nicht auf, sondern wird ins Grab gelegt. Für den Leib gilt also die Entzeitlichung nicht, die jenseits des Todes herrscht. Aber für wen gilt sie dann, wenn nichts am Menschen vom Leib abtrennbar ist? Oder gibt es da doch etwas, was im zeiträumlichen Zersetzwerden des Leibes von ihm unterscheidbar besteht und aus der Zeit heraustritt, die ihn nun erst vollends in Besitz nimmt? Wenn es aber ein solches Etwas gibt, warum darf man es dann eigentlich nicht Seele nennen? Und mit welchem Recht kann man es eigentlich Leib nennen, da es doch mit dem geschichtlichem Leib des Menschen und seiner Materialität offenkundig nichts zu tun hat? Wieso ist es nun eigentlich kein Dualismus, wenn man nach dem Tod einen zweiten Leib postuliert (das muß man doch wohl?), dessen Herkunft und Existenzart dunkel bleiben?"

Part Two: Crucial Distinctions in Ratzinger's Theology of Resurrection

Nonetheless, within this passage we can identify some characteristics that Ratzinger assumes to belong to the *Leib*. These include (1) spatio-temporality, (2) historicity and materiality, and (3) post-death disintegration (i.e., the *Leib* is equated with the corpse). Greshake, of course, would not accept that a dead body can properly be called a *Leib*, yet the rejection of this distinction (at least with respect to the dead body) is itself the key to Ratzinger's argument. The *Leib-Körper* distinction allows Greshake to maintain a resurrection of the body while simultaneously stating that (following Karl Rahner) "matter 'in itself' (as atom, molecule, organ . . .) is imperfectible."[42] Unwilling to deny the salvation of matter "in itself," Ratzinger's polemic with Greshake induced him to reject what could be considered the dualism of the *Leib-Körper* distinction.

In 1987, Ratzinger discussed Hengstenberg's distinction between *Körperlichkeit* and *Leiblichkeit* and considered Johann Auer's attempt to further develop it. Auer makes a distinction between *Leibhaftigkeit* and *konkretem Leib*.[43] In this case, the *Leib* dies and goes back to the earth, whereas *Leibhaftigkeit* (bodiliness) is a metaphysical property and is incorruptible.[44] Auer essentially replaces Hengstenberg's *Körper* with the idea of a material *Leib*.

Ratzinger writes that in following Hengstenberg, Auer

> distinguishes betweeen the concrete phenomenon *"Körper"* (*Leib*), and *"Leiblichkeit"* as the metaphysical principle of man's constitution. While the *Leib* dies, the metaphysical parameter *"Leiblichkeit"* remains as the reality that essentially determines man. The distinction between *"Leib"* (physical) and *"Leiblichkeit"* (metaphysical) is as such undoubtedly valid and helpful. But it does not solve the question of the concrete bearer of *"Leiblichkeit"* and therefore does not solve the current problem either. For the fact that metaphysical *"Leiblichkeit"* belongs to man even after death shows the constancy of a metaphysical constitution, but not the event of "resurrection." This distinction may be held

---

42. Greshake, *Auferstehung der Toten*, 386. "Die Materie 'in sich' (als Atom, Molekül, Organ . . .) ist unvollendbar." Also, *Auferstehung der Toten*, 379, where Greshake suggests that since the evolutionary process is not goal-oriented, the material world has no *telos*. Here, Greshake cites Rahner, "Transzendente Vollendung," 594: "die physische Welt als solche ist in sich grundsätzlich 'unvollendbar.'"

43. Auer, *Person*, 35.

44. Ibid.

and used, but one cannot derive from it the justification to assert a "resurrection in death."[45]

We will discuss this in more detail later in this book, but we may note here that for Ratzinger, resurrection is not the enduring of a metaphysical principle called *Leiblichkeit* (as it appears to be for Greshake)[46] but is an *event*. This strongly suggests a connection to the matter of this world, since in this conception, resurrection requires something *more* than the soul's own metaphysical constitution. Further, it is clear from the above that Ratzinger's new use of *Leib* cannot be reduced to the meaning of *Leib* in Auer's theology. For Ratzinger, *Leib* is material (as in Auer) as well as metaphysical (as in Greshake).

In "Jungfrauengeburt und leeres Grab" (2004), Ratzinger speaks of the dead *Leib* of Jesus, which must not be "left to rot in the tomb."[47] There is a close correlation between the corpse—the dead *Leib*—and the risen body of Jesus. Christian faith is certain "that Jesus's body did not remain in the tomb and did not undergo decay but was transformed by God's power into the new embodiment of the Risen One."[48] Ratzinger's repeated insistence in "Jungfrauengeburt und leeres Grab" on God's power over

---

45. Ratzinger, *Nachwort zur 6. Auflage* (*Eschatologie*, 192)."J. Auer . . . das Problem durch den Rückgriff auf die Philosophie von H. E. Hengstenberg zu lösen versucht, indem er mit ihm zwischen dem konkreten Phänomen 'Körper' (Leib) und 'Leiblichkeit' als metaphysischem Konstitutionsprinzip des Menschen unterscheidet. Während der Leib sterbe, bleibe die metaphysische Größe 'Leiblichkeit' als wesentlich den Menschen bestimmende Realität bestehen. Die Unterscheidung zwischen 'Leib' (physisch) und 'Leiblichkeit' (metaphysisch) ist als solche ohne Zweifel berechtigt und hilfreich. Sie löst indes nicht die Frage nach dem konkreten Träger von 'Leiblichkeit' und daher auch nicht das hier anstehende Problem. Denn der Tatbestand, daß zum Menschen auch nach dem Tod metaphysisch 'Leiblichkeit' gehört, zeigt die Konstanz einer metaphysischen Konstitution an, aber nicht das Ereignis 'Auferstehung'. So wird man diese Unterscheidung festhalten und nutzen, aber aus ihr nicht die Berechtigung der Behauptung einer 'Auferstehung im Tode' ableiten dürfen." Ratzinger misquotes Auer, who uses the term "Leibhaftigkeit" rather than "Leiblichkeit," although no significant semantic distinction exists between the two words. The published English version of this passage appears in *Eschatology*, 288 n. 4, but seems to be based on a slightly different German text.

46. Greshake, *Resurrectio Mortuorum*, 319–22.

47. Ratzinger, "Jungfrauengeburt." "Und deswegen ist es so wichtig, dass Auferstehung nicht zu einem Interpretament verflüchtigt wird, während man den Leib Jesu im Grab verwesen lässt."

48. Ibid. "Desgleichen gehört es zu diesen historischen Gewissheiten des Glaubens, dass Jesu Leib nicht im Grab geblieben und nicht der Verwesung verfallen, sondern durch die Kraft Gottes in die neue Leiblichkeit des Auferstandenen umgewandelt worden ist."

matter makes it crystal clear that—at least in the case of Jesus—there can be no denial of a material, numerical identity between the dead and risen body. In this way, no significant distinction between *Leib* and *Körper* is possible (nor is it employed). This same insistence is present in volume 2 of *Jesus von Nazareth* (2011), where he speaks of the dead and decomposing *Leib* which also must be raised.[49] Here, Ratzinger does not appear to be concerned in any way with the problems of bodily identity that arose with Thomas Aquinas.

Ratzinger, in the new foreword to the 6th edition of *Eschatologie* (2006), claims that "the bodiliness of Christ, who retains a body in eternity, signifies the taking seriously of history and of matter."[50] Given this and the other developments we have seen in Ratzinger's theology, it is evident that Ratzinger has developed his theology in a way similar to that in which Augustine modified his. This modification has meant "the taking seriously of history and of matter" to the point that Ratzinger now speaks only of the *Leib*, which both dies and is raised. Rather than posit two bodily elements in man (*Leib* and *Körper*), Ratzinger appears to have settled upon only one, the *Leib*. In this way, Ratzinger's development closely parallels that of Augustine, who eventually acknowledged that the flesh was a constitutive component of man and could not be abstracted away from the body, to be dispensed with in the resurrection.

The Document of the International Theological Commission and the *Leib-Körper* Distinction

As Prefect of the Congregation for the Doctrine of the Faith, Ratzinger was *ipso facto* the President of the International Theological Commission. In 1992, the Commission released a document titled *Some Current Questions in Eschatology*. The Commission wrote that "the conceptual separation between a body and a corpse, or the introduction into the notion of body of two diverse concepts (a difference is expressed in German by the words 'Leib' and 'Körper,' while in many other languages it cannot be expressed) are scarcely understood outside academic circles. Pastoral experience shows us that the Christian people are greatly perplexed when they hear sermons affirming that the dead person has already risen while his corpse

---

49. Ratzinger, *Jesus von Nazareth II*, 281 (*Jesus of Nazareth II*, 256).

50. *Vorwort Papst Benedikts XVI. zur Neuausgabe* (*Eschatologie*, 14; *Eschatology*, xxi). "Die Leibhaftigkeit Christi, der in Ewigkeit Leib behält, bedeutet das Ernstnehmen der Geschichte und der Materie."

The Body and the Flesh?

is still buried."[51] The argument here is essentially identical to that given by Ratzinger in *Eschatologie*[52] and "Zwischen Tod und Auferstehung,"[53] but in this case its attack is broadened to explicitly include the *Leib-Körper* distinction itself, which is intrinsically connected to "resurrection in death."[54] Given the similarities between Ratzinger's theology and this and other arguments in the Commission's document, and considering Ratzinger's praising of Pozo's treatment of this very question (only two years earlier),[55] it seems likely that the statements therein correspond to Ratzinger's theology at that time.

A Final Question on Memoria-*Time*

As a postscript to our discussion of the *Leib-Körper* distinction, we must ask whether Ratzinger's concept of *memoria*-time is not itself predicated upon this distinction. In "Jenseits des Todes" and in *Eschatologie*, Ratzinger distinguishes between physical time and *memoria*-time. The first belongs to man "inasmuch as he is *Körper*"[56] and is called *Körperzeit*.[57] One of the main purposes of Ratzinger's theory of *memoria*-time is to show how there can be time beyond death, since physical time (*Körperzeit*) will not exist there. Thus, even though Ratzinger does not explicitly claim that *memoria*-time is the *only* kind of time that might somehow be given "a

51. *Current Questions*, 2.1

52. Ratzinger, *Eschatologie*, 94 (*Eschatology*, 108).

53. Ratzinger, "Zwischen Tod und Auferstehung" (*Eschatologie*, 216; *Eschatology*, 254)

54. This conection is clearly stated by Greshake in "Parteiische Rückblick," 548 n. 40. "I am attempting, completely along the lines of modern anthropology, to differentiate between *Körper* and *Leib*. By '*Körper*' is understood simply that human materiality that is the object of empirical experience and science, which man is always newly 'disposing of' throughout his life, and which he 'disposes of' once and for all in death. By '*Leib*' is meant that concrete-historical impression of man which is irrevocably taken up in the soul as the fruit of being-in-the-world." Greshake then goes on to state that this has a Thomistic basis. [Ganz im Zuge neuzeitlicher Anthropologie versuche ich, zwischen Körper und Leib zu differenzieren, wobei unter Körper eben jene menschliche Materialität verstanden wird, die Gegenstand empirischer Erfahrung und Wissenschaft ist und deren sich der Mensch in seinem Leben stets neu und im Tod einmal endgültig 'entledigt', und unter Leib jene konkret-geschichtliche Prägung des Menschen, die al Frucht des In-der-Welt-Seins in der Seele unverwechselbar aufgehoben ist.]

55. Ratzinger, *Nachwort zur 6. Auflage* (*Eschatologie*, 190).

56. Ratzinger, *Eschatologie*, 147 (*Eschatology*, 183). "sofern er Körper ist."

57. Ibid., 147 (*Eschatology*, 183).

Part Two: Crucial Distinctions in Ratzinger's Theology of Resurrection

continuing existence on a new level,"[58] one could ask: if the resurrection is truly (as Ratzinger claims) a material event,[59] then must physical time, too, be outlawed from the eschaton? Or, does *memoria*-time, imprinted as it is by physical time, somehow include all kinds of time? As we noted above, Ratzinger has made no attempt to work out more systematically the implications of his theory of *memoria*-time.

It is worthy of note, however, that when discussing *memoria*-time in "Das Ende der Zeit" (1998), Ratzinger no longer speaks of *Körperzeit*, nor does he oppose physical time to *memoria*-time. In fact, he speaks of a multiplicity of levels of time such as cosmic time, and the time of history which includes both individuals and cultures.[60] In this more recent treatment of *memoria*-time, *memoria* is not placed in direct opposition to physical time but rather is seen as a possible way of finally summing up all time. It thus appears to have lost something of the dualistic edge present in *Eschatologie*.

Augustinian Evaluation

In the case of the *Leib-Körper* distinction there is a striking similarity between the theological development of both Augustine and Ratzinger. Augustine originally held a kind of Origenist view of resurrection in which the blessed will possess an immaterial body.[61] He derived this from his reading of 1 Cor 15:50, holding that there will be no flesh and blood in the risen body. Ratzinger (also apparently following 1 Cor 15:50) originally held a similar view in which the "resurrection of the body" was understood as a continuance of the whole person, and the body in its material, physical constitution (i.e., the *Körper*) appeared to be excluded from salvation. Both these thinkers, however, eventually came to the conclusion that such views were not consonant with Christian faith. Augustine realized

---

58. Ratzinger, "End of Time," 24.

59. Ratzinger, *Eschatologie*, 131 (*Eschatology*, 160). Ratzinger asks, "Is there such a thing as resurrection understood as a material event?" [Wie steht es denn mit der Auferstehung der Toten? Gibt es so etwas als ein materielles Ereignis?] He goes on to suggest that the answer is yes, and that modern theories are not so much afraid of the immortality of the soul as they are of the scandal of the resurrection.

60. Ratzinger, "End of Time," 4–6.

61. For example, Augustine, *f. et symb.* 10.24, where he states that "at that moment of angelic transformation it will no longer be flesh and blood but only a body" (quia illo tempore immutationis angelicae non iam caro erit et sanguis, sed tantum corpus).

The Body and the Flesh?

that Christ's incarnation meant that flesh and blood cannot be excluded from the resurrection. Ratzinger likewise recognized this, in large part through his controversy with Greshake.

In a sense, one might say that the direction of Greshake's theology represents the logical conclusion of Ratzinger's earlier considerations of resurrection (e.g., in *Einführung*). For if resurrection does not require the matter of this world, then there is no reason that it should not already happen while the history of this world continues on. Given that the *Leib-Körper* distinction is a fundamental presupposition of "resurrection in death," it is not surprising that during the course of the debate, Ratzinger abandoned it.

This raises another issue, namely that of the tension between what might be called Augustinianism and Thomism, since the *Leib-Körper* distinction finds certain support within Thomas' Aristotelian, hylomorphic anthropology (in which a dead body is not really a body at all). As we have already noted, one alternative is the Augustinian notion of a plurality of forms in man (as opposed to the Thomistic idea that the intellectual soul is *unica forma corporis*), most notably the *forma corporeitas*.[62] In this latter view, the body possesses its own form and is truly a counterpart to the soul, whereas in a strict hylomorphism the body is not a counterpart to the soul at all but rather its material expression. Ratzinger's abandonment of the *Leib-Körper* distinction, his arguments against "resurrection in death," and his rejection of a "strict Thomism" suggest that he holds something like the Augustinian view. Notably, Gallus Manser has written that "it would be hard to find an Augustinian who has not, either consciously or semi-consciously, argued for the *forma corporeitatis*."[63] Although Ratzinger nowhere connects his anthropology explicitly to the *forma corporeitatis*, his theology of resurrection undoubtedly points in its direction.[64]

Augustine's view—that the post-death soul awaits reunion with its body in the resurrection—presupposes not only the separability of body

---

62. Of course, in Augustine's own theology, soul and body are not simply accidentally united but are intrinsically ordered to each other. We have already shown earlier in this book how Augustine's anthropology overcomes the dualistic tendencies in Platonism and Gnosticism.

63. Manser, *Das Wesen des Thomismus*, 160. "Man wird schwerlich einen Augustinisten finden, der nicht bewußt oder halb bewußt die *forma corporeitatis* verteidigt hätte." It should be noted that *forma corporeitas* and *forma corporeitatis* are used interchangeably and should not be understood to indicate different concepts.

64. This is not to suggest that Ratzinger strictly holds the medieval notion of the *forma corporeitas*. There are numerous possible ways of conceiving man's body-soul unity within a dual anthropology that grants to the body its own existence.

Part Two: Crucial Distinctions in Ratzinger's Theology of Resurrection

and soul, but also the existence of a *body* (however decomposed it may be) for the soul to be joined to. In this Augustinian view, the Durandian solution (i.e., that the resurrection body is not "given back" but is the result of the soul again informing *materia prima*) is simply unacceptable. For Ratzinger, the duality of the Augustinian schema is to be preferred to the position of Durandus. This duality preserves the material aspect of the resurrection, guaranteeing that it still involves the matter of *this* world, and is the rising of *this* body to new life.

Part Three

Ratzinger the Realist

6

Matter in Ratzinger's Theology of Resurrection

Like Augustine's, Ratzinger's views on the role of matter in the resurrection have undergone development. We have seen how Augustine initially denied a material resurrection, yet later not only allowed this but also suggested that this material, risen body will be so glorified and enlivened by spirit that it will be capable of the divinizing *visio Dei*. In this vision, God is not only seen *by* glorified material bodies, but *in* these bodies as well.

Ratzinger's early thought on the materiality of the resurrection was strongly marked by a tendency to emphasize the spiritualization of matter as well as the perfection of the cosmos rather than the individual. This had begun to change around the time he wrote *Eschatologie*, however, when he began to place greater emphasis on material continuity and the salvation of matter as such.

In this chapter, we will examine this important development in Ratzinger's thought—a development which in many ways mirrors Augustine's own—and will see how Ratzinger's opposition to Greshake's theology of "resurrection in death" and to the denial of Christ's empty tomb led Ratzinger toward a more physical, material, and Augustinian understanding of resurrection. I will also attempt to show how some of the difficult

181

questions about the risen body might be approached by combining key insights of both Augustine and Ratzinger.

The Teilhardian and Rahnerian Influence in Ratzinger's Eschatology

We have seen that Ratzinger began his theological career by holding positions on the resurrection which are largely opposed to the mature theology of Augustine. What was the source of these ideas? Although Ratzinger has been influenced by a variety of thinkers, we will here examine the influence of Teilhard de Chardin (and, to a lesser extent, Karl Rahner) upon Ratzinger's early theology of resurrection. We will begin by noting that Ratzinger's earliest theology actually exhibits a certain realism highly akin to Augustine's, although this would quickly evaporate as Ratzinger began to emphasize the resurrection as the endpoint of a process of fulfillment. In this regard, he was highly influenced by Teilhard's evolutionary theology. It will be suggested that the tendency in Teilhard and Rahner to see matter mainly in terms of its potential to become spirit results in a devaluation of real matter, something which will have great repercussions on understanding the resurrection of the body. We will conclude by observing how Ratzinger has more recently become highly critical of the idea of eschatological fulfillment as a process, suggesting that the Teilhardian views espoused in *Einführung* and *Eschatologie* may no longer be held by Ratzinger.

Ratzinger's Earliest Writings: The Relics of Augustinianism?

Although it is true that in Ratzinger's early writings on resurrection—particularly *Einführung*—there is a marked de-emphasis on materiality and resurrectional realism, in his earliest works on the topic—"Auferstehung des Fleisches" and "Auferstehungsleib" (both 1957)—there seem to be present elements of a more materialist, Augustinian type. There, Ratzinger states that "just as now, matter determines the place of spirit, so in the new world spirit will be the place of matter. This means that the resurrection brings about a new, 'intelligible' spatiality and temporality."[1] In this view,

---

1. Ratzinger, "Auferstehung des Fleisches" (1957), 1051. "Wie gegenwärtig die Materie den Ort des Geistes bestimmt, so wird in der neuen Welt der Geist der Ort der Materie sein. Das heißt: Die A. schafft eine neue 'intelligible' Räumlichkeit u. Zeitlichkeit."

the fulfillment of the world will include space and time, even if these are both transfigured.

Further, when speaking of the discontinuity of the resurrection, Ratzinger nonetheless maintains that "in spite of the fundamental transformation it undergoes, the risen body remains a real human body, even retaining sexual difference."[2] This very Augustinian teaching on the persistence of sexual difference in the risen body, however, has never again been discussed by Ratzinger, nor does it play a role in the German resurrection debates of the twentieth century. It is in this same article that Ratzinger also admits that if the relics of a saint are present, they will participate in the risen body.[3] For these statements, he was later excoriated by Greshake as a "physicalist,"[4] even though two years previously (in 1967) Ratzinger's "new" view—hardly different from Greshake's at the time—had been published in *Sacramentum Mundi*.[5]

What are we to make of these very "physicalist" statements concerning resurrection which are present in 1957—before Ratzinger had received a teaching chair in theology—yet seem to be cast off only ten years later? Is it possible that they were written before the onset of Ratzinger's self-confessed flirtation with "anti-Platonism"? If Ratzinger encountered the then-popular "anti-Platonizing" tradition after he had completed his theological studies, it is possible that its influence did not make itself fully felt in his writings until after 1957. If this is the case, we can consider the above statements to be "relics" of a more traditional, Augustinian understanding of the resurrection originating in the period before his reception of a chair in theology.

The Teilhardian and Rahnerian Sources of Ratzinger's Early Theology

By the time Ratzinger wrote *Einführung*, he was strongly influenced by the theology of Teilhard de Chardin. This shows up in his discussion of resurrection there, and to a lesser degree in *Eschatologie*. Because of this, it will

---

2. Ratzinger, "Auferstehungsleib," 1053. "Der auferstandene Leib bleibt trotz der grundlegenden Verwandlung, die er erfährt, ein wahrer Menschenleib, auch der Unterschied der Geschlechter bleibt bestehen."

3. Ibid.

4. Greshake, *Auferstehung der Toten*, 386. Published in 1969.

5. Ratzinger, "Auferstehung des Fleisches" (1967).

be helpful to first briefly consider some of the main points of Teilhard's eschatology.

In Teilhard's theology, the cosmos is seen in an upward, evolutionary process of becoming, progressing toward a final point which Teilhard calls "Omega." He thus speaks of a process of "complexification" which occurs not only in the tendency of atoms to organize themselves into more complex unities, but in all things.[6] The evolution of human beings produces thought, so that from then on the earth not only has a lithosphere, stratosphere, biosphere, etc., but also develops a "noosphere" or a "thinking layer."[7] This can be called a sort of soul of the earth.[8]

In this view, all of creation—both spirit and matter—is undergoing a "mega-synthesis" which means the unification of matter and mind, bringing about a "spirit of the earth."[9] Because consciousness means freedom from material constraints, the mind will eventually be detached "from its material matrix, so that it will henceforth rest with all its weight on God-Omega."[10] In this respect, matter appears as something to be transcended.

Here, we clearly have a *process* understanding of eschatological fulfillment in which there is a steady progression toward spirit. Teilhard eschews the classical notion of a God who sets things into motion, opting instead for the evolutionarily-inspired image of "an organic Prime-Mover God, *ab ante*."[11] Clearly, evolution is the determinative factor of Teilhard's theology. It "is a general condition to which all theories, all hypotheses, all systems must bow and which they must satisfy henceforward if they are to be thinkable and true. Evolution is a light illuminating all facts, a curve that all lines must follow."[12]

Some aspects of Teilhard's theology of upward progress find echoes in the thought of Karl Rahner. Like Teilhard, Rahner sees the cosmos as becoming conscious of itself in man.[13] Out of the Teilhardian notion of the upward evolution of the cosmos, Rahner develops the idea of "active

---

6. Teilhard de Chardin, *Phenomenon of Man*, 48.

7. Ibid., 182.

8. Ibid.

9. Ibid., 244, 253.

10. Ibid., 287.

11. Teilhard de Chardin, "God of Evolution" (1953), 240.

12. Teilhard de Chardin, *Phenomenon of Man*, 218.

13. Rahner, *Foundations of Christian Faith*, 190.

Matter in Ratzinger's Theology of Resurrection

self-transcendence."[14] This is the basis for his oft-cited claim that matter is a kind of "frozen spirit."[15] Rahner likewise sees the resurrection as a way of describing the final unity and fulfillment of the cosmos.[16] And we have already noted Rahner's earlier view that "in death, the soul becomes not a-cosmic, but all-cosmic."[17]

An evaluation of Rahner's understanding of matter is far beyond the scope of this study. Nonetheless, it should be pointed out that there is in Rahner a certain tendency to view matter as a stage or level in the process of the fulfillment of spirit.[18] In this way, the distinction between matter and spirit can become blurred. This is not to say that Rahner does not also emphasize the distinction between matter and spirit (which he does),[19] but only that there is in Rahner's theology a strong trend toward viewing matter's eschatological fulfillment in terms of spirit. This is exemplified by his statement (seized upon by Greshake) that "the physical world as such is in itself fundamentally 'imperfectible.'"[20]

---

14. Rahner, "Unity of Spirit and Matter," 174–77. German text in "Einheit von Geist und Materie," 210–13.

15. "Unity of Spirit and Matter," 177; "Einheit von Geist und Materie," 213.

16. Rahner, *Foundations of Christian Faith*, 190. "But if we presuppose that evolution has any ultimate and one-way direction at all, then the process by which the cosmos becomes conscious of itself in man, in his individual totality and in the freedom which he actualizes, this process must also have a final result. . . . In Christian terminology we usually call it man's final and definitive state, his salvation, the immortality of the soul or the resurrection of the flesh, but in doing so we have to see clearly that, when correctly understood, all of these terms are describing a final and definitive state of fulfillment for the cosmos."

17. Rahner, *On the Theology of Death*, 28.

18. Rahner, "Unity of Spirit and Matter," 177. "We have seen, furthermore, that matter and spirit are not simply disparate things but that matter is, as it were, 'frozen' spirit whose only meaning is to render real spirit possible." German text in "Einheit von Geist und Materie," 213. Also, cf. Rahner, "Naturwissenschaft und vernünftiger Glaube," 42. "Materiality must ultimately . . . be understood as the lowest stage of spirit, because otherwise materiality could not be thought of as deriving from an absolute spirit." My translation. "Materialität muß letztlich . . . als unterste Stufe des Geistes verstanden werden, weil anders Materialität nicht von einem absoluten Geist herkünftig gedacht werden konnte."

19. Rahner, *Foundations of Christian Faith*, 184. There Rahner states that spirit and matter are not "reducible to each other" and that "there is an essential difference between spirit and matter."

20. Rahner, "Neuen Erde," 594. "die physische Welt als solche ist in sich grundsätzlich 'unvollendbar.'" My translation.

Part Three: Ratzinger the Realist

Ratzinger's Early Teilhardianism: Fulfillment as Process

Einführung in das Christentum

The influence of Teilhard's theology exerts itself most strongly in Ratzinger's *Einführung*. When discussing resurrection and eschatology, Ratzinger appeals to Teilhard repeatedly. He describes the overcoming of death by God's love (i.e., dialogical immortality) as a "decisive complexity or 'complexification'" which would be "a final stage of 'mutation' and 'evolution'" transcending biology.[21] This "mutation" of man and cosmos breaks down "the frontier of *bios*" so that in death, "the future dimension of mankind is opened up and its future has in fact already begun."[22]

In *Einführung*, Ratzinger sees the cosmos as "movement . . . it is not just a case of history *existing in it*, [but] that the cosmos itself *is* history."[23] Further, "in this cosmic movement, as we have already seen, spirit is not some kind of accidental by-product of development which has no meaning for the whole; on the contrary, we were able to establish that in this cosmic movement, matter and its development constitute the prehistory of spirit."[24] We can thus explain the idea of the second coming of Christ "as the conviction that our history is advancing to an 'omega' point" which will reveal to us that "mind [*Sinn*] holds being together, gives it reality, indeed *is* reality."[25] Faith in the return of Christ, then, can be thought of as "faith in the ultimate unification of reality by spirit."[26]

---

21. Ratzinger, *Intro.*, 304.

22. Ibid., 314. We will discuss later how such statements effectively support Greshake's theology of "resurrection in death."

23. Ibid., 320.

24. Ratzinger, *Einführung*, 303 (*Intro.*, 320). My translation. "In dieser kosmischen Bewegung aber ist, wie wir früher schon sahen, der Geist nicht irgendein zufälliges Nebenprodukt der Entwicklung, das fürs Ganze nichts zu bedeuten hätte; vielmehr konnten wir feststellen, dass in ihr die Materie und deren Entfaltung die Vorgeschichte des Geistes bilden." Foster here translates *Geist* first as "spirit" and then as "spirit or mind." He also first translates *Entwicklung* as "development" and then as "evolution."

25. Ratzinger, *Intro.*, 320–21 (*Einführung*, 303).

26. Ratzinger, *Einführung*, 304 (*Intro.*, 321). My translation. "Aber die Verschmelzung von Natur und Geist, die in ihr [i.e., in der Technik] geschieht, ermöglicht uns doch, auf neue Weise zu erfassen, in welcher Richtung die Wirklichkeit des Glaubens an die Weiderkunft Christi zu denken ist: als Glaube an die endgültige Vereinigung des Wirklichen vom Geist her." Again, Foster translates *Geist* as "spirit or mind," which is imprecise, as Ratzinger earlier uses *Sinn* to designate "mind." In this case, Ratzinger

Matter in Ratzinger's Theology of Resurrection

It need not be pointed out that these statements are Teilhardian. What is important, however, is that Ratzinger sees eschatological fulfillment as a process of "complexification" which is ultimately an upward evolution towards spirit. In such a view it must be asked whether matter can really be fulfilled *as matter*, since it appears as a stage in the evolution of spirit.

Eschatologie

The Teilhardian theology of fulfillment as process continues to play a role in *Eschatologie*. But given the high Teilhardian content of the eschatological section of *Einführung*, one might expect a similar situation in *Eschatologie*. This is not the case, however, as Ratzinger's use of Teilhard is almost entirely restricted to one brief section[27] which serves to connect Ratzinger's concept of post-death time to the ongoing history of the world, but which does not appear to be intrinsically connected to his other arguments on the resurrection from that work.

In this section, Ratzinger develops Rahner's thesis of the all-cosmic soul. He also continues in the view (also set forth in *Einführung*) that "the universe, matter, is as such temporally composed, it is a process of becoming. This temporality of the universe, which knows being only in the form of becoming, nonetheless has a direction which, in the gradual construction of the biosphere and noosphere, emerges out of and beyond the physical moments."[28] This cosmic movement is toward "a unity which encompasses all previous unities,"[29] corresponding effectively to Teilhard's idea of "pleromization."[30]

Ratzinger concludes this brief Teilhardian interlude by claiming that "the new world is unimaginable. Neither are there any kind of conceivable, concrete statements about the way humans will relate to matter in

---

is using *Geist* as a counterpart to "Materie." Ratzinger's attitude toward technology in *Einführung* is more open and positive than that found in his later works.

27. This section is found in *Eschatologie*, 154–56 (*Eschatology*, 191–94).

28. Ratzinger, *Eschatologie*, 154 (*Eschatology*, 191). "das All, die Materie ist als solches zeitlich verfaßt, ein Prozeß des Werdens. Diese Zeitlichkeit des Alls, die Sein nur in der Form des Werdens kennt, hat aber eine Richtung, die sich in dem allmählichen Aufbau der Biosphäre und der Noosphäre aus und über den physikalischen Momenten abzeichnet."

29. Ibid., 154 (*Eschatology*, 191). "Sie [i.e., diese Richtung] ist vor allem ein Voranschreiten zu immer komplexeren Einheiten und ruft damit nach der totalen Komplexität, nach einer Einheit, die alle bisherigen Einheiten übergreift."

30. Teilhard de Chardin, "Reflections on Original Sin" (1947), 198.

the new world, or about the 'risen body.' There is, however, the certainty that the dynamic of the cosmos is leading to a goal, to a situation in which matter and spirit will newly and finally belong to each other. This certainty remains the concrete content of the belief in the resurrection of the flesh even today, especially today."[31] Within this statement there are several points to consider. First, Ratzinger makes the claim that nothing concrete can be said about the materiality of the resurrection, or about the risen body. This is somewhat surprising, however, as the whole dispute with Greshake suggests that Ratzinger does have a particular view on the resurrection's materiality. Second, Ratzinger again claims that the true "content" of faith in the resurrection is simply the belief that the cosmos is moving toward a goal where "matter and spirit will newly and finally belong to each other." This concept of the reciprocal ordering of matter and spirit could be easily reconciled with a more classical, Augustinian view, but it is difficult to see how the classical view could be reduced to this concept. Third, as evidenced by Ratzinger's statement that such an explanation is valid "especially today," it appears that Ratzinger is attempting to extract what he considers to be the essential core of the doctrine of resurrection which can be held forth to the modern, scientific world. If this is the case, then we can understand this brief foray into Teilhardianism as part of Ratzinger's early attempt to bring resurrection theology closer to a modern worldview. But it is not clear that such a conceptual move harmonizes well with other statements on the resurrection made by Ratzinger in *Eschatologie* and in his later polemic with Greshake, as we will observe shortly.

Evolution, Ethics, and the Individual: Ratzinger's Later Critique of Teilhardianism and Fulfillment-as-Process

Although Ratzinger embraced the notion of fulfillment-as-process in *Einführung* and to a lesser extent in *Eschatologie*, his appetite for such schemata has diminished significantly since then. This is evident in his

---

31. Ratzinger, *Eschatologie*, 156 (*Eschatology*, 194). "Es gibt keine Vorstellbarkeit der neuen Welt. Es gibt auch keinerlei irgendwie konkretisierbaren und in die Vorstellung reichenden Aussagen über die Art des Materiebezugs der Menschen in der neuen Welt und über den 'Auferstehungsleib'. Aber es gibt die Gewißheit, daß die Dynamik des Kosmos auf ein Ziel zuführt, auf eine Situation, in der Materie und Geist einander neu und endgültig zugeeignet sein werden. Diese Gewißheit bleibt der konkrete Inhalt des Bekenntnisses zur Auferstehung des Fleisches auch heute, gerade heute."

more recent discussions of both Rahner, Teilhard, and the whole notion of progress.

Rahner and Process

Although in *Eschatologie* Ratzinger had adopted Rahner's thesis that the all-cosmic soul inaugurates a process of the ascending unification of spirit and matter, so that the resurrection is simply "the coming-to-an-end of this process,"[32] by the time of the afterword to the 6th edition of *Eschatologie* (1990) it appears that he has now parted ways with Rahner on this issue. There, he mentions Herbert Vorgrimler's use of "Rahner's idea of the soul . . . which in death becomes not acosmic, but all-cosmic. The soul's always already at-hand orientation to the world, beyond its own embodiment, could be interpreted as a new kind of embodiment, which accrues to it in death. In an early phase of his thought, Rahner tried to develop from this a sort of process-understanding of judgment and resurrection."[33]

But does Ratzinger still approve of this "process-understanding" of resurrection? The answer seems to be no, judging by his succeeding comments. In the following paragraph, he mentions that "in Medard Kehl I have been unable to find anything essentially new beyond Rahner and Greshake."[34] Ratzinger then proceeds to ridicule a plethora of ideas from Kehl's book (which ostensibly derive from Rahner and Greshake).[35] He continues, "Rahner rings through here as well, when it is said that the Parousia will not happen in the apocalyptic figures of judgment and catastrophe, but that it is 'the coming-to-an-end of the universal process

---

32. Ibid., 154 (*Eschatology*, 191). "'Jüngster Tag,' 'Ende der Welt,' 'Auferstehung des Fleisches,' wären dann Chriffren für das Zu-Ende-Kommen dieses Prozesses."

33. Ratzinger, *Nachwort zur 6. Auflage* (*Eschatologie*, 191). "K. Rahner's Gedanken von der Seele . . . die im Tode nicht akosmisch, sondern allkosmisch werde. Ihr immer schon vorhandener Weltbezug über die eigene Leiblichkeit hinaus würde sich so als eine neue Art von Leiblichkeit deuten lassen, die ihr im Tode zuwächst. Rahner hat in einer frühen Phase seines Denkens daraus eine Art von prozeßhaftem Verständnis des Gerichts und der Auferstehung zu entwickeln versucht."

34. Ibid. (*Eschatologie*, 191). "Nichts wesentlich Neues über Rahner und Greshake hinaus habe ich zu dieser Frage bei M. Kehl finden können."

35. These include (1) that in the death of the individual there is already the return of the Lord, resurrection, and judgment; (2) that the separation of body and soul in death is dualistic and based on Neoplatonic anthropology; (3) that this contradicts the holistic view of the Bible; (4) that man dies as a whole, but not wholly; and (5) that we have to bid farewell to apocalyptic images from the Bible like "Last Judgment," "Last Day," "Parousia of the Judge" (Ratzinger, *Nachwort zur 6. Auflage*, in *Eschatologie*, 191–92). Ratzinger here points to Kehl, *Eschatologie*, 163, 232.

of fulfillment, in which all men (prepared for it) die into the life of the resurrection."[36] Ratzinger believes that "here, an explosive consequence of the new eschatology comes into view: the attempt to rearrange the relationship between man's action in the world and the coming of the kingdom of God."[37] In this case, Ratzinger is clear that he has little regard for theologies of fulfillment as process.

Teilhard, Evolution, and Progress

During the 1980s and 1990s, Ratzinger became more and more suspicious of the melding of evolution with theology and philosophy. In 1986, he noted that evolution is now attempting to become a universal philosophy, in which case it must be countered by philosophy.[38] And, dissenting from the position articulated in John Paul II's 1996 message to the Pontifical Academy of Sciences, which stated that evolution is "more than an hypothesis,"[39] Ratzinger opined in 1998 that while John Paul II "had his reasons for saying this . . . at the same time, it is true that the evolution doctrine is still not a complete, scientifically verified theory."[40]

In an extended speech given at the Sorbonne in Paris in 1999, Ratzinger further discussed the danger of evolution becoming a philosophy of everything and thereby interpreting everything through the narrow lens of Darwinism. The chief problem here is that

---

36. Ratzinger, *Nachwort zur 6. Auflage* (*Eschatologie*, 192). "Auch hier klingt Rahner durch, wenn gesagt wird, die Parusie geschehe nicht in den apokalyptischen Zeichen des Gerichtes und der Katastrophe; sie sei 'das Zu-Ende-Kommen des universalen Vollendungsprozesses, in dem alle (dazu bereiten) Menschen in das Leben der Auferstehung hineinsterben.'" The internal quotation is from Kehl, *Eschatologie*, 249.

37. Ibid., (*Eschatologie*, 192). "weil hier eine brisante Konsequenz der neueren Eschatologie zum Vorschein kommt: der Versuch, das Welthandeln des Menschen und das Kommen des Gottesreiches auf neue Weise zueinander in Beziehung zu setzen."

38. This is from Ratzinger's 1986 foreword to the published acts of a 1985 symposium held in Rome, "Evolutionism and Christianity." Published in *Schöpfung und Evolution*, 9–10.

39. John Paul II, "Message to the Participants of the Plenary of the Pontifical Academy of Sciences," October 22, 1996, par. 4. Original (French) text in *Insegnamenti di Giovanni Paolo II* 19 (1996) 572. "Aujourd'hui, près d'un demi-siècle après la parution de l'encyclique [*Humani Generis*], de nouvelles connaissances conduisent à reconnaître dans la théorie de l'évolution plus qu'une hypothèse."

40. Ratzinger, *Schöpfung und Evolution*, 151. My translation. "Als der Papst dies sagte, hatte er seine Gründe. Aber zugleich gilt, daß die Evolutionslehre noch keine komplette, wissenschaftlich verifizierte Theorie ist."

> Every explanation of reality that cannot at the same time provide a meaningful and comprehensible basis for ethics necessarily remains inadequate. Now the theory of evolution, in the cases where people have tried to extend it to a *"philosophia universalis,"* has in fact been used for an attempt at a new ethos based on evolution. Yet this evolutionary ethic that inevitably takes as its key concept the model of selectivity, that is, the struggle for survival, the victory of the fittest, successful adaptation, has little comfort to offer. Even when people try to make it more attractive in various ways, it ultimately remains a bloodthirsty ethic. Here, the attempt to distill rationality out of what is in itself irrational quite visibly fails.[41]

This inability of evolution to ground a Christian ethic makes itself acutely felt in Teilhard's theology, in which physical and moral evil is "the *statistically inevitable by-product* of the unification of the multiple,"[42] while original sin "is everywhere, as closely woven into the being of the world as the God who creates us and the Incarnate Word who redeems us."[43] It is "an aspect or global modality of evolution,"[44] "the essential reaction of the finite to the creative act . . . it is the *reverse side* of all creation"[45] which "considered in its cosmic basis . . . tends to be indistinguishable from the sheer mechanism of creation—in which it represents the action of the negative forces of 'counter-evolution.'"[46]

Ratzinger's most overt critique of Teilhard's theology would come in 1998. Under the rubric "Faith in Progress," Ratzinger considers the view that there will arise a perfected state of humanity, wherein "history" has essentially come to an end. But, he asks, does this do justice to all those who have to suffer along the way?[47]

> These questions are also valid ones for the Christian variant of this faith in progress that Teilhard de Chardin developed. He

---

41. Ratzinger, "Vérité," lectured delivered on November 27, 1999, at the Sorbonne, Paris. English translation in Ratzinger, *Truth and Tolerance*, 162–83. Hereafter cited as "Vérité."

42. Teilhard de Chardin, "Reflections on Original Sin," 196.

43. Teilhard de Chardin, "Historical Representations of Original Sin" (prior to 1922), 54.

44. Teilhard de Chardin, "Christ the Evolver" (1942), 149.

45. Teilhard de Chardin, "Fall, Redemption, and Geocentrism" (1920), 40.

46. Teilhard de Chardin, "Christ the Evolver," 150.

47. Ratzinger, "End of Time," 14.

Part Three: Ratzinger the Realist

> described the cosmos as a process of upward development, as a journey of unification. From the very simple, this journey leads to ever greater and more complex units in which multiplicity is not canceled out but integrated into a growing synthesis, culminating in the Noosphere, where spirit and its understanding comprehend the whole, and everything is integrated into a kind of living organism. Based on Ephesians and Colossians, Teilhard envisages Christ as the energy that drives toward the Noosphere, an energy that finally incorporates everything in its fullness.[48]

Ratzinger has reservations, however:

> This impressive vision . . . has to face all those questions that have to be posed to the idea of progress in general. For Teilhard all of evolution's terrible aspects and so too, finally, all of history's atrocities, are inevitable mishaps in the process of upward movement toward the definitive synthesis . . . Thus, in the end human beings in their suffering appear as the material for evolution's experiment, the world's injustices as mishaps that you have to reckon for on such a journey. Humanity is subordinated to the cosmic process; but this is precisely when the age-old question that the Psalms put to God acquires a new urgency: "What are human beings, that you are mindful of them?" (Ps 8:5)
>
> Or is it that we have to reckon our sense of the direct relation of each and every person to God to be arrogance, and bow before the majesty of the cosmos, to the Godhead of evolution? Or is it that there is a God who is greater than the cosmos and before whom one single person is greater than the whole silent cosmos?[49]

Here, Ratzinger clearly stresses the salvation of the individual who is directly related to God rather then viewing the individual's salvation in the context of a cosmic process as he did in *Eschatologie*.[50] This criticism marks a significant turning point in Ratzinger's relationship to Teilhardian eschatology.

This is not to imply, however, that Ratzinger has rejected *every* idea proposed by Teilhard. For example, in a 2009 homily Benedict XVI approvingly described Teilhard's idea that "at the end we will have a true

---

48. Ibid., 14–15.

49. Ibid., 15. The themes of the majesty of the cosmos and the God of evolution are all themes in Teilhard's theology.

50. Ratzinger, *Eschatologie*, 154–55 (*Eschatology*, 191–92).

cosmic liturgy where the cosmos will become a living host."[51] Like the consecrated host that becomes the body of Christ, the material world too will be imbued with God's life. This, however, is in no way an endorsement of Teilhard's notion of process-fulfillment but rather is simply a presentation of what the final state will be. In this sense, it is very close to the vision presented by Augustine in *De Civitate Dei* XXII, 29.

It should also be mentioned that while Ratzinger still sometimes describes the resurrection using language whose ultimate origin lies in evolutionary biology, the emphasis now is on the radical discontinuity of the resurrection event, rather than on seeing resurrection as the culmination of a long process. For example, he can speak of the resurrection as "an ontological leap,"[52] "something like a radical 'mutative leap' which opens up a new dimension of life, of human existence."[53] In both these cases, however, the images used serve to emphasize the surpassing newness of resurrection without jettisoning the (material) continuity that also exists. In fact, the very idea of evolutionary "leaps" was coined by theorists attempting to describe the origins of species whose appearance seems inexplicable on the basis of gradual changes by natural selection. It is clear that Ratzinger does not have in mind any process vision of resurrection.

In any case, it is clear that by the end of the twentieth century Ratzinger had become highly critical of theologies of process-fulfillment, particularly those that predicate human fulfillment on progress or evolution. This is because the inability of evolutionary theology to ground a truly Christian ethic means the forsaking of the individual in the name of a greater cosmic process. It therefore appears that by the 1990s Ratzinger had moved beyond the Teilhardian idea of cosmic fulfillment as an evolutionary process that we find in *Einführung* and, to a lesser extent, in *Eschatologie*.[54]

---

51. Benedict XVI, Homily, July 24, 2009. My translation. "alla fine avremo una vera liturgia cosmica, dove il cosmo diventi ostia vivente."

52. Ratzinger, *Jesus of Nazareth II*, 274 (*Jesus von Nazareth II*, 300).

53. Ratzinger, *Jesus von Nazareth II*, 299 (*Jesus of Nazareth II*, 274). My translation. "Wir könnten ... die Auferstehung als so etwas wie einen radikalen 'Mutationssprung' ansehen, in dem sich eine neue Dimension des Lebens, des Menschseins auftut."

54. As Marchler notes in 2009, "Ratzinger's attitude toward Teilhard's overly optimistic progress-thought has become somewhat more critical over the years" ("Perspektiven," 183 n. 87). [Allerdings ist Ratzingers Stellung gegenüber Teilhards allzu optimistischem Fortschrittsdenken mit den Jahren etwas kritischer geworden.]

Part Three: Ratzinger the Realist

Internal Tensions in *Eschatologie*: Ratzinger's Move toward Physicalism

We have noted how, in 1968 and 1977, Ratzinger sometimes viewed "resurrection" as a metaphor for the completion of a process of fulfillment wherein matter and spirit would be unified in a final synthesis.[55] In this view, it is not clear that the resurrection touches physical bodies as such (cf. the *Leib-Körper* distinction), nor is it certain that risen embodiment will involve individual human bodies. All that is certain here is the continuance of the person in an ongoing relationship to matter which will be fulfilled in some way at the end. This abstract vision of resurrection, so different from Augustine's vivid imagery, successfully avoids any connotations of physicalism.[56] But might it also risk committing the same error that Ratzinger accuses the Origenists of, namely, transforming a "human" resurrection into an idealized one?[57]

Two Contrary Movements

Yet within *Eschatologie* there is another countervailing tendency of a more "realist" nature, which emphasizes the salvation of matter *as* matter and stresses the connection of the corpse to the risen *body*. Much of *Eschatologie* is a polemic against "resurrection in death." It is thus fascinating to note that when Ratzinger argues against Greshake, he reverts to what could be called a more physicalist, indeed, a more Augustinian view of resurrection. We have already discussed how Ratzinger moved in an Augustinian direction when he abandoned the *Leib-Körper* distinction due to the polemic with Greshake.

---

55. See, e.g., Ratzinger, *Eschatologie*, 154 (*Eschatology*, 191–92). "'Last Day,' 'End of the World,' and 'Resurrection of the Flesh' would then be figures for the coming-to-an-end of this process." "'Jüngster Tag,' 'Ende der Welt,' 'Auferstehung des Fleisches' wären dann Chiffren für das Zu-Ende-Kommen dieses Prozesses."

56. See, for example, Ratzinger, *Eschatologie*, 155 (*Eschatology*, 192). Ratzinger says that we cannot imagine the particularities of the world of the resurrection and "so far as Greshake opposes such 'physicalist' conceptual games, one must agree with him. We cannot attain any images of it [the world of the resurrection], nor do we need them. In fact, one should bid a final farewell to such attempts." [soweit Greshake sich gegen solche 'physizistischen' Denkspiele wendet, ist ihm völlig recht zu geben (*Auferstehung der Toten* 386). Wir können darüber keine Vorstellungen gewinnen und bedürfen ihrer auch nicht; von solchen Versuchen sollte man in der Tat endgültig Abschied nehmen.]

57. Ibid., 143 (*Eschatology*, 176–77).

Matter in Ratzinger's Theology of Resurrection

Already in 1972, however, Ratzinger had detected a certain spiritualism in the theology of "resurrection in death" and employed a line of reasoning that would eventually become his signature argument against Greshake[58]—namely, that "resurrection in death" is contradicted by the fact of the corpse in the grave. In *Eschatologie*, he argues that "resurrection in death" is simply a covert attempt to reintroduce the doctrine of the immortality of the soul, since it separates the idea of resurrection from the body of the person who has died.[59] Here, Ratzinger's understanding of matter is clearly a more "physicalist" one. He seizes upon the fact that Greshake's theology can speak of resurrection in spite of the presence of the corpse, pointing out what he sees as the absurdity of the idea. But this argument only holds, as Sonnemans has observed,[60] if there is a necessary connection between the corpse and the risen body. In other words, the argument is ultimately incompatible with the *Leib-Körper* distinction.

It is also difficult to imagine how this argument is compatible with the idea of the soul becoming all-cosmic at death. Ratzinger's appeal to the all-cosmic soul is designed to maintain the soul's ongoing orientation to matter and time even in death. In such a theology, however, the corpse can become irrelevant. For if risen embodiment is the fulfillment of an all-cosmic existence, then the only thing that matters is the ongoing, ascending synthesis and not any physical bodily remains. In fact, such bodily remains would be of no value whatsoever, since the corpse's decomposition (i.e., its breakdown into simpler material units) actually leads in the *opposite* direction of the upward process of the formation of more complex unities. This incompatibility has also been noticed by Thomas Marschler: "It could be critically asked whether Ratzinger might not have to work out more consistently the ontological implications of his criticism of Greshake's concept of eschatological matter. Upon this background, for example, does the the idea of an all-cosmic becoming of the beatified soul, as Ratzinger borrows it from Rahner, remain conceivable in the strict sense?"[61]

---

58. This argument is repeated in *Eschatologie*, in "Zwischen Tod und Auferstehung," and even found its way into the 1992 International Theological Commission document on eschatology.

59. Ratzinger, *Eschatologie*, 94 (*Eschatology*, 108). For Ratzinger's early use of the argument, see "Jenseits des Todes," 235 ("Beyond Death," 159).

60. Sonnemans, *Seele*, 441–42.

61. Marschler, "Perspektiven," 177 n. 63. "Kritisch wäre zu fragen, ob Ratzinger die ontologischen Implikate seiner Kritik an Greshakes eschatologischen Materie-Begriff nicht konsequenter hätte ausformulieren müssen. Bleibt auf ihrem Hintergrund z.B.

Part Three: Ratzinger the Realist

Ratzinger's concern in the "corpse-in-the-ground" argument, however, is twofold: On the one hand, it is kerygmatic. He does not believe that speaking of "resurrection" for people who have just died is in any way meaningful.[62] On the other hand, he fears that Greshake's view ultimately renders the real material world superfluous. Against this, Ratzinger wishes (as does Augustine) to assert a strong materiality in the resurrection. The explicit denial of any connection at all between the corpse and the risen body dilutes the full materiality of the resurrection.

This is why, in response to Greshake's statements that matter is imperfectible and that "if, therefore, man's freedom finalizes itself in death, then body, world, and the history of this freedom are permanently preserved in the concrete form of that freedom's finality,"[63] Ratzinger counters fiercely: "Such ideas may be meaningful. The only question is with what right one can still speak of 'bodiliness' when all connection to matter is explicitly denied and matter's participation in the final state only remains insofar as it was an 'ecstatic moment of the human act of freedom.'"[64] As we will see when we discuss in greater detail Ratzinger's dispute with Greshake over matter in the resurrection, Ratzinger clearly rules out the possibility of speaking of "resurrection" when there is no connection with matter, or when matter is only perfected as "an ecstatic moment of the human act of freedom." He later states that "Greshake's idea that the soul assimilates matter as the 'ecstatic moment' of the realization of its freedom and definitively leaves it behind *qua* matter to the eternally imperfectible would be inconceivable for Thomas."[65]

---

die Vorstellung eines Allkosmisch-Werdens der verherrlichten Seele, wie ihn Ratzinger von Rahner übernimmt, im strengen Sinn denkbar?"

62. Ratzinger, "Zwischen Tod und Auferstehung" (*Eschatologie*, 216; *Eschatology*, 254).

63. Greshake, *Auferstehung der Toten*, 387. Cited by Ratzinger in *Eschatologie*, 94 (*Eschatology*, 108). "Wenn sich mithin im Tode die Freiheit des Menschen verendgültigt, so ist in deren konkreter Gestalt der Endgültigkeit Leib, Welt, und Geschichte dieser Freiheit bleibend aufgehoben . . ."

64. Ratzinger, *Eschatologie*, 94 (*Eschatology*, 109). "Solche Gedanken mögen sinnvoll sein; es fragt sich nur, mit welchem Recht man dann noch von 'Leiblichkeit' sprechen kann, wenn ausdrücklich jede Beziehung zur Materie bestritten ist und ihr Anteil an der Endgültigkeit nur bleibt, sofern sie 'ekstatisches Moment des menschlichen Freiheitsaktes' war." Ratzinger is citing Greshake, *Auferstehung der Toten*, 386–87. Here, "moment" is used in the sense of natural physics, as in "moment of force."

65. Ibid., 144 (*Eschatology*, 179). "Die Vorstellung Greshakes, daß die Seele die Materie als 'ekstatisches Moment' ihres Freiheitsvollzugs in sich aufnimmt und sie als *Materie* im ewig Unvollendbaren dann definitiv hinter sich läßt, ist von Thomas her unvollziehbar."

Matter in Ratzinger's Theology of Resurrection

There are thus within *Eschatologie* two diverging currents of thought on human fulfillment. In the first, the individual and physical reality of bodily resurrection is deemphasized. This is evidenced by Ratzinger's occasional use of the *Leib-Körper* distinction, and by his description of the resurrection of the body as an all-cosmic union of matter and spirit, an idea whose provenance (Rahner and Teilhard) casts doubt on whether matter is really saved *as* matter, and in which it is difficult to recognize the "risen body" as a real, human one. In the second, however, he emphasizes the necessary connection between the corpse and the risen body, and insists on the fulfillment of matter *as* matter. This second view seems to show itself only when Ratzinger is refuting Greshake's theology of "resurrection in death."

Do Some Elements of Ratzinger's Theology Support "Resurrection in Death"?

It has just been asserted that already in *Eschatologie* (1977) there is present a more physical view of resurrection that is incompatible with statements made by Ratzinger in both *Einführung* and other parts of *Eschatologie*. This assertion is supported by the fact that while one of the central arguments of *Eschatologie* is the refutation of "resurrection in death," some elements of Ratzinger's eschatology (from 1968–1977) are compatible with, and suggestive of, "resurrection in death."

Discussing the Teilhardian content of *Eschatologie*, Nachtwei comments that "for Ratzinger, the all-cosmic becoming of the spirit is not a postulate of the intermediate-state. It is the dynamic event of the final state itself, which begins in death. This is fulfilled in an exchange of love between God, man, world."[66] The soul's becoming all-cosmic is "the first stage of risen embodiment itself."[67] But how is this ultimately different from "resurrection in death"? One of Ratzinger's chief objections to that theory is that it posits a resurrection immediately at death without the necessary respect for history entailed in "waiting" for the end. But in the "process" view of fulfillment sometimes adopted by Ratzinger in *Escha-*

---

66. Nachtwei, *Dialogische Unsterblichkeit*, 174. "Für Ratzinger ist das Allkosmischwerden des Geistes nicht Postulat des Zwischenzustandes. Es ist das dynamische Geschehen des im Tod beginnenden Vollendungszustandes selbst. Dies erfüllt sich in einem Austausch der Liebe zwischen Gott, Mensch, Welt." Also cf. Nachtwei, *Dialogische Unsterblichkeit*, 139.

67. Ibid. "Das mit dem Tod eintretende Allkosmischwerden ist die erste Stufe der Auferstehungsleiblichkeit selbst."

tologie, the "process" of resurrection begins in death. Even if final, definitive fulfillment must wait for the end of history (something Greshake also holds), the fact remains that resurrection *begins* in death. Thus, even with Nachtwei's clarification that "risen embodiment is fulfilled, then (as its highest 'stage') when 'matter belongs definitively to spirit in a completely new way, and spirit will be completely one with matter' [*Eschatologie*, 154],"[68] one still must ask what sort of *event* might be associated with the attainment of this "highest 'stage,'" and whether such a schema preserves the difference between death and resurrection. Such a view is similar to Ratzinger's assertion in *Einführung* that "with the crossing of the frontier of death, the future dimension of mankind is opened up and its future has in fact already begun."[69]

Wohlmuth repeatedly suggests that Ratzinger's theology is compatible with "resurrection in death."[70] Even Greshake has argued that in *Eschatologie*, Ratzinger is inconsistent in his criticisms since at times he appears to hold the *Leib-Körper* distinction.[71] In his 1998 article looking back on the resurrection debate, Greshake initially lays out the fundamental tenets of "resurrection in death," and as support for them he cites Ratzinger's *Einführung*.[72] Admittedly, Ratzinger's approach in *Eschatologie*

68. Ibid. "Das mit dem Tod eintretende Allkosmischwerden ist die erste Stufe der Auferstehungsleiblichkeit selbst, die sich dann erfüllt (als ihre höchste 'Stufe'), wenn die 'Materie ganz neu und definitiv dem Geist zu eigen und dieser ganz eins mit der Materie sein wird.'"

69. Ratzinger, *Intro.*, 314.

70. Wohlmuth, *Mysterium der Verwandlung*, 171. Also, Franz-Josef Nocke has attempted to unite Ratzinger's idea of dialogical immortality with "resurrection in death." This in itself does not prove much, however, since Ratzinger's notion of dialogical immortality can be easily separated from his emphasis on materiality. See Nocke, "Eschatologie," 377–478. Pages 459–61 are particularly relevant, although most of Nocke's citations of Ratzinger are prior to *Eschatologie*.

71. Greshake ("Leib-Seele-Problematik," 163 n. 16) is particularly frustrated that Ratzinger, who had himself claimed that "es wird eine Unterscheidung zwischen 'Körper' und 'Leiblichkeit' möglich" (*Eschatologie*, 144), nonetheless fails to appreciate Greshake's use of the *Leib-Körper* distinction, something Greshake claims finds support in Thomistic anthropology.

72. Greshake, "Parteiische Rückblick," 539. Greshake notes that a range of Catholic theologians have determined that there are two phases of the final fulfillment-event: (1) the fulfillment of the whole man (body and soul) *in death*, and (2) the fulfillment of the social totality of humanity *at the end of history*. "Seen thus, there is nothing to prevent one from understanding and describing the individual fulfillment in death as resurrection (of the individual)." At the end of this sentence is a footnote (n. 7) which states, "Even J. Ratzinger spoke this way in the beginning," and cites p. 294 of the 1st edition of *Einführung*. "So gesehen aber spricht nichts dagegen, die individuelle

marks a significant shift, but as we have noted, support for "resurrection in death" can still be gleaned from selections from that work.

We have also already noted Sonnemans' insightful criticism that Ratzinger's "corpse-in-the-ground" argument is incompatible with the *Leib-Körper* distinction.[73] Given the above examples, then, it must be admitted that within *Eschatologie* there is inconsistency in Ratzinger's thought on the risen body. Two different anthropological ideas are being held in tension, a tension which would be further strained by the controversy with Greshake which we will examine momentarily.

Augustinian Evaluation

Based on our deliberations thus far it should be clear which side of this tension corresponds to Augustine's thought. We can discern in Ratzinger's gradual movement away from those formulations that see resurrection as the fulfillment of a process, something of an Augustinian trajectory inasmuch as Ratzinger moves toward a view that sees resurrection as a material event that affects the individual *qua* individual. In *Eschatologie*, therefore, we can observe the maturation of Ratzinger's Augustinianism in the area of the resurrection, but that Augustinianism is still competing with opposing notions from his earlier thought. In Ratzinger's later works, which critique the view of fulfillment-as-process and emphatically repeat his "corpse-in-the-ground" argument, we see the ascendance of that Augustinian tendency often criticized as "physicalism."

It should be remembered, however, that although Augustine emphasizes the salvation of the individual, he does not neglect the cosmic element. The problem, from an Augustinian point of view, with Teilhardian eschatology is not so much its cosmic element as its "process" character, which derives from its evolutionary foundation. The fact of this "process" makes it very difficult to speak of resurrection as an *event*, instead making it appear as something that is attained by "stages" (which is actually how Nachtwei describes Ratzinger's view of risen embodiment).[74] In Augustine, of course, there can be found no support of any kind for a resurrection by stages. From an Augustinian point of view, therefore, we must

---

Vollendung im Tod als Auferstehung (des einzelnen) zu verstehen und bezeichnen." The footnote reads, "So sprach anfangs auch *J. Ratzinger*, Einführung 294."

73. Sonnemans, *Seele*, 441–42.

74. Nachtwei, *Dialogische Unsterblichkeit*, 174–75.

reject such a notion. Although Nachtwei often tends to read Ratzinger as a Teilhardian (and he cannot really be blamed for this, given that he wrote his book in 1985), it does appear that the conclusions he draws concerning the all-cosmic soul represent the true trajectory of the idea, whether Ratzinger was fully aware of it at the time or not.

Having determined which side of the tension present in *Eschatologie* is the Augustinian one, we will now examine the Augustinian direction Ratzinger took his understanding of risen materiality in the ongoing debate with Greshake and in the years following it.

The Question of the Resurrection's Materiality in the Ongoing Debate with Greshake

Having noted the tension in Ratzinger's theology of resurrection that still persists in *Eschatologie*, we will now explore the ways Ratzinger has developed this theology in the succeeding years. We will begin by recalling the important insights Augustine brings to the problem before we examine Ratzinger's insistence, against Greshake, on the salvation of matter "in itself." We will further see that Ratzinger's notion of matter's "spiritualization" articulated in the controversy with Greshake is in fact close to Augustine's.

Augustinian Background

Augustine gave matter an exalted role in his theology of resurrection. The matter of the body, no matter where it has been dispersed through postdeath decomposition, is always before the eyes of God and cannot be lost. In the resurrection, this matter will assume a new mode of existence; its substance will remain but it will receive the qualities proper to immortal bodies. The entire world, too, will be made "new and better" so that eschatological fulfillment will truly be a completion and perfection of the first creation rather than its abrogation. The risen body will then be truly material, and its matter will not come from an *ad hoc* new creation of matter specifically for the purposes of resurrection, but will be numerically one with the matter of the earthly body that once lived. In this way, continuity is preserved both on the spiritual and material planes, since both matter and spirit will be healed and elevated in the eschaton.

Underlying all this is Augustine's fundamental understanding that the resurrection will be a fulfillment of the first creation rather than a new one; to use a scholastic phrase, grace does not destroy nature but elevates it. This is further based on Augustine's distinction between matter as such, and the characteristics associated with the matter of this world: instability, decay, and ephemerality. Augustine is able to imagine a kind of matter possessed of new *qualitates* which would be elevated by God's grace and perfectly animated by the human spirit. While matter in the resurrection would be truly matter, it would be possessed of none of those negative characteristics we now associate with it.

When faced with doubts about the materiality of the resurrection, one of Augustine's favorite arguments is to point to the infinite power over matter of the God who made the universe from nothing.[75] For him, a decomposed body does not present a problem, nor does the transformation of this seemingly irredeemable world.

Some Initial Questions about Matter's Fulfillment

To begin with, several questions present themselves that will have to be examined as we consider Ratzinger's debate with Greshake. First of all, if matter is transformed in the resurrection, then *how* does this happen? Is *all* the matter of the universe transformed, or only that which has come into contact with human beings? And how is this matter implicated in the resurrection? Is it through its "interiorization" into the body of a human being? Or does it participate in the eschatological event independently of humanity? And finally, is *matter itself* actually redeemed, or only matter's meaning, its "finality"? Or, put differently, will heavenly existence actually include material, physical "stuff," however transformed and exalted it might be?

These are all important questions in the polemic between Ratzinger and Greshake. We will begin our discussion of that debate by locating some points of agreement between the two theologians before we consider their differences and attempt to identify the reasons for them.

The "Interiorization" of Matter in the Soul

Both Greshake and Ratzinger believe that Thomas' *anima forma corporis* doctrine implies the soul's irrevocable orientation to matter, as we have already noted. But they also believe that matter is "interiorized" by the soul during its life. Thus, Greshake can say that "in the process

75. Examples include Augustine, *civ. Dei* 21.7, 22.5; *s.* 240.2, 242.7, 362.15.18.

of self-becoming, man transforms the material dimension (of his body, of the world . . .) into his personal life by virtue of his spiritual nature."[76] Greshake directly relates this notion to Teilhard's idea of "hominization" in which man becomes the leading edge of evolution's trajectory, bringing the material world upward to God.[77]

For Greshake, "man . . . interiorizes matter in himself, but that matter does not cease to be matter (it is in fact matter mediated in and through man!)."[78] Matter should not be understood as the stuff of immediate sensory experience but rather as an energy, capable of being transformed into higher complexities.[79] This higher level is attained when matter is interiorized into the human spirit.

Ratzinger's position on the interiorization of matter is, on the surface, similar to Greshake's. In reference to Thomas' understanding that the soul is *forma corporis*, Ratzinger declares: "It is absolutely clear from this starting point that man 'interiorizes' matter during his entire life and that consequently, even in death, he does not relinquish this connection but rather bears it within himself. Only in this way does the connection to resurrection also begin to make sense."[80] Here Ratzinger agrees with Greshake on matter's "interiorization" in the human spirit. He also agrees that this "interiorization" is not annulled by the event of death. For even then, "the soul is not held down by any sort of body, but rather the soul, which endures, holds interiorly within itself the matter of its life and thus rests upon the risen Lord—upon the new unity of spirit and matter which is inaugurated in him."[81] In this view, however, the soul is not said to be

76. Greshake, "Leib-Seele-Problematik," 170. "Im Prozeß des Selbstwerdens verwandelt der Mensch kraft seiner Geistnatur die Dimension des Materiellen (seines Leibes, der Welt . . .) in sein persönliches Leben hinein."

77. Ibid.

78. Ibid., 171. "Der Mensch macht sich mithin die Wirklichkeit zu eigen, indem er Materie in sich verinnerlicht, ohne daß diese aufhört, Materie zu sein (freilich Materie in und durch den Menschen vermittelt!)."

79. Ibid. In a note, Greshake claims that he is following Heisenberg in this regard.

80. Ratzinger, "Zwischen Tod und Auferstehung" (*Eschatologie*, 219; *Eschatology*, 258). "Daß der Mensch sich in seinem ganzen Leben Materie 'verinnerlicht' und daß er folglich auch im Tod diesen Zusammenhang nicht abstreift, sondern in sich trägt, ist von diesem Ansatz her durchaus klar; nur so wird die Beziehung auf Auferstehung hin auch sinnvoll."

81. Ibid. (*Eschatologie*, 219; *Eschatology*, 258). "Nicht irgendeine Art von Leib hält die Seele fest, sondern die Seele, die fortbesteht, hält verinnerlicht die Materie ihres Lebens in sich und ist so ausgespannt auf den auferstandenen Christus—auf die neue Einheit von Geist und Materie hin, die in ihm eröffnet ist."

risen. It "holds within itself the matter of its life" without yet possessing a risen body. We will discuss what all this may mean shortly.

We conclude our introduction to the concept of matter's "interiorization" by citing again, in full, Ratzinger's description of the soul in "dialogical" terms: "Soul is nothing other than man's ability for relationship to the truth, to eternal love. And now the order of realities lines up properly: the truth which is love, which we call God, gives man eternity, and because matter is integrated into the human spirit, into the human soul, in him this matter thereby attains perfectibility in the resurrection."[82] In this way, Ratzinger connects the question of the salvation of matter with his idea of dialogical immortality. The soul interiorizes matter, and thereby draws it into a saving relationship with God. This is in fact very close—on the surface at least—to Greshake's position.

The Bodiliness (Leiblichkeit *or* Leibhaftigkeit) *of the Soul*

Because of the soul's irrevocable "interiorization" of the matter of its life and its unique relationship to the body, it can be said to possess "bodiliness" (*Leiblichkeit, Leibhaftigkeit*). And since this bodily orientation does not end in death, even the soul of a dead man can be said to possess this characteristic. Greshake can therefore say that "body constitutes man as being-in-the-world . . . This 'transcendental sense' of bodiliness actuates itself under the conditions of space and time, in what is known to us empirically as physical corporeality. But this 'transcendental sense' need not as such be bound to physical corporeality."[83] The distinction between *Leib* and *Körper* is here clearly evident, where the transcendental sense of *Leiblichkeit* is viewed phenomenologically and is clearly distinct from *Körperlichkeit*, a material and physical condition. In this schema, the soul possesses *Leiblichkeit* even beyond death.

---

82. Ibid. (*Eschatologie*, 219–20; *Eschatology*, 259). "Seele ist nichts anderes als die Beziehungsfähigkeit des Menschen zur Wahrheit, zur ewigen Liebe. Und nun wird die Abfolge der Realitäten richtig: Die Wahrheit, die Liebe ist, das heißt Gott, gibt dem Menschen Ewigkeit und weil in den menschlichen Geist, in die menschliche Seele Materie integriert ist, darum erreicht in ihm die Materie die Vollendbarkeit in die Auferstehung hinein."

83. Greshake, *Resurrectio Mortuorum*, 321. "Leib konstituiert den Menschen als In-der-Welt-Sein . . . Dieser 'transzendentale Sinn' von Leiblichkeit verwirklicht sich unter den Bedingungen von Raum und Zeit in der uns empirisch bekannten Körperlichkeit. Aber der 'transzendentale Sinn' muß als solcher nicht daran gebunden sein."

Part Three: Ratzinger the Realist

Ratzinger, as we have seen, holds that the soul's orientation to matter does not end in death.[84] And he agrees with Greshake that one cannot speak univocally of a "bodiless soul."[85] In 1990, he approvingly cites Raphael Schulte, stating that in death, "we must not speak of a total disembodiment of the soul, but rather what remains is 'the soul's essential *relation* to its (fully valid) embodiment.'"[86] Sonnemans correctly notes that in Ratzinger, "this 'soul'-concept must include a 'bodiliness,' which, once again, is to be distinguished from 'materiality.'"[87]

Is "Bodiliness" Resurrection?

But if a soul can be said to possess "bodiliness" even after death, an obvious question arises: does this mean that the human being is already risen, or does resurrection involve more than simply "bodiliness"? For Greshake, the answer is clear: the soul's "bodiliness" means a "resurrection in death":

> Body (and thus history and world) are not simply left behind in death but rather come to finality in the subject: In death, and in the encounter with God that takes place there, man is precisely the outcome of his "bodiliness," i.e., his boundness and interwovenness with the world and history. From this point of view, in its fulfillment the soul bears within itself the risen and transfigured body (and thus the past worldly expression). Or, put another way: "Risen bodiliness is the whole living, organic ensemble of relations and reciprocal interconnections which— open to the whole of reality—our body has molded by means of its essential, particular individuality."[88]

---

84. E.g., Ratzinger, *Eschatologie*, 144 (*Eschatology*, 179). "If it is the essence of the soul to be 'form,' then its orientation to matter is irrevocable. One would have to dissolve the soul itself to take this orientation away from it." [Wenn es das Wesen der Seele ist, 'forma' zu sein, dann ist ihre Zuordnung auf Materie hin unaufhebbar und man müßte sie selber auflösen, um ihr dies zu nehmen.]

85. Ratzinger, "Zwischen Tod und Auferstehung" (*Eschatologie*, 219; *Eschatology*, 258).

86. Ratzinger, *Nachwort zur 6. Auflage* (*Eschatologie*, 193). "Schulte . . . läßt aber doch deutlich erkennen, daß es einerseits die Konstanz die Seele im Tode gibt und daß anderseits nicht von einer totalen Entleiblichung der Seele gesprochen werden muß, vielmehr 'der Wesens*bezug* der Seele auf ihre (vollgültige) Verleiblichung' bleibt." Ratzinger is citing Schulte, *Leib und Seele*, 57 (1980).

87. Sonnemans, *Seele*, 459. "in diesem 'Seelen'-Begriff muß eine 'Leiblichkeit' enthalten sein, die von einer 'Materialität' nochmals zu unterscheiden ist." Sonnemans discusses this further on 462–63.

88. Greshake, *Resurrectio Mortuorum*, 264–65. The same passage later appears in

Matter in Ratzinger's Theology of Resurrection

In this view, "bodiliness" represents the finality or summation of one's personal relation to the world and history and is not necessarily a physical state or constitution. There can even be a "risen bodiliness" which is contained within the soul. And since this is not annulled in death, it can be called resurrection:

> If thereby the material dimension—mediated and transformed in and through the spiritual subject—is not stripped away even in death, and if—as stated earlier—the relationality to the whole creation given with bodiliness is also not taken away but rather confirmed, then the assertion can be accounted for: the resurrection of the body happens *in death*, i.e., in death a soul does not separate from a body to partake in God's life, but rather in death the one and entire man suffers the loss of every relationship capable of being experienced, but through the crisis of death the person, one and entire, is saved by God.[89]

It should by now be clear that what we are dealing with in Greshake's theology is a risen embodiment which is a property of the soul, deriving from its relation to the world and history during its life, but not necessarily requiring the ongoing existence of matter *qua* matter. This is why such a hypothesis is sometimes referred to as "body-in-soul."[90] The issue is summed up well by the title of chapter 7 of Sonnemans' book: "Auferste-

---

"Parteiische Rückblick," 539. "Leib (und damit Geschichte und Welt) werden im Tod nicht einfach zurückgelassen, sondern kommen im Subjekt zur Endgültigkeit: Der Mensch ist im Tode und in der hier stattfindenden Gottsebegegnung genau das, was aus seiner 'Leibhaftigkeit,' d. h. Welt- und Geschichtsverwobenheit und -gebundenheit, geworden ist. So gesehen, trägt die Seele in ihrer Vollendung den erweckten verklärten Leib (und damit den vergangenen welthaften Ausdruck) in sich. Oder anders gesagt: 'Die auferweckte Leiblichkeit ist das ganze lebendige, organische Ensemble von Relationen und gegenseitigen Abhängigkeiten, die—offen auf das Ganze der Wirklichkeit—unser Leib von seiner wesenhaften partikulären Individualität her geprägt hat.'" The internal citation is from Moingt, "Immortalité de l'âme et/ou résurrection," 73.

89. Greshake, *Tod und Auferstehung*, 117–18. "Wenn somit die Dimension des Stofflichen—in und durch das geistige Subjekt vermittelt und verwandelt—auch im Tod nicht abgestrift wird und wenn—wie unter 'erstens' gesagt—auch die mit der Leiblichkeit gegebene Relationalität zur gesamtes Wirklichkeit nicht aufgehoben, sondern bestätigt wird, dann kann die Aussage verantwortet werden: *Im Tod* geschieht Auferstehung des Leibes, d. h., im Tod trennt sich nicht nur eine Seele vom Leib, um an Gottes Leben teilzunehmen, sondern im Tod erleidet der eine und ganze Mensch den Verlust aller erfahrbaren Beziehungen, wird aber von Gott her durch die Krise des Todes hindurch als eine und ganze Person gerettet."

90. E.g., Greshake, *Resurrection Mortuorum*, 253. There, Greshake suggests this idea goes back to Romano Guardini, who wondered if the body could be in the soul since it holds in itself the fruit of its historical *Dasein*. See Guardini, *Die letzten Dinge*, 59.

Part Three: Ratzinger the Realist

hung im Tod. Leiblichkeit statt Leib?" (Resurrection in Death: Bodiliness instead of a Body?). Sonnemans identifies the key differences between Ratzinger and Greshake in this regard: "The only part of the controversy between Greshake and Ratzinger that is merely verbal is the soul-concept; in reality their disagreement is about the understanding of bodiliness and materiality, of the fulfillment of matter and the cosmos. Here we must ask whether the concept of 'bodiliness,' as Greshake uses it, has anything at all to do with 'matter,' and whether Ratzinger's accusation that Greshake is proposing an 'aggravated Platonism' is to the point or misconstrues what Greshake means by 'bodiliness.'"[91]

We can bring this difference into sharper contrast by observing an exchange between Ratzinger and Greshake. Writing in response to Ratzinger's *Eschatologie*, Greshake asserts that the concept of a bodiless soul waiting in an "intermediate state" is nonsensical. He suggests that man "interiorizes" his body and his world throughout life. Thus, if in death man is not annihilated but saved by God, then that body and world also come to fulfillment. Greshake sums up: "With this point of difference, there is a difference of substance in which I would like to hold unconditionally to my position (*salvo meliore iudicio in futuro*), since the converse opinion [i.e., Ratzinger's], despite all assurances, is dualistic and only results in contradictions which can only be concealed with difficulty."[92]

Ratzinger responds in "Zwischen Tod und Auferstehung":

> If Greshake sees here a "difference of substance" with me, in which he "would like to hold unconditionally" (p. 180) to his position, then the point of difference will probably have to be narrowed down yet again. I have always taught, based on the *anima forma corporis* formula, the enduring body-orientation of the soul which has "produced" itself in the body and has thus integrated bodiliness into itself. That it has already "come to

---

91. Sonnemans, *Seele*, 459. "Die kontroverse zwischen Greshake und Ratzinger geht nur verbal um den Seelenbegriff; sachlich geht es in ihr um das Verständnis von Leiblichkeit und Materialität, von Vollendung der Materie und des Kosmos. Hier stellt die Frage, ob der Begriff der 'Leiblichkeit', wie Greshake ihn verwendet, überhaupt etwas mit 'Materie' zu tun hat, und ob Ratzingers Vorwurf, bei Greshake liege ein 'verschärfter Platonismus' vor, zutreffend ist oder an dem vorbeigeht, was Greshake unter 'Leiblichkeit' versteht." The internal citation from Ratzinger is from *Eschatologie*, 96 (*Eschatology*, 112).

92. Greshake "Leib-Seele-Problematik," 180. "Mit diesem Differenzpunkt ist eine Sachdifferenz gegeben, bei der ich unbedingt an meiner Position (salvo meliore iudicio in futuro) festhalten möchte, da die gegenteilige Meinung allen Versicherungen zum Trotz dualistisch ist und in nur mühsam überdeckte Widerspruche gerät."

fulfillment" with death (p 180), I consider to be incompatible with the openness of history, in which the resurrection has simply *not* happened yet, as 2 Tim 2:18 emphasizes.[93]

Ratzinger thus corrects what appears to be a misunderstanding of his position on Greshake's part, but the point of difference remains: although a soul may retain "bodiliness," this is not equivalent to resurrection. This becomes clearer in Ratzinger's later discussion of Johann Auer's eschatology:

> While the body dies, the metaphysical parameter "bodiliness" remains as the reality which essentially determines man. The distinction between "body" (physical) and "bodiliness" (metaphysical) is as such undoubtedly valid and helpful. But it does not solve the question of the concrete bearer of "bodiliness" and therefore does not solve the current problem either. For the fact that metaphysical "bodiliness" belongs to man even after death shows the constancy of a metaphysical constitution, but not the event of "resurrection." This distinction may be held and used, but one cannot derive from it the justification to assert a "resurrection in death."[94]

---

93. Ratzinger, "Zwischen Tod und Auferstehung" (*Eschatologie*, 222 n. 17; *Eschatology*, 287 n. 17). "Wenn Greshake hier eine 'Sachdifferenz' zu mir sieht, bei der er 'unbedingt' an seiner Position 'festhalten möchte' (180), so müßte der Differenzpunkt wohl nochmals eingeengt werden. Die bleibende Leibbezogenheit der Seele, die sich im Leib 'gezeitigt' und so Leiblichkeit in sich integriert hat, habe ich von der anima-forma-corporis-Formel her immer gelehrt. Daß sie bereits mit dem Tod 'zur Vollendung gekommen' sei (180), halte ich mit der Offenheit der Geschichte für unvereinbar, in der die Auferstehung eben noch *nicht* geschehen ist, wie 2 Tim 2,18 mit Nachdruck betont." Second Timothy 2:16–18 states, "Avoid such godless chatter . . . among them are Hymenaeus and Philetus, who have swerved from the truth by holding that the resurrection is past already."

94. Ratzinger, *Nachwort zur 6. Auflage* (*Eschatologie*, 192). An earlier English version of this passage (*Eschatology*, 288 n. 4) seems to be based on a slightly different German text and will not be followed here. "Während der Leib sterbe, bleibe die metaphysische Größe 'Leiblichkeit' als wesentlich den Menschen bestimmende Realität bestehen. Die Unterscheidung zwischen 'Leib' (phyisisch) und 'Leiblichkeit' (metaphysisch) ist als solche ohne Zweifel berechtigt und hilfreich. Sie löst indes nicht die Frage nach dem konkreten Träger von 'Leiblichkeit' und daher auch nicht das hier anstehende Problem. Denn der Tatbestand, daß zum Menschen auch nach dem Tod metaphysisch 'Leiblichkeit' gehört, zeigt die Konstanz einer metaphysischen Konstitution an, aber nicht das Ereignis 'Auferstehung'. So wird man diese Unterscheidung festhalten und nutzen, aber aus ihr nicht die Berechtigung der Behauptung einer 'Auferstehung im Tode' ableiten dürfen." As noted previously, Ratzinger here misquotes Auer, who uses the term "Leibhaftigkeit" rather than "Leiblichkeit," although no significant semantic distinction exists between the two words.

For Ratzinger, therefore, resurrection is more than a "metaphysical constitution" of the soul. Not even "interiorized" matter can count as a risen body. The resurrection requires more than an ongoing material *orientation* or *configuration*; it requires the *real matter* of the *real world*. And this real matter will not be transformed until the event of resurrection at the end of time. The fact of history's incompleteness therefore disallows a "resurrection in death" because of the intimate connection between the resurrection's materiality and ongoing history. It is therefore interesting that Greshake is essentially in agreement with Ratzinger (in his later writings at least) in that he allows an intermediate state between the fulfillment of the individual and the fulfillment of the entire human community at the end of history.[95] But for Greshake, the existence of "bodiliness" means that even this waiting period can be seen as a risen state.

At this point, an obvious question arises that points to the heart of the Ratzinger-Greshake difference: why does Ratzinger not allow that a soul's "bodiliness" could amount to resurrection? What more is required? The question could also be turned around and directed to Greshake: why does he hold a "resurrection in death" if he admits that there will be a greater fulfillment at the end of history? These questions point to the core issue dividing Ratzinger and Greshake: the *materiality* of the resurrection.

Matter in the Eschaton: "In Itself," or Only in Human Beings?

At the center of the whole debate lies the concept of "Materie an sich," or "matter in itself."[96] The term entered the debate via Greshake's 1969 book, *Auferstehung der Toten*, when Greshake stated (following Rahner) that "Die Materie 'an sich' (als Atom, Molekül, Organ . . .) ist unvollendbar."[97] In *Eschatologie*, Ratzinger attacked this statement, suggesting that it would entail "a partitioning of creation and in this respect would imply an ultimate dualism in which the entire realm of matter is excluded from creation's goal and relegated to a second-order reality."[98]

95. Greshake, "Leib-Seele-Problematik," 177–78.

96. The term "an sich" could also be translated "by itself."

97. Greshake, *Auferstehung der Toten* ["Matter 'in itself' (as Atom, molecule, organ . . .) is imperfectible"], 386. The corresponding passage from Rahner is in "Immanente und transzendente Vollendung," 594. Rahner, however, stated that "*die physische Welt als solche*" ["the physical world as such"] is imperfectible. The term "Materie 'an sich'" originates with Greshake, who nonetheless believes that it expresses Rahner's meaning.

98. Ratzinger, *Eschatologie*, 155 (*Eschatology*, 192). "Das würde, den gegenteiligen

Matter in Ratzinger's Theology of Resurrection

Greshake responded to this passage two years later:

> I cannot for the life of me understand how Ratzinger can make the accusation that in my interpretation, no fulfillment of matter can be thought, unless one gazes spellbound—like a deer in the headlights—upon a "matter in itself," which is itself left behind like a burnt-out rocket stage if matter is "interiorized" in spirit. But this view is misleading, for if matter is conceived strictly *ontologically* in its relation to man and his history of freedom (and this is the only way matter has meaning and being, cf. 114f., 169f.), then in this *ontological* view, no "matter in itself" is left behind, if all matter has interiorized itself in spirit and thereby has come to fulfillment.[99]

In a similar vein, Greshake later rhetorically asks, "what is such a perfection of matter 'in itself' supposed to mean? Isn't such a postulate absurd, as Rahner has already shown?"[100]

For Greshake, then, matter's ontological status is phenomenologically determined; it receives ontological status inasmuch as it is related to man and his history of freedom. To further illustrate his point, he claims that a solar system that no one ever saw would in itself be meaningless.[101] For this reason, matter cannot be fulfilled by itself; it needs (the human) spirit. Greshake can therefore ask Ratzinger, "Is it really so hard to distinguish between the perfection of matter 'in itself' *and* 'in the other'?"[102] The Teilhardian principle of hominization is strongly in play here.

Versicherungen zum Trotz, eine Teilung der Schöpfung und insofern einen letzten Dualismus bedeuten, bei dem der ganze Bereich der Materie aus dem Schöpfungsziel herausgenommen und zu einer Wirklichkeit zweiter Ordnung gemacht wird."

99. Greshake, "Leib-Seele-Problematik," 174–75. "Ich verstehe beim besten Willen nicht, wieso Ratzinger mir vorwirft, in meinen Interpretation könne keine Vollendung der Materie gedacht werden, es sei denn, man blicke gebannt—wie das Kaninchen auf die Schlange—auf eine 'Materie-an-sich', die gleich einer ausgebrannten Raketenstufe selbst dann zurückbleibt, wenn die Materie im Geist 'verinnerlicht' ist. Aber gerade diese Sicht führt in die Irre. Wird nämlich Materie *ontologisch* strikt gedacht in bezug auf den Menschen und seine Freiheitsgeschichte (und nur so hat Materie Sinn und Sein, vgl. 114f, 169f), dann bleibt—in dieser *ontologischen* Sicht—keine 'Materie-an-sich' zurück, wenn sich alle Materie im Geist 'verinnerlicht' hat und damit zur Vollendung gekommen ist." To stare at something "wie das Kaninchen auf die Schlange" means to be paralyzed by fear.

100. Ibid., 176. "Aber was soll eine solche Vollendung der Materie 'an sich' sein? Ist ein solches Postulat nicht widersinnig, wie das bereits Rahner gezeigt hat?"

101. Ibid., 177.

102. Ibid., 163. "Ist es wirklich so schwierig zwischen der Vollendung der Materie 'an sich' oder 'in sich' *und* 'im andern' zu unterscheiden?" It should be noted here that

Part Three: Ratzinger the Realist

But at this point an important distinction is in order. By stating that "Materie 'an sich' . . . ist unvollendbar," Greshake means on the one hand that matter cannot reach full perfection "by itself" or "in itself," but that its true fulfillment requires human beings, the crown of God's creation. But Greshake *also* understands this dictum in a second sense in which it implies that matter *itself* (i.e., matter *qua* matter) is simply imperfectible. It will be left behind like a "burnt-out rocket stage."[103] It is not clear whether this meaning was intended by Rahner as well. It is this second sense, however, which Ratzinger perceives when he objects that "Greshake's idea that the soul assimilates matter as the 'ecstatic moment' of the realization of its freedom and definitively leaves it behind *qua* matter to the eternally imperfectible would be inconceivable for Thomas."[104] Ratzinger objects here not so much to the idea that matter can only be fulfilled through man, but to the idea that matter, as a substance, cannot be saved.

Nachtwei has pointed out that within Ratzinger's dialogical-relational theology, there can really be no such thing as matter "in itself" since matter can never be utterly detached from everything and is therefore always in relation.[105] This is an important insight, but it has no effect on the second sense in which Greshake understands matter "in itself," which is the real crux of the disagreement with Ratzinger.

We can see this disagreement in clearer outline when we consider the following exchange over the materiality of the risen body. In "Zwischen Tod und Auferstehung," Ratzinger argues that the human subjectivity posited by Greshake, which lives on after death (Greshake later called this entity a "'leibhaftige' Seele"),[106] "clearly has nothing to do with man's

---

"an sich" and "in sich" mean essentially the same thing in this case and so have been rendered together as "in itself" in order to avoid a confusing English translation.

103. It should be noted, of course, that it is not, strictly speaking, Greshake's position that matter "in itself" is left behind like a burnt-out rocket stage. Greshake does believe, however, that what Ratzinger is so fixated upon (i.e., Ratzinger's understanding of matter "in itself") *is* in fact left behind like a burnt-out rocket stage.

104. Ratzinger, *Eschatologie*, 144 (*Eschatology*, 179). "Die Vorstellung Greshakes, daß die Seele die Materie als 'ekstatisches Moment' ihres Freiheitsvollzugs in sich aufnimmt und sie als *Materie* im ewig Unvollendbaren dann definitiv hinter sich läßt, ist von Thomas her unvollzeihbar."

105. Nachtwei, *Dialogische Unsterblichkeit*, 137. Sonnemans (*Seele*, 449) makes the same point, but within the context of Rahner's theology.

106. Greshake, "Römische Lehrschreiben," 189.

historical body and its materiality."¹⁰⁷ Greshake's response reveals his position more clearly:

> This could be the remaining substantial difference between Ratzinger's position and my own: Ratzinger still thinks (as before, cf. *Eschatologie* 62ff.) of a fulfillment of matter "in itself" and a fulfillment of time "in itself," or put another way: Ratzinger thinks the space-time schema also holds for the eschaton. But if one assumes that in death not time "in itself" but rather time's *finality* is preserved and saved—not existence in matter (i.e., in body and world) "in itself," but rather the *finality* of this existence—then we can dispense with Ratzinger's desideratum to hold open the soul for a (yet again!) new unity of spirit and matter which is not already reached in death.¹⁰⁸

Greshake, then, holds the eternal preservation of matter's *finality*, but not of its existence *as matter*. He states that "the fact that space and time *in themselves* will not be fulfilled excludes nothing from the final fulfillment except the *mode* of the spatio-temporal realization of the person's life."¹⁰⁹ But this statement appears rather disingenuous, if one accepts that matter itself is a real *thing*. For if matter has being in itself (and surely it does in the scholastic theology to which Greshake makes such frequent appeal), then what is excluded from the eschaton is real being, a real part of God's creation. Greshake, however, only considers matter's relevance inasmuch as it represents the "mode" in which a person's life is realized in this spatio-temporal world which will pass away. But is matter not a *thing* as well as

---

107. Ratzinger, "Zwischen Tod und Auferstehung" (*Eschatologie*, 215; *Eschatology*, 252–53). "Und mit welchem Recht kann man es eigentlich Leib nennen, da es doch mit dem geschichtlichen Leib des Menschen und seiner Materialität offenkundig nichts zu tun hat."

108. Greshake, "Römische Lehrschreiben," 189–90. "Hier dürfte die bleibende Sachdifferenz zwischen Ratzinger und der hier vertretenen Position liegen: Ratzinger denkt nach wie vor (vgl. S.62ff.) eine Vollendung der Materie 'in sich' und eine Vollendung der Zeit 'in sich', oder anders: Ratzinger denkt das Raum-Zeit-Schema auch für die Vollendung weiter. Wenn man aber davon ausgeht, daß im Tod nicht die Zeit 'in sich', sondern die *Endgültigkeit* der Zeit aufbewahrt und gerettet wird, nicht das Sein in Materie (d.h. in Leib und Welt) 'in sich', sondern die *Endgültigkeit* dieses Seins, so entfällt das Desiderat Ratzingers, die Seele für eine (nochmals!) neue Einheit von Geist und Materie offenzuhalten, die nicht schon im Tod erreicht ist." Greshake's internal citation is from the 1st edition of *Eschatologie*, whose page numbers differ from the current 6th edition.

109. Ibid., 189. "Dadurch, daß Zeit und Raum *in sich* nicht vollendet werden, bleibt nicht etwas von der Vollendung ausgeschlossen, es sei denn die *Weise* des zeit-räumlichen Lebensvollzugs der Person."

a *mode* of human existence? Is it not more than a kind of matrix in which the human person actuates himself?

In Greshake, however, matter is only considered in its relation to the human spirit. His assertion that only matter's *finality* is saved and not the matter itself is predicated on the presupposition that matter's *ontological* status is derived from its *meaning*. Here, ontology is determined phenomenologically. This is why Greshake can say that matter only has being in relation to man and his history of freedom.[110]

The result of all this is a heaven which contains the perfected "finalities" of material things, but not the material things themselves, which are in themselves "imperfectible." For this reason, we must ask whether Ratzinger does not score a direct hit when he denounces "resurrection in death" as an "aggravated Platonism."[111] For doesn't such a view represent the upshot of Plato's doctrine of the ideas in its most dualistic interpretation?[112]

The Spiritualization of Matter

In fact, Greshake's understanding of matter is derived in large part from Teilhard de Chardin. Greshake makes frequent reference to Teilhard's idea that matter and spirit are "no longer two things, but two *states*, or two aspects of one and the same cosmic stuff."[113] He is also deeply influenced by Leo Scheffczyk's view of matter, in which matter undergoes a process of "spiritualization" in the body, making it clear that "matter is on a path to fulfillment which more and more escapes the attachment to corporeality,

---

110. Greshake, "Leib-Seele-Problematik," 175.

111. Ratzinger, *Eschatologie*, 96 (*Eschatology*, 112). "Im übrigen muß man hier wiederum in doppelter Hinsicht einen verschärften Platonismus anprangern."

112. Nachtwei (*Dialogische Unsterblichkeit*, 129) notes that even if Ratzinger's accusation that *no* matter is saved is an overstatement, it is still the case that in Greshake, "matter is . . . dualistically disjoined into one area where it is perfected in man, and into another area where it is left to its own fate." [Materie wird, schärfer formuliert, dualistisch zertrennt in einen Bereich, der im Menschen vollendet wird, und in einen Bereich, der seinem eigenen Schicksal überlassen bleibt.]

113. Greshake, *Resurrectio Mortuorum*, 319. I have used the English translation found in Teilhard de Chardin, *Heart of Matter*, 26. This work dates from 1950.

measurability and rigidity."[114] Matter's value lies in its ability to be the "expression" and "revelation" of something that lies behind it—spirit.[115]

But in Greshake it is not so much that matter and spirit become united (so that matter *itself* becomes implicated in spirit and spiritualized), but rather that only matter's meaning or finality (and not its substance) is preserved. "Matter, then, is forever inscribed in the subject . . . even if matter's self-actualizing bondage to space and time, as sensory reality or as corporeality, ends in death."[116] In *Tod und Auferstehung*, Greshake cites a passage from Teilhard on "hominization" and then offers his interpretation: "the 'interiorization' of matter into the self-realization of the human spirit brings forth, in fact, another form of 'matter' than that which is known to us from the objective world of the senses or from our own corporeality. It is transformed, liberated, 'unbounded' matter."[117] But since for Greshake, what is "interiorized" is not matter in itself but only matter's finality, this new "liberated" form of matter can only be a way of expressing the change brought about in the human spirit by its contact with the body and matter. It is not matter as commonly understood. It is not a counterpart to spirit but rather a modality or modification of spirit.

---

114. Ibid., 321. "Diese anfanghafte 'Vergeistigung' der Materie, die sie schon im Leibe erfährt, erlaubt nun den Schluß, daß die Materie in dieser Schöpfung auf einem Vollendungsweg begriffen ist, der sie immer mehr der Verhaftung an Körperlichkeit, Massigkeit und Starre entzieht." This entire passage is a citation from Scheffczyk, *Auferstehung*, 291. Interestingly, Scheffczyk notes that this very passage is actually based on Hengestenberg's *Der Leib und die letzten Dinge*, 59. Greshake also follows Scheffczyk in "Leib-Seele-Problematik," 172–73. It should be pointed out, however, that even Scheffczyk holds a fulfillment of the material world apart from man—e.g., Scheffczyk, *Auferstehung*, 287–88.

115. Ibid., 320.

116. Greshake, "Leib-Seele-Problematik," 171. This passage is found in virtually identical form in "Verhältnis 'Unsterblichkeit der Seele' und 'Auferstehung des Leibes,'" 117 and in *Tod und Auferstehung*, 117. "Materie ist dann für immer im Subjekt (nicht in der Seele!) eingeschrieben, auch wenn die als sinnenhafte Wirklichkeit oder als Körperhaftigkeit sich realisierende Raum-Zeit-Gebundenheit der Materie im Tod ein Ende findet." I have omitted Greshake's parenthetical interjection because he admits the term *soul* in later works.

117. Greshake, *Tod und Auferstehung*, 117. "Die 'Verinnerlichung' von Materie in den Selbstvollzug des menschlichen Geistes hinein bringt freilich eine andere Gestalt von 'Materie' hervor als die, welche uns aus der sinnenhaften Objektwelt oder von der eigenen Körperlichkeit her bekannt ist. Es ist verwandelte, befreite, 'entgrenzte' Materie."

Part Three: Ratzinger the Realist

Augustine and Spiritualization

What, then, can we say about this debate from the Augustinian perspective? Greshake asserts a real salvation of matter, yet restricts this salvation to matter's *finality* so that matter is saved by becoming interiorized into spirit while matter "in itself" is imperfectible. Greshake, of course, believes that matter only has meaning and significance in relation to the human spirit and thus believes that matter's true *telos* is to become spiritualized (through interiorization). As internally coherent as this may be, it is hard to imagine a position that more strongly contradicts Augustine's view. For according to Augustine, the risen body will be called spiritual "not because flesh will be converted into spirit, which is what some have inferred [from 1 Cor 15:44]."[118] On the contrary, "it will still be flesh and not spirit."[119]

The Greshakian concept of "interiorization" into spirit against which Ratzinger sets himself stands in stark contrast to the Augustinian notion of the risen body's spiritualization. In both cases, it is the human spirit that spiritualizes the body. In Augustine, spiritualization happens in the risen body so that the matter of that body is elevated by the human spirit and belongs completely to it. In Greshake, however, matter and the body make a sort of imprint upon the soul so that matter achieves lasting fulfillment by the mark it leaves in the human spirit, which is the only thing that endures. But in this case, what is saved is neither matter nor the earthly body, but a sort of fossilized impression of it while the actual matter of this world is left to decay and annihilation.[120]

By arguing for the salvation of matter "in itself," Ratzinger instinctively places himself on the side of Augustine. Although Greshake's intent is to hold a close relationship between matter and spirit, the resultant

---

118. Augustine, *civ. Dei* 13.20.

119. Ibid., 22.21.

120. Greshake, "Parteiische Rückblick," 548 n. 40. "I am attempting, completely along the lines of modern anthropology, to differentiate between *Körper* and *Leib*. By '*Körper*' is understood simply that human materiality that is the object of empirical experience and science, which man is always newly 'disposing of' throughout his life, and which he 'disposes of' once and for all in death. By '*Leib*' is meant that concrete-historical impression of man which is irrevocably taken up in the soul as the fruit of being-in-the-world." [Ganz im Zuge neuzeitlicher Anthropologie versuche ich, zwischen Körper und Leib zu differenzieren, wobei unter Körper eben jene menschliche Materialität verstanden wird, die Gegenstand empirischer Erfahrung und Wissenschaft ist und deren sich der Mensch in seinem Leben stets neu und im Tod einmal endgültig 'entledigt', und unter Leib jene konkret-geschichtliche Prägung des Menschen, die als Frucht des In-der-Welt-Seins in der Seele unverwechselbar aufgehoben ist.]

Matter in Ratzinger's Theology of Resurrection

schema is what Ratzinger would call a "monistic solution" since matter is not fulfilled *as* matter but only inasmuch as it becomes "interiorized" by spirit. Out of fear of "dualism," Greshake refuses to allow matter any ongoing existence in its own right and therefore proposes a position which, contrary to his intentions, leads in the direction of an eschatological spirit-monism.

Just as Augustine saw in the incarnation the primary reason for taking matter seriously,[121] so Ratzinger notes in the 2006 foreword to *Eschatologie* that "the bodiliness of Christ, who retains a body in eternity, means the taking seriously of history and matter."[122] Christ's assumption and retention of the entirety of human nature—including its material aspects—led both Augustine and Ratzinger to the ultimate conclusion that matter's final goal—spiritualization—lies not in being converted into spirit but in belonging perfectly to it.

The Salvation of the World

When discussing Greshake's statement that matter "in itself" is imperfectible, we noted two possible meanings. The first implies that matter can only be perfected in and through man (and not by itself), while the second implies that only matter's finality (and not matter *qua* matter) is perfected by being interiorized in the human spirit. As we have seen, Ratzinger emphatically rejects the second meaning. As to the first, Ratzinger clearly affirms that matter is perfected by being "integrated into the human spirit."[123] Yet he does not make "interiorization" in the human spirit a *sine qua non* of matter's salvation. He does not deny the meaning and salvific potential of unseen solar systems. Nachtwei rightly observes that "against any Gnostic truncation of the faith, Ratzinger wants to hold to the fulfillment of matter as an independent, ongoing reality in reciprocal relationship to man. Simply put: in the eschaton, matter and the cosmos will be present not only as

---

121. Augustine, *civ. Dei* 10.24. "Thus, [by his incarnation] the good and true Mediator showed that it is sin which is evil, and not the substance or nature of flesh. He showed that a body of flesh and a human soul could be assumed and retained without sin, and laid aside at death, and changed into something better by resurrection."

122. Ratzinger, *Vorwort Papst Benedikts XVI. zur Neuausgabe* (*Eschatologie*, 14; *Eschatology*, xxi). "Die Leibhaftigkeit Christi, der in Ewigkeit Leib behält, bedeutet das Ernstnehmen der Geschichte und der Materie."

123. Ratzinger, "Zwischen Tod und Auferstehung" (*Eschatologie*, 219–20; *Eschatology*, 249). "Weil in den menschlichen Geist, in die menschliche Seele Materie integriert ist, darum erreicht in ihm die Materie die Vollendbarkeit in die Auferstehung hinein."

an *interiorized* moment of human history but also as an additional counterpart in the relational-dialogical unity of creation."[124] Ratzinger can thus declare that "it is the entire creation that will become a vessel of divine glory. The whole created reality is included in beatitude. God's creature, the world, is—as the Scholastics say—an 'accidental' part of the final joy of the saved."[125] And in 1992, he states that the reason we cannot imagine the resurrection at the end of time is because "we know neither the potential of matter nor the potency of the Creator. But since the resurrection of Christ we do know that not only the individual will be saved, but that God also wants to—and is able to—save his entire creation."[126]

Ratzinger's understanding of the salvation of the world, then, hangs upon a rejection of both senses of Greshake's dictum. For, if the world can only attain fulfillment *through man* then it is difficult to imagine how that world could become an "accidental" element in beatific joy (it would instead be intrinsic to man, having become part of the human spirit). And if the physical world itself is not saved except as a fossilized impression in the human spirit, then what is saved is not actually *the world*. This is why Ratzinger declares that "denying the soul and asserting a resurrection in death means a spiritualistic theory of immortality which considers as impossible an actual resurrection and the salvation of the world as a whole."[127]

---

124. Nachtwei, *Dialogische Unsterblichkeit*, 171. "Ratzinger will gegen eine gnostische Verkürzung den Glauben an die Vollendung der Materie als eigenständiger in wechselseitiger Bezogenheit zum Menschen stehender Wirklichkeit festhalten. Vereinfacht gesagt: Materie und Kosmos wird es in der Vollendung nicht nur als *verinnerlichtes* Moment der Menschheitsgeschichte geben, sondern auch als äußeres Gegenüber in der relational-dialogischen Einheit der Schöpfung."

125. Ratzinger, *Eschatologie*, 188 (*Eschatology*, 237). "daß die gesamte Schöpfung dazu bestimmt ist, Gefäß göttlicher Herrlichkeit zu werden. Die ganze geschaffene Wirklichkeit wird in die Seligkeit einbezogen; Gottes Geschöpf Welt ist—wie die Scholastiker sagen—ein 'akzidentelles' Stück der endgültigen Freude der Geretteten."

126. Ratzinger, "Mein Glück," 157–58. My tranlation. "Wir können es uns nicht vorstellen, weil wir weder die Möglichkeiten der Materie noch die des Schöpfers kennen. Aber seit der Auferstehung Christi wissen wir, daß nicht nur die einzelnen gerettet werden, sondern daß Gott seine ganze Schöpfung retten will und daß er es kann."

127. Ratzinger, *Nachwort zur 6. Auflage* (*Eschatologie*, 194; *Eschatology*, 267). "Leugnung der Seele und Behauptung der Auferstehung im Tode bedeuten eine spiritualistische Unsterblichkeitstheorie, die wirkliche Auferstehung und Heil der Welt als Ganzes nicht für möglich hält."

Augustine and the Cosmic Process

Ratzinger's appropriation of Rahner's concept of the all-cosmic soul and his use of Teilhardian terminology, incomplete as these models may be, was intended to provide a supporting structure for his assertion that matter "in itself" will be saved. In effect, what Ratzinger expresses in Teilhardian terms—that in heaven there will be a more complex unity of matter and spirit and that this matter's new state will be brought about by spirit[128]—coincides well with Augustine's idea that in heaven, the body will be "spiritual" and that "we shall see Him [God] by the spirit in ourselves, in one another, in Himself, in the new heavens and the new earth, and in every created thing which shall then exist."[129]

The key difference, however, is that the Teilhardian system employed in a rather *ad hoc* way by Ratzinger is bound up with the notion of cosmic *process*, while Augustine's system is not. Or, put another way: the end result of Teilhard's vision is roughly equivalent to Augustine's, but the path to that goal differs tremendously. One could say that the problem with the view is not so much that the soul becomes "all-cosmic" (since the precise metaphysical nature of this world-orientation is nowhere specified and so could be interpreted in varying ways), but rather that the event "resurrection" appears to lie on a continuum with the gradually increasing union of matter and spirit. Further, resurrection not only thereby loses its unique character as a dramatic event of grace, but also appears to be so abstracted from lived human existence that it is not even clear that there will be individual, risen *bodies*. Augustine wanted to stress nothing more than the fact that each person will receive his own body back in the resurrection. Dissolving the distinct resurrection of discrete bodies into a more generic and general unification of spirit and matter contradicts the heart of Augustine's resurrection theology.

We have seen, however, that Ratzinger later became aware of the problems associated with theologies that view fulfillment as an upward evolutionary process and criticized Teilhard in this regard. In spite of the inadequacies of the "Teilhardian section" of *Eschatologie*, however, we must recognize Ratzinger's intention. He wants to affirm the final salvation of the entire universe so that nothing of the material world is excluded from the eschaton. The use of Teilhardian terms like "complexification" is intended to provide an alternative to Greshake's view, in which matter

128. Ratzinger, *Eschatologie*, 154 (*Eschatology*, 191).

129. Augustine, *civ. Dei* 22.29.

is only saved by being "spiritualized." Ratzinger still wants to maintain a real event of resurrection which is more than the final step of a gradual evolutionary process toward greater spiritualization, even if his discussion on pp. 154–56 of *Eschatologie*, taken alone, may suggest otherwise.

Augustinian Evaluation

We have already noted the differences between the idea held by Ratzinger in *Einführung* and, to a lesser extent, in *Eschatologie*, which saw eschatologial fulfillment as a process, and Augustine's view of resurrection as an event. We have seen that Ratzinger has moved in the direction of Augustine's thought. We also observed that Augustine's concept of "spiritualization" corresponds better to Ratzinger's than to Greshake's. For Augustine, what is saved is real matter and not only the fossilized impression that matter leaves in the human spirit. This brings us to another important aspect of Augustine's theology of resurrection: his emphasis on *nature*.

Earlier in this book, we saw that Augustine actually places an extraordinary emphasis on *nature* in the question of the resurrection. It is thus *this* body which will be raised, and *this* world which will be transformed. The *substantia* of created things will remain but they will be given new *qualitates*. We can thus locate Ratzinger's increasing emphasis on resurrectional physicality and materiality within the Augustinian stream that stresses the redemption of *natura*. Although both Ratzinger and Augustine see the resurrection as a *new* creation, neither emphasizes grace so strongly that nature becomes obscured.

The modern tendency to downplay the physicality of the resurrection, in part out of respect for the autonomy and proper territory of modern science, ultimately leads either to a disproportionate emphasis on grace (as in the *Ganztod* theory) or to a dualistic fission within nature, so that matter *as* matter ("Materie an sich") is left to the scientists while "resurrection" is ultimately reduced to the ongoing existence of spirit. Ratzinger, however, wants to hold the salvation of *this* world and of matter "in itself" and in this respect shares in the Augustinian emphasis on nature.

Some Remaining Questions

We have now established that Ratzinger views the resurrection as a material event involving matter "in itself," and that the eschatological fulfillment will encompass the entire created world. But several difficult questions remain. If the soul possesses an enduring "bodiliness" after death, then what is the relationship of that "bodiliness" to the future risen body, if that body will in fact be a material one (although elevated to a new mode of existence)? This also raises again the question of bodily identity. On the basis of Ratzinger's theology, can we speak of a true numerical identity between the earthly body and the risen one? And what is the place in this schema of the image of resurrection as fulfillment of a cosmic process, and of the "corpse-in-the-ground" argument employed by Ratzinger against "resurrection in death"?

Jesus' Resurrection and Ours: The Question of Material Continuity

Much light can be shed on these questions by examining Ratzinger's view of Jesus' resurrection. This is because for Ratzinger, as for Augustine, Jesus' resurrection and ours are bound inseparably together. Ratzinger notes, following 1 Cor 15:16, that if the dead are not raised, then Christ has not been raised either. Thus, "Christ's resurrection and the resurrection of the dead are not two realities but rather only one, which ultimately is nothing other than the verification of faith in God before the eyes of history."[130] This is consonant with the 1979 document of the Congregation for the Doctrine of the Faith, *Certain Questions*, which stated that the general resurrection "is nothing other than the extension to human beings of the Resurrection of Christ itself."[131]

After the publication of *Eschatologie*, however, Ratzinger became more and more suspicious that "resurrection in death" and the general anti-material sentiment it expressed might endanger the reality of Jesus' empty tomb. In "Zwischen Tod und Auferstehung," he expressed concern that "in radically following through on this model [i.e., 'resurrection in death'], Christ's resurrection becomes problematic as well. For if it is said

---

130. Ratzinger, *Eschatologie*, 100 (*Eschatology*, 116). "Auferstehung Christi und Auferstehung der Toten sind nicht zwei Wirklichkeiten, sondern eine einzige, die letztlich nichts anderes als eben Verifikation des Gottesglaubens vor den Augen der Geschichte ist."

131. Congregation for the Doctrine of the Faith, *Certain Questions* 2. In 1992, ITC's *Current Questions* (11.3) would connect resurrectional realism with Christ's resurrection: "Such a resurrection is envisaged in a thoroughly realistic way both because of the parallelism with Christ's own resurrection and because of the relationship with the dead body in the sepulchre."

that what befalls every Christian is what happened with Christ when he was raised, then we are approaching a disembodiment and de-historicization of the Lord's resurrection as well."[132] Given the close connection between Christ's resurrection and ours, it would seem natural that "resurrection in death" would also assert that Jesus rose when he died, thus eliminating the need for an empty tomb.

In 1987, Ratzinger lamented what he perceived as a "new Docetism," noting that "in many areas the force of this Docetism has become so potent that to maintain a virgin birth and an actual resurrection from the grave is considered by not a few to be positively undignified."[133] What happens, then, if Jesus' empty tomb is denied? "Naturally, then, *our* bodies cannot count on resurrection either, and the world may peacefully go on forever, since everyone rises in death."[134]

Given, then, the inextricable connection between Christ's resurrection and ours, a "resurrection in death" theology would deny not only any connection between the decaying corpse and the risen body, but could also lead to the denial of Jesus' empty tomb. For Ratzinger, this is another compelling reason for rejecting such a theory.

Greshake, Rahner, and the Empty Tomb

Ratzinger's suspicions were unequivocally confirmed when in 1998 Greshake published another article on "resurrection in death." In defending his theory, he notes that Christoph Schönborn has criticized "resurrection in death" as being incompatible with faith in Jesus' empty tomb.[135] But

132. Ratzinger, "Zwischen Tod und Auferstehung" (*Eschatologie*, 222 n. 12; *Eschatology*, 287 n. 12). "Darüber hinaus wird bei radikaler Durchführung dieses Modells auch die Auferstehung Christi problematisch. Denn wenn gesagt wird, jedem Christen widerfahre, was mit Christus in seiner Auferweckung geschehen ist, so liegt eine Entleiblichung und Entgeschichtlichung auch der Auferstehung des Herrn mindestens nahe."

133. Ratzinger, *Nachwort zur 6. Auflage* (*Eschatologie*, 201; *Eschatology*, 273). "An der Gestalt Christi wird weithin nur noch sein Wort wichtig genommen, nicht sein Fleisch (Jungfrauengeburt und wirkliche Auferstehung aus dem Grab zu vertreten, gilt bei nicht wenigen als geradezu unschicklich, so stark ist der Druck dieses Doketismus mancherorts geworden)."

134. Ibid (*Eschatologie*, 201; *Eschatology*, 273). "Natürlich kann dann auch *unser* Leib nicht mit Auferstehung rechnen, und die Welt mag ruhig unendlich so weitergehen, weil ja ein jeder im Tod aufersteht."

135. Greshake is citing Schönborn, "Auferstehung des Fleisches," where Schönborn states that Jesus' resurrection illustrates several things about our own. First, there is a

Matter in Ratzinger's Theology of Resurrection

Greshake sees such criticism as inconsequential because for him, Jesus' risen body has *no direct relation to his earthly body*. This is ultimately based on the idea—derived from Thomistic hylomorphism—that a dead body is not a real body, and is not directly involved in resurrection.[136] In Jesus' case, "only the personal identity of the earthly with the raised ('transfigured') Jesus is required. What is not essential is that some or all of the bodily material (the bodily remains), which in the moment of Jesus' death had been informed by his soul and was laid in the tomb, participates in the existence that Jesus brings into the world of God."[137] Greshake then cites Hans Kessler, asserting that "rising from the dead has nothing directly and absolutely to do with the cadaver.... Therefore the idea of the empty tomb is not a necessary component of Christian resurrection faith."[138]

---

clear distinction between death and resurrection. "The idea that resurrection already happens in the moment of death is incompatible with the basic fact of Jesus being laid in the tomb and his 'resurrection on the third day'" (23). [Die Idee, die Auferstehung geschehe bereits im Moment des Todes, stößt sich an der elementaren Tatsache der Grablegung Jesu und der 'Auferstehung am dritten Tag.'] Schönborn's second point is that "the risen body is really identical with the earthly body" (23). [der Auferstehungsleib ist real identisch mit dem irdischen Leib.]

136. Greshake, "Parteiische Rückblick," 539–40. After stating that "resurrection in death" rejects the idea of the reanimation of a corpse, he notes that "this idea already results from a consistent Thomistic anthropology, whereby the reality of the body is mediated through the soul and is not understood as a distinct empirical-physical reality" (539 n. 8). [Dies ergibt sich bereits aus einer konsequenten thomanischen Anthropologie, wonach die Wirklichkeit des Leibes durch die Seele vermittelt und nicht als empirisch-physikalische Eigenwirklichkeit zu verstehen ist.] Greshake (540) also cites Georg Scherer to show that Thomistic anthropology supports "resurrection in death" (Scherer, "Das Leib-Seele-Problem," 78–79). On p. 549 of "Parteiische Rückblick," Greshake laments that the Church's magisterium (particularly the 1992 document of the International Theological Commission) is not taking Thomas seriously enough.

137. Greshake, "Parteiische Rückblick," 550. "Erforderlich hierfür [i.e., für die Auferstehung Jesu] ist streng genommen nur die Personalidentität des irdischen mit dem erhöhten ('verklärten') Jesus. Nicht erforderlich ist, daß etwas oder gar alles von der Leibesmaterie (den Leibesresten), die im Augenblick des Todes Jesu von seiner Seele informiert und ins Grab gelegt war, an dem Aufgensmmensein der Person Jesu in die Welt Gottes teilnimmt." This entire passage is a citation from Kolping, *Fundamentaltheologie*, vol. III/1, 635. Greshake maintains that Kolping is "in no way a particularly 'progressive' fundamental theologian" (550). [Schon 1981 bemerkte der keineswegs sonderlich 'progressive' Fundamentaltheologe Adolf Kolping ...]

138. Ibid. "Das Auferstehen hat mit der Leiche nicht direkt und unbedingt etwas zu tun. ... Darum ist der Gedanken des leeren Grabes kein notwendiger Bestandteil des christlichen Auferstehungsglaubens." Greshake is citing Kessler, *Die Auferstehung Jesu Christi*, 334. There, Kessler bases this on his interpretation of 1 Cor 15:50 ("flesh and blood cannot inherit the kingdom of God, nor does the perishable inherit the imperishable"). The corpse is corruptible, and so is doomed to decomposition. Kessler states that

Part Three: Ratzinger the Realist

Greshake cites other theologians whom he claims hold this view,[139] but the most important authority appealed to is Rahner, who states that

> as a common concept . . . resurrection says nothing about a future for that materiality which we know as the corpse which is left behind, since the saved finality of the one man can also be imagined and granted without a sort of total substantial change to the abandoned materiality which is only its own as long as it is part of the whole of the man. Neither, then, does resurrection . . . imply the idea of an empty, evacuated tomb.[140]

And in 1975, Rahner had similarly declared that the identity of the risen body cannot in any way be based on the matter of the earthly body:

> What good would it do the identity of the earthly and transfigured body if one tried to imagine into the risen body some kind of material particle that had once belonged to the earthly body? This kind of thing can simply no longer be imagined or thought today. We, however, consider from here on that identity is given through the identity of the spiritual subject of freedom, through what we call the 'soul.' Therefore even the empirical experience of the corpse in the grave no longer supplies any argument at all that the 'resurrection' has not yet taken place.[141]

---

such a view concerning the decomposition of Jesus' body is not contradicted by Acts 2:27, 31 ("For thou wilt not abandon my soul to Hades, nor let thy Holy One see corruption . . . He was not abandoned to Hades, nor did his flesh see corruption") because in this passage avoiding corruption simply means being saved from death.

139. Greshake ("Parteiische Rückblick," 550 n. 53) names Georg Essen's *Historische Vernunft und Auferweckung Jesu*, 352ff.; Hansjürgen Verweyen's *Gottes letztes Wort*, 441ff.; and Karl-Heinz Menke's *Die Einzigartigkeit Jesu Christi*, 148ff.

140. Rahner, *Das große Kirchenjahr*, 256. My translation. "Auferstehung sagt . . . als allgemeiner Begriff von sich aus nichts von einer Zukunft jener Materialität aus, die wir als zurückgelassenen Leichnam kennen, da die gerettete Endgültigkeit des einen Menschen auch gedacht und gegeben sein kann ohne die in einem gewissermaßen totalen Stoffwechsel aufgegebene Materialität, die die eigene nur ist, solange sie im Ganzen des Menschen west. Auferstehung . . . impliziert darum auch nicht die Vollendung eines leeren, geleerten Grabes." A more paraphrastic English translation can be found in Rahner, *Great Church Year*, 174. This particular excerpt is from a sermon Rahner gave at the Easter Vigil in 1970. Greshake cites this passage in "Parteiische Rückblick," 547-48.

141. Rahner, "Über den Zwischenzustand," 461-62. My translation. This work dates from 1975. "Was würde es überhaupt der Identität zwischen dem irdischen und dem verklärten Leib nützen können, wenn man irgendeine solche materielle Partikel in den Auferstehungsleib hineindenken würde, die früher einmal zum irdischen Leib gehört hätte? So etwas läßt sich doch heute einfach nicht mehr vorstellen und denken. Identität ist für uns vielmehr durch die Identität des geistigen Freiheitssubjekts, das 'Seele'

Matter in Ratzinger's Theology of Resurrection

Greshake rejects the idea that Jesus had a bodiless existence for three days. The proclamation that Jesus was raised on the "third day" is thus a "formula" for a miraculous intervention of God, indicating his resurrection *pro nobis*.[142] This does not mean that Greshake absolutely denies the *possibility* of an empty tomb, however. "In any case, I would not want to *a priori* rule out that the 'empty tomb' was perhaps, in the context of the Jewish ideas of the time, a 'necessary' *sign* placed by God, to stand for the resurrection realized on the cross."[143] Yet the fact remains that for Greshake, the empty tomb "is not a necessary component of Christian resurrection faith" but rather "a 'sign,' a 'signpost,' a 'symbol,' a 'signal' without which resurrection faith could, presumably, have hardly permeated into the worldview of that time period."[144] From all this, Greshake concludes that "Jesus' resurrection and its exemplarity for ours is no argument against the thesis of 'resurrection in death.'"[145]

Therefore, "resurrection in death" does in fact apply to Jesus, who rises when he dies on the cross. In such a schema, it is difficult to see how the dead body of Jesus laid in the tomb bears any salvific significance. It does not become transfigured or elevated into a higher state of being and is essentially another "burnt-out rocket stage." The identity between Jesus' dead and risen body that Thomas Aquinas had taken pains to defend on the basis of the Fathers[146] is here abandoned in the name of Thomas himself.

---

genannt wird, jetzt und künftig gegeben. Darum kann auch die empirische Erfahrung des Leichnams im Grab gar kein Argument mehr abgeben, daß die 'Auferstehung' noch nicht stattgefunden habe." For another English translation, see "Intermediate State," 120.

142. Greshake, "Parteiische Rückblick," 550.

143. Ibid., 550 n. 53. "Ich möchte jedenfalls nicht apriori ausschließen, daß das 'leere Grab' ein von Gott gesetztes, im Kontext der damaligen jüdischen Vorstellungen vielleicht sogar 'notwendiges' *Zeichen* für die am Kreuz realisierte Auferstehung war."

144. Ibid., 552. "Angesichts dessen ist die Überzeugung von einer Auferstehung Jesu erst nach drei Tagen sowie von einem leeren Grab kein notwendiger Bestandteil des christlichen Auferstehungsglaubens. Vielmehr ist letzteres 'Zeichen', 'Wegzeichen', 'Symbol', 'Signal', ohne welches der Auferstehungsglaube sich unter den Bedingungen der damaligen Vorstellungswelt vermutlich kaum hätte durchsetzen können." Greshake ("Parteiische Rückblick," 552 n. 61) claims to have drawn these ways of describing the empty tomb from Heinrich Schlier, Walter Kasper, Jacob Kremer, Jürgen Moltmann, and Hans Kessler; he provides no references, however.

145. Ibid. "Somit spricht der Blick auf die Auferstehung Jesu und deren Exemplarität für unsere Auferstehung nicht gegen die These von der 'Auferstehung im Tod.'"

146. Aquinas took pains to formulate his system so that it would agree with the Fathers. In *Quodl.* IV, q. 5 he cites John Damascene against the possibility of Christ's body

Part Three: Ratzinger the Realist

Ratzinger's Recent Statements on Resurrectional Realism

We have now glimpsed a certain tendency in modern theology to view Jesus' bodily resurrection as independent of the empty tomb. Already by the time of *Eschatologie*, Ratzinger considered that a strict Thomistic hylomorphism was untenable due in part to its inability to maintain the identity of the earthly body of Jesus with the one laid in the tomb.[147] It was during this time that he also appears to have abandoned the *Leib-Körper* distinction which, along with the Thomistic-Aristotelian understanding of *materia prima* connected with it, forms the foundation for Greshake's metaphysical devaluation of the corpse.

Ratzinger had already stated in 1987 that if Jesus' tomb was not empty, "then *our* bodies cannot count on resurrection either."[148] Such a statement certainly suggests what could be called a strongly "realist" (or even "physicalist") view of resurrection since it implies that our resurrection will also involve empty graves. And regarding Ratzinger's accusation that Greshake's use of the term *resurrection* is "a classic case of *lingua docta*, the language of historicist scholars" which could never convince a believer "that his dead friend has just risen from the dead,"[149] Greshake responds caustically that "in these statements, Ratzinger reveals just how 'physicalistically' he understands the resurrection, seeing it fundamentally as the restoration of the *Körper*, so that faced with the corpse one may not, according to him, speak of resurrection."[150]

Given this relatively recent criticism by Greshake, along with his denial of the necessity of the empty tomb, one would expect that Ratzinger

---

decaying, and in *Summa* III, q. 50, a. 5 he follows Athanasius' statement that it was the same body that was laid in the tomb. Of course, we must distinguish between Aquinas' intent (to follow the Fathers) and the adequacy of his Aristotelian-hylomorphic system to realize that intent.

147. Ratzinger, *Eschatologie*, 145–46 (*Eschatology*, 180–81).

148. Ratzinger, *Nachwort zur 6. Auflage* (*Eschatologie*, 201; *Eschatology*, 273). "Natürlich kann dann auch *unser* Leib nicht mit Auferstehung rechnen."

149. Ratzinger, "Zwischen Tod und Auferstehung" (*Eschatologie*, 216; *Eschatology*, 254). "Daß aber sein toter Freund soeben auferstanden sei, das kann ihm keine Sprache der Verkündigung einsichtig machen, weil diese Verwendung von 'Auferstehung' typische *lingua docta*, historistisches Gelehrtensprache, aber kein möglicher Ausdruck gemeinsamen und gemeinsam verstandenen Glaubens ist."

150. Greshake, "Parteiische Rückblick," 541. "In diesen Ausführungen zeigt sich, wie 'physizistisch' Ratzinger Auferstehung versteht, nämlich im Grunde doch als Wiederhinzugabe des Körpers, so daß angesichts des Leichnams nach ihm nicht von Auferstehung gesprochen werden kann."

Matter in Ratzinger's Theology of Resurrection

would clarify his own position relative to such issues if he were to write again on resurrection. This happened in 2004, when Ratzinger published "Jungfrauengeburt und leeres Grab," in which he took the opportunity to make clear his own position on Jesus' empty tomb. From that point on, we see clear and consistent affirmations of the physical realism of the resurrection.

"Jungfrauengeburt und leeres Grab": The Context

This very short document is, on the surface, primarily concerned with the theologians of the Katholische Integrierte Gemeinde,[151] which had opened a theological academy in Rome in 2003. Ratzinger had begun a friendly association with this community in 1976, shortly before he was made archbishop of Munich and Freising. The community's theologians include Gerhard Lohfink (Greshake's former coauthor) and Rudolf Pesch. Pesch's 2002 book, *Über das Wunder der Jungfrauengeburt*, essentially argues that the virgin birth of Jesus is to be interpreted primarily ecclesiologically. It also seems to suggest that Joseph was the biological father of Jesus.[152]

Ratzinger begins by stating that

> For a long time now, but particularly since the appearance of Rudolf Pesch's book *Über das Wunder der Jungfrauengeburt* (2002), the question has been posed to me over and over again whether the theologians of the Integrated Community actually accept the Church's belief in the virginal conception and birth of Jesus (*natus ex Maria virgine*), and in his bodily resurrection. Since my friendly connection with this circle of theologians is well-known, this was at the same time also a question to me which I couldn't leave unclarified.[153]

---

151. The Katholische Integrierte Gemeinde (KIG), or Catholic Integrated Community, is composed of Catholic priests as well as married and single laypeople who generally live in communal households. Rudolf Pesch and his family joined the community in 1990.

152. Pesch, *Über das Wunder der Jungfrauengeburt*, 175. "Luke makes it unmistakably clear—as the fourth evangelist does in an even clearer way (cf. Jn 1:45; 6:42)—that God's fatherhood alone constitutes Jesus' divine sonship, but does not necessarily exclude the human fatherhood of Joseph." [Lukas macht—wie übrigens noch deutlicher der vierte Evangelist (vgl. Joh 1,45; 6,42)—unmissverständlich klar, dass die Vaterschaft Gottes die göttliche Sohnschaft Jesu exklusiv konstituiert, aber nicht die menschliche Vaterschaft Josefs ausschließen muss.]

153. Ratzinger, "Jungfrauengeburt." "Schon seit längerer Zeit, besonders aber seit dem Erscheinen des Buches von Rudolf Pesch, 'Über das Wunder der Jungfrauengeburt' (2002), wurde immer wieder die Frage an mich gerichtet, ob denn die Theologen

Part Three: Ratzinger the Realist

Ratzinger seems to have felt the need to publish this document (which is the summary of an address he gave privately to the theologians of the KIG) because he recognized that all the questions he had received about the virgin birth and the empty tomb were directed toward him as well. With respect to the virgin birth, this could be partly due to the fact that he himself had held a position quite close to Pesch's in his *Einführung* (1968),[154] even if he had changed that position in *Die Tochter Zion* (1977) (where he criticized Pesch for misappropriating his statements on the virgin birth).[155]

What is particularly interesting, however, is the fact that Ratzinger raises the question of the empty tomb. Why does he bring it up here? While Greshake's 1998 article was certainly not the primary motivation, we can say that the theological tendency (in both the systematic and exegetical fields) manifested in that article was an impetus behind Ratzinger's decision to publish a "clarification" of his personal views on the topic. The membership in the KIG of Lohfink (who had co-authored several works on resurrection with Greshake) could also have played a role. That

---

der Integrierten Gemeinde wirklich das Bekenntnis der Kirche zur jungfräulichen Empfängnis und Geburt Jesu ('natus ex Maria virgine') und die leibliche Auferstehung Jesu annähmen. Da meine freundschaftliche Verbundenheit mit diesem Kreis von Theologen bekannt ist, war dies zugleich auch eine Frage an mich selbst, die ich nicht ungeklärt stehen lassen durfte."

154. Ratzinger, *Intro.*, 274–75 (*Einführung*, 258–59). "According to the faith of the Church, the Divine Sonship of Jesus does not rest on the fact that Jesus had no human father; the doctrine of Jesus' divinity would not be affected if Jesus had been the product of a normal human marriage."

155. Ratzinger, *Daughter Zion*, 51 n. 11. German text in *Die Tochter Zion*, 50 n. 9. "I would like to emphasize clearly the limits of my frequently cited observation in *Einführung in das Christentum* (Munich, 1968), 225, that Jesus' divine sonship would not of itself exclude an origin in a normal marriage. I wanted only to emphasize very clearly the distinction of biological and ontological levels of thought and to clarify that the ontological statements of Nicaea and Chalcedon are not as such identical with the statements about the virgin birth. This should not be used to deny that, despite the distinction of levels, a deep, even an indissoluble correspondence exists between the two levels, between Jesus' unity of person with the eternal Son of the eternal Father and the earthly fatherlessness of the man Jesus. Yet I admit that I did not make the point clearly enough; to that degree von Balthasar's critique, ibid., 43, [Balthasar, "Empfangen durch den Heiligen Geist," 43] is justified. But to everyone who reads not only the cited passage of my book (225) but also the whole section (222–30) it must otherwise be crystal clear that the use of my remarks in R. Pesch, *Das Markusevangelium* I (Freiburg, 1976), 323, contradicts my meaning." More recently, cf. Benedict XVI, Angelus, December 18, 2011. "Not only did the Virgin Mary conceive, but she did so through the work of the Holy Spirit, that is, God Himself. The human being who came to life in her womb took Mary's flesh, but his existence derived totally from God. . . . In this sense, the virginity of Mary and the divinity of Jesus guarantee each other."

Ratzinger chose to publish such a clarification suggests that he recognized that the issue of Jesus' empty tomb had not been sufficiently addressed in his previous writings on resurrection. In fact, apart from various passing remarks, this is Ratzinger's first explicit, extensive treatment of the question of what happened to Jesus' body after it was laid in the tomb.

Ratzinger's Resurrectional Realism in "Jungfrauengeburt und leeres Grab"

In "Jungfrauengeburt," Ratzinger (in true Augustinian fashion) frames the question of a material resurrection in terms of God's power. He begins by noting that most modern science confines religion to the realm of subjectivity, disallowing any intervention of God in the material world.[156] He notes that such a view is proposed in the midst of what deceptively appears to be an exaltation of matter but is really "a subtle new Gnosticism."[157] When God is forbidden from acting upon matter, we are left with

> a God who is no God at all but only a product of psychology and wishful thinking. This is why Jesus' conception of the virgin is so important: God's Spirit can bring about something new and can intervene in the real world, in the world of the body. This is why it is so important that resurrection not be evaporated away into a hermeneutical construct while the body of Jesus is left to rot in the tomb. No, matter is God's! This insight is so pivotal precisely because our subtle Gnosticism cannot tolerate it anymore.[158]

---

156. Ratzinger, "Jungfrauengeburt." "In the view of most modern science, religion belongs strictly in the realm of subjectivity. There, everyone can experience and feel whatever they want. But the world of matter—the objective world which obeys other laws—God has no business there." [Die Religion gehört gerade nach der Vorstellung des Großteils der modernen Wissenschaft in den Bereich der Subjektivität: Da kann jeder empfinden und fühlen, was er mag. Aber die Welt der Materie—die objektive Welt, die gehorcht anderen Gesetzen, da hat Gott nichts zu suchen.]

157. Ibid. "Heute gibt es bei aller Lobpreisung der Materie einen subtilen neuen Gnostizismus, der Gott die Materie wegnimmt."

158. Ibid. "Ein solcher Gott ist jedoch kein Gott, sondern nur noch ein Element der Psychologie und der Vertröstung. Deshalb ist die Empfängnis Jesu aus der Jungfrau so wichtig: Gottes Geist kann Neues schaffen, in der leibhaftigen Welt, in die Welt des Leibes eingreifen. Und deswegen ist es so wichtig, dass Auferstehung nicht zu einem Interpretament verflüchtigt wird, während man den Leib Jesu im Grab verwesen lässt. Nein, die Materie ist Gottes; das ist gerade deswegen so zentral, weil unser subtiler Gnostizismus dies nicht mehr vertragen kann."

Part Three: Ratzinger the Realist

The question of the resurrection is thus immediately reframed as a question of whether God is powerful enough to raise up the matter of a dead body. This is precisely the line of argumentation used by Augustine in *De Civitate Dei*.[159] Ratzinger recalls a statement made by the more conservative Protestant theologian Adolf Schlatter in a conversation with his more liberal colleague Adolf von Harnack: "the question of miracles is actually a question of whether God is God,"[160] because an impotent God who cannot do miracles would be no God at all.

Ratzinger then proceeds to deal with the preliminary question of whether faith can give us certainty about historical events. He declares that a historically acting God is an essential part of biblical faith, and "thus some foundational historical facts belong to faith as faith, whose certainty is completely different from hypothetical probability."[161] Among these facts are Jesus' virginal conception and his bodily resurrection.

With respect to the first, we see that Jesus is a "new creation" not only on the ontological level but also on the *biological* level.[162] Thus, Jesus' dead body "did not remain in the tomb and did not undergo decay but has been transformed by God's power into the new embodiment of the Risen One."[163]

---

159. Cf. *civ. Dei* 22.26. "In any case, why can He not cause the flesh to rise again, and live eternally? . . . Of His omnipotence, which causes so many unbelievable things to happen, we have already said a great deal. If our adversaries wish to know what the Almighty cannot do, here they have it; I will tell them: He cannot lie." Also, *civ. Dei* 22.20, 21.7.

160. Ratzinger, "Jungfrauengeburt." "'Nein, uns trennt die Gottesfrage, denn in der Wunderfrage geht es in der Tat darum, ob Gott Gott ist oder ob er nur dem Bereich der Subjektivität zugehört.'" Ratzinger also recalls this conversation (with slightly different wording) in *God and the World*, 60–61. German version in *Gott und die Welt*, 68.

161. Ratzinger, "Jungfrauengeburt." "Dem biblischen Glauben ist es eigen, dass er von einem geschichtlich handelnden Gott redet, und deswegen gehören einige grundlegende historische Fakten zum Glauben als Glauben, dessen Gewissheit ganz anders geartet ist als die Wahrscheinlichkeit der Hypothese."

162. Ibid. "He is truly son of a human mother and truly man. But he is also simultaneously the beginning of a new creation coming forth—biologically, even—from God himself." [Für die glaubende Kirche war es von Anfang an eine zum Glaubenskern gehörende Gewissheit, dass Jesus nicht aus der Verbindung eines Mannes und einer Frau hervorgegangen ist, sondern dass Gott ihn aus und in Maria, der 'heiligen Erde ihres Leibes' (wie die Väter sagen) als den zweiten Adam geschaffen hat, so dass er wahrhaft Sohn einer menschlichen Mutter und wahrhaft Mensch ist, aber doch auch und zugleich Anfang einer neuen Schöpfung, von Gott selbst auch biologisch herkommend.]

163. Ibid. "Desgleichen gehört es zu diesen historischen Gewissheiten des Glaubens, dass Jesu Leib nicht im Grab geblieben und nicht der Verwesung verfallen, sondern durch die Kraft Gottes in die neue Leiblichkeit des Auferstandenen umgewandelt worden ist." Also, cf. *Gott und die Welt*, 363 (*God and the World*, 337). This dates from

Matter in Ratzinger's Theology of Resurrection

Again, God's power over matter is strongly affirmed. It is also interesting that in this case, the dead *Leib* (*not* the *Körper*) is itself transformed into a new form of embodiment. This is not a case of "spiritualization" through "interiorization" but truly involves matter "in itself."

Ratzinger again drives the point home, connecting God's power to a material resurrection:

> A God who cannot also act on matter would be a powerless God. Matter would, so to speak, belong to a sphere beyond God's action. This idea is radically opposed to the biblical faith articulated by the confession of the Church. It ultimately denies divinity to God. This is why the Church's faith does not find it surprising but on the contrary consistent and reasonable that God, in his central historical action—in the incarnation, death, and resurrection of the Lord—has shown his power over matter, and has brought about the conception of Jesus in Mary's womb. It is not surprising either that after Jesus's burial he acted again on the dead body of Jesus, snatching it from decay and bringing it into the new mode of existence of those who are risen, which Jesus himself had described to the Sadducees as the mode of existence of the sons of God (Lk 20:36): its archetype and beginning is the risen Son.[164]

2000. "Christ has stepped out of this world and its life, into a new mode of embodiment which is no longer subject to physical laws. This embodiment belongs to the world of God, from which Christ shows himself to men and opens his heart to them so that they might recognize him and touch him." My translation. [Christus ist aus dieser Welt und ihrem Leben herausgetreten in eine neue Weise von Leiblichkeit, die nicht mehr den physikalischen Gesetzen unterliegt. Sie gehört der Welt Gottes zu, von der aus er sich den Menschen zeigt und ihnen das Herz aufschließt, damit sie ihn erkennen und berühren.]

164. Ratzinger, "Jungfrauengeburt." "Ein Gott, der nicht auch an der Materie handeln könnte, wäre ein ohnmächtiger Gott—die Materie wäre sozusagen eine dem Handeln Gottes entzogene Sphäre. Diese Vorstellung ist dem biblischen Glauben, den das Bekenntnis der Kirche artikuliert, radikal entgegengesetzt. Sie spricht letztlich Gott das Gottsein ab. Deswegen ist es für den Glauben der Kirche nicht verwunderlich, sondern im Gegenteil konsequent und einsichtig, dass Gott in seinem zentralen geschichtlichen Handeln—in Menschwerdung, Sterben und Auferstehung des Herrn—seine Macht bis in die Materie hinein gezeigt, die Empfängnis Jesu im Mutterleib Mariens bewirkt und dass er wieder nach dem Begräbnis am toten Leib Jesu gehandelt, ihn der Verwesung entrissen und ihn in die neue Seinsweise der Auferstandenen hineingeführt hat, die Jesus selbst den Sadduzäern gegenüber als die Seinsweise der Söhne Gottes bezeichnet hatte (Lk 20, 36): Ihr Urbild und Anfang ist der auferstandene Sohn." Luke 20:36: "For they cannot die any more, because they are equal to angels and are sons of God, being sons of the resurrection."

Part Three: Ratzinger the Realist

This is by far the most explicit affirmation by Ratzinger of the material, numerical continuity between the dead body of Jesus and his risen body. Like Augustine, Ratzinger maintains that this dead body has been transformed and brought into a "new mode of existence." That God has *brought* Jesus' earthly body into this new mode of existence suggests a direct material continuity since the earthly body does not give rise to, but is itself drawn into, the exalted form of heavenly existence. Jesus' body was snatched from decay, which is a material, biological process.

The second point to note—which is very important—is that Ratzinger states that Jesus' body was brought into "the new mode of existence of those who are risen." The form of Jesus' risen embodiment, then, is identified with ours. Ratzinger further connects this to Jesus' words to the Sadducees about the nature of the resurrection. Jesus—the "risen Son"—is the archetype for the resurrection of all of us who are made God's sons by adoption. This is a point to which we will have to return: if Jesus' resurrection is the archetype for ours, and if his risen embodiment (from a material standpoint) is identical to ours, then we have moved closer to answering some of the questions we raised earlier about Ratzinger's theology. It would thus seem, then, that there must (in some way at least) be material continuity between our earthly and risen bodies. In this case, the *Leiblichkeit* of a "separated" soul would only be complete when it is again coupled with the "real" matter of its body, which would be elevated into a new mode of existence in the resurrection. This is fully consistent with the statement by the Congregation for the Doctrine of the Faith that the separated soul lacks full embodiment.[165]

In "Jungfrauengeburt," then, Ratzinger, by means of a certain polemical reorientation of the question, responds to the position of Greshake and other theologians who deny the necessity of Jesus' empty tomb. Ratzinger believes that the fundamental cause of this position is a "subtle new Gnosticism" which is uncomfortable with the scandal of God acting upon the material world. He therefore frames his response in terms of God's power over his creation, which includes matter. Within this context, Ratzinger finds it not scandalous but perfectly reasonable that there would be a direct, numerical, material identity between the dead and risen body of Jesus, even if the earthly body is transformed into a new kind of embodiment. The material realism expressed in *Die Tochter Zion* (1977) regarding Christ's virginal conception is now extended to his bodily resurrection as well.

---

165. Congregation for the Doctrine of the Faith, *Certain Questions* 3.

Ratzinger's Resurrectional Realism after His Election to the Papacy in 2005

Much of the material contained in "Jungfrauengeburt" was later used by Ratzinger in his discussion of the resurrection of Jesus in the second volume of his *Jesus of Nazareth* series (2011),[166] as well as in his discussion of Jesus' virginal conception in the corresponding volume on the infancy narratives (2012).[167] In these works, he strenuously affirms the physicality and materiality both of Jesus' bodily resurrection, and of his conception in Mary's womb.

This new emphasis on physicality is also present in some of his later pronouncements as Pope Benedict XVI. Consider, for example, his new appraisal of 1 Cor 15:50 in his homily at the 2012 Easter Vigil: "'Flesh and blood cannot inherit the kingdom of God,' as Saint Paul says in the First Letter to the Corinthians (15:50). On the subject of Christ's resurrection and our resurrection, the Church writer Tertullian in the third century was bold enough to write: 'Rest assured, flesh and blood, through Christ you have gained your place in heaven and in the Kingdom of God' (CCL II, 994). A new dimension has opened up for mankind. Creation has become greater and broader."[168]

---

166. For example, *Jesus of Nazareth II*, 257 (*Jesus von Nazareth II*, 282): "Resurrection essentially implies that Jesus' body [*Leib*] was not subject to corruption. . . . Theological speculations arguing that Jesus' decomposition and Resurrection could be mutually compatible belong to modern thinking and stand in clear contradiction of the biblical vision." Also, *Jesus of Nazareth II*, 254 (*Jesus von Nazareth II*, 279): "Today, notions of resurrection have been developed for which the fate of the corpse is inconsequential. Yet the content of the Resurrection becomes so vague in the process that one must ask with what kind of reality we are dealing in this form of Christianity."

167. Cf. Ratzinger, *Infancy Narratives*, 56–57. Here, he outlines (as in "Jungfrauengeburt") the problem with the modern worldview: that in restricting God to the subjective sphere, it ultimately denies him his divinity. However, if God is God, then he has power over matter, and has acted on matter in the conception and resurrection of Christ, e.g., p. 56: "Karl Barth pointed out that there are two moments in the story of Jesus when God intervenes directly in the material world: the virgin birth and the resurrection from the tomb, in which Jesus did not remain, nor see corruption." Also, p. 57: "If God does not have power over matter, then he simply is not God. But he does have this power, and through the conception and resurrection of Christ he has ushered in a new creation."

168. Benedict XVI, Homily, April 7, 2012. Also cf. Ratzinger, *Jesus of Nazareth II*, 274, where Ratzinger cites the same passage by Tertullian: "Indeed, matter itself is remolded into a new type of reality. The man Jesus, complete with his body [*Leib*], now belongs totally to the sphere of the divine and eternal. From now on, as Tertullian once said, 'spirit and blood' have a place within God (cf. *De Resurrect. Mort.* 51:3)." Here,

Part Three: Ratzinger the Realist

Here, the interpretation expressed decades earlier in *Einführung* is explicitly rejected in favor of the realism of Tertullian, the same realism which likely influenced Augustine. Flesh and blood now have a place in heaven, even if the way that flesh and blood participate in the resurrection is here left unexplained.

Further, in his homily for Ash Wednesday in 2012, Benedict XVI cited a passage from Origen to support the participation of "dust and ashes" in the resurrection of the body. There, he spoke of

> the unthinkable closeness of God who beyond death, opens the way to resurrection, to paradise finally regained. There is a similar text by Origen that says: "What was initially flesh, from the earth, a man of dust (cf. 1 Cor 15:47), and was destroyed by death and returned to dust and ashes—as is written: *you are dust, and to dust you shall return*—is made to rise again from the earth. Later, according to the merits of the soul that inhabits the body, the person advances towards the glory of a spiritual body" (*Sui Prìncipi* 3, 6, 5: S.Ch, 268, 248).[169]

In this homily, Benedict XVI does not further develop the idea of the participation of dust and ashes in the resurrection of the body. It is interesting, however, that in this case it is the flesh, the man of dust, that rises again from the earth before its transformation into a spiritual body. Whatever Ratzinger's opinion of Origen's theology of resurrection, it is notable that the text he chooses to cite involves the participation of bodily remains in the resurrection. Although the resurrection is not the focal point of the homily, the passing reference above implies a physical realism that cuts against the grain not only of Ratzinger's earlier theology, but of a large segment of modern theology.

There is also the recent claim by Ratzinger that in Jesus' resurrection, "*matter itself* [*Materie selbst*] is remolded into a new type of reality . . . since we ourselves have no experience of such a renewed and transformed type of matter [*Materialität*] . . . it is not surprising that it oversteps the boundaries of what we are able to conceive."[170] Here again, "matter itself" is saved by being drawn up into a new kind of existence.

---

however, Ratzinger's text misquotes Tertullian (the error is in the German text itself), who did not speak of "spirit and blood" but "caro et sanguis," i.e., flesh and blood. Probably the error arose during transcription (Ratzinger writes his books by hand) due to the orthographical similarity between "Fleisch" and "Geist."

169. Benedict XVI, Homily, February 22, 2012.

170. *Jesus of Nazareth II*, 274 (*Jesus von Nazareth II*, 299).

Yet neither in "Jungfrauengeburt" nor in his *Jesus of Nazareth* series does Ratzinger discuss any of the (Thomistic) metaphysical issues underpinning those theologies that have no need for an empty tomb. This may be due to the non-technical nature of these works, but it is more likely an indication that Ratzinger—as already suggested in *Eschatologie*[171]—believes such metaphysical conclusions (including the *Leib-Körper* distinction and the non-identity between Jesus' living and dead body) to be invalid. Ratzinger therefore addresses what he believes to be the root cause of the denial of the empty tomb, which is an overly zealous allegiance to the so-called "modern worldview" and its *a priori* exclusion of the miraculous.

Augustinian Evaluation

Although in *Eschatologie* there appeared to be a tension in Ratzinger's theology of resurrection, this tension has been eliminated in Ratzinger's later works, where he opts for a more realist, Augustinian view of resurrection. Ratzinger is no longer concerned (as he once was) with the "modern worldview" and its emphasis on science and evolution. While not rejecting either science or evolution outright, he does not believe that they can form the basis of a theology. In his later, more realist eschatology, we also see something of a move away from the transcendental theology of Rahner, occasionally employed in *Einführung* and *Eschatologie*. Writing in 1997, Ratzinger recalled the experience of working with Rahner at Vatican II:

> As we worked together, it became obvious to me that, despite our agreement in many desires and conclusions, Rahner and I lived on two different theological planets.... Despite his early reading of the Fathers, his theology was totally determined by Suarezian scholasticism and its new reception in the light of German idealism and of Heidegger. His was a speculative and philosophical theology in which Scripture and the Fathers in the end did not play an important role and in which the historical dimension was really of little significance. For my part, my whole intellectual formation had been shaped by Scripture and the Fathers and profoundly historical thinking. The great difference between the Munich school, in which I had been trained, and Rahner's became clear to me during those days, even though it still took a while for our parting of ways to become outwardly visible.[172]

---

171. Ratzinger, *Eschatologie*, 145–46 (*Eschatology*, 180–81).

172. Ratzinger, *Milestones*, 128–29.

Part Three: Ratzinger the Realist

This "parting of ways" is nowhere more explicit than in Ratzinger's resolute rejection of the assertion that the resurrection does not require an empty tomb.[173] Whereas the key influences on Greshake's eschatology appear to be Rahner and Teilhard (who also play a strong role in Ratzinger's early eschatological works), their influence disappears in Ratzinger's more recent works on the resurrection. His more recent insistence on the reality of miracles and on the biological character of Jesus' virginal conception and bodily resurrection consciously opposes the scientific worldview that both Rahner and Greshake wish to take seriously.

We can see the change in boldness of theological expression by comparing different statements from Ratzinger. In the first, from *Eschatologie* (1977), he defines "the concrete content of the faith in the resurrection" as "the certainty that the dynamic of the cosmos is leading to a goal . . . in which matter and spirit will newly and finally belong to each other."[174] Such an assertion, in all its generality, says nothing at all about what risen embodiment might be like. In "Jungfrauengeburt" (2004), however, Ratzinger declares that in Jesus' resurrection, God provides "the certainty . . . that his action reaches all the way to the body"[175] wherein he "has proven himself as Lord over death, which is ultimately a biological phenomenon, a phenomenon of the body."[176] Ratzinger graphically describes that "after Jesus' burial [God] acted again on the dead body of Jesus, snatching it from decay and bringing it into the new mode of existence of those who are risen."[177] We can see that Ratzinger's earlier reserved formulations asserting a general union of spirit and matter as the climax of a cosmic process have given way to bold statements declaring that the resurrection is a biological, physical *event* whereby God's power acts upon individual

---

173. Rahner makes this claim in *Das große Kirchenjahr*, 256.

174. Ratzinger, *Eschatologie*, 156 (*Eschatology*, 194). "Aber es gibt die Gewißheit, daß die Dynamik des Kosmos auf ein Ziel zuführt, auf eine Situation, in der Materie und Geist einander neu und endgültig zugeeignet sein werden."

175. Ratzinger, "Jungfrauengeburt." "Dieses auf dem Zusammenhang von Prophetie und geschehener Geschichte beruhende Stichwort von der Rettung des Leibes Jesu vor der Verwesung gehört zentral zum biblischen Auferstehungszeugnis und bleibt zentral in der Theologie der Väter. Es hat der Kirche die Glaubensgewissheit vermittelt, dass Jesus wirklich leiblich auferstanden ist, dass Gottes Handeln bis in den Leib hinein reicht."

176. Ibid. "er [Gott] . . . sich als Herr über den Tod erwiesen hat, der ja schließlich ein biologisches Phänomen, ein Phänomen des Leibes ist."

177. Ibid. "er [Gott] wieder nach dem Begräbnis am toten Leib Jesu gehandelt, ihn der Verwesung entrissen und ihn in die neue Seinsweise der Auferstandenen hineingeführt hat."

Matter in Ratzinger's Theology of Resurrection

human bodies.[178] In this respect, his newfound "realism" represents a clear move in the direction of the Augustinian theology of *De Civitate Dei* XXII.

Ratzinger: Visualizing Heaven

Ratzinger and the Visio Dei

We have now considered the questions of bodily identity and materiality, but a final question remains: what will heaven be like? What will we do there? We have already seen how Augustine came to understand the divinizing *visio Dei* as taking place through the risen body. Augustine variously describes the state of beatitude as perpetual adoration of God, unending

---

178. In this regard, Marschler's comments ("Perspektiven," 176–77 n. 61) are somewhat puzzling. Concerning the "corpse-in-the-ground" argument used by Ratzinger in *Eschatologie*, Marschler warns that "one should certainly not interpret this criticism of Ratzinger's as if he himself considered the resurrection as a 'resumption' of the materially identical earthly body—even in his later works in the debate he has not fallen back into that 'physical transfiguration' of the Tradition, which he has criticized again and again." [Man darf diese Kritik Ratzingers gewiss nicht so verstehen, als postuliere er selbst Auferstehung als 'Zurücknahme' des material identischen irdischen Leibs—auch in seinen späteren Beiträgen zur Debatte ist er nicht in jene 'Verklärungsphysik' der Tradition zurückgefallen, die er ausdrücklich immer wieder kritisiert hat.] Perplexingly, however, the only evidence provided by Marschler from these "later works" is a brief article from 1972 ("Die Auferstehung Christi und christliche Jenseitshoffnung," 34–37) in which Ratzinger (as he had often done up until 1977) emphasized that the only certainty about eschatological fulfillment was that at the end of time, creation as a whole would be fulfilled. Marschler then continues, "One could hardly call such statements 'physicalist.'" Marschler, however, nonetheless exhibits a certain awareness of that development of Ratzinger's which has been argued for in the present work: "Whether over the course of the years Ratzinger's theses exhibit at least a tendency toward more traditional-physicalist formulations would require a more exact study.... some formulations, as for example the cautious opinion in favor of the thesis that 'God could have intervened in biological or physical processes' ("Damit Gott alles in allem sei," 122 [English "My Joy"]), seem to point in this direction." ['Physizistisch' wird man solche Aussagen wohl kaum nennen können. Ratzingers eigentliches Anliegen ist hier die Auferstehung 'am Ende der Zeiten', nicht die Betonung einer irgendwie identischen Leiblichkeit. Ob im Laufe der Jahre Ratzingers Thesen zumindest eine Tendenz hin zu eher traditionell-physizistischen Formulierungen erkennen lassen, würde eine exaktere Untersuchung erfordern.... manche Formulierungen, wie z.B. das vorsichtige Votum zugunsten der These, dass 'Gott in biologische oder physikalische Vorgänge eingegriffen haben' könnte, in diese Richtung deutbar scheinen (*Damit Gott alles in allem sei* [sic], 122).] Given the difficulty of condensing Ratzinger's entire eschatology into a single book chapter, it is not surprising that Marschler's treatment of the resurrection is limited in scope and on the whole only superficially deals with many of the issues.

song,[179] and eternal rest.[180] And although he acknowledges that "I do not know what the nature of that occupation, or rather of that rest and repose, will be,"[181] Augustine nonetheless feels authorized to state that we will see God by means of our own bodies, and in the bodies of others.[182] In his theology, the human body and the whole creation is filled with God's presence, although the human body remains a human body. In heaven, we will see and know all the other blessed, seeing God with them and in them.[183]

Ratzinger, however, has surprisingly little to say about the risen state in most of his writings. Although he began in 1957 by graphically asserting that "the risen body remains a real human body, even retaining sexual difference"[184] and that "the resurrection does not bypass the 'relics' of the old earthly body, insofar as they are still recognizably present as such,"[185] by the time of *Einführung* there is virtually no talk of the characteristics of the risen body or of heaven. There, Ratzinger emphasizes that heaven "is not to be understood as an everlasting place above the world or simply as an eternal metaphysical region."[186] Rather, it "is to be defined as the contact of the being 'man' with the being 'God'; this confluence of God and man took place once and for all in Christ when he went beyond *bios* through death to new life."[187] In *Einführung*, then, the reticence to speak of what happens in heaven is consistent with Ratzinger's position at that time, which downplayed the individual and material aspects of resurrection and so would not be expected to have much to say about heaven.

In *Eschatologie* we also find little said about the risen state. Ratzinger contends that we can ascertain a sense *that* there will be eternal life, but "the *what* of this new life remains completely out of our area of experience and thus, from our point of view, absolutely unknowable."[188] Although he

179. Augustine, *s.* 243.8.

180. Augustine, *civ. Dei* 22.30; *s.* 362.27.28.

181. Augustine, *civ. Dei* 22.29.

182. Ibid., 22.30.

183. Ibid.; *s.* 243.5.

184. Ratzinger, "Auferstehungsleib," 1053. "Der auferstandene Leib bleibt . . . ein wahrer Menschenleib, auch der Unterschied der Geschlechter bleibt bestehen."

185. Ibid. "die ganze kirchl. (doktrinelle u. liturg.) Tradition zwingt jedoch zu der Einschränkung, daß die Auferstehung an den 'Reliquien' des alten Erdenleibs nicht vorbeigeht, soweit sie noch eindeutig als solche vorhanden sind."

186. Ratzinger, *Intro.*, 313.

187. Ibid.

188. Ratzinger, *Eschatologie*, 132 (*Eschatology*, 161). "Dagegen bleibt das *Was* dieses

Matter in Ratzinger's Theology of Resurrection

speaks in Teilhardian terms of the new union of spirit and matter that Christ will bring about, from this he concludes that "the new world is unimaginable. Neither are there any kind of conceivable, concrete statements about the way humans will relate to matter in the new world, or about the 'risen body'. There is, however, the certainty that the dynamic of the cosmos is leading to a goal, to a situation in which matter and spirit will newly and finally belong to each other."[189] Here, the impression is given that the only thing we can know about heavenly existence is that matter and spirit will be united. It is therefore not so surprising when the reader discovers that in this manual on eschatology, the section on "heaven" is only 3.5 pages long (in the German edition). In that section Ratzinger develops a Christological notion of heaven as the place in God that is created for us by Jesus' humanity.[190]

> Heaven, as becoming one with Christ, thus has the character of adoration; the clear sense of every form of worship is fulfilled in it: Christ is the eschatological temple (Jn 2:19), heaven is the new Jerusalem, the shrine where God is worshiped. The movement toward the Father of a humanity united to Christ is a response to the opposite movement of God's love which offers itself to man. Thus, worship in its heavenly, fulfilled form, involves the uninterrupted immediacy of God and man which the theological tradition has described as the vision of God. The controversial issue between the Thomists and the Scotists of whether this fundamental action is better described as vision of God or as love, depends on the anthropological starting point; but ultimately it

---

neuen Lebens gänzlich außerhalb unseres Erfahrungsraumes und somit von uns her gesehen schlechthin unwißbar."

189. Ibid., 156 (*Eschatology*, 194). "Es gibt keine Vorstellbarkeit der neuen Welt. Es gibt auch keinerlei irgendwie konkretisierbaren und in die Vorstellung reichenden Ausagen über die Art des Materiebezugs der Menschen in der neuen Welt und über den 'Auferstehungsleib'. Aber es gibt die Gewißheit, daß die Dynamik des Kosmos auf ein Ziel zuführt, auf eine Situation, in der Materie und Geist einander neu und endgültig zugeeignet sein werden."

190. Ibid., 185 (*Eschatology*, 234). This same notion is expressed again in *Jesus of Nazareth II*, 274 (*Jesus von Nazareth II*, 299–300): "Even if man by his nature is created for immortality, it is only now [i.e., with the resurrection of Jesus] that the place exists in which his immortal soul can finds its 'space', its 'bodiliness' ['*Leiblichkeit*'], in which immortality takes on its meaning as communion with God and with the whole of reconciled mankind. This is what is meant by those passages in Saint Paul's prison letters (cf. Col 1:12–23 and Eph 1:3–23) that speak of the cosmic body of Christ, indicating thereby that Christ's transformed body is also the place where men enter into communion with God and with one another and are thus able to live definitively in the fullness of indestructible life."

comes down to this: the sheer permeation of the whole man by God's fullness, and man's pure openness, which God—"all in all" and thus in man himself—allows to be filled boundlessly.[191]

The description of the *visio Dei* here is eloquent, but undeniably visually restrained. We will be one with God and filled with him, but beyond that little is delineated. On the contrary, Ratzinger urges caution in the use of heavenly images.[192] This is in stark contrast to Augustine's lengthy and moving description in *De Civitate Dei* of how we will see God. Ratzinger's reticence to speak of the particulars of heavenly existence, at least in *Eschatologie*, is in all likelihood motivated by his discomfort at that time with overly physicalist or "mythological" representations of heaven and of the risen body. Although Ratzinger has not explicitly treated the topic of the *visio Dei* since *Eschatologie*, he has certainly shown an openness to greater physical realism in eschatological imagery. In this respect, there is a certain shift toward Augustine's position. On the whole, however, Ratzinger has avoided Augustinian speculation on the details of the risen body and the *visio Dei*.

While such restraint is undeniably advantageous in avoiding embarrassment, from the perspective of proclamation it paradoxically risks having the opposite effect, that is, of making the Christian message overly intellectual and abstract. The vivid imagery of Augustine provides the believer with concrete images to take hold of, and in which to hope. A martyr may well offer up his life in the knowledge that he will one day see his God face to face, in his own flesh. But it is less likely that he would give his life for "the certainty that the dynamic of the cosmos is leading to a goal, to a situation in which matter and spirit will newly and finally belong to each other."[193] The problem from a kerygmatic point of view is that

---

191. Ibid., 186 (*Eschatology*, 234–35). "Himmel als Einswerden mit Christus hat somit den Charakter der Anbetung; in ihm ist der vordeutende Sinn jedes Kultes erfüllt: Christus ist der endzeitliche Tempel (Joh 2,19), der Himmel das neue Jerusalem, die Kultstätte Gottes. Der Bewegung der mit Christus vereinten Menschheit auf den Vater hin antwortet die Gegenbewegung der Liebe Gottes, die sich dem Menschen schenkt. So schließt der Kult in seiner himmlischen Vollendungsform die trennungslose Unmittelbarkeit von Gott und Mensch ein, die von der theologischen Überlieferung als Anschauung Gottes bezeichnet wird. Die zwischen Thomisten und Skotisten umstrittene Frage, ob dieser Grundakt besser als Anschauung Gottes oder als Liebe zu bezeichnen ist, hängt vom anthropologischen Ansatz ab; im letzten geht es immer um das eine— die reine Durchdringung des ganzen Menschen von der Fülle Gottes und seine reine Offenheit, die Gott 'alles in allem' und so ihn selbst grenzenlos erfüllt sein läßt."

192. Ibid., 187–88 (*Eschatology*, 237).

193. Ibid., 156 (*Eschatology*, 194). "Aber es gibt die Gewißheit, daß die Dynamik des

the excision of potent visual imagery (like Augustine's) from resurrection theology may make the Christian faith less ridiculous in the eyes of the world, but it ultimately robs that faith of its truly *human* hope. Of course there must be a recognition that heaven will ultimately surpass anything we can imagine—even Augustine, in all his concrete realism, recognized that his speculations were not certainties[194]—yet the fact remains that the absence of compelling heavenly imagery can only fail to capture the human imagination, and therefore human hope.

Ratzinger's *Eschatologie* is a dogmatic handbook rather than a spiritual guide, yet the difference here between Ratzinger and Augustine is not for that reason dissolved. Augustine, as an active pastor, recognized that hope for heaven could not be grounded in abstractions and principles. In his eschatology, that hope is based on being with Christ and with the other saints, possessing our own bodies, and seeing God in a new, exalted world. While Ratzinger does not reject these images, his approach is to caution against "the autarchy of only one image"[195] since no image can capture the whole. He acknowledges the conditional validity of images, but ultimately refuses to employ any himself. Perhaps the difference between Augustine and Ratzinger in this regard could be summed up simply by stating that there is little homiletic material in *Eschatologie*. There are scintillating polemics and deep insight, but nothing to compare to Augustine's ability to inspire wonder and awe.

In a possible nod to Augustine, Ratzinger concludes *Eschatologie* by declaring that at the end, "the whole creation will become 'song,' a self-forgetful gesture of the breaking forth of being into the whole and simultaneously the entry of the whole into the particular. It will be joy, in which all questioning is resolved and satisfied."[196] Yet even here, the metaphor "song" is not left to stand on its own but is immediately interpreted in terms of the interpenetration of the whole and the particular. In Ratzinger's eagerness to flee mythology, he unconsciously neuters the power of the image. In this regard, Ratzinger's theology could benefit greatly from an Augustinian emphasis on the beauty and glory of the resurrection.

Kosmos auf ein Ziel zuführt, auf eine Situation, in der Materie und Geist einander neu und endgültig zugeeignet sein werden."

194. Augustine, *civ. Dei* 22.20.

195. Ratzinger, *Eschatologie*, 188 (*Eschatology*, 237). "Die Schrift hat demgemäß nie eine Alleinherrschaft eines einzigen Bildes geduldet."

196. Ibid., 188 (*Eschatology*, 238). "Dann wird die ganze Schöpfung 'Gesang' sein, selbstvergessene Gebärde der Entschränkung des Seins ins Ganze hinein und zugleich Eintreten des Ganzen ins Eigene, Freude, in der alles Fragen aufgelöst und erfüllt ist."

Part Three: Ratzinger the Realist

Ratzinger and Beauty

At this point, one might ask: why does Ratzinger neglect the aesthetic element in his theology of resurrection? Although any answer to this question will remain in the realm of speculation, it might be pointed out that much of Ratzinger's work is a defense of the transcendental of *truth*, whereas beauty is not a pressing issue for him. This is not to say that one cannot focus on both, but only that Ratzinger's particular *forte* lies in a defense of truth, as is clear in so many of his publications.

On the other hand, Tracey Rowland argues that there *is* a strong aesthetic element in Ratzinger's theology.[197] Yet if this is so, why have we not uncovered it in our study of Ratzinger's theology of resurrection? The reason may be that "in the works of Ratzinger discussions about beauty most often arise in the specific context of liturgy."[198] While there are likely many parallels between Augustine's and Ratzinger's ecclesiology and liturgical theology, our concern here is with the resurrection of the body. We can therefore say that although Ratzinger may be sensitive to the Augustinian concern for beauty in certain areas of his theology, this is not carried over into his theology of resurrection.

In this regard, we might also ask why Augustine was so interested in beauty. In his case, the answer is likely due to a number of factors, including his own personality, the ancient culture he lived in, and even the Platonic tendency to value beauty and harmony. As regards this last reason, we have another positive characteristic of Platonism that was retained by Augustine. Ratzinger, however, does not (in his works on the resurrection at least) exhibit the emotional spontaneity evident in Augustine's admiration for beauty. His is a more reserved theology, which seeks after the truth without that exuberant Augustinian delight in the beautiful.

Concerning our fourth Augustinian characteristic (beauty), then, we unfortunately have remarkably little to say. Beauty is simply not a motivating theological concern in Ratzinger's theology of the resurrection of the body. While he certainly displays a deep desire to maintain the salvation of the whole creation, the *beauty* of that creation and of the human body does not play a role in his eschatology at all. From the Augustinian point of view, this can only be considered a deficiency.

---

197. Rowland, *Ratzinger's Faith*, 8. "Ratzinger's focus on the transcendental of beauty is therefore part of his Augustinian heritage and also one of the many points of convergence between him and Hans Urs von Balthasar and John Henry Newman."

198. Ibid., 8–9.

Matter in Ratzinger's Theology of Resurrection

An Augustinian-Ratzingerian Synthesis

Having established that Ratzinger's current thought on the resurrection lies much closer to Augustine's than did his earlier thinking, can we meld together some of the key insights of both Ratzinger and Augustine in a way that could offer a provisional explanation in response to some of the difficult questions that have been raised about the resurrection? I will attempt to do so here, not as a definitive conclusion but as an example of the possibilities of such a synthesis.

The Soul's Material Orientation after Death

Both Ratzinger and Augustine agree that in death, the soul separates from the body. This separation, producing an anguish *contra naturam*,[199] emphasizes well the seriousness and horror of death. If the person did not undergo such a separation, death would become trivialized. The concept of the soul's becoming all-cosmic risks such a trivialization, as it effectively declares death to be the opening up of a greater form of embodiment rather than a loss of one's own body.[200] This "*anima separata*," then, is separated from the real matter that once formed its earthly body, yet due to the process of "interiorization" during the person's life, that soul (in which the person subsists) has been imprinted by and permanently configured to the earthly body to which it was once united. It therefore can be said to possess the metaphysical character of "bodiliness" [*Leiblichkeit*].

This "bodiliness," however, is not itself resurrection but is rather an irrevocable orientation or configuration to the matter of the body that once lived. It represents the totality of the individual's relations to his body and to the material world, but does not thereby overcome the need for the real body and the real world to which this person was once related. We can say with Ratzinger that "the soul, which endures, holds interiorly within itself the matter of its life and thus rests upon the risen Lord—upon the new unity of spirit and matter which is inaugurated in him."[201]

---

199. Augustine, *civ. Dei* 13.6.

200. This is suggested in Ratzinger's statement in *Eschatologie*, 154–55 (*Eschatology*, 192) that "that all-cosmic existence inaugurated by death would lead to universal interchange, universal openness, and so to the overcoming of all alienation." [jenes Allkosmisch-Sein, welches der Tod eröffnet, würde dann zu universalem Austausch, universaler Offenheit und so zur Überwindung aller Entfremdung führen.]

201. Ratzinger, "Zwischen Tod und Auferstehung" (*Eschatologie*, 219; *Eschatology*,

The post-death soul, then, remains oriented to "the matter of its life" (not necessarily the matter of the entire cosmos) and can truly be said to be "at rest" since in the risen Lord, the resurrection has already happened. The general resurrection, however, is more than the soul's resting in the bosom of Christ. It requires the matter of one's own life. We will be raised as distinct individuals, and this distinction holds for our risen bodies as well.

The soul, which possesses a kind of "bodiliness" even after death, remains not simply imprinted by the matter of its life (as if it were only a fossil) but rather remains oriented, in an irrevocable manner, to the real matter of its body which remains in the real world. "Bodiliness," then, indicates a *relation* and in fact a "longing" for that real matter which is the true complement to the soul's "bodiliness." Without the real matter of its body, the soul's "bodiliness" remains a mere shadow, or rather a foreshadowing, of what the human being will become in the resurrection.

Soul, Matter, and Dialogical Immortality

As regards the question of the dispersion of matter after death, we can here make use of Ratzinger's concept of dialogical immortality. If the soul is the basis for the whole person's relationship to God, then we must say (as Ratzinger does) that "the truth which is love, which we call God, gives man eternity, and because matter is integrated into the human spirit, into the human soul, in him this matter thereby attains perfectibility in the resurrection."[202] In other words, dialogical immortality touches not only the soul, but also the matter of one's body. Through the soul, the body (and its matter) is related directly to God, inscribed in his memory, and can therefore never be lost, for "how can anything either lie hidden from Him Who perceives all things, or irrevocably escape Him Who moves all things?"[203]

---

258). "die Seele, die fortbesteht, hält verinnerlicht die Materie ihres Lebens in sich und ist so ausgespannt auf den auferstandenen Christus—auf die neue Einheit von Geist und Materie hin, die in ihm eröffnet ist."

202. Ibid. (*Eschatologie*, 219–20; *Eschatology*, 259). "Die Wahrheit, die Liebe ist, das heißt Gott, gibt dem Menschen Ewigkeit und weil in den menschlichen Geist, in die menschliche Seele Materie integriert ist, darum erreicht in ihm die Materie die Vollendbarkeit in die Auferstehung hinein."

203. Augustine, *civ. Dei* 22.20.

For this reason, the souls of the departed saints need not worry about the problem of receiving again their body in the resurrection, for "their flesh rests in hope."[204] By the soul's (dialogical) power of "interiorization," it is not only the body's "finality" that is retained, but also the link to that real matter itself, which continues to exist in this world of flux and change until the Last Day, when it will be transfigured and elevated into a new form of existence and united again (how, precisely, we do not know) with the soul that once gave it life.

Here, we must emphasize, as both Augustine and Ratzinger do, that what is really at stake is our image of God and his power over matter. Modern physics and its view of the universe have impressed upon modernity the infinite complexity of any sort of resurrectional "reassembly." Considering, however, that modern science does not have any definitive and conclusive understanding of what matter *is*, we need not concern ourselves with questions of quantum mechanics when considering the resurrection. In the end, it does not really matter which physical model we follow; what counts is that the material part of "me" that was a part of this world will not be ultimately abandoned but will again be a part of me in the resurrection. Here, as is often the case, the supposed difficulties posed by science are not really difficulties at all. One may as well say that the modern discovery of the immense size of the universe suggests that God could not have created it. For if God can simultaneously animate every element in the entire, expanding universe then we ought not to worry about the "problem" of material continuity in the risen body but rather entrust that difficulty to him, who is eminently capable of dealing with it.

In this case, the difficulty of the decaying corpse and the identity of the risen body is similar to the difficulty of the Maccabean martyrs faced by Israel.[205] There, the question was posed as to whether a God who rewards the righteous could let them die so horribly. There, as in our current case, the solution lay in God's power, and his love. The Maccabean martyrs could still experience God's love and reward because death was not the end; God has power even there and will raise them up on the Last Day. Our dead bodies appear to be lost, but God has the power (in a way known to himself) to give them back to us. If we wish to hold a fundamental continuity between this world and the next, then the source of our risen bodies must lie in *this* world and not in an *ex nihilo* re-creation or in a spiritualized version of bodiliness.

204. Ibid., 13.20.

205. 2 Macc 2–12.

Part Three: Ratzinger the Realist

Jesus' Resurrection and Ours

In an Augustinian-Ratzingerian synthesis, we will have to maintain the close connection between the resurrection of Jesus and our own resurrections. If "Jesus' body did not remain in the tomb and did not undergo decay but has been transformed by God's power into the new embodiment of the Risen One,"[206] then we must expect our own bodies to be transformed into a new form of embodiment as well. The key problem here is that Jesus' body did not decay, whereas ours obviously do. Augustine was aware of this when he cited Ps 15:9 (LXX), claiming that the flesh of the faithful departed rests in hope. This is because before God's eyes, our bodies are not lost at all.

We might therefore say that if the chief difference between the state of Jesus' body at his resurrection, and the state of our bodies at the final resurrection, is one of decomposition, then our resurrection will—in a way known to God and enabled by his power—mean a certain *recomposition* of our bodies. We therefore need not concern ourselves with the dispersion of particles, for God already knows how he will recompose and glorify our risen bodies. If it is true that Jesus' body did not undergo decay, and if our resurrection is truly our inclusion in his resurrection, then even decay—which is part of that "biological phenomenon" known as death[207]—can pose no difficulty to our real, material resurrection.

Augustine and Thomas

The position articulated here clearly opts for an Augustinian duality rather than the narrow Thomistic view characterized by Durandus and Greshake, in which the body is *only* the soul's expression and not a counterpart to it. In this Augustinian-Ratzingerian synthesis, the post-death soul requires, for its complete fulfillment, more than the regained ability to express itself in matter but rather that real matter of its erstwhile body.

---

206. Ratzinger, "Jungfrauengeburt." "Desgleichen gehört es zu diesen historischen Gewissheiten des Glaubens, dass Jesu Leib nicht im Grab geblieben und nicht der Verwesung verfallen, sondern durch die Kraft Gottes in die neue Leiblichkeit des Auferstandenen umgewandelt worden ist."

207. Ibid. "God . . . has really acted in history all the way to the bodily sphere and has proven himself as Lord over death, which is ultimately a biological phenomenon, a phenomenon of the body." [Es geht darum, ob Gott Gott ist und ob er wirklich in der Geschichte bis ins Leibliche hinein gehandelt und sich als Herr über den Tod erwiesen hat, der ja schließlich ein biologisches Phänomen, ein Phänomen des Leibes ist.]

Such a schema therefore necessarily places greater emphasis on duality than would a strict hylomorphic view, but I believe that it better allows for the connection of this world to the next since it necessitates the salvation of this-worldly matter.

Because it requires the reunion of two substances, such a "dual" view therefore safeguards the resurrection as a final, eschatological event. The elision of duality can lead to the elimination of the event of resurrection, for if resurrection is not a re-union then it need not be a discrete event. If it concerns only one thing (rather than two) then resurrection becomes merely a characteristic of being dead (as in "resurrection in death").

The Beauty of the Resurrection

An Augustinian-Ratzingerian theology of resurrection would defend the reality of the resurrection from spiritualistic formulations by insisting on the beauty of the exquisite body-soul ordering of the human being. The mode of this union, as ineffable as it is, is nonetheless startling in its complexity and beauty. That a spiritual substance (the soul) can be united to a material body is itself wonderful and remarkable. That these two could be again united in a perfect way so that the soul's tendency to sinfulness, as well as the body's tendency to decay and corruption, will be forever removed, is even more worthy of awe.

Given on the one hand the immense complexity of the body unearthed by modern science, and on the other the fact that the body is an expression of the soul, we certainly have grounds for admiration. If, as Augustine says, all the workings of the body will be made perfectly manifest to us in the resurrection so that none of its intricacies will be hidden, then the resurrection becomes an event of beauty. This extends to the natural world as well, which will be made "new and better"[208] so that our ability to contemplate creation will be perfected rather than annulled.

One difficulty, which Benedict XVI has admitted, is that many people do not find the prospect of eternal life very exciting.[209] In many cases, this may be due to the fear that heaven means sitting on a cloud, blinded by rays of light emanating from God, never again to see the beauty of this world. A more Augustinianized view of resurrection, however, will stress that the world to come will include all those beautiful things present in

---

208. Augustine, *civ. Dei* 22.16.
209. Benedict XVI, *Spe Salvi* 10.

Part Three: Ratzinger the Realist

the world here and now. Yet these things will be hyper-present; not only will their qualities be perfected so that they will express their intrinsic beauty even more perfectly, but our ability to perceive that beauty will be heightened as well so that our enjoyment of those "accidental" elements of beatific joy will be enjoyment of the Lord himself. There need be no strict separation between the *visio Dei* and our appreciation for creation's beauty, for "we shall see Him by the spirit in ourselves, in one another, in Himself, in the new heavens and the new earth, and in every created thing which shall then exist."[210]

Ratzinger's theology of resurrection contains many forceful assertions and powerful arguments. When observed along its proper trajectory, it provides a strong defense against attempts to spiritualize the resurrection and to dissolve the statements of the Church's tradition into mythology. Yet Ratzinger's formulations on the nature of risen embodiment require additional "filling out" if they are to "defend a human resurrection against a mathematical one."[211] This is because of Ratzinger's reticence (at least since 1957) to say anything concrete about the risen body. Given, however, Ratzinger's more recent openness to physical realism, which is a central component in the aesthetic approach of Augustine, I believe that Ratzinger's current thought would be compatible with a more aesthetic approach to the resurrection of the body. In this way, one would be free to explore the beauty that will arise when "the whole creation will become 'song.'"[212]

---

210. Augustine, *civ. Dei* 22.29.

211. Ratzinger, *Eschatologie*, 143 (*Eschatology*, 177). "Es [i.e., das kirkliche Lehramt] mußte eine menschliche Auferstehung gegen eine mathematische verteidigen."

212. Ibid., 188 (*Eschatology*, 238). "Dann wird die ganze Schöpfung 'Gesang' sein."

7

Conclusion

We began this book by asking about the Augustinian nature of Joseph Ratzinger's theology of the resurrection of the body. This has led us through the theologies of both Augustine and Ratzinger and has necessitated delving into a considerable amount of detail. As a conclusion to this book, we will simply discuss some of the more significant and relevant issues that have arisen from the present study, rather than attempt an exhaustive summary. Although the research carried out here has consequences for a range of issues, this conclusion will discuss three of particular relevance and import: (1) the problem of defining Ratzinger's Augustinianism, (2) the relationship between Platonic dualism and scientific materialism, and (3) the problem of Thomistic hylomorphism and Augustinian duality.

Ratzinger's Augustinianism

Defining Ratzinger the Augustinian: Avoiding Ambiguities

Although it is often remarked that Ratzinger's theology is highly Augustinian, we have seen that such statements are relatively meaningless unless properly qualified. First of all, it would be hard to find a single characteristic or set of characteristics that play an equally important role in every

Part Three: Ratzinger the Realist

area of Augustine's theology. For this reason, the objective content of the adjective "Augustinian" can change as one moves into different areas of Augustine's thought. This means, for example, that one cannot take a characteristic of Augustine's theology of predestination and use it as an arbiter of whether someone's Trinitarian theology is Augustinian or not. Second, a description of Ratzinger's theology as "Augustinian" becomes nebulous unless confined to a specific area of that theology. It may thus be true that Ratzinger's epistemology is Augustinian (in that it shares much in common with Augustine's epistemology) but this should not be stated of Ratzinger's theology as a whole.

Third, it is notable that few theologians seem to be aware of Ratzinger's theological development. This is particularly true concerning his eschatology. As this work has shown, Ratzinger's theology of resurrection cannot be considered uniformly Augustinian over time. The eschatological vision of *Einführung*, for example, with its emphasis on resurrection as the fulfillment of a cosmic process and its denial of the salvation of the *Körper*, is stridently discordant with Augustine's view of the transfiguration of matter and the world that will occur in the resurrection.

Thus, although Ratzinger undoubtedly moved toward a more Augustinian position which stressed the resurrection of the individual, the salvation of matter "in itself," the connection of resurrection to the corpse in the ground, and God's power to intervene in the material world, one must be cognizant that Ratzinger's more recent theology does not form one seamless whole with his earlier work. It is therefore hoped that this study might contribute to a greater awareness of, and sensitivity toward, the development of Ratzinger's thought on the resurrection. We must therefore be wary of overly-broad statements, such as Joseph Komonchak's claim (approved of by Tracey Rowland)[1] that "from Ratzinger's *Introduction to Christianity* (1968) down to the homily he delivered on his installation as Pope Benedict XVI, a distinctive and consistent approach has been visible. . . . Theology cannot count on any help from contemporary philosophy or the human and natural sciences. In Ratzinger's writings, there are very few positive references to intellectual developments outside the Church; they almost always appear as antithetical to the specifically Christian."[2] Komonchak, admittedly, restricts his analysis to the relationship between the Church and the world and does not consider Ratzinger's anthropology. Nonetheless, such a statement would be better qualified either by avoiding

1. Rowland, *Ratzinger's Faith*, 13–14.
2. Komonchak, "Church in Crisis," 13.

Conclusion

its reference to *Einführung* or by explicitly limiting itself to the realm of ecclesiology, since *Einführung*, in its eschatological treatment at least, *is* open to intellectual developments outside the Church as well as natural science.[3]

On the whole, it seems that the general tendency in English-language Ratzinger scholarship is to view him in light of his later, more "conservative" works. Generally, however, little theological development is acknowledged. This could be partly due to the fact that English-language literature has mainly dealt with his ecclesiology,[4] in which there may have been less of an intellectual development than in his eschatology. In the German literature, however, we have a similar, yet strikingly different situation with respect to Ratzinger's eschatology. There, the majority of publications appeared in the 1980s during the debate with Greshake, and more recent works have continued to focus heavily on Ratzinger's early publications.[5]

---

3. For example, *Intro.*, 320–21 where Ratzinger claims that the process of "complexification" of matter and spirit whose culmination can be described as Christ's second coming "can already be seen today in a certain sense in the remodeling of the world through technology." Such a statement, of course, contrasts with many of Ratzinger's later statements on technology.

4. As noted in the introduction of this work, there has been no English work at all on Ratzinger's eschatology. The chapter dedicated to eschatology in Nichols' *The Theology of Joseph Ratzinger* is simply a synopsis of the book *Eschatologie*. It provides no analysis and does not mention any of Ratzinger's other works at all. As previously noted, the new (2007) edition reproduces the original eschatology chapter in unaltered form.

5. For example, in 2005, Wohlmuth only deals with Ratzinger with respect to the controversy with Greshake (*Mysterium der Verwandlung*, 164–81), and does not refer to any works by Ratzinger after the *Nachwort zur 6. Auflage* (1990). Marschler ("Perspektiven") does not even cite the *Nachwort zur 6. Auflage* and almost exclusively cites works from the 1960s and 1970s, with the exception of a few brief references to "Ende der Zeit" and one reference to Ratzinger's 1992 address to the Catholic Academy in Prague. Quy (*Theologische Verwandtschaft*), in his chapter comparing the eschatology of Augustine and Ratzinger, manages to avoid the topic of the resurrection of the body entirely. Notwithstanding Marschler's intuition that Ratzinger may be more recently tending toward a more physicalist theology of resurrection (176–77 n. 61), none of the above authors recognizes any development in Ratzinger's eschatological thought. Even Verweyen's *Joseph Ratzinger—Benedikt XVI. Die Entwicklung seines Denkens* (2007) does not acknowledge any development of Ratzinger's thought in the area of resurrection. Verweyen simply comments that concerning "resurrection in death," "The multi-layered debate which ensued even after 1977 cannot be retraced again here," thus avoiding the topic of the resurrection of the body entirely (73). [Die vielschichtige, auch nach 1977 weitergehende Debatte kann hier nicht noch einmal verfolgt werden.] Here, Verweyen simply points the reader to Ratzinger's *Nachwort zur 6. Auflage*. Although Verweyen's book includes a section titled "Der Mythos der großen Wende" (The Myth of the Great Turning Point), 39–42, the section is entirely restricted to Ratzinger's views

Part Three: Ratzinger the Realist

The result is that in the German literature, Ratzinger's theology of resurrection still tends to be viewed in terms of its earlier Rahnerian and Teilhardian elements. We have seen, however, that Augustine is often wrongly criticized as a Platonist based solely on his very early works. Similarly, a proper theological appreciation of Ratzinger's work is impossible without a correct recognition of the development of his thought.

Possible Reasons for Ratzinger's Shift toward Augustinian Resurrectional Realism

Given, then, that Ratzinger's position on the resurrection has shifted over time toward a more traditional, realist, Augustinian one, the obvious question arises: Why? While a definitive determination is probably impossible, a number of factors could have played a role in that change. It might be suggested that after 1968, Ratzinger simply became more conservative in general, and that his eschatology followed this trend. Yet many aspects of his earlier theology remained (e.g., the notion of dialogical immortality), and so this still leaves unanswered the question of why Ratzinger might have become more "conservative" on the particular issue of the risen body.

It is also possible that the change was occasioned by Ratzinger's move from the life of a professor to pastoral life when he was made Archbishop of Munich and Freising in 1977. His attention to pastoral issues regarding the resurrection, however (as in the "corpse-in-the-ground" argument), was present before this.[6] The most "physicalist" statements on the resurrection, however, came after Ratzinger had moved to Rome in 1981. In this regard, it is possible that his time as Prefect for the Congregation for the Doctrine of the Faith might have impelled him toward the more traditional formulations characteristic of Augustine's theology. It is also possible that by stepping away from the German Catholic theological environment, highly influenced at that time by Rahner (and, to a certain extent, Teilhard), Ratzinger became more open to other ways of developing his theology.

What seems to me most likely, however, is that through the reception of criticisms of his early work[7] and his own theological reflection,

---

on ecclesiology and Vatican II.

6. E.g., in "Jenseits des Todes" (1972) and *Eschatologie*, which was written by 1976.

7. For example, both Pozo and Kasper accused Ratzinger of advocating in *Einführung* a Platonism that devalued the flesh. And von Balthasar accused him of creating a

Conclusion

Ratzinger came to recognize that when speaking of the resurrection, the real issue is the realism of Christian faith. He realized that the incarnation and resurrection of the Lord require that matter be taken seriously,[8] and reveal that "God's action reaches all the way to the body."[9] Thus, rather than locating the reason for Ratzinger's more recent position in any episcopal or curial responsibilities, it would seem more probable that he came to it simply because his own reflection on the fundamentals of Christian faith led him in that direction.

Ratzinger's Augustinian Trajectory

Although one may (for purposes of convenience) speak of "early" and "late" positions of Ratzinger, there is no particular point at which Ratzinger's theology suddenly changed direction. He did not have a sudden conversion experience. I therefore believe it to be helpful to describe Ratzinger as being, from the early days of his theology, on an Augustinian *trajectory*. Although his discussion of the resurrection in *Einführung* has little in common with Augustine's, one still discerns there a certain resistance to theologies that utterly demythologize the resurrection (even if, as Kasper suggests, Ratzinger himself at times indulged in demythologizing). With each of his successive works on the resurrection, however, we see a gradual movement *in the direction of* that theology of resurrection articulated by the mature Augustine. This is not to say, however, that Ratzinger would eventually end up in the precise position expressed in *De Civitate Dei* XXII. It does mean, however, that the defining characteristics of Ratzinger's theology of resurrection have come to more closely approximate those key characteristics of Augustine's.

---

split between biology and ontology in his discussion of the virgin birth.

8. See Ratzinger, *Eschatologie*, 14 (*Eschatology*, xxi). "The bodiliness of Christ, who retains a body in eternity, means the taking seriously of history and matter." [Die Leibhaftigkeit Christi, der in Ewigkeit Leib behält, bedeutet das Ernstnehmen der Geschichte und der Materie.]

9. Ratzinger, "Jungfrauengeburt." "Dieses auf dem Zusammenhang von Prophetie und geschehener Geschichte beruhende Stichwort von der Rettung des Leibes Jesu vor der Verwesung . . . hat der Kirche die Glaubensgewissheit vermittelt, dass Jesus wirklich leiblich auferstanden ist, dass Gottes Handeln bis in den Leib hinein reicht."

Part Three: Ratzinger the Realist

Ratzinger, Platonic Dualism, and the Modern Worldview

We have already noted the surprising fact that those theologies of resurrection that attempt to be "anti-Platonic" often end up asserting what is in fact a dualism that can also be considered an eschatological monism (since only spirit is saved and not matter). Ratzinger admits that he attempted to construct a "de-Platonized eschatology" (in apparent reference to *Einführung*) yet eventually rejected it upon greater study.[10] A connection that often goes unnoticed, however, is that between Ratzinger's rejection of "anti-Platonism" and his devaluation of the role of the modern scientific worldview in his theology.

In *Einführung*, after raising the question of a risen, material body, Ratzinger asks rhetorically, "is this not all completely absurd, quite contrary to our understanding of matter and its modes of behavior, and therefore hopelessly mythological?"[11] This is similar to the position of Greshake, who opposes the inclusion of matter "in itself" in the resurrection because, according to science, such matter is marked by flux and finitude. Since matter falls under the purview of natural science (which cannot envisage an eschatological fulfillment), matter "in itself" is excluded from the eschaton.

What we have here is a striking similarity between Platonic dualism and modern natural science. Although Etienne Gilson has suggested that modern science is highly Platonic with respect to its attention to perfect ideal laws and mathematical precision,[12] it is also Platonic in another sense. The Platonic tradition attempted to envision perfect, unchanging

---

10. Ratzinger, *Eschatologie*, 15 (*Eschatology*, xxv).

11. Ratzinger, *Intro.*, 348.

12. Gilson, *Being and Some Philosophers*, 41. "When they philosophize, modern scientists usually fall into some sort of loose Platonism. Plato's world precisely is the very world they live in, at least *qua* scientists." Ratzinger agrees with this assessment when he states, following Jacques Monod, that "modern natural science is ultimately Platonism, based on the priority of what is thought over what is experienced, of the ideal over the empirical. Its fundamental assertion is that reality is built from ideal structures and thus can be known more precisely in thought than in mere perception." My translation. [Jacques Monod hat . . . gezeigt, daß die moderne Naturwissenschaft letztlich Platonismus ist, auf dem Vorrang des Gedachten vor dem Erfahrenen, des Idealen vor dem Empirischen beruht und von der Grundvorstellung lebt, daß die Wirklichkeit aus gedanklichen Strukturen gebaut ist und daher im Denken genauer erkannt werden kann als im bloßen Wahrnehmen.] Ratzinger, "Erfahrung und Glaube," 62–63. This was originally a lecture delivered to the Munich diocesan school teachers on February 23, 1978.

Ideas apart from material, mutable beings and thus located beatitude in an immaterial state. In this system, matter can be neither saved nor ultimately united with spirit. Likewise, in modern natural science, a materialism is asserted in which spirit is allowed no interaction with matter, which only obeys predetermined physical laws. Nature has been decisively severed from grace. For the theologian who accepts such a worldview, religion and theology are prevented from acting upon the material world. God is, as Ratzinger recently stated, "reduced to the interiority of our subjectivity"[13] and is therefore no God at all.

But faith in the resurrection means a rejection of both reductive scientific materialism and eschatological docetism, two extremes which have more in common with each other than it may at first appear. As Ratzinger states in *Eschatologie*, "the modern theories [of the resurrection] which we have encountered, despite their contrary starting points, do not shun the immortality of the soul so much as the resurrection, which is still the real scandal for the intellect. In this respect, modern theology is much closer to the Greeks than it wants to admit."[14] It might be added that modern theology did not get to this point by attempting to be Greek; it got there by means of a "scientific" worldview that separates the spiritual from the physical world. In "Jungfrauengeburt," Ratzinger describes the view of most modern science as "subtle Gnosticism."

Inasmuch as the modern scientific worldview—like Platonism— rejects the possibility of spirit truly being united with matter, its union with theology results in a view of matter that bears all the problematic components of Platonic dualism. Seen in this light, Ratzinger's gradual rejection of the modern scientific worldview can be seen as corresponding to Augustine's gradual rejection of those problematic Platonic elements of his theology that he initially accepted.[15] It is Ratzinger's early work— which seeks to take seriously the modern scientific worldview—which bears the marks of Platonic dualism. It is his later work—which discounts that worldview—which truly insists on the salvation of matter *qua* matter.

13. Ratzinger, "Jungfrauengeburt."

14. Ratzinger, *Eschatologie*, 131 (*Eschatology*, 160). "Mit diesen Fragen wird endgültig sichtbar, daß die modernen Theorien, denen wir begegnet sind, trotz ihres gegenteiligen Ausgangspunktes weniger der Unsterblichkeit der Seele als der Auferstehung ausweichen, die der wahre Skandal des Denkens geblieben ist. Insofern ist die moderne Theologie den Griechen viel näher, als sie wahrhaben will."

15. For example, Augustine's early denial that the risen body would contain flesh, or his belief that God could not be seen with the eyes of the risen body.

Augustinian Duality and Hylomorphism

Augustine and the Salvation of Matter

Augustine made a clear distinction between matter's empirical qualities (or *qualitates*), which are marked by decay, finitude, and mutability, and its substance, which will be preserved and fitted with new *qualitates* in the resurrection.[16] The Platonists of his day (like modern materialists) could not imagine how something as mutable as matter could be raised up in the resurrection. Yet Augustine's insight lay in realizing that matter need not be determined solely by its *qualitates*, or, to use Aristotelian terminology, by its accidents. By distinguishing between matter's substance (ontological) and its *qualitates* (phenomenological), Augustine opens the door to the salvation of matter without reducing the resurrection to a mere resuscitation of corruptible bodies. Earthly matter's empirical properties will be replaced with new, incorruptible properties but that matter will remain *substantially* matter. This means that matter "in itself" is truly saved, even if it may not look or feel like the matter we currently know. As we have seen, Ratzinger argues this point vigorously against Greshake. Yet we can agree with Greshake that physical bodiliness (or, to use his term, *Körperlichkeit*)[17] in its current empirical finitude will not exist in the resurrection. We must simultaneously maintain, however, that the physical earthly body (i.e., the *Körper*), finite and corruptible as it is, will be in some way transformed into the glorified, risen body. There will be a radically new quality to the risen body, but if the resurrection is to be a true "*re*-surrection" then it must be the raising up of that which fell asleep in death, that is, the substance of the earthly body. If Paul can declare that "flesh and blood cannot inherit the kingdom of God, nor does the perishable inherit the imperishable" (1 Cor 15:50), he does not thereby exclude the perishable (i.e., the earthly body) from the hope of salvation. Rather, he emphasizes that it cannot enter heaven *as* perishable. For, at the end, "this perishable nature must put on the imperishable, and this mortal nature must put on immortality" (1 Cor 15:53). The assertion that what dies will be raised naturally leads to the question of Thomistic hylomorphism and the problems that proceed from it.

---

16. Augustine, *civ. Dei* 20.16.

17. For example, Greshake, "Verhältnis 'Unsterblichkeit der Seele' und 'Auferstehung des Leibes,'" 117.

Conclusion

The Problem of Thomistic Hylomorphism

When we considered Ratzinger's understanding of the body-soul distinction, we observed that he is critical of the Thomistic hylomorphic theory inasmuch as it "cannot maintain any identity at all between the body before and after death."[18] Since for Thomas, the intellectual soul is the *only* substantial form of the human body, this means that when the soul leaves the body at death, the matter of that body reverts to *materia prima*. We have already noted the various problems that such an idea, left unmodified, poses to Catholic doctrine. What is perhaps most interesting in this controversy, however, is the fact that the "Augustinian" position—which by some accounts appears more "dualistic" since it posits body and soul as distinct entities which can be separated in death—is actually better able to account for the identity between Jesus' living and dead body. It also avoids other problems raised by the hylomorphic theory.[19]

To be sure, Ratzinger has high praise for Thomas' formulation that the soul is *forma corporis*,[20] but he also makes clear that this cannot be interpreted in a "strict" way.[21] For if, as Greshake holds, Thomistic anthropology necessitates that "the reality of the body is mediated through the soul and is not understood as a distinct empirical-physical reality,"[22] then the *Leib-Körper* distinction as employed by Greshake is unavoidable and there can be no material identity between dead and risen bodies.

Ratzinger's approach, however—like Augustine's—is to connect the resurrection with the corpse. Yet Ratzinger, apart from suggesting that the Thomistic synthesis "must today be carried out anew,"[23] does not offer

---

18. Ratzinger, *Eschatologie*, 145 (*Eschatology*, 180). "Insofern kann die thomistische Lehre, streng durchgeführt, überhaupt keine Identität zwischen dem Leib vor und nach dem Tod festhalten." See also Schneider, *Die Einheit des Menschen*, 61–62.

19. For example, the question of parenthood: if the body has an existence alongside the soul, then biological parenthood can be genuine since the body of the child does indeed derive from the parents rather than the child's soul alone (which is created directly by God).

20. Ratzinger, "Zwischen Tod und Auferstehung" (*Eschatologie*, 218–19; *Eschatology*, 257–58).

21. Ratzinger, *Eschatologie*, 146 (*Eschatology*, 181).

22. Greshake, "Parteiische Rückblick," 539 n. 8. "Dies ergibt sich bereits aus einer konsequenten thomanischen Anthropologie, wonach die Wirklichkeit des Leibes durch die Seele vermittelt und nicht als empirisch-physikalische Eigenwirklichkeit zu verstehen ist."

23. Ratzinger, *Eschatologie*, 146 (*Eschatology*, 181). "Die Synthese, die Thomas unter den Bedingungen seines Jahrhunderts auf geniale Weise formuliert hat, muß heute neu vollzogen werden."

Part Three: Ratzinger the Realist

any new metaphysical framework upon which to build his theology of resurrection. This represents a significant lacuna and problem not only in Ratzinger's theology of resurrection, but in any modern eschatology that wishes to take Thomas Aquinas seriously while avoiding what could be called the monism of a strict hylomorphism. The unsolved question is how to envision the soul as *forma corporis* without giving up material identity between this world and the next and between the earthly and risen body. It is a question of how to preserve the body-soul *unity* achieved by Thomas' formulation, as well as the real *duality* of Augustine's system.

In Greshake's system, Thomistic hylomorphic *unity* means that the body does not exist apart from the soul; thus the body's salvation is understood as its interiorization in the soul, which alone endures. The resurrection, then, means the saving of the whole person, whose soul has already interiorized his body, in death. For Ratzinger, however, Augustinian *duality* means that the body is not simply a modality of, or impression upon, the soul. The body possesses a separable existence. For this reason, the resurrection must necessarily involve two things: the soul, *and* the body. The resurrection is thereby connected to the fate of the entire universe since the resurrection is in fact a material event. This is why resurrection cannot happen "in death" but must await the Last Day. The resurrection requires the matter of this universe, and thus cannot happen until that universe is brought to an end. Only in this way do we avoid "an ultimate dualism in which the entire realm of matter is excluded from creation's goal and relegated to a second-order reality."[24]

The ongoing challenge for theological anthropology and eschatology, then, is to maintain the connection to matter present in Augustinian duality, while simultaneously taking seriously the Council of Vienne, which stated that the intellectual soul is "the form of the human body of itself and essentially [*per se et essentialiter*]."[25] Following Augustine, matter and spirit must be properly distinguished so that the former is not converted or subsumed into the latter.[26] But this must be done in a way that acknowl-

---

24. Ibid., 155 (*Eschatology*, 192). "Das würde, den gegenteiligen Versicherungen zum Trotz, eine Teilung der Schöpfung und insofern einen letzten Dualismus bedeuten, bei dem der ganze Bereich der Materie aus dem Schöpfungsziel herausgenommen und zu einer Wirklichkeit zweiter Ordnung gemacht wird."

25. Denzinger 481; Tanner, 361. It is of note, however, that the council did not state that the soul is the *only* form of the body, as Thomas did in *Summa* I, q. 76, a.4, where he states, "Ergo impossibile est quod in homine sit aliqua alia forma substantialis quam anima intellectiva."

26. Augustine, *civ. Dei* 13.20. "So shall the flesh rightly be called spiritual when it

Conclusion

edges the intimate body-soul union described by Thomas' *anima forma corporis* formula. This, however, will necessitate something of a fresh interpretation of Thomas' formula, as Ratzinger points out. It might involve envisioning anew the relationship between *forma* and *materia prima*, or perhaps the *way* that the soul functions as *forma corporis*.[27] In any case, such a task has not been carried out by Ratzinger, and would first require an in-depth examination of Thomas Aquinas, something carried out neither here nor in any of Ratzinger's works.

Ratzinger's theology of resurrection can be termed "Augustinian" in that the key characteristics of Augustine's mature eschatology come more and more to the fore in each successive Ratzingerian writing on the resurrection. Of course, Ratzinger brings his own unique approach to eschatology, and in his theology of resurrection it is not simply a case of Ratzinger imitating Augustine. We observe, however, a common trajectory shared by the two theologians. Both began with a theology partly influenced by certain dualistic elements, and both had to gradually purify that theology throughout their lives. In this way, Ratzinger's correspondence to Augustine is not static, but dynamic. Their similarity lies not only in shared ideas, but in a shared trajectory. As Benedict XVI stated in 2008, "Augustine's conversion was not sudden nor fully accomplished at the beginning, but . . . can be defined rather as a true and proper journey that remains a model for each one of us."[28]

If, however, Ratzinger followed in the footsteps of Augustine, this has not meant a reversion to the world of sixteen hundred years ago. Rather, it has meant a recognition of "the everlasting timeliness of [Augustine's] faith; of the faith that comes from Christ, the Eternal Incarnate Word, Son of God and Son of Man."[29] We see this Augustinian faith ring forth clearly when Ratzinger defends the realism of Christ's resurrection and ours:

> What is really in question is the core of the image of God and the realism of God's historical action. It is a question of whether faith really extends into history. It is a question of whether matter is or is not beyond God's power, of whether God is God and

serves the spirit. This is not because flesh will be converted into spirit."

27. This might raise the question of how the body is a complete entity. For example, would Thomas want to hold that the intellectual soul provides the form to the electrons and molecules that continually pass into, and out of, the body? Or might there be a certain hierarchy of forms in the body, with the intellectual soul governing all the others but not necessarily "micro-managing" them all?

28. Benedict XVI, General Audience, February 27, 2008, par. 2.

29. Benedict XVI, General Audience, January 16, 2008, par. 7.

whether he has really acted in history all the way to the bodily sphere and has proven himself as Lord over death, which is ultimately a biological phenomenon, a phenomenon of the body. And so it is a question of whether we can entrust ourselves to the word of faith, whether we trust God and whether we can live and die on the ground of faith.[30]

---

30. Ratzinger, "Jungfrauengeburt." "So wird sichtbar . . . dass vielmehr der Kern des Gottesbildes und der Realismus von Gottes geschichtlichem Handeln in Frage steht. Es geht darum, ob der Glaube wirklich in die Geschichte hineinreicht. Es geht darum, ob die Materie der Macht Gottes entzogen ist oder nicht. Es geht darum, ob Gott Gott ist und ob er wirklich in der Geschichte bis ins Leibliche hinein gehandelt und sich als Herr über den Tod erwiesen hat, der ja schließlich ein biologisches Phänomen, ein Phänomen des Leibes ist. Und so geht es darum, ob wir uns dem Wort des Glaubens anvertrauen können, ob wir Gott trauen und ob wir auf dem Grund des Glaubens leben und sterben können."

Bibliography

Alfaric, Prosper. *L'évolution intellectuelle de saint Augustin.* Paris: E. Nourry, 1918.
Alfeche, Mamerto. "Augustine's Discussions with Philosophers on the Resurrection of the Body." *Augustiniana* 45 (1995) 95–140.
———. "The Rising of the Dead in the Works of Augustine (1 Cor 15,35–57)." *Augustiniana* 39 (1989) 54–98.
———. "The Transformation from *Corpus Animale* to *Corpus Spirituale* according to St. Augustine." *Augustiniana* 42 (1992) 239–310.
Althaus, Paul. *Die letzten Dinge.* Unaltered, 8th ed. Gütersloh: C. Bertelsmann, 1961.
———. "Retraktationen zur Eschatologie." *Theologische Literaturzeitung* 75 (1950) 254–60.
Auer, Johann. *Person: Ein Schlüssel zum christlichen Mysterium.* Regensburg: Friedrich Pustet, 1979.
———. *"Siehe, ich mache alles neu." Der Glaube an die Vollendung der Welt.* Regensburg: Friedrich Pustet, 1984.
Augustine. *Against the Academics.* Translated by John J. O'Meara. Ancient Christian Writers 12. New York: Paulist, 1951.
———. *De anima et eius origine.* In vol. 44 of *Patrologia Latina,* edited by Jacques-Paul Migne, 475–548. Paris: Migne, 1845.
———. "Answer to Adimantus, a Disciple of Mani." In *The Manichean Debate,* translated by Roland Teske, edited by Boniface Ramsey, 166–223. Works of Saint Augustine: A Translation for the 21st Century I/19. Hyde Park, NY: New City, 2006.
———. *Answer to Faustus, a Manichean (Contra Faustum Manichaeum).* Translated by Roland Teske. Edited by Boniface Ramsey. Works of Saint Augustine: A Translation for the 21st Century I/20. Hyde Park, NY: New City, 2007.
———. *The Christian Combat.* Translated by Robert P. Russell. In *The Fathers of the Church: A New Translation,* edited by Ludwig Schopp et al., 4:309–53. New York: Cima, 1947.
———. *The City of God against the Pagans.* Translated by R. W. Dyson. New York: Cambridge University Press, 2007.
———. *The Confessions.* Translated by Maria Boulding. Edited by John E. Rotelle. Works of Saint Augustine: A Translation for the 21st Century I/1. Hyde Park, NY: New City, 1997.
———. "The Enchiridion on Faith, Hope, and Charity." In *On Christian Belief,* translated by Bruce Harbert, edited by Boniface Ramsey, 273–343. Works of Saint Augustine: A Translation for the 21st Century I/8. Hyde Park, NY: New City, 2005.

Bibliography

———. *Expositions of the Psalms (Ennarationes in Psalmos) 73-98*. Translated by Maria Boulding. Edited by John E. Rotelle. Works of Saint Augustine: A Translation for the 21st Century III/18. Hyde Park, NY: New City, 2002.

———. *Expositions of the Psalms (Ennarationes in Psalmos) 99-120*. Translated by Maria Boulding. Edited by Boniface Ramsey. Works of Saint Augustine: A Translation for the 21st Century III/19. Hyde Park, NY: New City, 2003.

———. "Faith and the Creed." In *On Christian Belief*, translated by Michael Campbell, edited by Boniface Ramsey, 149–74. Works of Saint Augustine: A Translation for the 21st Century I/8. Hyde Park, NY: New City, 2005.

———. *Letters 1-99*. Translated by Roland Teske. Edited by John E. Rotelle. Works of Saint Augustine: A Translation for the 21st Century II/1. Hyde Park, NY: New City, 2001.

———. *Letters 100-155*. Translated by Roland Teske. Edited by Boniface Ramsey. Works of Saint Augustine: A Translation for the 21st Century II/2. Hyde Park, NY: New City, 2003.

———. *The Literal Meaning of Genesis*. Vol. 2, *Books 7-12*. Translated by John Hammond Taylor. Ancient Christian Writers 42. New York: Newman, 1982.

———. *The Magnitude of the Soul*. Translated by John J. McMahon. In *The Fathers of the Church: A New Translation*, edited by Ludwig Schopp et al., 2:51–149. New York: Cima, 1947.

———. *De Moribus Ecclesiae catholicae et de Moribus Manichaeorum*. In vol. 32 of *Patrologia Latina*, edited by Jacques-Paul Migne, 1309–78. Paris: Migne, 1845.

———. *On Music*. Translated by Robert Catesby Taliaferro. In *The Fathers of the Church: A New Translation*, edited by Ludwig Schopp et al., 2:153–379. New York: Cima, 1947.

———. *The Retractations*. Translated by Mary Inez Bogan. Washington, DC: Catholic University of America Press, 1968.

———. *Sermons (148-183)*. Translated by Edmund Hill. Edited by John Rotelle. Works of Saint Augustine: A Translation for the 21st Century III/5. New Rochelle, NY: New City, 1992.

———. *Sermons (230-272B) on the Liturgical Seasons*. Translated by Edmund Hill. Edited by John Rotelle. Works of Saint Augustine: A Translation for the 21st Century III/7. New Rochelle, NY: New City, 1993.

———. *Sermons (273-305A) on the Saints*. Translated by Edmund Hill. Edited by John E. Rotelle. Works of Saint Augustine: A Translation for the 21st Century III/8. Hyde Park, NY: New City, 1994.

———. "Sermons 361 and 362." Translated by John A. Mourant. In John A. Mourant, *Augustine on Immortality*. Villanova, PA: Augustinian Institute, Villanova University, 1969.

———. "Sermon 362A." In Isabella Schiller, Dorothea Weber, and Clemens Weidmann, "Sechs neue Augustinuspredigten: Teil 1 mit Edition dreier Sermones." *Wiener Studien* 121 (2008) 227–84.

———. *The Soliloquies of Augustine*. Translated by Rose Elizabeth Cleveland. Boston: Little, Brown, 1910.

———. *Teaching Christianity (De Doctrina Christiana)*. Translated by Edmund Hill. Edited by John Rotelle. Works of Saint Augustine: A Translation for the 21st Century I/11. Hyde Park, NY: New City, 1996.

Bibliography

———. *Tractates on the Gospel of John, 11–27*. Translated by John Rettig. Washington, DC: Catholic University of America Press, 1988.
———. *The Trinity*. Translated by Edmund Hill. Edited by John E. Rotelle. Works of Saint Augustine: A Translation for the 21st Century I/5. Brooklyn, NY: New City, 1990.
Balthasar, Hans Urs von. "Empfangen durch den Heiligen Geist, geboren von der Jungfrau Maria." In *Ich glaube: Vierzehn Betrachtungen zum Apostolischen Glaubensbekenntnis*, edited by Wilhelm Sandfuchs, 39–49. Würzburg: Echter, 1975.
Bavel, Tarsicius Johannes van. "The Anthropology of Augustine." *Louvain Studies* 5:1 (1974) 34–47.
Benedict XVI, Pope. Angelus of December 18, 2011. http://www.vatican.va/holy_father/benedict_xvi/angelus/2011/documents/hf_ben-xvi_ang_20111218_en.html.
———. Encyclical Letter *Spe Salvi*. 2007. http://www.vatican.va/holy_father/benedict_xvi/encyclicals/documents/hf_ben-xvi_enc_20071130_spe-salvi_en.html.
———. General Audience of January 16, 2008. http://www.vatican.va/holy_father/benedict_xvi/audiences/2008/documents/hf_ben-xvi_aud_20080116_en.html.
———. General Audience of February 27, 2008. http://www.vatican.va/holy_father/benedict_xvi/audiences/2008/documents/hf_ben-xvi_aud_20080227_en.html.
———. Homily for Ash Wednesday. February 22, 2012. http://www.vatican.va/holy_father/benedict_xvi/homilies/2012/documents/hf_ben-xvi_hom_20120222_ceneri_en.html.
———. Homily for the celebration of vespers with the faithful of Aosta (Italy). July 24, 2009. http://www.vatican.va/holy_father/benedict_xvi/homilies/2009/documents/hf_ben-xvi_hom_20090724_vespri-aosta_en.html.
———. Homily for the Easter Vigil. April 7, 2012. http://www.vatican.va/holy_father/benedict_xvi/homilies/2012/documents/hf_ben-xvi_hom_20120407_veglia-pasquale_en.html.
———. Homily for the souls of Cardinals and Bishops who died over the course of the year. November 3, 2012. http://www.vatican.va/holy_father/benedict_xvi/homilies/2012/documents/hf_ben-xvi_hom_20121103_suffragio_en.html.
———. *Schöpfung und Evolution: Eine Tagung mit Papst Benedikt XVI. in Castel Gandolfo*. Edited by Stephan Otto Horn and Siegfried Wiedenhofer. Augsburg: Sankt Ulrich, 2007.
Bonaventure. *II Sent*. d. 17, a. 1, q. 2. In Quaracchi 1885, 413–16.
Börresen, Kari Elisabeth. "Augustin, interprète du dogme de la résurrection: Quelques aspects de son anthropologie dualiste." *Studia Theologica* 23 (1969) 141–55.
Bowery, Anne-Marie. "Plotinus, *The Enneads*." In *Augustine Through the Ages: An Encyclopedia*, edited by John Fitzgerald and John C. Cavadini, 654–57. Grand Rapids: Eerdmans, 1999.
Bultmann, Rudolf. *Kerygma und Mythos: ein theologisches Gespräch*. Hamburg: H. Reich, 1965.
Bynum, Caroline Walker. *The Resurrection of the Body in Western Christianity, 200–1336*. New York: Columbia University Press, 1995.
Clarke, Thomas E. *The Eschatological Transformation of the Material World according to Saint Augustine*. Woodstock, MD: Woodstock College Press, 1956.
———. "St. Augustine and Cosmic Redemption." *Theological Studies* 19 (1958) 133–64.

Bibliography

Congregation for the Doctrine of the Faith. "Epistula de Quibusdam Quaestionibus ad Eschatologiam Spectantibus." Vatican City State: Typis Polyglottis Vaticanis, 1979. Original letter accessed from the archives of the Archdiocese of Ottawa, Canada.

———. "Epistula de Quibusdam Quaestionibus ad Eschatologiam Spectantibus." *Acta Apostolicae Sedis* 71 (1979) 939–43.

———. "Letter on Certain Questions Regarding Eschatology." *L'Osservatore Romano* (English Edition), July 23, 1979, 7.

———. "Schreiben der Kongregation für die Glaubenslehre zu einigen Fragen der Eschatologie." Edited by Sekretariat der Deutschen Bischofskonferenz. *Verlautbarungen des Apostolischen Stuhls* 11: 1979.

Copleston, Frederick. *A History of Philosophy.* Vol. 1, *Greece and Rome.* Westminster, MD: Newman, 1950.

Corkery, James. *Joseph Ratzinger's Theological Ideas: Wise Cautions and Legitimate Hopes.* New York: Paulist, 2009.

Cullmann, Oscar. *Immortality of the Soul or Resurrection of the Dead? The Witness of the New Testament.* London: Epworth, 1958. Given in English as the Ingersoll Lecture on the Immortality of Man at Harvard University, 1955.

Decrees of the Ecumenical Councils. Vol. 1, *Nicaea I to Lateran V.* Edited by Norman P. Tanner. Washington, DC: Georgetown University Press, 1990.

Dodds, Eric R. *The Greeks and the Irrational.* Berkeley: University of California Press, 1951.

Duns Scotus, John. *Lib IV Sent.,* d. 11, q. 3. In *Johannes Duns Scotus: Opera Omnia,* 8:604–57. Hildesheim: Georg Olms, 1968.

Duchrow, Ulrich. *Christenheit und Weltverantwortung. Traditionsgeschichte und systematische Struktur der Zweireichelehre.* Stuttgart: Ernst Klett, 1970.

———. "Der sogenannte psychologische Zeitbegriff Augustins im Verhältnis zur physikalischen und geschichtlichen Zeit." *Zeitschrift für Theologie und Kirche* 63 (1966) 267–88.

Duquesne, Jacques, and Giancarlo Zizola. *Benôit XVI ou le Mystère Ratzinger.* Second part (pp. 109–238) translated from Italian by Jean-Pierre Bagot and Anna Colao. Paris: Édition du Seuil, 2005.

Eccles, John C. "Hirn und Bewusstsein." *Mannheimer Forum* 77/78 (1978) 9–65.

Eccles, John C., and Daniel N. Robinson. *The Wonder of Being Human: Our Brain and Our Mind.* New York: Free Press, 1984.

Essen, Georg. *Historische Vernunft und Auferweckung Jesu: Theologie und Historik im Streit um den Begriff geschichtlicher Wirklichkeit.* Mainz: M. Grünewald, 1995.

Evangeliou, Christos. "Porphyry's Criticism of Christianity and the Problem of Augustine's Platonism." *Dionysius* 13 (1989) 51–70.

Ferrisi, Pietro Antonio. "La resurrezione della carne nel *De fide et symbolo* di S. Agostino." *Augustinianum* 33 (1993) 212–32.

Finan, Thomas. "Modes of Vision in St. Augustine: De Genesi ad litteram XII." In *The Relationship between Neoplatonism and Christianity,* edited by Thomas Finan and Vincent Twomey, 141–54. Dublin: Four Courts, 1992.

Fitzgerald, John, and John C. Cavadini. *Augustine Through the Ages: An Encyclopedia.* Grand Rapids: Eerdmans, 1999.

Gilson, Etienne. *Being and Some Philosophers.* Toronto: Pontifical Institute of Mediaeval Studies, 1949.

Gregory of Nyssa. *De hominis opificio.* In vol. 44 of *Patrologia Graeca,* edited by Jacques-Paul Migne, 123–256. Paris: Migne, 1863.

Greshake, Gisbert. *Auferstehung der Toten: Ein Beitrag zur gegenwärtigen theologischen Diskussion über die Zukunft der Geschichte*. Essen: Ludgerus-Verlag Hubert Wingen, 1969.

———. "Auferstehung im Tod: Ein 'parteiischer' Rückblick auf eine theologische Diskussion." *Theologie und Philosophie* 73 (1998) 538–57.

———. "Die Leib-Seele-Problematik und die Vollendung der Welt." In Gisbert Greshake and Gerhard Lohfink, *Naherwartung—Auferstehung—Unsterblichkeit: Untersuchungen zur christlichen Eschatologie*, 4th ed., 156–84. Freiburg im Breisgau: Herder, 1982.

———. "Seelenwanderung oder Auferstehung? Ein Diskurs über die eschatologische Vollendung des Heils." In Gisbert Greshake, *Gottes Heil—Glück des Menschen. Theologische Perspektiven*, 236–44. Freiburg im Breisgau: Herder, 1983.

———. *Tod und Auferstehung*. In *Christlicher Glaube in moderner Gesellschaft*, 5:63–133. Freiburg im Breisgau: Herder, 1980.

———. "Das Verhältnis 'Unsterblichkeit der Seele' und 'Auferstehung des Leibes' in problemgeschichtlicher Sicht." In Gisbert Greshake and Gerhard Lohfink, *Naherwartung—Auferstehung—Unsterblichkeit*. 4th ed., 82–120. Freiburg im Breisgau: Herder, 1982.

———. "Zum römischen Lehrschreiben über die Eschatologie (17.5.1979)." In Gisbert Greshake and Gerhard Lohfink, *Naherwartung—Auferstehung—Unsterblichkeit*, 4th ed., 185–92. Freiburg im Breisgau: Herder, 1982.

Greshake, Gisbert, and Jacob Kremer. *Resurrectio Mortuorum: Zum theologischen Verständnis der leiblichen Auferstehung*. Darmstadt: Wissenschaftliche Buchgesellschaft, 1986.

Guardini, Romano. *Die letzten Dinge*. 5th ed. Würzburg: Echter, 1952.

Hengstenberg, Hans-Eduard. *Das Band zwischen Gott und Schöpfung*. 3rd ed., newly revised. New York: Peter Lang, 1991.

———. *Der Leib und die letzten Dinge*. Regensburg: Friedrich Pustet, 1955.

Houghton, Hugh A. G. "Augustine's Adoption of the Vulgate Gospels." *New Testament Studies* 54 (2008) 450–64.

Hugo, John. *St. Augustine on Nature, Sex, and Marriage*. 1969. Reprint, Princeton: Scepter, 1998.

Husserl, Edmund. *Cartesianische Meditationen und Pariser Vorträge*. Edited by S. Strasser. 2nd ed. The Hague: Martinus Nijhoff, 1963.

International Theological Commission. "De quibusdam quaestionibus actualibus circa eschatologiam." *Gregorianum* 73 (1992) 395–435.

———. "Some Current Questions in Eschatology." *Irish Theological Quarterly* 58 (1992) 209–43.

Irenaeus of Lyons. *Adversus Haereses*. Vol. I of *The Ante-Nicene Fathers: The Apostolic Fathers with Justin Martyr and Irenaeus*, edited by Alexander Roberts and James Donaldson. Grand Rapids: Eerdmans, reprinted 2001.

Jones, Beth Felker. *Marks of His Wounds: Gender Politics and Bodily Resurrection*. New York: Oxford University Press, 2007.

Kasper, Walter. "Das Wesen des Christlichen. Ein Fundamental-Theologe und ein Dogmatiker zu dem Buch von Joseph Ratzinger: *Einführung in das Christentum*." *Theologische Revue* 65 (1969) 182–88.

Kehl, Medard. *Eschatologie*. Würzburg: Echter, 1986.

Bibliography

Kessler, Hans. *Sucht den Lebenden nicht bei den Toten: Die Auferstehung Jesu Christi in biblischer, fundamentaltheologischer und systematischer Sicht*. 2nd ed. Düsseldorf: Topos Plus, 1987.

Kolping, Adolf. *Fundamentaltheologie*. Vol III/1. Münster: Regensberg, 1981.

Komonchak, Joseph. "The Church in Crisis: Pope Benedict's Theological Vision." *Commonweal* 132 (June 3, 2005) 11–14.

Küng, Hans. *Eternal Life? Life after Death as a Medical, Philosophical, and Theological Problem*. Translated by Edward Quinn. Garden City, NY: Doubleday, 1984.

———. *Ewiges Leben?* Munich: Piper, 1982.

Kunzelmann, Adalbert. "Die Chronologie der Sermones des Hl. Augustinus." In *Miscellanea Agostiniana: Testi e Studi*, 2:427–520. Rome: Tipografia Poliglotta Vaticana, 1931.

Lambot, Cyril. "Lettre inédite de S. Augustin relative au 'de Civitate Dei.'" *Revue bénédictine* 51 (1939) 109–21.

Lawless, George. "Augustine and Human Embodiment." *Augustiniana* 49 (1990) 167–86.

Lohfink, Gerhard. "Das Zeitproblem und die Vollendung der Welt." In Gisbert Greshake and Gerhard Lohfink, *Naherwartung—Auferstehung—Unsterblichkeit: Untersuchungen zur christlichen Eschatologie*, 4th ed., 131–55. Freiburg im Breisgau: Herder, 1982.

Manser, Gallus. *Das Wesen des Thomismus*. Freiburg in der Schweiz: Paulusverlag, 1949.

Marrou, Henri. *The Resurrection and St. Augustine's Theology of Human Values*. Translated by Maria Consolata. Villanova, PA: Augustinian Institute, Villanova University, 1966.

Marschler, Thomas. "Perspektiven der Eschatologie bei Joseph Ratzinger." In *Joseph Ratzinger: Ein theologisches Profil*, edited by Peter Hofmann, 161–91. Munich: Ferdinand Schöningh, 2008.

McEvoy, James J. "Neoplatonism and Christianity: Influence, Syncretism or Discernment?" In *The Relationship between Neoplatonism and Christianity*, edited by Thomas Finan and Vincent Twomey, 155–70. Dublin: Four Courts, 1992.

Menke, Karl-Heinz. *Die Einzigartigkeit Jesu Christi im Horizont der Sinnfrage*. Freiburg: Johannes, 1995.

Moingt, Joseph. "Immortalité de l'âme et/ou résurrection." *Lumière et Vie* 107 (1972) 65–78.

Moisuc, Cristian. "Aristotélisme et christologie au XIII-ème siècle. Le problème du corps du Christ dans les derniers écrits de saint Thomas d'Aquin." *Meta: Research in Hermeneutics, Phenomenology, and Practical Philosophy* 1 (2009) 137–54.

Mourant, John A. *Augustine on Immortality*. Villanova, PA: Augustinian Institute, Villanova University, 1969.

Nachtwei, Gerhard. *Dialogische Unsterblichkeit. Eine Untersuchung zur Joseph Ratzingers Eschatologie und Theologie*. Leipzig: St. Benno Verlag, 1986.

Nichols, Aidan. *The Theology of Joseph Ratzinger: An Introductory Study*. Edinburgh: T. & T. Clark, 1988.

———. *The Thought of Pope Benedict XVI: An Introduction to the Theology of Joseph Ratzinger*. 2nd ed. London: Burns & Oates, 2007.

Nocke, Franz-Josef. "Eschatologie." In *Handbuch der Dogmatik*, edited by Theodor Schneider, 2:377–478. Düsseldorf: Patmos, 1992.

———. *Eschatologie*. Leitfaden Theologie 6. Düsseldorf: Patmos, 1982.

Bibliography

O'Collins, Gerald. "Augustine on the Resurrection." In *Saint Augustine the Bishop: A Book of Essays*, edited by Fannie LeMoine and Christopher Kleinhenz, 65–75. New York: Garland, 1994.

O'Donoghue, N. D. "The Awakening of the Dead." *Irish Theological Quarterly* 56 (1990) 49–59.

O'Meara, John J. *Charter of Christendom: The Significance of* The City of God. New York: Macmillan, 1961.

———. "Parting from Porphyry." In *Congresso Internazionale su S. Agostino nel XVI centenario della Conversione, Roma, 15-20 settembre 1986, Atti* 2, 357–69. Rome: Institutum Patristicum Augustinianum, 1987.

Pesch, Rudolf. *Über das Wunder der Jungfrauengeburt: Ein Schlüssel zum Verstehen*. Bad Tölz: Urfeld, 2002.

Phan, Peter C. "Current Theology: Contemporary Context and Issues in Eschatology." *Theological Studies* 55 (1994) 507–36.

Plato. *Phaedo*. In *Five Dialogues*. Translated by G. M. A. Grube. Indianapolis: Hackett, 1981.

Popper, Karl R., and John C. Eccles. *The Self and Its Brain: An Argument for Interactionism*. Berlin: Springer, 1977.

Porphyry. *Sentences: Études d'Introduction: Texte Grec et Traduction Française, Commentaire*. Edited by Luc Brisson. English translation by John Dillon. Paris: J. Vrin, 2005.

Pozo, Candido. "Problemática en la teología católica." In *Resurrexit. Actes du symposium international sur la résurrection de Jésus (Rome 1970)*, 489–531. Rome: Libreria Editrice Vaticana, 1974.

Quy, Joseph Lam C. *Theologische Verwandtschaft: Augustinus von Hippo und Joseph Ratzinger/Papst Benedikt XVI*. Würzburg: Echter, 2009.

Rahner, Karl. "Christianity within an Evolutionary View of the World." In vol. 5 of *Theological Investigations*, translated by Karl-H. Kruger, 157–92. Baltimore: Helicon, 1966.

———. "Die Einheit von Geist und Materie im christlichen Glaubensverständnis." In vol. 6 of *Schriften zur Theologie*, edited by Karl Rahner, 185–214. Einsiedeln: Benziger, 1965.

———. *Foundations of Christian Faith*. Translated by William V. Dych. New York: Seabury, 1978.

———. *The Great Church Year*. Translated by Harvey D. Egan. New York: Crossroad, 1993.

———. *Das große Kirchenjahr*. Freiburg im Breisgau: Herder, 1987.

———. "Immanente und transzendente Vollendung der Welt." In *Schriften zur Theologie*, edited by Karl Rahner, 8:593–609. Einsiedeln: Benziger, 1967.

———. "The Intermediate State." In vol. 17 of *Theological Investigations*, translated by Margaret Kohl, 114–24. New York: Crossroad, 1981.

———. "Natural Science and Reasonable Faith." In vol. 21 of *Theological Investigations*, translated by Hugh M. Riley, 16–55. New York: Crossroad, 1988.

———. "Naturwissenschaft und vernünftiger Glaube." In vol. 15 of *Schriften zur Theologie*, edited by Karl Rahner, 24–62. Einsiedeln: Benziger, 1983.

———. *On the Theology of Death*. Translated by Charles Henkey. New York: Herder and Herder, 1961.

———. "Über den 'Zwischenzustand.'" In vol. 12 of *Schriften zur Theologie*, edited by Karl Rahner, 455–66. Einsiedeln: Benziger, 1975.

Bibliography

———. "Über die theologische Problematik der 'neuen Erde.'" In vol. 8 of *Schriften zur Theologie*, edited by Karl Rahner, 580–609. Einsiedeln: Benziger, 1967.

———. "Unity of Spirit and Matter in Christian Faith." In vol. 6 of *Theological Investigations*, translated by Karl-H. Kruger and Boniface Kruger, 153–77. Baltimore: Helicon, 1969.

Ratzinger, Joseph. "Die Auferstehung Christi und christliche Jenseitshoffnung." In *Christlich—was heißt das?*, edited by Gerhard Adler, 34–37. Düsseldorf: Patmos, 1972.

———. "Auferstehung des Fleisches." *Lexikon für Theologie und Kirche* 1, 2nd ed. (1957) 1048–52.

———. "Auferstehung des Fleisches." *Sacramentum Mundi* 1 (1967) 397–402.

———. "Auferstehung und ewiges Leben." In *Dogma und Verkündigung*, edited by Joseph Ratzinger, 310–14. Munich: Wewel, 1973.

———. "Auferstehungsleib." *Lexikon für Theologie und Kirche* 1, 2nd ed. (1957) 1052–54.

———. "Beyond Death." *Communio* 1 (1974) 157–65.

———. "Concerning the Notion of Person in Theology." Translated by Michael Waldstein. *Communio* 17 (1990) 439–54.

———. *Daughter Zion: Meditations on the Church's Marian Belief*. Translated by John M. McDermott. San Francisco: Ignatius, 1983.

———. "Dammit Gott alles in allem sei." In *Kleines Credo für Verunsicherte*, edited by Wolfgang Beinert et al. Freiburg: Herder, 1993.

———. *Einführung in das Christentum: Vorlesungen über das Apostolische Glaubensbekenntnis*. 9th ed. Munich: Kösel, 2007.

———. "The End of Time." In *The End of Time? The Provocation of Talking about God*, edited by Tiemo Rainer Peters and Claus Urban, 4–25. English edition translated and edited by J. Matthew Ashley. Mahwah, NJ: Paulist, 2004.

———. "Das Ende der Zeit." In *Ende der Zeit? Die Provokation der Rede von Gott*, edited by Tiemo R. Peters and Claus Urban, 13–31. Mainz: M.-Grünewald, 1999.

———. "Erfahrung und Glaube." *Internationale katholische Zeitschrift Communio* 9 (1980) 58–70.

———. *Eschatologie—Tod und Ewiges Leben*. 6th ed. Regensburg: Friedrich Pustet, 2007.

———. *Eschatology: Death and Eternal Life*. 2nd ed. Translated by Michael Waldstein. Translation edited by Aidan Nichols. Washington, DC: Catholic University of America Press, 2007.

———. "Glaube, Geschichte und Philosophie. Zum Echo auf *Einführung in das Christentum*." *Hochland* 61 (1969) 533–43.

———. *Glaube—Wahrheit—Toleranz: Das Christentum und die Weltreligionen*. Freiburg im Breisgau: Herder, 2003.

———. *God and the World: Believing and Living in Our Time: A Conversation with Peter Seewald*. Translated by Henry Taylor. San Francisco: Ignatius, 2002.

———. *Gott und die Welt: Glauben und Leben in unserer Zeit. Ein Gespräch mit Peter Seewald*. Munich: Knaur Taschenbuch, 2005.

———. *In the Beginning . . . : A Catholic Understanding of the Story of Creation and the Fall*. Translated by Boniface Ramsey. Grand Rapids: Eerdmans, 1986.

———. *Introduction to Christianity*. Translated by J. R. Foster. San Francisco: Ignatius, 2004.

Bibliography

———. "Jenseits des Todes." *Internationale katholische Zeitschrift Communio* 1 (1972) 231–44.
———. *Jesus of Nazareth: The Infancy Narratives*. Translated by Philip Whitmore. New York: Image, 2012.
———. *Jesus of Nazareth. Part Two: Holy Week. From the Entrance into Jerusalem to the Resurrection*. Translated by the Vatican Secretariat of State. San Francisco: Ignatius, 2011.
———. *Jesus von Nazareth. Zweiter Teil: vom Einzug in Jerusalem bis zur Auferstehung*. Freiburg: Herder, 2011.
———. "Joseph Cardinal Ratzinger: Bibliography as of February 1, 2002." In *Pilgrim Fellowship of Faith: The Church as Communion*, edited by Stephan Otto Horn and Vinzenz Pfnür, translated by Henry Taylor, 299–379. San Francisco: Ignatius, 2005.
———."Joseph Ratzinger im Gespräch mit Martin Lohmann." Transcript of interview on September 4, 1998, on television station Bayern-Alpha. http://www.br.de/fernsehen/br-alpha/sendungen/alpha-forum/joseph-ratzinger-gespraech100.html.
———. "Jungfrauengeburt und leeres Grab: Eine Klarstellung zur Orientierung der von Theologen der Katholischen Integrierten Gemeinde geführten 'Akademie für die Theologie des Volkes Gottes.'" *Die Tagespost: Katholische Zeitung für Politik, Gesellschaft, und Kultur*, November 10, 2004.
———. "Mein Glück ist, in deiner Nähe zu sein: Vom christlichen Glauben an das ewige Leben." In *Gott ist uns nah: Eucharistie: Mitte des Lebens*, edited by Stephan Otto Horn and Vinzenz Pfnür, 139–58. Augsburg: Sankt Ulrich, 2001.
———. *Milestones: Memoirs, 1927–1977*. Translated by Erasmo Leiva-Merikakis. San Francisco: Ignatius, 1998.
———. "My Joy Is to Be in Your Presence: On the Christian Belief in Eternal Life." In *God Is Near Us: The Eucharist, the Heart of Life*, edited by Stephan Otto Horn and Vinzenz Pfnür, translated by Henry Taylor, 130–48. San Francisco: Ignatius, 2003.
———. "Zum Personverständnis in der Theologie." In Joseph Ratzinger, *Dogma und Verkündigung*, 205–23. Munich: Wewel, 1973.
———. "Resurrection: Theological." In *Sacramentum Mundi: An Encyclopedia of Theology*, edited by Karl Rahner et al., 5:340–42. London: Burnes & Oates, 1968–70.
———. *Die sakramentale Begründung christlicher Existenz*. Freising: Kyrios, 1966.
———. *Skandalöser Realismus? Gott handelt in der Geschichte*. Bad Tölz: Urfeld, 2005.
———. *Die Tochter Zion: Betrachtungen über den Marienglauben der Kirche*. Einsiedeln: Johannes, 1977.
———. *Truth and Tolerance: Christian Belief and World Religions*. Translated by Henry Taylor. San Francisco: Ignatius, 2004.
———. "Vérité du Christianisme?" Translated by Henry Taylor. In Joseph Ratzinger, *Truth and Tolerance*, 162–83. San Francisco: Ignatius, 2004.
———. *Volk und Haus Gottes in Augustins Lehre von der Kirche*. Munich: Karl Zink, 1954.
———. "Zwischen Tod und Auferstehung." *Internationale katholische Zeitschrift Communio* 9 (1980) 209–26.
Rausch, Thomas. *Pope Benedict XVI: An Introduction to His Theological Vision*. New York: Paulist, 2009.

Bibliography

Richey, Lance Byron. "Porphyry, Reincarnation and Resurrection in *De Ciuitate Dei*." *Augustinian Studies* 26 (1995) 129–42.

Ricoeur, Paul. *Husserl: An Analysis of His Phenomenology*. Translated by Edward G. Ballard and Lester E. Embree. Evanston: Northwestern University Press, 1967.

———. *Oneself as Another*. Translated by Kathleen Blamey. Chicago: University of Chicago Press, 1992.

Roberts, Christopher C. *Creation and Covenant: The Significance of Sexual Difference in the Moral Theology of Marriage*. New York: T. & T. Clark, 2007.

Rowland, Tracey. *Ratzinger's Faith: The Theology of Pope Benedict XVI*. New York: Oxford University Press, 2008.

Scheffczyk, Leo. *Auferstehung: Prinzip des christlichen Glaubens*. Einsiedeln: Johannes, 1976.

Scherer, Georg. "Das Leib-Seele-Problem in seiner Relevanz für die individuelle Eschatologie." In *Tod, Hoffnung, Jenseits: Dimensionen und Konsequenzen biblisch verankerter Eschatologie*, edited by Ferdinand Dexinger, 61–88. Freiburg im Breisgau: Herder, 1983.

Schiller, Isabella, Dorothea Weber, and Clemens Weidmann. "Sechs neue Augustinuspredigten: Teil 1 mit Edition dreier Sermones." *Wiener Studien* 121 (2008) 227–84.

Schneider, Theodor. *Die Einheit des Menschen: Die anthropologische Formel "anima forma corporis" im sogenannten Korrektorienstreit und bei Petrus Johannis Olivi: Ein Beitrag zur Vorgeschichte des Konzils von Vienne*. Münster: Aschendorff, 1973.

Schönborn, Christoph. "'Auferstehung des Fleisches' im Glauben der Kirche." *Internationale Katholische Zeitschrift Communio* 19 (1990) 13–29.

Schulte, Raphael. *Leib und Seele*. Freiburg im Breisgau: Herder, 1980.

Sonnemans, Heino. *Seele: Unsterblichkeit—Auferstehung: Zur griechischen und christlichen Anthropologie und Eschatologie*. Freiburg im Breisgau: Herder, 1984.

Te Selle, Eugene. "Porphyry and Augustine." *Augustinian Studies* 5 (1974) 113–48.

Teilhard de Chardin, Pierre. "Christ the Evolver" (1942). In *Christianity and Evolution*, translated by René Hague, 138–50. New York: Harcourt Brace Jovanovich, 1971.

———. "Fall, Redemption, and Geocentrism" (1920). In *Christianity and Evolution*, translated by René Hague, 36–44. New York: Harcourt Brace Jovanovich, 1971.

———. "The God of Evolution" (1953). In *Christianity and Evolution*, translated by René Hague, 237–43. New York: Harcourt Brace Jovanovich, 1971.

———. *The Heart of Matter*. Translated by René Hague. New York: Harcourt Brace Jovanovich, 1978.

———. "Note on Some Possible Historical Representations of Original Sin" (prior to 1922). In *Christianity and Evolution*, translated by René Hague, 45–55. New York: Harcourt Brace Jovanovich, 1971.

———. *The Phenomenon of Man*. Translated by Bernard Wall. New York: Collins, 1961.

———. "Reflections on Original Sin" (1947). In *Christianity and Evolution*, translated by René Hague, 187–98. New York: Harcourt Brace Jovanovich, 1971.

Tertullian. *Tertullian's Treatise on the Resurrection*. Translated by Ernest Evans. London: SPCK, 1960.

Teske, Roland J. "Soul." In *Augustine Through the Ages: An Encyclopedia*, edited by John Fitzgerald and John C. Cavadini, 807–12. Grand Rapids: Eerdmans, 1999.

Thomas Aquinas. *In Epistolam I ad Corinthios*, chapter 15. In vol. 21 of Thomas Aquinas, *Opera Omnia*, edited by Stanislas Edouard Fretté, 27–53. Paris: P. Larousse, 1876.

———. *Quaestiones Quodlibetales*. Edited by Raymundi Spiazzi. 9th ed. Rome: Marietti, 1949.

———. *Summa Theologiae*. Vol. 54. Blackfriars edition. Translated by Richard T. A. Murphy. New York: McGraw-Hill, 1965.

Trapè, Agostino. "Escatologia e antiplatonismo di sant'Agostino." *Augustinianum* 18 (1978) 237–44.

Van Fleteren, Frederick. "Augustine and the Resurrection." *Studies in Medieval Culture* 12 (1978) 9–15.

Verweyen, Hansjürgen. *Joseph Ratzinger—Benedikt XVI. Die Entwicklung seines Denkens*. Darmstadt: Primus, 2007.

Vorgrimler, Herbert. *Hoffnung auf Vollendung. Aufriß der Eschatologie*. Freiburg: Herder, 1980.

Watson, Gerard. "St. Augustine, the Platonists and the Resurrection Body: Augustine's Use of a Fragment from Porphyry." *Irish Theological Quarterly* 50 (1983/84) 222–32.

Welch, Lawrence J. "The Augustinian Foundations of a Nuptial Theology of the Body: 'He Who Created Both Sexes Will Restore Them Both,'" In *Essays in Honor of Matthew L. Lamb*, edited by Michael Dauphinais and Matthew Levering, 353–74. Naples, FL: Sapientia, 2007.

Wohlmuth, Joseph. *Mysterium der Verwandlung: Eine Eschatologie aus katholischer Perspektive im Gespräch mit jüdischem Denken der Gegenwart*. Munich: Ferdinand Schöningh, 2005.

Wolfson, Harry A. "Immortality and Resurrection in the Philosophy of the Church Fathers." In *Doctrines of Human Nature, Sin, and Salvation in the Early Church*, edited by Everett Ferguson, 301–36. New York: Garland, 1993.

Yudin, Victor. "Refutando a Porfirio mediante Platón: lectura agustiniana de 'Timeo' 41 A-B." *Augustinus* 52 (2007) 245–51.

www.ingramcontent.com/pod-product-compliance
Lightning Source LLC
Chambersburg PA
CBHW030614230426
43661CB00053B/1976